THE BIG BOOK OF

SERIAL KILLERS

Volume 2

150 Serial Killer Files of

the World's Worst Murderers

An Encyclopedia of Serial Killers

JACK ROSEWOOD

REBECCA LO

FREE BOOK

CONTENTS

Introduction 1

John Bodkin Adams 5

Howard Allen 10

Lowell Amos 12

Benjamin Atkins 15

Atlanta Ripper 17

Joseph D. Ball 20

Velma Barfield 23

Juana Barraza 25

Herb Baumeister 27

Levi Bellfield 29

Manuel Octavio Bermúdez 31

Donato Bilancia 34

Jake Bird 36

David and Catherine Birnie 39

Wayne Boden 43

Gary Ray Bowles 46

Ian Brady and Myra Hindley 49

Carl "Charlie" Brandt 54

Briley Brothers 57

Peter Bryan 61

Judias Buenoano 63

Harvey Carignan 66

Michael Bear Carson and Suzan Carson 69

Steven David Catlin 72

George Chapman 74

John Christie 77

Joseph Christopher 81

Cynthia Coffman 83

Daniel Conahan 86

Rory Enrique Conde 88

Eric Edgar Cooke 90

John Cooper 95

Ray and Faye Copeland 97

Juan Vallejo Corona 100

Andre Crawford 103

John Martin Crawford 106

Charles Cullen 108

Andrew Cunanan 111

Death Angels 114

Bandali Debs 117

Thomas Dillon 119

Westley Allan Dodd 121

Ronald Dominique 124

The Doodler 126

John Duffy and David Mulcahy 128

Peter Dupas 131

Paul Durousseau 134

Volker Eckert 137

Edward Edwards 139

Mack Ray Edwards 142

Bevan Spencer von Einem 144

Scott Erskine 149

Richard Evonitz 152

Raymond Fernandez and Martha Beck 154

Michel Fourniret 157

Kendall Francois 160

Frankford Slasher 163

Joseph Paul Franklin 165

Leonard Fraser 168

Gerald and Charlene Gallego 171

Michael Gargiulo 176

Carlton Gary 178

Sean Vincent Gillis 181

David Alan Gore and Fred Waterfield 184

Mark Goudeau 187

Gwendolyn Graham and Catherine May Wood 190

Harrison Graham 193

Ricky Lee Green 196

Vaughn Greenwood 199

Belle Gunness 201

Fritz Haarmann 207

John George Haigh 213

Archibald Hall 217

William Henry Hance 220

Charles Ray Hatcher 222

Dale Hausner and Samuel Dieteman 226

William Heirens 230

Loren Herzog and Wesley Shermantine 233

Johann Otto Hoch 236

Michael Hughes 241

Colin Ireland 243

Leslie Irvin 246

Phillip Carl Jablonski 248

M. Jaishankar 251

Vincent Johnson 253

Gilbert Paul Jordan 256

Joseph and Michael Kallinger 259

Béla Kiss 262

Timothy Krajcir 265

Peter Kürten 267

Allan Joseph Legere 271

Edward 'Eddie' Leonski 274

Samuel Little 276

Henry Lee Lucas 281

Maoupa Cedric Maake 284

Patrick Mackay 286

Michael Madison 288

Ramadan Abdel Rehim Mansour 290

David Mason 292

Gennady Mikhasevich 295

Blanche Taylor Moore 297

Peter Moore 300

Dontae Morris 302

Herbert Mullin 304

Robert Napper 307

National Socialist Underground 309

Earle Nelson 312

New Bedford Highway Killer..316

Colin Norris...319

Original Night Stalker - Golden State Killer...322

Rudolf Pleil...326

Stephen Port..329

Dorothea Puente..331

Wang Qiang...334

Ángel Maturino Reséndiz..336

Ripper Crew...340

James Dale Ritchie...343

Michael Bruce Ross..345

Sergei Ryakhovsky...347

Altemio Sanchez..349

Gerard John Schaefer...352

Charles Schmid...355

Juan Segundo..357

Tommy Lynn Sells..359

Anthony Allen Shore..362

Angus Sinclair...364

Moses Sithole..366

Erno Soto..368

Lyda Southard...370

Richard Speck...372

Alexander Spesivtsev...375

Gerald Stano...377

Paul Michael Stephani...380

John Straffen...382

William Suff..384

Igor Suprunyuck and Viktor Sayenko...388

Ahmad Suradji..391

Joseph Taborsky..393

Serhiy Tkach...395

Ottis Toole..397

Jane Toppan..400

Chester Turner..402

Jack Unterweger..404

Darren Deon Vann...406

Robert Joe Wagner...409

West Mesa Killer 413

Christopher Wilder...415

Peter Woodcock..418

Christopher Worrell and James Miller 420

Robert Zarinsky 423

Conclusion..425

INTRODUCTION

In a world with over *7 billion* human beings, it's no surprise that a few of them have turned out to be troubled people with a penchant for violence. Loud bullies or silent menaces, these men and women can be dangerous for the people around them, and they often get into trouble with the law sooner or later because of these behaviors.

However, it is important to note that there is a big stretch between solving your problems with anger and actually going out and taking lives of innocents because of a twisted desire within you that takes control of your urges.

This is the definition of a serial killer. Serial killers are not necessarily psychopaths or pariahs of society, as we have been taught by television – many times, they are the next-door neighbor who smiles at us every morning or joins us as we walk our dog. Sometimes, they're even the uncle, cousin or nurse taking care of our children, believe it or not. There are countless examples of these deadly individuals walking among us with impunity.

Yet, even though we should be programmed to fear them, serial killers cause some sort of curiosity among us. Why is this?

According to experts, there are a few valid reasons behind this fascination that we demonstrate toward serial killers:

1. **We can be victims at any time** – Serial killers, regardless of the profiles they select for their victims (ethnicity, skin color, gender, occupation), often strike randomly. This leads many of us to feel that we're always in danger of being murdered by one of these deadly criminals. In fact, we may even know somebody who had a close encounter with one of these murderers.

2. **They are human beings, just like us** – Even if they have done terribly horrific things, serial killers were still children once, had to go to school and grow up as teenagers just like we did. We empathize with them, even when we hate them for what they've done at one point or another in their lives. Even if it is just to judge their actions. They are men and women of varying ages and motivations, not simple monsters.

3. **We wish to understand the horror** – Regardless of whether we *like* serial killers or not, we consume content related to them because we want to know *why* and *how* they have done what they've done. We wish to place a human, logical reason behind the act of murdering dozens of victims, and it helps us to do so by reading books like this one, watching documentaries and listening to interviews. It's a matter of curiosity, but also of learning.

4. **It can help us stop or protect ourselves from them** – The victims of serial killers were never voluntarily in the path of one of these dangerous individuals. Most of them were unaware of what they were facing until it was too late. Many readers of True Crime titles are simply seeking to gather the information necessary to recognize a potential serial killer and stop them from harming somebody or at least avoiding them before their own lives are taken.

Whatever the reasons we provide for our attraction towards serial killers, it's this curiosity which leads readers to the True Crime genre in books, and which has led us to produce these encyclopedias on serial killers across the United States and the entire planet – we want you to know exactly everything there is on these deadly and unpredictable human beings.

What The Big Book of Serial Killers Volume 2 is about

The True Crime genre in writing is often overlooked or underappreciated as being created to satisfy the morbid curiosity of its fans; some of our friends and family members judge us heavily when we confess our love for this particular category of writing, and frankly, it is very unfair.

This book has been created for more than just a trip into the tales surrounding the crimes of sick, twisted individuals that took lives for fun. It brings value in ways that very few other books of the genre can do on their own: by educating its readers on the dark underground of murderers across the world, providing all of the details that would typically be tough to find separately, and which would require months of research to replicate.

From a scientific perspective, this book is what a chemical encyclopedia is to a fan of science, or what a history title is to an anthropology student. This title, which serves as a sequel to the best-selling *"The Big Book of Serial Killers"*, is an educational written work for True Crime enthusiasts who see the potential of study in this field.

You could be a law enforcement officer wishing to learn of precedents for a tough case you're working on; a university student that has been assigned one or more of these killers for an important course project; or simply somebody who enjoys the thrill of learning about these individuals for the fun of it; there is no lack of utility for this book.

Each chapter in this book has been structured in the following way for your benefit:

- **Table of contents** - Ordered alphabetically by surname to allow for improved searching.

- **Summary of the killer's details** – Their date of birth, nicknames, characteristics, number of victims, date of murders, date of arrest, victim profile, method of murder, location and current status are all listed here for your ease.

- **Background of the killer's life** – The killer was more than just that: this section has been created to allow you to grasp what their family was like, how they began their lives, and what led them to become murderers.

- **Murders: the killer's crimes** – The main section of each killer's chapter, the "Murders" section speaks of all of the atrocities each person committed while actively murdering, describing with detail what they did to each and every victim.

- **Trial** – Following the killer's arrest (if there was one, of course), the chapter will cover what took place from the moment they were handcuffed to the instant they were found guilty of a crime or crimes.

- **Outcome** – The killer may still be alive, whether behind bars or now a free man or woman. Here, we find out how their story ended, or if maybe there's still something more still to happen to them.

- **Trivia** – Interesting facts on each killer, as well as a list of books, movies and TV series based on them.

As you may have noticed by now, this powerful and very detailed encyclopedia of serial killers is the perfect resource in investigating any of the 150 names found across its pages.

Use each chapter and its sections to your advantage, and don't feel obliged to read it in any particular order.

Final Notes

It doesn't matter what you've bought this book for: a ton of effort has been put into it to ensure the best in detail and accuracy – please enjoy it for what it is, and don't feel satisfied by simply reading what information can be found here.

Venture out and perform your own research, discover more content online and continue to buy our books to learn more about the most infamous killers who have lived in human history.

Finally, if you haven't read the first volume of The Big Book of Serial Killers yet, I recommend you to visit www.JackRosewood.com/books to grab your copy today!

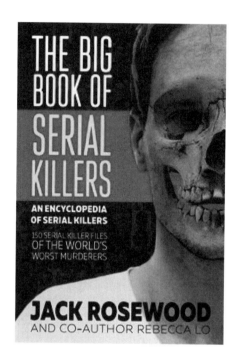

With that said, we leave you to dig into the criminal cases of these 150 serial killers that we didn't cover in the first volume.

Enjoy the fascinating read of The Big Book of Serial Killers Volume 2!

JOHN BODKIN ADAMS

Date of birth: January 21, 1899

Aliases/Nicknames: Doctor Death

Characteristics: Doctor, killed for greed

Number of victims: 0 - 163 +

Date of murders: 1935 - 1956

Date of arrest: December 19, 1956

Victim profile: Elderly female patients

Method of murder: Poisoning

Location: Eastbourne, East Sussex, England, United Kingdom

Status: Acquitted of murder on April 15, 1957. Died on July 4, 1983

Background

In 1899, Adams was born into a deeply religious family of Plymouth Brethren in Ulster, Ireland. He would remain a member of the Brethren for the rest of his life. His father was a watchmaker by profession and also a preacher in the local congregation; he died from a stroke in 1914. Adams had a younger brother, William, who died in 1918 during the influenza pandemic.

Adams spent several years attending Coleraine Academical Institution, then The Queen's University of Belfast. His teachers described him as a lone wolf and a "plodder." He graduated in 1921 and was offered a position as an assistant houseman at Bristol Royal Infirmary by surgeon Arthur Rendle Short. This wasn't a successful position for Adams, and after a year he applied for a job as a general practitioner at a Christian practice in Eastbourne, Sussex.

Attention and suspicion began to arise about Adams during the mid-1930s, and gossip spread concerning his methods, which were perceived as unconventional. In 1935, a patient of Adams, Matilda Whitton, left him £7,385 in her will. Though this was contested by her family, as it was a large amount of money at the time, the will was upheld in court.

Adams gained a diploma in anesthetics in 1941 and began working one day a week at a local hospital. There, he was known as a "bungler," who would eat food, count his money, or fall asleep during operations. At times, he mixed up the tubes for the anesthetic gas, and the patients would turn blue or even wake up during surgery.

Despite all of this, Adams' career was rather successful, leading him to become very wealthy. But in 1956, suspicions about his behavior were reported to the police by Leslie Henson, after his friend Gertrude Hullett died unexpectedly under Adams's care. By this time, Adams had been made a beneficiary in 132 wills of his patients, and rumors were rife about the numerous deaths of Adams' patients.

Murders

The investigation was taken over by the Metropolitan Police's Murder Squad on August 17, 1956, and the two officers assigned were Detective Superintendent Herbert Hannam (Scotland Yard) and Detective Sergeant Charles Hewett. They decided to focus only on cases from 1946 to 1956, which included 310 death certificates written by Adams. Of these, 163 were determined to be suspicious. As the investigation continued, nurses that had been involved in treating the patients were interviewed. Some stated Adams had given patients a "special injection," and wouldn't disclose the contents to the nurses. He would also ask nurses to leave the patient's room before he gave them one of these injections.

Adams' house was searched on November 24, 1956, mainly to look for dangerous drugs such as morphine, heroin, and pethidine. When this was stated to Adams, he declared there were no drugs of that sort in his house. Upon being questioned about his drug register, he admitted he hadn't kept one since 1949.

During the search of his home, Adams was seen to remove two items from a cupboard when he thought nobody was looking. When investigators challenged him on this, he pulled two bottles of morphine out of his pocket. He claimed they were for two of his patients, but pharmacy records showed that one of them had never been prescribed morphine.

Victims

<u>Edith Alice Morrell</u>

On June 24, 1948, wealthy widow Edith Alice Morrell suffered a stroke, leaving her partially paralyzed. Because she was visiting her son in Cheshire, she was admitted to a hospital nearby. Her regular doctor was Adams; he came to visit Morrell on June 26, and she was transferred to Eastbourne on July 5. Adams began giving her morphine on July 9, then added heroin to the mix on July 21.

Morrell died on November 13, 1950, at the age of eighty-one. The death certificate was filled out as "stroke" by Adams. Originally in her will, Adams was removed from it on September 13, 1950. However, after her death, her son gifted Adams her Rolls-Royce and a chest of silver cutlery. Adams also kept a lamp that had belonged to Morrell, and billed her estate £1,674 for eleven hundred medical visits. Police later found that Adams had only visited her 321 times.

<u>Gertrude Hullett</u>

Another patient of Adams was Gertrude Hullett, who passed away on July 23, 1956, at the young age of fifty. Her husband had died months earlier, and she had been depressed since, so she had been prescribed sodium phenobarbitone and sodium barbitone. According to Adams, he administered two barbiturate tablets to her every morning, and over time reduced the dosage from two tablets of 7.5 grains each to two tablets of 5 grains.

Adams received a check for one thousand pounds from Hullett on July 17, supposedly so he could purchase a car her deceased husband had promised him. Two days later, Hullett appeared to have taken an overdose, and slipped into a coma. She was seen by another doctor in Adams' absence and, on conferring, they decided she had most likely suffered from a cerebral hemorrhage. The following morning, Adams contacted the coroner to organize a private postmortem, despite the fact Hullett was still alive. She then developed bronchopneumonia, and finally died on July 23. An analysis of a urine sample taken from Hullett on July 21 later revealed she had twice the fatal dose of barbitone in her system.

Five days before her alleged overdose, Hullett had altered her will, leaving Adams her Rolls-Royce Silver Dawn which was worth around twenty-nine hundred pounds.

Other Possible Victims

Agnes Pike was being treated by Adams in August 1939, when her solicitors became concerned at how much hypnotic medication Adams was giving her. Another doctor was asked to take over her care and, on examination, could find no disease or ailment afflicting her. Pike was incoherent and strongly under the influence of drugs and, during the examination, Adams administered an injection of morphia (morphine). When questioned, Adams stated that he had given her the drug in case she became violent. The doctor hired by the solicitors noted that Adams seemed to have kept the patient away from all family, banning them from visiting her. Under the new doctor's care, Pike eventually regained her faculties and was able to take care of herself.

Emily Louise Mortimer died on December 24, 1946, at the age of seventy-five. Following her death, Adams removed a clock and a bottle of brandy from her room. He also received money from Mortimer's will in the form of shares, totaling nineteen hundred fifty pounds in dividends by 1957.

On February 23, 1950, Adams' patient, Amy Ware, died aged seventy-six years. Like Pike, she had also had family banned from visiting. In her will, she left Adams one thousand pounds, though he wrote on her cremation form that he was not a beneficiary.

Anabelle Kilgour, eighty-nine, died on December 28, 1950. Adams had been taking care of her following a stroke she had suffered in July. She went into a coma after Adams began giving her sedative medication and died five days later. In her will, Kilgour left him a clock and two hundred pounds.

Adams convinced his patient Julia Bradnum, eighty-five, that she should sell her home and leave the proceeds in her will to whoever she wanted. During his treatment of Bradnum, he was often seen holding her hand. The day before her death, she had been up and about, taking care of household chores, and on the morning she died, Adams came to see her after he was informed she wasn't feeling well. He injected her with an unknown substance and stated that she would be dead in three minutes. Bradnum died on May 11, 1952, leaving Adams six hundred sixty-one pounds in her will. On the death certificate, Adams listed the cause of death as cerebral hemorrhage, but no evidence of this was found when her body was exhumed and reexamined.

Seventy-two-year-old Julia Thomas received treatment for depression from Adams in early November 1952. Adams gave her sedatives on November 19, saying she would feel better the next morning. The following day, after he had given her more tablets, she went into a coma. Adams told Thomas' cook on November 21 that she had promised him her typewriter and that he was going to take it, even though she hadn't yet passed away. She died in the early hours of the next morning.

Another patient to die under suspicious circumstances was Hilda Neil Miller, aged eighty-six. She lived in a guest house with her sister Clara and, on occasion, Adams was seen to pick up items in their room and pocket them. The sisters were cut off from their relatives, and when Hilda died on January 15, 1953, Adams organized her funeral and burial site.

Then on February 22, 1954, Hilda's sister Clara, then aged eighty-seven, also passed away. On an extremely cold day, a nurse entered Clara's room and noticed that all of her bedding had been taken off, her nightgown was up around her chest, and the window was wide open, letting in the freezing air. She was later determined to have died from bronchopneumonia. Adams received twelve hundred seventy-five pounds in her will and charged her estate another seven hundred pounds for treatment. Once again, like her sister before her, Adams arranged the funeral.

James Downs was the brother-in-law of previous patient Amy Ware, and he died under Adams' care on May 30, 1955, aged eighty-eight. He had suffered a broken ankle four months prior, which led to his admission to a nursing home. Adams gave him a sedative containing morphia, which had the effect of making Downs forgetful. On April 7, Adams instructed his nurse to give Downs a tablet to make him more alert, and two hours later, a solicitor arrived to amend Downs' will. Adams told the solicitor that he was to inherit one thousand pounds, and after the amendment was made, another doctor was brought in to declare the patient alert. Following Downs' death, Adams charged his estate two hundred sixteen pounds.

Gertrude Hullett's husband, Alfred John Hullett, died on March 14, 1956, at the age of seventy-one. He left five hundred pounds to Adams in his will.

The final suspicious case was that of Annie Sharpe, who had been the owner of the guest house where Hilda and Clara Neil Miller had lived before their deaths. According to Adams, she died suddenly on November 15, 1956, from cancer of the peritoneal cavity. Adams had made the diagnosis five days before her death and prescribed her morphine and pethidine. Her cremation took place quickly, so no investigation into her death could be made.

Trial

On November 24, 1956, Adams was arrested and charged with thirteen offenses, including false representation on cremation certificates. He was granted bail while the investigation continued. He was arrested again on December 19, 1956, and formally charged with the murder of Morrell.

Hannam believed he had enough evidence to charge Adams with the murders of Morrell, Clara Neil Miller, Gertrude Hullett, and Julia Bradnum. But he was only charged with the one count of murder, that of Morrell's. The information regarding these deaths, and that of Hullett's husband, could be used in court to prove a "system" of deaths associated with Adams.

The committal hearing began on January 14, 1957 and concluded on January 24. Taking only five minutes to deliberate, Adams was committed for trial.

On March 18, 1957, the trial began. If he was found guilty, Adams could have faced the death penalty. The trial went on for seventeen days, which at that point was the longest in Britain. It concluded on April 9, 1957, and after deliberating for forty-four minutes, the jury declared Adams not guilty of the murder of Morrell.

Outcome

Following the trial, Adams resigned from the National Health Service. He returned to court for the other charges, eight counts of forging prescriptions, four counts of making false statements on cremation forms, and three offenses under the Dangerous Drugs Act, 1951. He was found guilty, fined twenty-four hundred pounds, and required to pay the court costs of four hundred fifty-seven pounds. His license to prescribe dangerous drugs was revoked, and he was struck off the medical register on November 27.

Adams returned to practicing medicine in Eastbourne after his reinstatement as a general practitioner on November 22, 1961. The following July he was given authority to prescribe dangerous drugs again.

On June 30, 1983, Adams fell and fractured his hip. He developed a chest infection while in the hospital, and on July 4, he died from heart failure. He had amassed a substantial wealth of £402,970 and continued to receive legacies from his former patients right up until his own death.

Trivia

A documentary made for television in 1986, "The Good Doctor Bodkin Adams," starred Timothy West as the lead character.

Adams would travel to see his patients in the back of his Rolls-Royce, driven by a chauffeur. He liked to snack on a sweet treat, Violet Creams, which he kept on standing order with Charbonnel et Walker.

In August 1962, Adams applied for a visa so he could travel to America, but he was refused because of his convictions.

HOWARD ALLEN

Date of birth: February 10, 1949
Aliases/Nicknames: Nil
Characteristics: Arson, robberies
Number of victims: 3 +
Date of murders: 1974 / 1987
Date of arrest: August 4, 1987
Victim profile: Opal Cooper, 85; Laverne Hale, 87; Ernestine Griffin, 73
Method of murder: Stabbing with a knife, beating
Location: Marion County, Indiana, USA
Status: Sentenced to death June 11, 1988

Background

Allen invaded a home in August 1974 to commit burglary. During the act, he beat to death the elderly resident Opal Cooper, eighty-five. He was arrested, convicted of manslaughter, and sentenced to two to twenty-one years in state prison. In January 1985, he was paroled and returned to Indianapolis, where he began working at a car wash. It wasn't long, however, before he started looking for more victims.

Murders

Allen entered the home of a seventy-three-year-old woman on May 18, 1987, most likely to burglarize it. He beat the woman and choked her before fleeing; luckily, she survived the attack. Two days later, Laverne Hale, eighty-seven, wasn't so lucky. Although she initially survived the attack, she succumbed to her injuries and died on May 29.

On June 2, another home was broken into just five blocks away from where Laverne Hale was killed. Fortunately, the tenant of the home, an elderly man, wasn't there when the burglar entered. Out of frustration, Allen set the house on fire before he left.

Ernestine Griffin, seventy-three, was the next known victim. On July 14, Allen broke into her home in Indianapolis and stabbed Griffin eight times with a large butcher knife. He then smashed her skull repeatedly with a toaster. His total gains from the robbery amounted to a camera and about fifteen dollars.

Trial

On August 4, 1987, Allen was arrested when witnesses from the May 18 attack were able to identify him. He was charged with burglary, unlawful confinement, and battery. He was then linked to the other robberies and attacks and was charged with burglary and arson from the June 2 robbery, as well as the murder of Ernestine Griffin.

Police discovered Allen had been a neighbor of Laverne Hale, and they suspected him of being responsible for her murder. His modus operandi in known cases matched the murder of Hale, and he had lived directly across from her house.

Allen became a suspect in eleven more cases, where each victim had been assaulted and robbed. All of these events took place in close proximity to his other crimes. Allen was known for committing local crimes, staying within Indianapolis.

Allen went on trial, and in 1988, he was convicted of the felony battery and burglary from the assault on May 18. He was also found guilty of habitual criminal behavior. For these charges, he was sentenced to 88 years in prison.

Then on June 11, 1988, he was found guilty of the murder and robbery of Ernestine Griffin. For this crime, the jury recommended the death penalty.

Outcome

Allen received the death penalty for Griffin's murder and was placed on death row. He has made numerous appeals citing issues with his legal representation in court and the inappropriateness of a juror, who, despite marking on the questionnaire she had never been in court or charged with any crimes, had in fact been convicted of crimes such as traffic violations.

To date, all of his appeals have been rejected.

Trivia

At his trial, family members of Allen testified that his mother was a heavy drinker on weekends and would often stay away for several days at a time. They also claimed the children would stand outside the local tavern and beg adults going inside to ask for money from their mother so they could get some food.

LOWELL AMOS

Date of birth: January 4, 1943
Aliases/Nicknames: Nil
Characteristics: Killed for insurance money, poisoning
Number of victims: 4
Date of murders: 1979 -1994
Date of arrest: 1994
Victim profile: His mother and three wives
Method of murder: Poisoning
Location: Detroit, Michigan, USA
Status: Sentenced to life imprisonment without the possibility of parole on October 24, 1996

Background

Amos was born and raised in Anderson, Indiana, a relatively small town with a population of around fifty-five thousand. A quarter of the residents worked at one of the General Motors plants, including Amos, who was a plant manager there.

Amos decided to enter politics, and in January 1979, he announced himself as a candidate for the mayoralty of Anderson. However, his wife Saundra, 36, was found dead in their home just days after the announcement.

Murders

Amos told police that he had found Saundra dead in the bathroom. He claimed she had been mixing alcohol with sedatives, which led to her falling and striking her head. The coroner ruled her death as indeterminate. Following Saundra's death, Amos received a life insurance payout of three hundred fifty thousand.

A short time after his wife's death, Amos met and married Carolyn. He purchased large insurance policies on her life, a fact that instigated many arguments between the two of them. She demanded he cancel the policies, but he refused. She kicked him out of the house in 1988.

Amos left Carolyn's and moved in with his mother. Just a few weeks later, she was rushed to the hospital, where it was noted she seemed "stupefied." Doctors were unable to diagnose a specific problem, however, so she was discharged and sent back home. She died several days later. Amos rang Carolyn, who rushed over and discovered him throwing his belongings into his car. When she asked him what he was doing, he stated he didn't want people knowing he had been living with his mother. No autopsy was performed on the elderly woman because of her age, and it was presumed that she had died of natural causes. Amos inherited more than one million dollars from his mother's death.

Carolyn allowed Amos to move back in with her. She was found dead in the bathroom nine months later. According to Amos, he had gone into the bathroom to give her a glass of wine, and she was using a hairdryer right next to the bathtub full of water. He returned to check on her later and found her dead, presumably from electrocution; however, the cause of death was never identified. The wine glass he had supposedly given her was found clean in the dishwasher, not in the bathroom. Amos received an insurance payout of eight hundred thousand dollars.

In December 1994, Amos and his latest wife, Roberta, went to a company party at the Atheneum Hotel in Detroit. They retired to their room at the hotel around 4:30 a.m., and four hours later, Amos placed a call to one of his colleagues, Bert Crabtree, in a panicked state. Crabtree and another guest, Danial Porcasi, went to Amos' room and were told that Roberta had died after an accident. Amos stated he needed to clean before he called the police, and he asked Porcasi to take his coat. While driving home later that morning, Porcasi looked in the coat pocket and found a small, black leather case. Inside was a syringe missing the needle and a washcloth with a foul odor.

Amos took the coat back from Porcasi, and the black case disappeared. When questioned by the police about Roberta, Amos said they had taken cocaine during sexual acts, and Roberta was still taking the drug when he fell asleep. He said she couldn't snort the drug because she had a sinus problem, so she took it "inside" her body instead. He claimed that when he woke up, she was already dead.

During the inspection, cocaine was found on the bed linen, including the part that tucked under the mattress. Roberta's autopsy revealed she had more than fifteen times the lethal dose of cocaine in her body; there was even cocaine inside her vagina. Police strongly suspected Amos of washing Roberta's body before they arrived because no cocaine was found on her externally. Also, there were makeup marks on the pillow and linen, but none on her face.

Although police didn't have enough evidence to charge Amos, they were suspicious enough to start investigating his background, and they put him under surveillance. Two days after losing his wife, Amos went out with two women and paid one thousand dollars for dinner and drinks before proceeding to have sex with both of them. When the story of Roberta's death was made public, several women came forward claiming they believed Amos had drugged them before sex.

Trial

After looking thoroughly into Amos' personal life and discovering the suspicious pattern of deaths and life insurance payouts, the police arrested him for the murder of Roberta. Unfortunately for Amos, the law had changed in Michigan, which allowed previous incidents to be presented in court during trials.

Although Amos wasn't going to receive a payout from Roberta's death, prosecutors argued that the marriage was coming to an end anyway; Roberta had purchased a house for herself and had told people close to her that she wanted to be rid of Amos.

The prosecution argued that Amos had killed Roberta because he couldn't stand to be rejected. They alleged he had given her a glass of wine with sedatives crushed into it. Once she had passed out from the sedatives, he injected cocaine dissolved in water into her vagina. Then he smothered her with the pillow, which is how the traces of makeup ended up on it.

13

On November 4, 1996, Amos was found guilty of premeditated murder and a second charge of murder using a toxic substance.

Outcome

Amos was sentenced on November 4, 1996, to life imprisonment without the possibility of parole.

To date, Amos has not been charged in relation to the other deaths.

Trivia

The television movie *Black Widower* was made in 2006, with Amos as the subject.

Sometimes people spelled his name as "Lowel."

BENJAMIN ATKINS

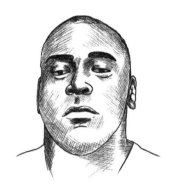

Date of birth: August 26, 1968

Aliases/Nicknames: The Woodward Corridor Killer

Characteristics: Rape, homeless, drug addict

Number of victims: 11

Date of murders: December 1991 - August 1992

Date of arrest: August 21, 1992

Victim profile: Darlene Saunders, 35; Debbie Ann Friday, 30; Bertha Jean Mason, 26; Patricia Cannon George, 36; Vickie Truelove, 39; Valerie Chalk, 34; Juanita Hardy, 23; Unknown female; Brenda Mitchell, 38; Vicki Beasley-Brown, 43; Joanne O'Rourke, 40; Ocinena Waymer, 22

Method of murder: Strangulation

Location: Detroit, Michigan, USA

Status: Sentenced to 11 life terms on May 11, 1994. Died in prison on September 17, 1997

Background

Born on August 26, 1968, Atkins experienced a tortured childhood. He grew up in Detroit, Michigan, with his mother, an alcohol abuser who worked as a prostitute and was addicted to heroin. When he couldn't stay with her, he was sent to live in boys homes. Throughout his childhood, he was subjected to sexual, physical, and psychological abuse.

Murders

For nine months, Atkins attacked and killed eleven women, most of whom were prostitutes or drug abusers. Many of his victims were found in derelict buildings and abandoned motels. His victims were:

October 1991
Darlene Saunders, thirty-five - raped and beaten in Highland Park, but she survived.

December 14, 1991
Debbie Ann Friday, thirty - strangled to death in Highland Park.

December 30, 1991
Bertha Jean Mason, twenty-six - strangled to death in Detroit.

January 3, 1992
Patricia Cannon George, thirty-six - strangled to death in Detroit.

January 25, 1992
Vickie Truelove, thirty-nine - strangled to death in Detroit.

February 17, 1992
Valerie Chalk, thirty-four - strangled to death and found at the Monterey Motel, Highland Park.

February 17, 1992
Juanita Hardy, twenty-three - strangled to death and found at the Monterey Motel, Highland Park.

April 9, 1992
Brenda Mitchell, thirty-eight - strangled to death in Highland Park.

April 15, 1992
Vicki Beasley-Brown, forty-three - strangled to death in Highland Park.

June 15, 1992
Joanne O'Rourke, forty - strangled to death in Highland Park.

August 21, 1992
Ocinena Waymer, twenty-two - strangled to death in Highland Park.

As the number of victims increased, a task force was created to find the killer. Of great assistance was a survivor, who had been attacked by a man she knew as Tony. With her help, the task force was able to identify Atkins as the suspect, and he was arrested on August 21, 1992.

Trial

When Atkins was questioned about his possible involvement in the murders, he denied any involvement, stating that he was homosexual and had no interest in women. Watching the interrogation was Sergeant Ronald Sanders, a Detroit homicide detective. He asked to have a shot at Atkins to see if he could get him to confess.

Sanders told Atkins that he knew he had never had a father figure and that he also had a son the same age as Atkins; the sergeant continued to tell him that he needed to get everything off his chest. Remarkably, this worked, and Atkins confessed to all of the murders, including another, that nobody knew about. He told the investigators he killed them, so he wouldn't have to worry about them pressing charges against him.

At Atkins' trial, his attorney tried to convince the jurors that Atkins was a product of his environment and the harshness of society. The jury, however, still found Atkins guilty. A sheriff's deputy in court that day said that Atkins was more concerned about being able to have a cigarette than his conviction.

Outcome

Convicted of eleven murders, Atkins received eleven life sentences. He would only serve a very small fraction of time, though. Atkins was HIV positive, and on September 17, 1997, he died from an infection related to HIV.

Trivia

His mother abandoned him when he was aged two.

Atkins was allegedly raped by a caseworker when he was ten years old and living in a boys home in Detroit.

When Atkins was a young child, his mother would have sex in the car with clients while he was in the back seat.

ATLANTA RIPPER

Date of birth: Unknown

Aliases/Nicknames: Atlanta Ripper

Characteristics: Women (black or dark-skinned), mutilation

Number of victims: 15 - 21

Date of murders: 1911

Date of arrest: Never apprehended

Victim profile: Rosa Trice; Belle Walker; Addie Watts; Lena Sharpe; Sadie Holley; plus many others

Method of murder: Stabbing, beating

Location: Atlanta

Status: Unknown

Background

Throughout 1911 and part of 1912, Atlanta was rocked by multiple murders of young black or mulatto women. Body after body turned up, some horribly mutilated, with no apparent end to the killings. Police would eventually arrest six men and charge them with some of the murders, but only one was convicted, and that case was dubious to start with.

No specific perpetrator was identified, and the murder cases remained unsolved. It's believed there could be as many as twenty-one victims, though investigators couldn't say categorically that they were committed by one man.

Murders

Belle Walker, an African-American cook, failed to come home after work on May 27, 1911. Her sister went out to search for her and found her body the following day, just twenty-five yards away from her home. Her assailant had cut her throat. Then on June 15, the body of Addie Watts, another black woman, was found with her throat cut. Days later, on June 27, the body of Lizzie Watkins was discovered with the same type of injuries.

On July 1, 1911, Emma Lou Sharpe, twenty, was waiting for her mother to come home from grocery shopping. When she didn't return, Emma Lou decided to go looking for her. When Emma Lou reached the grocery store, she learned her mother had never arrived there. As she walked back home, a tall black man approached her and asked how she was feeling. Trying to walk past him, Emma Lou replied that she was well.

The man blocked her from passing him, and told her not to be afraid because he didn't "hurt girls like you." Then, without warning, he stabbed her in the back. Emma Lou managed to run from the man, screaming for someone to help her. She soon learned that her mother was already dead, her throat cut so severely she was almost beheaded.

A group of men working on July 11 discovered a large pool of blood on the road. There was a trail leading away from it, so they followed it to a small gully, around thirty feet away. There they found the body of Sadie Holley, a worker at the laundry nearby. She, too, had been nearly decapitated when her throat was cut.

The next body found belonged to Mary Ann Duncan. She was discovered lying among the railroad tracks in Blantown, in the western area of Atlanta, on August 31. Her shoes were missing, and her throat had been cut.

The body of Minnie Wise was found in an alleyway on November 10, with her shoes missing, her throat cut, and a finger severed. The newspapers described her as "a comely mulatto girl."

More bodies were found throughout the winter of 1912, all with their throats cut. One of the victims was a 19-year-old described as an "octoroon" girl; her body was found in some bushes with a stab wound to the throat. In the spring, another "octoroon" girl was found in the Chattahoochee River. The fifteen-year-old's body had been mutilated and her throat cut.

Then, in March 1913, Laura Smith, a mixed-race young woman who worked as a servant, was found with her throat cut.

Trial

Within twenty-four hours of the discovery of Sadie Holley's body, police arrested twenty-seven-year-old laborer Henry Huff. He had been seen with her the night she died and, according to police, he had blood on his clothes and scratches on his arms when they arrested him.

Soon after, police picked up another man, Todd Henderson, whom a witness claimed had been with Holley the night she was murdered. Police brought Emma Lou Sharpe into the station to see if she could identify him as her attacker. She later said that she was certain he was the man who had stabbed her. Police were also suspicious that Henderson told them he didn't have a razor or pocketknife; they later found he had dropped a razor off at a barbershop to be sharpened.

Another man arrested and charged with one of the murders was John Daniel. He and Henry Huff were indicted on August 9, 1913, by a grand jury. Huff was charged with the murder of Holley. There is no information regarding what murder Daniel was charged with.

Police continued to arrest suspects, namely black men. Charlie Owens, one of the suspects, was convicted of one of the murders, though it wasn't stated which one. He received a life sentence.

Huff was found not guilty.

Henry Brown, also known as Lawton Brown, was arrested on August 10, 1912, for the murder of Eva Florence, who had been killed the previous November. His wife told police that when he came home on Saturdays, his clothes were always bloody. When police questioned Brown, he told them specific details about some of the other murders, so detectives were sure they had the right man.

Brown went on trial in October 1912, for the murder of Florence. However, a black man named John Rutherford testified in court that Brown had been abused during the interrogation. He claimed that

Brown had been struck in the head numerous times while tied to a chair, and the beating only stopped when he confessed. The jury believed that this would have made Brown confess to anything, and he was acquitted on October 18.

Outcome

The official murder tally for the Ripper killings was twenty, but the newspapers in Atlanta brought the murders and the unknown suspect into the public eye over the years that followed. In 1914, three years after the murders had begun, firefighters discovered notes pinned to fireboxes around Atlanta. Whoever had written them promised to cut the throats of all African-American women who were found on the streets after a certain hour of the night.

Despite a reward being offered for the identity of the Ripper, nobody ever came forward.

Trivia

The shoes of several of the Ripper's victims were cut from their feet, and sometimes located near the body. Some of the shoes were never found. Because of the language used in newspapers at the time, one article reported that "the woman's shoes were not molested."

"Octoroon" was the term used to describe someone who was one-eighth black.

JOSEPH D. BALL

Date of birth: January 7, 1896

Aliases/Nicknames: Joe Ball, The Butcher of Elmendorf, The Alligator Man

Characteristics: Fed his victim's bodies to alligators

Number of victims: 5 - 14 +

Date of murders: 1936 - 1938

Date of arrest: Unsuccessful

Victim profile: Young women

Method of murder: Shooting

Location: Elmendorf, Bexar County, Texas, USA

Status: Committed suicide by shooting himself to avoid arrest on September 24, 1938

Background

As a young child, Ball kept to himself, preferring to spend his time alone exploring the outdoors and fishing. As he grew older, he developed a fascination with guns and would practice shooting them for several hours each week.

When America entered World War I on April 6, 1917, Ball enlisted and fought on the front lines in Europe. In 1919, at the end of the war, he received an honorable discharge and returned to Elmendorf, his hometown. He tried working with his father for a while, but that didn't last long.

It was the prohibition era, and Ball—figuring out there was a huge demand for illegal alcohol—became a bootlegger. Ball would drive his Model A Ford around the area selling whiskey out of a barrel. He eventually set up a bar and hired Clifton Wheeler, a young African-American man, to work for him.

In addition to featuring live alligators, the bar also had the prettiest and youngest girls on staff to serve the customers. They didn't seem to stay long though, and Ball would often say they had been simply drifting through town looking to make quick money.

Ball met Minnie Gotthardt, known as "Big Minnie," in 1934. She began to help him with running the bar and they were together for three years when Ball developed an eye for his young waitress Dolores "Buddy" Goodwin. Apparently, he had once thrown a bottle at her, leaving a scar on her face and neck. She fell in love with him nonetheless.

Now Ball was involved with two women, and a third was about to come onto the scene. He hired Hazel "Schatzie" Brown, twenty-two, to work for him, and before long, Ball was in love with her. Trying to juggle the three women became complicated. In the summer of 1937, Minnie disappeared. When her family questioned Ball, he said she had given birth to a black baby and left town.

Ball and Dolores were married a few months after that. She later said that he had told her he had shot Minnie in the head and buried her in the sand at a local beach. Dolores didn't believe it and never spoke of it to Ball again.

Dolores disappeared in April 1938, and Hazel went missing not long afterward.

Murders

Minnie's family started asking questions again in mid-1938, and they requested that Bexar County Sheriff's office investigate her disappearance. They questioned Ball on several occasions but never found any evidence to suggest foul play, and he was consequently dismissed as a suspect in Minnie's disappearance.

The family of Julia Turner, twenty-three, went to the police a few months later, stating the young girl had gone missing while working at Ball's bar. Once again, Ball was interviewed. He told the police Turner was having some personal problems and had moved on. They searched her home, and when they found all of her belongings still there, they went back to Ball. This time, he said she had been in a desperate state and he had left her some money because she didn't want to go back home due to problems with her roommate.

Two more employees went missing, and the police continued to question Ball. Then, a previous neighbor of Ball's went to the police on September 23, 1938, with a startling story. He claimed he had seen Ball cut the flesh off a human body and feed it to his alligators. Another man then went to the police and said he had found a barrel that Ball had left behind his sister's barn, and that it was foul-smelling.

By the time police went to check on the barrel, it had vanished. When the man's sister corroborated the story, however, they decided it was time to pay Ball another visit.

Trial

Two deputies from the sheriff's office went to the bar and advised Ball that they needed him to come in for questioning. Ball asked if he could close the bar first, and the deputies agreed. As they waited, Ball quickly slammed down a beer, walked over to the cash register, and opened it. Inside was a .45 caliber revolver, which he waved at the deputies, then pointed to his heart. Before the deputies could stop him, he shot himself.

Following his death, the bar's premises was searched. Near the alligator pond, they found rotting meat and an axe with hair and blood on it. The investigators surmised that Ball had mutilated his victims and then fed them to the alligators.

Investigators tracked down Wheeler and took him to the sheriff's office for questioning. At first, he claimed he knew nothing about the circumstances of the women's disappearances. As the day progressed though, he finally admitted that he knew more than he had told them.

According to Wheeler, Hazel Brown had gotten into a relationship with another man and was going to move away. Ball was enraged and killed her. To prove the story, investigators asked Wheeler to show them where her body was.

The next day, Wheeler led them to an area near the San Antonio River, about three miles from town. He started to dig up some loose soil and, a few minutes later, blood and a terrible smell began to ooze out of the dirt. Wheeler dug up two legs, two arms, and a torso, but the head had been burned in a campfire close by. In the remains of the campfire, they found some teeth, pieces of skull, and a jawbone, all belonging to Hazel Brown.

Wheeler told the investigators that Ball had forced him to dig the grave and empty the large barrel that contained the body of Hazel Brown. This was the same barrel that had reportedly been left behind a barn that police had been unable to locate. At first, Wheeler refused to help Ball cut up the body, but he was eventually forced to.

He further told police that Ball had taken Minnie to Ingleside near Corpus Christi, found an isolated area, and shot her in the head. Apparently, Ball had killed her because she was pregnant, and he didn't want a baby to interfere with the relationships he was having with the other women. Investigators went to the area and, using machinery and hired laborers, they found her body on October 14, 1938.

Wheeler denied any knowledge of what had happened to the other women who had gone missing.

He was charged with assisting with the disposal of the bodies, and in 1939, he pled guilty.

Outcome

Wheeler was sentenced to just two years in prison. After he was released, he opened his own bar. Due to constant pressure from the press and the locals, however, he eventually left the area.

Dolores was found in California, alive and well. She had simply left to start a new life. Another one of the allegedly missing women was found in Phoenix, Arizona.

The rotting flesh found around the alligator pond proved to be animal and not human.

Trivia

Ball was the inspiration for Tobe Hooper's film *Eaten Alive*.

Locals used to joke that waitresses had been fed to Ball's alligators.

Sometimes Ball would feed dogs or cats to his alligators as a "treat."

Years later, Ball's third wife resurfaced. She claimed she had run away after she figured out about Ball's involvement in four possible murders.

The San Antonio Zoo became the home for Ball's alligators.

VELMA BARFIELD

Date of birth: October 23, 1932

Aliases/Nicknames: Death Row Granny

Characteristics: Poisoner

Number of victims: 5 - 7

Date of murders: 1969 - 1978

Date of arrest: May 13, 1978

Victim profile: Husbands, fiancés, and her own mother

Method of murder: Arsenic poisoning

Location: Robeson County, North Carolina, USA

Status: Executed by lethal injection in North Carolina on November 2, 1984

Background

Although Barfield (née Bullard) was born in South Carolina, she was raised by her family in Fayetteville, North Carolina. Her father was allegedly physically violent, and her mother did nothing to stop the abuse. In 1949, Barfield escaped her violent home and married Thomas Burke. After they had two children, Barfield underwent a hysterectomy; the procedure led her to suffer from back pain. Eventually, the pain drove her to develop an addiction to drugs.

Murders

The marriage became fraught with arguments due to Burke's consumption of alcohol and Barfield's pain issues. On April 4, 1969, Barfield took the children with her on an errand and left Burke passed out in the home. When they came back, the house was on fire, and Burke was deceased. Barfield purchased another home, and a few months later, it too burned to the ground. This time there was an insurance policy though, so Barfield was not left out of pocket.

In 1970, Barfield met and married Jennings Barfield, a widower. Jennings died from heart complications on March 22, 1971, within a year of their marriage.

Barfield and her mother, Lillian Bullard, ended up living together. In 1974, Bullard became ill with vomiting, diarrhea, and nausea. Though she recovered within a few days, she developed the same illness during the Christmas season. This time she didn't recover, and she died in the hospital on December 30, 1974, just hours after she had been admitted.

Barfield began caring for elderly couple Montgomery and Dollie Edwards in 1976. On January 29, 1977, Montgomery died after a period of illness. Dollie subsequently developed the same symptoms and died on March 1, a little over a month after her husband. Barfield then moved on to another elderly client, Record Lee, seventy-six. Lee had broken her leg and needed care. Her husband, John Henry, became ill on June 4, 1977, and died soon afterward. His symptoms were vomiting, diarrhea, abdominal and chest pain, and nausea.

The next person to fall victim to Barfield was Rowland Stuart Taylor, who was in a relationship with Barfield and was also a relative of Dollie's. Barfield had been forging checks from his account and, frightened she would be caught, she mixed arsenic-based rat poison into his tea and beer. Taylor died on February 3, 1978, and the subsequent autopsy revealed the arsenic in his system. Barfield was arrested and charged with his murder. She confessed to all of the murders but was only charged with Taylor's.

Trial

Barfield was convicted of Taylor's murder and sentenced to death. At the time, there wasn't a designated death row for women in North Carolina, so she was held at Central Prison in an area designated for mentally ill prisoners and those who were prone to escape attempts.

Outcome

While awaiting her execution, Barfield became a devout born-again Christian, and her last years were spent ministering to fellow inmates. Her religious efforts resulted in an appeal for her death sentence to be commuted to life. Also, a professor of psychiatry claimed Barfield had dissociative identity disorder, and that it was her other personality, "Billy," who had committed the murders.

Barfield's appeal was denied, and she decided not to pursue any further appeals. She was executed on November 2, 1984.

Trivia

After capital punishment resumed in 1976, Barfield became the first woman to be executed; she was the first woman executed since 1962.

Barfield was also the first woman to receive the lethal injection.

Her final statement was: "I know that everybody has gone through a lot of pain, all the families connected, and I am sorry, and I want to thank everybody who has been supporting me all these six years."

She dined on a bag of Cheetos and Coca-Cola for her last meal.

Her body was buried near Thomas Burke, her first husband.

The grandson of Jennings and his first wife, Jonathan Byrd, wrote the song "Velma" which is about the murders.

JUANA BARRAZA

Date of birth: December 27, 1958

Aliases/Nicknames: The Old Lady Killer, The Lady of Silence

Characteristics: Robbery

Number of victims: 42 - 48

Date of murders: 1998 - 2006

Date of arrest: January 25, 2006

Victim profile: María de la Luz González Anaya, 64; Guillermina León Oropeza, 84; María Guadalupe Aguilar Cortina, 86; María Guadalupe de la Vega Morales, 87; María del Carmen Muñoz Cote de Galván, 78; Lucrecia Elsa Calvo Marroquín, 85; Natalia Torres Castro, 85; Alicia Cota Ducoin, 76; Alicia González Castillo, 75; Andrea Tecante Carreto, 74; Carmen Cardona Rodea, 76; Socorro Enedina Martínez Pajares, 82; Guadalupe González Sánchez, 74; Esthela Cantoral Trejo, 85; Delfina González Castillo, 92; María Virginia Xelhuatzi Tizapán, 84; María de los Ángeles Cortés Reynoso, 84; Margarita Martell Vázquez, 72; Simona Bedolla Ayala, 79; María Dolores Martínez Benavides, 70; Margarita Arredondo Rodríguez, 83; María Imelda Estrada Pérez, 76; Julia Vera Duplan, 60; María Elena Mendoza Vallares, 59; María Elisa Pérez Moreno, 76; Arturo Patiño Barranco, 74; Carolina Robledo, 79; Ana María Velázquez Díaz, 62; Celia Villaliz Morales, 78; María Guadalupe Núñez Almanza, 78; Julia Vargas, 64; Mario Cruz Flores, 84; Emma Armenta Aguayo, 80; Emma Reyes Peña, 72; Carmen Sánchez Serrano, 76; Dolores Concepción Silva Calva, 91; María del Carmen Camila González Miguel, 82; Guadalupe Oliver Contreras, 85; María de los Ángeles Repper Hernández, 92; Ana María de los Reyes Alfaro, 84

Method of murder: Manual and ligature strangulation, beating, bludgeoning, stabbing

Location: Mexico City, Mexico

Status: Sentenced to 759 years in prison on March 31, 2008.

Background

Barraza was born in Epazoyucan, Hidalgo, north of Mexico City. Her childhood was horrendous after her alcoholic mother sold her to a man for three beers. The man repeatedly raped Barraza, and she ended up becoming pregnant, giving birth to a boy. She had four children, but lost her eldest son after he was killed during a mugging.

Barraza went on to become a professional wrestler, performing under the ring name of La Dama del Silencio, The Lady of Silence. She was especially interested in the Mexican masked professional wrestling called Lucha libre. Somewhere along the line, however, Barraza discovered other ways of making money and left the ring.

Murders

Elderly women were being violently murdered in Mexico City, and the authorities initially thought the killer was a man. They profiled the killer and believed "he" was clever, intelligent, careful, and was able to gain the trust of the intended victims. There was a theory that the killer may have posed as a government official, possibly pretending to register the women for welfare programs.

The Mexican authorities reported they had received witness statements that the killer wore women's clothing. After one murder, a person wearing a red blouse was seen leaving the victim's house. The big breakthrough came on January 25, 2006, when a suspect was apprehended while fleeing the home of Ana María de Los Reyes Alfaro, the latest victim. Alfaro, eighty-two, had been strangled to death in her home by a stethoscope.

Both the authorities and the public were shocked when they discovered the suspect was a woman. Previous witnesses had described the killer as a masculine-looking woman, which led police to search for a transvestite. Nobody considered the violent murderer could actually be a woman.

Fingerprint evidence linked Barraza to ten murders, and up to forty murders were eventually attributed to her. She confessed to four murders but denied the others.

Trial

In the spring of 2008, Barraza went on trial. The prosecution alleged there were forty victims in total, but Barraza denied that figure. She told the police her motive was the deep resentment she felt toward her mother; this was why she killed and robbed only elderly women.

Outcome

On March 31, 2008, she was convicted of sixteen counts of murder and aggravated burglary, and another eleven counts of murder. She received a sentence of 759 years in prison. Sentences doled out in Mexican courts are usually served concurrently, with the maximum being sixty years. Barraza will most likely serve the full sentence.

Trivia

"When I saw them, I felt much anger and more when they acted uppity or believed that because of their money, they could humiliate me." — ***Barraza***

Portrayal on television

Barraza was the topic of a television series in the early 2000s, called *Mujer casos de la Vida Real*. The episode she is featured in is called "Maggie, Pensionada," and she is portrayed by Leticia Perdigón, a Mexican actress.

Barraza was mentioned in *Instinto Asesino*, a documentary which aired in 2010. The episode was called "La Mataviejitas."

Barraza was featured in the television series *Deadly Women*, in the episode called "Payback."

The episode "Machismo," from the television series *Criminal Minds*, is based in part on Barraza.

Herb Baumeister

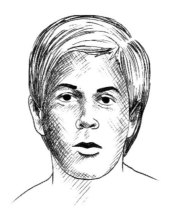

Date of birth: April 7, 1947

Aliases/Nicknames: Herb, The I-70 Strangler

Characteristics: Lust killer, torture, gay male victims

Number of victims: 8 - 16

Date of murders: 1980 - 1996

Date of arrest:

Victim profile: Johnny Bayer, 20; Allen Wayne Broussard, 28; Roger A. Goodlet, 33; Richard D. Hamilton, 20; Steven S. Hale, 26; Jeff Allen Jones, 31; Michael Kiern, 46; Manuel Resendez, 31

Method of murder: Strangulation

Location: Indiana, Ohio, USA

Status: Committed suicide to avoid arrest on July 3, 1996, in Ontario, Canada

Background

Baumeister was the eldest of four children born to Herbert and Elizabeth Baumeister in Indianapolis, Indiana. Although he had a normal childhood, his behavior changed quite dramatically as he approached adolescence. At one point, he was caught urinating on a teacher's desk at school. There also were reports Baumeister liked to play with dead animals. As a teen, he was diagnosed with schizophrenia but did not receive treatment.

As an adult, Baumeister had a variety of jobs, none of which ever lasted. His work ethic was great, but his behavior gradually became more bizarre. Despite this, he married Juliana Saiter in November 1971, and the couple had three children. His wife later stated they were only sexually intimate six times in the twenty-five years they were married. Baumeister was committed to a psychiatric facility in the 1970s by his father.

Murders

There had been numerous disappearances of gay men in the Indianapolis area in the early 1990s, and all were similar in height, weight, and age. Investigators were contacted in 1992 by Tony Harris, who claimed a patron at a gay bar had killed a friend of his and had also tried to kill him during an erotic asphyxiation session. The man was calling himself, "Brian Smart."

In August 1995, Harris saw "Brian Smart" again and took down his car's license plate number, giving it to the police. From the number, they were able to identify "Brian Smart" as Baumeister. They went to Baumeister's home and, after informing him he was a suspect in the disappearances, asked to search the property. Both Baumeister and his wife refused to allow police to search the house.

Juliana had become frightened enough by Baumeister's behavior and mood swings that she filed for divorce in June 1996. She then consented to allow police to search the house. The property, Fox Hollow Farm, consisted of eighteen acres. Police conducted the search while Baumeister was away on vacation; the search produced the remains of eleven men, eight of whom were later identified.

Trial

After learning there was a warrant out for his arrest, Baumeister fled the area and made his way to Ontario, Canada. Once there, he went to the Pinery Provincial Park and shot himself in the head. He left a suicide note which mentioned his failing business and marital problems as the reason for killing himself. He made no confession or statements regarding the bodies found on his property.

Outcome

In addition to the victims located at Baumeister's home, police also suspected him of killing another nine men. These victims were found in rural areas along Interstate 70 between Indianapolis and Columbus, Ohio. The murders had occurred in the 1980s.

Trivia

The scene of the murders became a favored area for paranormal investigators.

Baumeister was always in trouble at school and was very disruptive, which led to him being diagnosed with schizophrenia.

He urinated on a letter for the Governor while working at the State Bureau of Motor Vehicles. After he was fired for this, it was discovered that he had also been responsible for urinating on his supervisor's desk.

LEVI BELLFIELD

Date of birth: May 17, 1968

Aliases/Nicknames: The Bus Stop Killer, Levi Rabetts, Yusuf Rahim

Characteristics: Stalker, sadist

Number of victims: 2 - 3 +

Date of murders: 2002 - 2004

Date of arrest: November 22, 2004

Victim profile: Marsha McDonnell, 19; Amelie Delagrange, 22; Amanda Dowler, 13

Method of murder: Hitting with a hammer

Location: London, England, United Kingdom

Status: Sentenced to life imprisonment, with a recommendation that he should never be released, on February 26, 2008

Background

Bellfield was born in Isleworth, Greater London, to parents Joseph and Jean. Joseph died from leukemia at the young age of fifty-two, when Bellfield was just 10. The family, including Bellfield's four siblings, was brought up on a council estate in southwest London. By all accounts, the rest of his childhood was relatively normal.

As an adult, Bellfield fathered eleven children with three women; his first criminal conviction was in 1981 for burglary. In 1990, he was convicted of assault against a police officer, and he also picked up convictions for driving offenses and theft. By 2002, he had spent nearly a year in prison and had nine convictions.

Bellfield ran a wheel-clamping business in the West Drayton area of west London, where he was living when the murders took place.

Murders

The first victim, Amanda Jane "Milly" Dowler, was just thirteen years old when she went missing. She was last seen leaving the railway station in Walton-on-Thames on March 21, 2002. Her body was discovered six months later in Yateley Heath Woods.

In February 2003, Marsha Louise McDonnell, nineteen, was beaten in the head with a blunt instrument and died two days later in hospital. She had been attacked in Hampton, London, near her home after she got off a bus from Kingston upon Thames. Suspiciously, Bellfield sold his car six days after the murder for a quarter of what he had paid for it just five months prior.

Kate Sheedy, eighteen, was crossing the road near an industrial estate in Isleworth on May 28, 2004, when she was run over by a vehicle. Although she suffered multiple injuries, she survived after spending weeks in the hospital.

The final known victim was Amélie Delagrange, twenty-two, a French student who was visiting the country. On August 19, 2004, she was found with terrible head injuries at Twickenham Green; she died that same night in the hospital.

Trial

Police had been surveilling Bellfield and noted he liked to drive around and talk to young girls at bus stops. He became a suspect in the murder of Delagrange and was arrested on November 22, 2004. Three days later, he was charged with three counts of rape in west London and Surrey. On December 9, 2004, he was also charged with assaulting a woman in Twickenham years earlier and was held in custody.

On March 2, 2006, Bellfield was formally charged with the murder of Delagrange, the attempted murder of Kate Sheedy, and attempted murder and grievous bodily harm to another woman, Irma Dragoshi. On May 25, he was charged with McDonnell's murder.

Bellfield was also charged with the kidnapping and murder of Dowler and the attempted kidnapping of another young girl, Rachel Cowles, twelve, which had occurred on March 20, 2002. Bellfield denied the murder of Dowler and refused to take the stand at his trial.

Bellfield received another charge of abduction and false imprisonment following an attack on Anna-Maria Rennie on October 14, 2001.

Outcome

Bellfield was convicted of killing McDonnell and Delagrange, and of attempting to murder Sheedy, on February 25, 2008. He was sentenced to life imprisonment; the judge recommended he never be released. He was also convicted of killing Dowler and received the same sentence and recommendation.

Police suspected Bellfield had been responsible for numerous other murders and attacks on women, including the murder of Patsy Morris, fourteen, his childhood girlfriend, who had been killed in 1980.

In early 2015, Bellfield admitted his responsibility for some unsolved murder and rape cases. These were investigated, but in 2016, the decision was made to close the investigation as they could not find any links to Bellfield in any of the cases.

In 2016, Bellfield admitted to killing Dowler, and then later recanted.

Trivia

Bellfield's daughter presented a documentary, called *My Dad the Serial Killer,* on January 30, 2009. His other children and his wife also featured on the documentary.

Bellfield was featured on the television program *Britain's Most Evil Killers* in 2017.

MANUEL OCTAVIO BERMÚDEZ

Date of birth: October 15, 1961

Aliases/Nicknames: El Monstruo de los Cañaduzales (The Monster of the Cane Fields)

Characteristics: Rape, children

Number of victims: 21 - 50 +

Date of murders: 1999 – 2003

Date of arrest: July 18, 2003

Victim profile: Children

Method of murder: Rape and strangle them to death, while sometimes injecting them with a syringe to weaken their legs.

Location: Valle del Cauca, Colombia

Status: Sentenced to 40 years in prison

Background

Manuel Octavio Bermúdez was born in Trujillo, Valle del Cauca, Colombia in 1961. After his birth, he was orphaned and then tragically was adopted by an abusive woman. There are reports that she once threw him off the balcony of the home, and his foot and hand were broken, leaving him with a permanent limp. He was then handed over to another family in Palmira, but that home wasn't any better. The new parents were alcoholics, and the father was also abusive.

Murders

Between 1999 and 2003, Bermúdez raped and killed at least twenty-one children in several towns of Valle del Cauca. He would lure the children into cornfields, promising to pay them money for picking the corn, and then attack them. Sometimes he injected them with a drug to weaken their legs so they couldn't run away. Then he would rape and strangle them. The known victims are as follows:

April 6, 1999
In Palmira, the body of a ten-year-old boy was found but was not identified.

September 17, 1999
The body of another ten-year-old boy was found in Palmira.

May 5, 2000
The skeleton of a child was found on the Cascajal de Palmira farm.

December 30, 2001
The body of Javier Sánchez Fernández, eleven years old, was found in Palmira. He had disappeared two days earlier.

February 14, 2002
In Palmira, the body of another dead child was found but not identified.

April 1, 2002
The body of José Évert Sinisterra, who was thirteen years old, was found in Palmira.

April 9, 2002
On the Cascajal farm, they found the remains of another child.

July 27, 2002
Edwin Andrés Pérez, twelve years old, was found in Tuluá.

December 3, 2002
The remains of Miguel Ángel Arce, eleven years old, were found in the Aguaclara de Palmira village. He had gone missing a month earlier.

December 13, 2002
The body of Nahún Candelo was found in Palmira.

January 15, 2003
The body of Carlos Alfonso Fajardo Morcillo was found in Palmira.

January 25, 2003
On the Cascajal farm, they found the remains of Cristian Fabián Torres, nine years old. He had gone missing on December 10, 2002.

April 19, 2003
José Miguel Figueroa, twelve years old, was found in Yotoco.

May 16, 2003
In Pradera, they found the remains of another unidentified child.

May 26, 2003
Jorge Enrique Rodríguez, thirteen years old, was found in Pradera.

June 11, 2003
The body of Luis Carlos Galvis was found on the road to the corregimiento of Tablón, Pradera.

Trial

Bermúdez was identified by the mother of Luis Carlos Gálvez as being with the young boy the last time she had seen him. She reported this to the police, and he was arrested on July 18, 2003. When his rented room was searched, police found newspaper clippings regarding the murders, the drug Lidocaine, syringes, and the wristwatch Luis had been wearing the last time he was seen alive.

Outcome

Following his arrest, Bermúdez confessed to the murders of twenty-one children, seventeen of whom were found. He was convicted and sentenced to forty years in prison on March 20, 2004. Authorities suspect him of killing more than fifty children.

Trivia

Bermúdez identified his potential victims while selling ice cream.

Because of Columbian law, the maximum time a person can spend in prison is forty years.

DONATO BILANCIA

Date of birth: July 10, 1951

Aliases/Nicknames: Walter, The Monster of Liguria

Characteristics: Robbery, revenge, gambling

Number of victims: 17

Date of murders: 1997 - 1998

Date of arrest: May 6, 1998

Victim profile: Giorgo Centanaro, 58; Maurizio Parenti; Carla Scotto; Bruno Solari; Maria Luigia Pitto; Luciano Marro; Giangiorgio Canu, 52; Bodejana Almerina; Ljudmila Zubskova; Enzo Gorni; Massimo Gualillo; Candido Randò; Evelyn Esohe Endoghaye, 27; Elisabetta Zoppetti, 32; Mema Valbona; Maria Angela Rubino; Giuseppe Mileto, 51

Method of murder: Shooting with a .38 caliber revolver

Location: Italy

Status: Sentenced to 13 terms of life imprisonment, with no possibility of release, on April 12, 2000

Background

Bilancia was born in Potenza, Basilicata, Italy, in 1951. His family moved to northern Italy when he was about five years old, first to Piedmont and then to Genoa in the Liguria area. A chronic bed wetter until he was nearly twelve years old, his mother humiliated him by putting his wet mattress on the balcony of the house so the neighbors could see it. His aunt was just as mentally damaging. When getting him ready for bed, she would pull down his underwear in front of relatives and make fun of his penis, which was underdeveloped.

When Bilancia was fourteen years old, he began referring to himself as Walter. He left school and worked a variety of jobs until he was arrested for stealing a motor scooter and a truck that was carrying sweets. He was still a minor at this stage. Then, in 1974, he was arrested for having an illegal gun.

Bilancia spent some time in a mental unit at the local hospital, but he managed to escape. When police found him, they arrested him and charged him with robbery. He spent eighteen months in prison, but this was only the beginning. He was sent to prison a number of times, in both Italy and France, for armed robbery and robbery. However, up until he was forty-seven years old, he had never been arrested or charged for any violent crime.

Murders

Bilancia, a compulsive gambler, committed his first murder in October 1997 after a friend lured him into what he believed was a rigged card game. He strangled the friend to death after losing about one hundred eighty-five thousand pounds. Originally, the death was believed to be the result of a heart attack.

The next two murder victims were the operator of the card game and his wife. He shot them to death and then robbed their safe. He later told authorities that these murders gave him a taste for it. Bilancia left the bodies where they could be easily found, without making any attempt to conceal them.

He committed his next two murders the same month. He followed a jeweler home, planning to rob him. When they got to the man's house, however, he fatally shot both him and his wife after she had started screaming. He stole all the jewelry that was in the safe.

The sixth victim was a money changer who he killed while robbing him. Two months later, he murdered a night watchman simply because he didn't like them. He murdered two prostitutes shortly after, one from Russia and the other from Albania. Next, he shot, killed, and robbed another money changer.

In March of 1998, Bilancia held a prostitute at gunpoint while she performed oral sex on him. When two night watchmen interrupted, he killed them both and then shot the prostitute. She survived and gave a description to police. Bilancia killed two more prostitutes, one Ukrainian and the other Nigerian. He robbed and assaulted a third prostitute but let her live.

Bilancia boarded a train from Genoa to Venice on April 12, 1998, wanting to kill someone. He noticed a young woman who was traveling alone, followed her to the bathroom, and shot her in the head. Six days later, he followed another young woman to the toilet on a train and shot her. He found her black underwear exciting and masturbated, using her clothing to clean up afterward.

The last murder he committed was that of a service station attendant. He filled his car up with petrol and then stole the money.

Trial

Bilancia was the number one suspect after a description of his car was given to police on the night one of the prostitutes was murdered; the victim had been seen getting into his car before she was killed. Police followed Bilancia for several days, collecting his DNA from a coffee cup he threw away as well as discarded cigarette butts. The test results came back; his DNA matched the DNA found at some of the crime scenes.

Bilancia was arrested at his home on May 6, 1998. He had been in police custody for just over a week when he decided to confess. His confession took two days, during which he drew seventeen diagrams for the police regarding his crimes.

Bilancia's trial lasted eleven months, and on April 12, 2000, he was found guilty.

Outcome

Bilancia received a sentence of thirteen terms of life imprisonment, plus an extra twenty years for the attempted murder. The judge made an order that he should never be released.

Trivia

In prison, Bilancia has regularly been described by guards as a "model prisoner."

While in prison, he has achieved a diploma in accounting; he is also studying tourism.

He was given a temporary permit to leave the prison in 2017, so he could visit the graves of his parents.

JAKE BIRD

Date of birth: December 14, 1901

Aliases/Nicknames: The Tacoma Ax-Killer

Characteristics: Rape, robbery

Number of victims: 11 - 44

Date of murders: 1930s - 1947

Date of arrest: October 30, 1947

Victim profile: Bertha Kludt, 53; Beverly June Kludt, 17; at least nine others, unnamed

Method of murder: Beating with an ax, stabbing with a knife

Location: Several States, USA

Status: Executed by hanging at the Washington State Penitentiary in Walla Walla on July 15, 1949

Background

Bird was born somewhere in Louisiana, but couldn't recall the exact location. He worked as a manual laborer on the railroad, laying and maintaining tracks. He had a lengthy criminal record and had spent a cumulative total of thirty-one years in prison. His previous crimes included attempted murder and burglary.

Murders

Police were called to a residence early in the morning of October 30, 1947, after reports were made of a woman screaming. When they approached the residence, a man ran out the back door, through the backyard, and crashed through a fence. The police chased after the man, over several more fences, until a high wire fence stopped him. Cornered by the officers, he pulled a switchblade knife out and swung at them. One was stabbed in the back; the other suffered an injury to his hand.

Unfortunately for the suspect, one of the officers had been a former prizefighter and was able to subdue him with a punch to the jaw and a kick to the groin. Upon entering the residence they were initially called to investigate, they found two murder victims - Bertha Kludt, fifty-three, and her daughter, Beverly June Kludt, seventeen. Both had been struck several times in the head with an axe, and the weapon was still on the kitchen floor.

Trial

The man who had led police on a foot chase was Bird. Once at the city jail, he confessed to killing the two women but stated he had only broken into the home to rob it. When Bertha caught him, he tried to escape. She allegedly tried to stop him though, so he hit her with the axe. Then June woke and came to her mother's aid, so he killed her as well. However, detectives discovered Bird had made an attempt to sexually assault Bertha before she was killed.

Bird was charged on October 31, 1947, but only for the murder of Bertha. This was because the prosecution had to prove her murder was premeditated so Bird would qualify for the death penalty. Bird entered a plea of not guilty and was held without bail.

An incredibly short trial, it started on November 24, 1947, and ended two and a half days later. Evidence showed brain and blood tissue from both women were found on Bird's clothes, and his fingerprints were found on the axe and in the house. Bird's attorney tried to have his signed confession ruled inadmissible, claiming it had been made under duress; the judge disagreed and allowed it.

The jury deliberated for just thirty-five minutes before finding Bird guilty of first-degree murder. They recommended the death penalty.

Outcome

The judge agreed with the jury and sentenced Bird to death by hanging.

To delay his execution, Bird claimed he could solve at least forty-four murders he had committed or participated in. The governor awarded him a sixty-day reprieve to do so. He was interviewed by investigators from all over the country, but out of the forty-four he claimed, they could only substantiate eleven. Bird did have a lot of information about the murders, however, which made him the prime suspect.

Bird admitted to killing mainly female victims in Illinois, Nebraska, Kansas, Kentucky, Oklahoma, Ohio, South Dakota, Florida, Michigan, Wisconsin, Washington, and Iowa.

During the sixty-day reprieve, Bird lodged an appeal for a retrial, but his request was denied. He was executed by hanging on July 15, 1949 and buried in an unmarked grave in the prison cemetery.

Trivia

Bird was the seventh African-American inmate executed since the establishment of the death penalty in 1904, with the execution carried out in Washington State.

Bird's final statement following his conviction lasted for twenty minutes. He claimed his lawyers had been against him and he had not had the opportunity to represent himself.

Bird also said, "I'm putting the Jake Bird hex on all of you who had anything to do with my being punished. Mark my words, you will die before I do."

Five people who had been involved with Bird's trial died within a year of his conviction. Many believed this was due to the hex Bird had threatened to put on them.

The five men connected with Bird's trial who died within a year of the "Jake Bird Hex":

- Edward D. Hodge, Pierce County Superior Court Judge, age sixty-nine, died January 1, 1948.

- Joseph E. Karpach, Pierce County Under-sheriff, age forty-six, died April 5, 1948.

- George L. Harrigan, Pierce County court reporter, age sixty-nine, died June 11, 1948.

- Sherman W. Lyons, Tacoma Police Detective Lieutenant, age forty-six, died October 28, 1948.

- James W. Selden, Bird's defense attorney, age seventy-six, died on November 26, 1948.

Apparently, they all died from heart attacks, except for one who died from pneumonia.

DAVID AND CATHERINE BIRNIE

David Birnie

Date of birth: February 15, 1951

Aliases/Nicknames: The Moorhouse Murders

Characteristics: Rape

Number of victims: 4

Date of murders: October - November 1986

Date of arrest: November 10, 1986

Victim profile: Mary Francis Neilson, 22; Susannah Candy, 15; Noelene Patterson, 31; Denise Karen Brown, 21

Method of murder: Strangulation, stabbing with knife

Location: Freemantle, Western Australia, Australia

Status: Sentenced to four consecutive sentences of life imprisonment in 1987. Committed suicide by hanging himself in his cell on October 7, 2005.

Catherine Birnie

Date of birth: May 23, 1951

Aliases/Nicknames: The Moorhouse Murders

Characteristics: Rape

Number of victims: 4

Date of murders: October - November 1986

Date of arrest: November 10, 1986

Victim profile: Mary Francis Neilson, 22; Susannah Candy, 15; Noelene Patterson, 31; Denise Karen Brown, 21

Method of murder: Strangulation, stabbing with knife

Location: Freemantle, Western Australia, Australia

Status: Four terms of life imprisonment.

Background

David John Birnie

Birnie was the oldest of five children and grew up in Wattle Grove, east of Perth, Australia. The family was described by many as dysfunctional, with rumors of alcoholism, promiscuity, and incest. The house was filthy and unkempt, and meals were never cooked for the children.

Birnie's father was a small, unattractive man, and his mother was coarse, known for her profane language and inappropriate sexual behavior, such as exchanging sexual favors for taxi rides. The family moved to another suburb in the early 1960s, and Birnie met Catherine through friends. When he was fifteen, he left school and gained work as an apprentice jockey at Ascot racecourse. While there, he injured the horses and developed a habit of exhibitionism. Naked, and wearing stockings over his head, he broke into the room of an elderly lady in the house he was boarding at. He tried to rape her but was unsuccessful.

Birnie was convicted of numerous crimes and spent time in and out of prison. As an adult, he became addicted to pornography and sex. He married in his early twenties, and a daughter was born. The marriage ended, and he crossed paths with Catherine again. By the late 1980s, Birnie and Catherine were working out how to enact their sexual fantasies of rape and murder.

Catherine Margaret Harrison

Born in 1951, Catherine was two years old when her mother died during childbirth; her newborn sibling died two days later. Catherine's father sent her to live with her grandparents as he was unable to care for her. At the age of ten, there was a custody dispute, and she was sent back to live with her father. She met Birnie when she was twelve years old, and by fourteen, they were in a relationship together. Her father tried to get her to leave Birnie when she started getting into trouble with the police because of him.

Catherine spent time in prison during adolescence, and this gave her an opportunity to get away from Birnie. A parole officer encouraged her to work for the McLaughlin family as a housekeeper, and on her twenty-first birthday, she married Donald McLaughlin. The marriage produced seven children. Their first child, a son, was killed after being struck by a vehicle when he was an infant.

Catherine left her husband and children in 1985 and returned to Birnie. They never married, but she adopted his surname.

Murders

Over a five-week period, the Birnies abducted five women. The victims were aged between fifteen and thirty-one, and only one managed to escape. The others were raped and murdered. The lone survivor led police to the Birnies.

Victims

Mary Neilson

Neilson was twenty-two years old and studying psychology at the university. She also worked part-time in a delicatessen. She met Birnie when she was looking for tires for her car; since he worked at a spare parts yard, he gave her his phone number. Neilson went to the Birnies' house on October 6, 1986, to purchase tires from them. Once inside, she was gagged and chained to the bed. Catherine watched as Birnie raped Neilson. She was then taken to Gleneagles National Park near Albany Highway and raped again. She begged for her life before Birnie strangled her with a nylon cord. Birnie then stabbed her as well, believing that would make the body decompose quicker. They buried her in a shallow grave.

Susannah Candy

Two weeks after Neilson was murdered, the Birnies abducted Candy, fifteen, who was hitchhiking along the Stirling Highway in Claremont. As soon as she was inside their car, a knife was put to her throat, and her hands were tied. The couple took her back to their house in Willagee and forced her to write letters to her family, telling them she was okay. Then they gagged her and chained her to the bed. Birnie raped her, and then Catherine got into the bed with them. They both proceeded to assault the young girl until Birnie attempted to strangle her with a nylon cord. She went berserk, so they forced sleeping pills down her throat.

Once she was asleep, Birnie told Catherine that if she loved him, she would prove it by strangling the girl. Catherine didn't hesitate. While Birnie watched, she strangled the girl with the cord until she was no longer breathing. Candy was buried in the State Forest near the body of Neilson.

Noelene Patterson

Patterson, thirty-one, had run out of gas on her way home from work when the Birnies came across her on the Canning Highway. Once in the car, a knife was held to her throat, and she was tied up. Patterson was taken to their house on Moorhouse Street, and Birnie raped her repeatedly while she was chained to the bed and gagged. Initially, they had planned to kill her that same night, but Birnie decided to keep her longer. After three days, Catherine felt Birnie had become attached to Patterson, so she gave him an ultimatum - either kill Patterson, or she would do it herself.

Birnie forced sleeping pills down Patterson's throat and, while she was asleep, he strangled her. She was buried in the forest but not near the other graves.

Denise Brown

The Birnies abducted Brown, twenty-one, while she was waiting for a bus on November 5. They offered her a ride which she accepted and was soon at knifepoint in the back of the car. Like the others, she was chained to the bed and raped by Birnie. They took her to the Wanneroo pine plantation the next day and, while they waited for nightfall, Birnie raped her again in the car. He then raped her once more as they dragged her from the car. He thrust the knife into her neck to kill her and, when they thought she had died, they placed her body into a shallow grave. She wasn't dead though and sat upright in the grave, so Birnie struck her twice in the head with an axe.

Kate Moir

The only victim to escape was Moir, seventeen. She had accepted a ride from the Birnies and was taken back to the house at knifepoint. Once there, she was forced to dance for the Birnies and sleep in the same bed while handcuffed to Birnie. She was also forced to ring her mother and say she was staying at a friend's home for the night. When Birnie went to work the next morning and Catherine was busy at the front door conducting a drug deal, Moir—who had not been chained to the bed—escaped through a window. She knocked on neighbors' doors without luck and then ran down the road and into a shop, informing the owner that she had been raped.

When police arrived on the scene, Moir told them what had happened. At first, they didn't believe her. But she was able to give them a lot of details, including the address and phone number, and told them she had left a drawing in the house to prove she was there. When police went to the Birnie house, they discovered the drawing and confirmed every other detail Moir had given them.

The Birnies were arrested, and although they initially denied everything, saying the sex was consensual, Birnie eventually confessed.

Trial

At his trial, Birnie pleaded guilty to four counts of murder, along with one count each of rape and abduction. He was sentenced to four terms of life imprisonment.

Catherine was found guilty as well and also received four life sentences. They both would have to serve a minimum of twenty years before they could be eligible for parole.

Outcome

Birnie started his sentence at the maximum-security Fremantle Prison, but because he was at risk of harm from the other inmates, he was moved to solitary confinement for his own safety. The prison converted the old death row cells and moved him into there until 1990 when the prison closed. While they were incarcerated, the Birnies exchanged more than twenty-six hundred letters between them but were not allowed any other form of contact.

On October 7, 2005, Birnie was found dead in his cell. He had used a length of cord to hang himself from an air vent. He was fifty-four years old.

Catherine worked as a prison librarian during her incarceration. She applied for parole in 2007, but it was rejected. Her next possible parole date was meant to be in 2010, but, following requests from the families of the victims, the Attorney-General Christian Porter determined she would stay in prison for the rest of her life.

Another parole application was denied in 2016; she may be able to apply again in 2019.

Trivia

While in prison David was accused of rape but no charges were ever filed.

The Moorhouse Street house where the crimes were committed became available to rent in December 2018.

Peter, the son of Catherine, has stated his mother should "never be released."

After David's death, his body went unclaimed for over a month, so he was cremated as a pauper, with the taxpayers footing the bill.

WAYNE BODEN

Date of birth: January 1, 1948

Aliases/Nicknames: The Vampire Rapist

Characteristics: Rape, sexual sadism

Number of victims: 4

Date of murders: 1969 - 1971

Date of arrest: May 19, 1971

Victim profile: Shirley Audette, 20; Marielle Archambault, 20; Jean Wray, 24; Elizabeth Pourteous, 33

Method of murder: Strangulation

Location: Montreal, Quebec, Calgary, Alberta, Canada

Status: Sentenced to four life sentences in prison on February 16, 1972. Died in prison on March 25, 2006.

Background

Boden was born in Dundas, Ontario, in 1948. Little is known about his childhood and adolescence, other than he was fairly quiet and played school football. Between 1969 and 1971, he began raping and killing women; he earned his nickname from biting the breasts of his victims.

Murders

Boden's first known victim was Shirley Audette, who was found murdered on October 3, 1969. Her body was located behind an apartment complex in Montreal, Quebec. She was still fully clothed, though an examination showed she had been raped, bitten on the breasts, and then strangled to death. The lack of skin or blood under her fingernails suggested she made no attempt to fight off her attacker. Boden had lived next door to Audette and her boyfriend.

The next victim was Marielle Archambault. She left work on November 23 with a man she introduced to her work colleagues as "Bill." They reported she looked happy with "Bill" when she left work that night. The next morning she failed to turn up at work, so her employer went to her home to check on her in case she was unwell. Archambault's landlady helped the employer gain entry, and they discovered her dead on the couch. She was fully clothed, and the room was tidy, suggesting there hadn't been a struggle. The medical examination reported she had been raped and bitten in the same manner as Audette. A photograph of a man, identified as "Bill" by her coworkers, was found in the apartment. However, police were unable to locate the man.

Jean Way's boyfriend went to her apartment on January 16, 1970, to pick her up for a date. There was no answer at the door, so he left and returned later. On his second visit, he discovered the door was unlocked. He entered the apartment and found Way naked and dead on the bed. It was later believed that Boden was still in the apartment when Way's boyfriend knocked on the door the first time, and he fled before he could complete his routine of biting and then dressing his victim.

Elizabeth Anne Pourteous, a thirty-three-year-old schoolteacher in Calgary, Alberta, did not turn up for work on the morning of May 18, 1971. A call was made to her apartment manager, who then discovered her body on the floor of her bedroom. Porteous had been raped, her breasts bitten, and she had been strangled. There were signs of a struggle in the apartment, and a broken cufflink was found beneath her body. During the investigation, police discovered she had been seen in a blue Mercedes Benz on the night they believed she was killed. Witnesses described a decal in the back window of the vehicle, and a friend of Porteous stated she had been dating a man named "Bill."

Trial

The day after the body of Pourteous was found, police spotted a blue Mercedes near the murder scene. Half an hour later, Boden was arrested as he returned to his car. He admitted he had been dating Porteous and was with her the night she was killed; he also told them he had moved from Montreal the year before. When shown the cufflink, he admitted it belonged to him. But he claimed Pourteous was fine when he left her that night.

Police looked at the photograph found in Archambault's apartment and compared it to Boden. Because they looked similar, they held him in custody under suspicion of killing Pourteous.

A local orthodontist, Gordon Swann, was asked by police to examine the bite marks on Pourteous' body and compare them to Boden's teeth. There was little literature in Canada on comparing bite marks, so Swann contacted the FBI in America. They, in turn, directed him to a man in England who had experience in forensic odontology.

After receiving the information needed, Swann was able to show a comparison between Boden's teeth and the bite marks, with twenty-nine points of similarity.

At his trial, the evidence provided by Swann played a major part in convincing the jury Boden was guilty of murdering Pourteous. He was sentenced to life imprisonment.

Boden was then sent back to Montreal to face the judge and jury regarding the murders of Audette, Archambault, and Way. He was convicted and sentenced to three more terms of life imprisonment.

Outcome

Remarkably, Boden was granted an American Express credit card in 1977. During a day pass from prison, he used the card to flee. But he was caught again thirty-six hours later while having lunch in a restaurant. Because of this, three prison guards were disciplined, and an internal investigation was conducted by American Express to determine how a prisoner was able to get a credit card.

On March 27, 2006, Boden died from skin cancer.

Trivia

Boden had once been a fashion model.

His teachers, and fellow children at school, liked and admired him.

Because of his escape, the policy for outings for offenders who were classed as dangerous was changed.

Boden said he fled prison because the system had overlooked his grievances for more than thirteen years.

GARY RAY BOWLES

Date of birth: January 25, 1962

Aliases/Nicknames: Nil

Characteristics: Robberies, gay men

Number of victims: 5 - 6

Date of murders: March - October 1994

Date of arrest: October 22, 1994

Victim profile: John Hardy Roberts, 59; David Jarman, 38; Milton Bradley, 72; Alverson Carter Jr., 47; Albert Morris, 38; Walter Hinton, 47

Method of murder: Blunt force injury, strangulation, and/or shooting

Location: Maryland, Georgia, Florida, USA

Status: Sentenced to death in Florida on September 6, 1996. Resentenced to death on September 7, 1999 and was finally executed on August 22, 2019.

Background

Bowles was born into a turbulent family environment. His father, a coal miner, had died from black lung disease, and his mother went on to remarry several times. His second stepfather was an abusive and violent alcoholic who took out his anger on the whole family. When Bowles was thirteen years old, he finally fought back, causing his stepfather severe injuries. Soon after, Bowles left the house, angry that his mother had chosen to stay with a violent man. Over the next few years, Bowles was homeless and he supported himself through prostitution.

In 1982, Bowles was arrested after sexually assaulting and beating his girlfriend. He was convicted and sentenced to six years. He was released in 1991, and soon after was arrested again after stealing an elderly woman's purse. He was sentenced to four more years in prison but only served two before he was released again.

Murders

On April 14, 1994, police in Daytona were alerted to the home of John Hardy Roberts, fifty-nine. He had been viciously murdered, his body lying on the living room floor. There was a rag stuffed into his mouth, with signs of trauma about his head, and he had been strangled. The state of the room indicated there had been a violent struggle, and blood was spattered all over the place. A glass lamp was shattered, and police discovered Roberts' car and wallet, including credit cards and cash, were missing.

A plethora of evidence was found directing the police to a suspect. Fingerprints and probation papers belonging to Bowles were present, and when police checked the phone records, they discovered numerous calls had been made to his family members. There was also evidence that Bowles had tried to use the stolen credit cards.

Investigators knew who they were looking for but were unable to catch him. They followed the trail of evidence, and it led to Maryland, where another murder had occurred.

The decomposing body of David Jarman, thirty-eight, was found on April 14, 1994, by a building maintenance man. The body was in the basement of Jarman's home, and he had also been beaten and strangled, with a rag stuffed into his mouth. His wallet and his car were also missing.

Witnesses stated they had seen Jarman at a gay bar in Washington D.C. the night before his death with a man who matched the description of Bowles. The stolen credit cards had been used, and the signature matched Bowles'. Still unable to catch Bowles, investigators were next lead to Savannah, Georgia.

World War II veteran Milton Bradley, seventy-two, was found at a golf club, behind a shed. Like the other victims, he had material stuffed into his throat and he had been asphyxiated. He had also suffered a severe beating before he died. Bradley had previously suffered a brain injury which slightly impaired his mental capacity, and this most likely made him an easy target for Bowles.

A palm print found at the scene belonged to Bowles, and Bradley had been seen with a man matching his description in the days before he was killed.

The television show *America's Most Wanted* aired a segment about the murders and Bowles. Immediately after the airing, numerous tips came in from viewers. But the elusive Bowles had moved on again, this time to Florida.

The body of Albert Morris, thirty-seven, was discovered on May 19, in his trailer in Nassau County, Florida. A towel had been stuffed into his mouth and also tied around his head. He had been beaten about the head, shot in the chest, and then strangled to death. Like the other murders, his car and wallet were missing.

Bowles was immediately suspected of killing Morris. Authorities believed Bowles had met Morris in a gay bar and was invited to stay at the trailer. The night before the body of Morris was found, they were seen at a bar arguing, and were thrown out.

The next known victim was Alverson Carter Jr. The forty-seven-year-old had been killed in May, in Atlanta, and the crime scene and injuries sustained by the victim were similar to the previous murders. Later, forensic evidence found at the scene would link the murder to Bowles.

On November 18, 1994, a woman was concerned about the well-being of her brother, Walter Jamelle (Jay) Hinton; he hadn't contacted her on her birthday, even though he had promised to do so days earlier. She sent her fiancé to Hinton's mobile home in Duval County, Florida, to see if everything was all right. Though lights were on in the home, Hinton was nowhere to be seen.

Two days later, Hinton failed to turn up to work, and his sister became increasingly worried. They went back to Hinton's mobile home and were determined to get inside to have a good look this time.

As soon as they entered, they noticed a foul odor. The bedroom was a mess, as though a physical altercation had taken place in there. Then they entered the bathroom and noticed a strange mound covered by blankets on the floor. When a piece of the blanket was pulled back, they immediately recognized the decomposing body of Hinton.

When police arrived, they noticed Hinton's personal papers and wallet had been thrown on the bed. On the floor beside the bed was a large bloodied stepping-stone hidden under a pile of sheets. A receipt was found with the name "Timothy Whitfield" on it, and the car and watch belonging to Hinton was missing.

The medical examiner determined Hinton's head had been crushed by the large stone. Other injuries included broken ribs and abrasions on his limbs. It was clear there had been a violent struggle before Hinton was killed. In his mouth were toilet paper and a rag, pushed down into his throat; his cause of death was strangulation.

Witnesses stated a man had been staying at the home with Hinton and, based on their descriptions, Bowles was main suspect. The investigation continued and, finally, Bowles was arrested on October 22, 1994, for the murder of Hinton. Once in custody, he confessed to the six murders.

Trial

At his trial for the murder of Hinton in May 1996, Bowles pled guilty. He received the death sentence.

In August 1997, Bowles pled guilty to the 1994 murder of Roberts.

Eventually, Bowles was convicted of three counts of murder and sentenced to death, but this decision was reversed by the Florida Supreme Court after it was determined that information regarding the victim being gay—and Bowles' hatred of homosexuals—should not have been given to the jury.

At a new sentence hearing in 1999, he was once again given the death penalty.

Outcome

During the resentencing trial, information about Bowles' previous convictions, including the murders of Roberts and Morris, were included in the state's presentation of the case. It took the jury just one hour to reach a verdict, and he again was sentenced to die in the electric chair.

Bowles lodged numerous other appeals, all of which were rejected.

He was executed on August 22, 2019.

Trivia

A handmade card bearing his signature sold for forty dollars.

Bowles would offer himself as a prostitute to his victims before killing and robbing them.

Bowles was raised in Clifton Forge, Virginia.

IAN BRADY AND MYRA HINDLEY

Ian Brady

Date of birth: January 2, 1938

Aliases/Nicknames: The Moors Murderer, Ian Duncan Stewart

Characteristics: Rape

Number of victims: 5

Date of murders: July 1963 - October 1965

Date of arrest: October 7, 1965

Victim profile: Pauline Reade, 16; John Kilbride, 12; Keith Bennett, 12; Lesley Ann Downey, 10; Edward Evans, 17

Method of murder: Cutting the throat, strangulation with a piece of string

Location: Greater Manchester, England, United Kingdom

Status: Sentenced to three terms of life imprisonment on May 6, 1966. Died May 15, 2017.

Myra Hindley

Date of birth: July 23, 1942

Aliases/Nicknames: The Moors Murderer, The Most Evil Woman in Britain

Characteristics: Rape

Number of victims: 5

Date of murders: July 1963 - October 1965

Date of arrest: October 11, 1965

Victim profile: Pauline Reade, 16; John Kilbride, 12; Keith Bennett, 12; Lesley Ann Downey, 10; Edward Evans, 17

Method of murder: Cutting the throat, Strangulation with a piece of string

Location: Greater Manchester, England, United Kingdom

Status: Sentenced to two concurrent life sentences on May 6, 1966. Died in prison on November 16, 2002.

Background

Ian Brady

Born in Glasgow, Scotland, Brady's name at birth was Ian Duncan Stewart. His mother worked in a tearoom, and his father's identity was uncertain, though his mother claimed he had been a reporter who died before Brady's birth. Unable to care for Brady as a child, his mother left him with a local couple, John and Mary Sloan. Though his mother visited often in the beginning, these visits waned as he grew older.

Disturbingly, Brady began to torture and kill animals when he was around twelve years old. At one point he even set a dog on fire. It wasn't long before he started attacking other children; at school, he usually kept to himself.

In his teens, Brady developed an interest in the Nazis and World War II and tried to learn the German language. From the age of thirteen, he was caught breaking into houses. After the third instance, he went to live with his mother and stepfather in Manchester. He continued committing crimes and spent some time in juvenile centers.

Brady eventually settled down and learned how to do bookkeeping while in the juvenile institutions. He got a job in 1957 as a stock clerk at Millwards Merchandising and, a year later, he met Myra Hindley.

Myra Hindley

Born in Manchester, Hindley's childhood was more normal and stable than Brady's. Her father, however, was an alcoholic who would physically abuse her. He also taught her how to stand up for herself and fight.

When Hindley's younger sister was born in August 1946, Hindley was sent to live with her grandmother. Her attendance wasn't good at school because her grandmother often kept her home for minor reasons. Despite this, she maintained good grades. As a teenager, she became a popular babysitter in the area.

At fifteen, Hindley's friend tragically drowned, a loss that traumatized her. It wasn't long afterward that she left school and went to work as a junior clerk at an electrical engineering firm. In 1961, when she was eighteen, she changed jobs and went to work at Millwards Merchandising as a typist. On meeting Brady, she fell instantly in love, but he didn't reciprocate the feelings until a year later.

Brady enjoyed teaching Hindley about the Nazis and Hitler and talked about his beliefs that murder and rape weren't wrong. Hindley did whatever she could to make Brady happy, and after he said there was no god, she gave up going to church. Her devotion to Brady was absolute.

Murders

The first victim was Pauline Reade, a sixteen-year-old neighbor of Hindley. She was on her way to a dance on July 12, 1963, when Brady and Hindley saw her walking. Hindley drove in a van, and Brady followed behind on his motorcycle. From the mirror, Hindley saw Brady signal for her to pick up Reade.

Because Reade knew Hindley, she didn't hesitate to get into the van, at which point Hindley used the ruse of needing help to find an expensive glove she had lost on Saddleworth Moor. When they reached the Moor, Hindley introduced Brady to Reade and told the girl he had come to help look for the glove as well. Here, the story changes depending on who is telling it, Brady or Hindley.

Hindley claimed that she waited in the van while Brady took Reade onto the Moor. She said he returned after about a half an hour and told her to come to where Reade was. There, Reade lay on the ground, dying, her throat cut. Brady told Hindley to stay with Reade while he fetched a spade he had hidden previously, so he could bury the body. Hindley said Reade's clothes were undone and in disarray, so she assumed Brady had sexually assaulted her.

Brady had a different account. He said that not only was Hindley standing there when Reade was attacked, but that she also helped him sexually assault the poor girl.

The next victim was John Kilbride, a twelve-year-old boy. On November 23, 1963, in the early evening, Hindley saw Kilbride at a market and offered him a ride home. She convinced him by saying his parents would probably be worried that he was out so late. Once in the car, Brady told Kilbride there was a bottle of sherry at their home, and they would have to go there first to get it. But, before they got to the house, they had to take a detour to the Moor to find a glove Hindley had lost. When they got to the Moor, Brady took Kilbride away while Hindley stayed in the car. The young boy was sexually assaulted by Brady and, when cutting his throat didn't work, Brady strangled him with a piece of string, possibly a shoelace.

Another twelve-year-old boy, Keith Bennett, was picked up by Brady and Hindley early in the evening of June 16, 1964, as he was walking to his grandmother's house. Hindley had asked the boy to help load some boxes and said she would drive him home afterward. Instead, she drove to the Moor, and Brady went off with Bennett under the pretense of looking for a glove. Brady returned to Hindley a half an hour later and told her he had sexually assaulted Bennett and strangled him with a piece of string.

On December 26, 1964, Brady and Hindley went to a local fairground to find another victim; they came across Lesley Ann Downey, ten, standing near one of the rides. Once they were certain she was on her own, they walked near her, dropping some shopping, and then asked her to help them carry the packages to their car. They said she would have to come back to their home and help them unload the shopping there as well, and she obliged. Inside the house, they stripped her, gagged her, and forced her to pose for pornographic photographs. Then she was raped and killed. The next morning, her body was taken to the Moor and buried, still naked, with her clothes buried at her feet.

Searching for their next victim, the couple went to the Manchester Central railway station on the evening of October 6, 1965. While Hindley waited in the car, Brady went looking for a suitable victim, and soon returned to the car with Edward Evans. They went back to the house and shared a bottle of wine; then Brady told Hindley to go get her brother-in-law, David Smith.

When Hindley and Smith returned, Hindley told her brother-in-law to wait outside for a signal from her, a flashing light, before knocking on the door. He did as he was told. When the time came, he knocked on the door only for it to be opened by Brady. Smith was taken into the kitchen by Brady and told to wait while Brady got the wine. Minutes later, Smith heard a scream, followed by Hindley shouting for him to come and help. On entering the living room, Smith saw Brady striking Evans repeatedly with the flat of an axe. Then Brady strangled Evans with some electrical cord. Brady, suffering from a sprained ankle during the struggle, was unable to help take the body out to the car, so they wrapped it in plastic sheeting and left it in the spare bedroom.

Smith agreed to come back the next night to help get rid of the body, but, when he told his partner what he had seen, she insisted he inform the police. They went to a phone box and made the call.

Trial

Police were quick to act after receiving the call from Smith, and they went to the back door of Brady and Hindley's home. Hindley answered the door, and Superintendent Bob Talbot said he wanted to speak to Brady. Hindley allowed him inside, and Brady was in the living room. Talbot told them he was investigating a report of violence involving guns, to which Hindley denied there had been any violence the night before.

They allowed the police to look around the house, but when they came to the spare bedroom, they found the door locked. When asked for the key, Hindley claimed it was at work. When the police offered to drive her there to retrieve it, however, Brady told her to just give it to them. After discovering the body in the room, they returned to the living room and placed Brady under arrest on suspicion of committing a murder.

Although Hindley wasn't arrested, she insisted she go to the police station with Brady. When questioned about Evans' murder, she refused to make a statement, instead claiming it was an accident. There was no real evidence that she was involved, so she was released on the condition that she come back the next day for more questions.

On October 11, Hindley was charged as an accessory and remanded to prison.

On further questioning, Smith told police that Brady had packed items into suitcases that may be incriminating. He didn't know where they were, but he mentioned Brady had a "thing" about railway stations. After a search of all of the left-luggage offices in Manchester, the suitcases were finally found at the Manchester Central railway station on October 15.

When the suitcases were opened, they found nine pornographic photographs of a naked young girl with a scarf tied across her mouth. There was also a sixteen-minute tape recording of her pleading for help and screaming. The girl in the photos and on the tape was later identified as Lesley Ann Downey.

Another piece of evidence that was found in the house was an old exercise book with the name John Kilbride scribbled in it. This led police to believe there were more potential murders attributable to Brady and Hindley. A large collection of photos were found, all taken at Saddleworth Moor, so police decided to try to match the photos with locations on the Moor.

A huge band of officers was involved in the search and, on October 16, an arm bone was found sticking out of the ground. It belonged to Downey. Five days later, they found another shallow grave with the severely decomposed body of John Kilbride. Due to the state of the remains, he was identified by his clothing.

That very same day, Brady and Hindley appeared in court charged with the murder of Downey. Both had already been charged with the murder of Evans. On December 2, charges were added to both for the murder of John Kilbride.

The trial began on April 19, 1966, and lasted for fourteen days, with Mr. Justice Fenton Atkinson presiding. They both pleaded not guilty, and both gave evidence, with Brady's testimony lasting more than eight hours, and Hindley's six.

The jury took just two hours to deliberate on May 6; the jurors found Brady guilty of the murders of Evan, Downey, and Kilbride. Hindley was found guilty of the murders of Downey and Evans only. By that time in England, the death penalty had been abolished, so the only option was life imprisonment. Brady received three life sentences; Hindley was given two, along with an additional concurrent seven years for harboring Brady with the knowledge he had murdered Kilbride. Brady started his sentence at Durham Prison, and Hindley went to Holloway Prison.

Outcome

While in Durham, Brady requested he live in solitary confinement. After nineteen years in prison, he was diagnosed a psychopath. In November 1985, he was moved to what was then Park Lane Hospital, a high-security unit. It then became Ashworth Psychiatric Hospital. Brady stated he never wanted to be released.

During an alleged attack by staff in 1999, Brady broke his wrist,. Not long afterward, he went on a hunger strike. Those being treated under the Mental Health Act could not refuse food or treatment, however, so he was force-fed. Brady became ill and was sent to another hospital, and once he recovered, he requested a judicial review of how legal or illegal it was to force-feed him. The review was refused.

In 2001, Brady wrote a book, *The Gates of Janus*, which was his opinion and analysis of serial murder and specific serial killers. It was published, which caused major outrage throughout England.

Brady asked to be sent back to prison in 2012 but was refused.

On May 15, 2017, Brady died from restrictive pulmonary disease. His body was cremated without ceremony. During the night, his ashes were disposed of at sea.

Hindley lodged an appeal against her conviction immediately after the trial and sentencing but was unsuccessful. She wrote letters back and forth with Brady up until 1971, then ended things with him. She soon fell in love with Patricia Cairns, one of her prison warders. With the assistance of Cairns and another prisoner, Hindley planned an escape but failed. Cairns was charged and sentenced to six years for trying to help Hindley.

On November 15, 2002, Hindley died from bronchial pneumonia, due to heart disease. She was sixty years old. Nobody from her family attended the short funeral service. It was a difficult situation, with twenty of the local undertakers refusing to perform her cremation because hatred of her crimes was still so strong. Cairns scattered her ashes less than ten miles from Saddleworth Moor.

Trivia

Under Brady's influence, Hindley constantly bleached her hair and dressed in boots and miniskirts.

Hindley was affected by a brain aneurysm in 1999.

Hindley admitted in 1987 that her previous parole plea had been "on the whole ... a pack of lies."

Up until her death in February of 1999, Lesley Ann Downey's mother, Ann West, was a staunch campaigner of Hindley not receiving parole.

Numerous times throughout his incarceration, Brady went on hunger strikes that would last around forty-eight hours. On some occasions, he had to be fed through a nasogastric tube.

Brady had offered to donate a kidney to anyone who needed it, but his offer was refused.

"Myra gets the potentially fatal brain condition, whilst I have to fight simply to die. I have had enough. I want nothing, my objective is to die and release myself from this once and for all. So you see my death strike is rational and pragmatic. I'm only sorry I didn't do it decades ago, and I'm eager to leave this cesspit in a coffin." - *Brady*

CARL "CHARLIE" BRANDT

Date of birth: February 23, 1957

Aliases/Nicknames: Charlie

Characteristics: Juvenile murder, parricide, mutilation

Number of victims: 3 - 6 +

Date of murders: January 3, 1971, September 15, 2004

Date of arrest: 1971; died before arrest in 2004

Victim profile: His pregnant mother; his wife Teresa "Teri" Brandt, 46; his niece Michelle Jones, 37

Method of murder: Shooting, stabbing with knife

Location: Indiana, Florida, USA

Status: Spent a year in an Indiana mental institution. Was released in 1972. Committed suicide by hanging himself on September 15, 2004.

Background

Brandt was the second child of German immigrants Herbert and Ilse Brandt. Herbert was a laborer for the company International Harvester and later became a project engineer. The family moved often, so Brandt and his sister attended numerous schools. Although he was regarded as a good student, Brandt had trouble adjusting to new schools. The family moved to Fort Wayne, Indiana, in September 1968.

When Brandt was thirteen, he walked into his parents' bathroom on the night of January 3, 1971, with a gun. While his father was shaving, and his heavily pregnant mother was taking a bath, Brandt opened fire on them. His mother died at the scene, but his father survived. Brandt tried to kill his sister, but the gun wouldn't fire. She managed to calm Brandt down, and then fled the house seeking help from the neighbors. Brandt also left, and went to the house next door, telling the girl there that he had just shot his parents.

Under Indiana law, Brandt was too young to be charged with murder. Instead, he had to undergo three psychiatric evaluations. None of these resulted in identifying the underlying reason as to why Brandt shot his parents. He showed no signs or symptoms of mental illness. Brandt was kept at a psychiatric hospital for a year then was released back to the family. The shooting was never spoken of again.

The family moved to Florida after Brandt was released from the hospital. A year later, his father remarried and moved away, taking Brandt's sister with him. Brandt stayed with his grandparents. He went on to get a degree in electronics in 1984 and became a radar specialist. He married his girlfriend Teri in 1986, and no family members were invited to the wedding. The couple moved into a beach house in the Florida Keys in 1989.

Murders

Hurricane Ivan was bearing down on Florida in September 2004, when Brandt and his wife evacuated from their house. Michelle Lynn Jones, their niece, invited them to stay with her near Orlando. While they were visiting, Jones stayed in contact with her mother regularly and spoke with several friends. One of her friends, Lisa Emmons, had intended to visit on September 13, but Jones put her off, saying the Brandts had been drinking and had had an argument. It was the last time anyone heard from Jones.

Another of Jones' friends went to the house on September 15 to check on her. She was on the phone with Jones' mother when she approached the house. The front door was locked, so she entered through the garage, which was unlocked. There, she found the decomposing body of Brandt hanging from the rafters. She called the police and then went inside the house, where she found the bodies of Teri and Jones. Teri had suffered seven stab wounds to the chest. The body of Jones had been disemboweled and decapitated, and her internal organs had been removed. Jones' head had been placed beside her body.

Police searched the Brandts' home and found a variety of strange items. These included a collection of books about surgery and posters. It was clear that Brandt was a subscriber to Victoria's Secret catalogs, and an analysis of the home computer showed a history of looking for snuff film websites and autopsy photos.

Because Brandt regularly traveled for his job, cold cases throughout Florida were looked at as crimes he had potentially committed. Investigators launched requests all over the United States and overseas to search for murders that matched Brandt's modus operandi. Brandt was consequently linked to twenty-six unsolved murders in Florida dating back to 1973.

Possible Victims

Carol Sullivan, twelve, was abducted on September 20, 1978, from a bus stop in Volusia County. Only her skull was found, located in a bucket. Brandt was living in the area at the time, but investigators weren't able to link him to the murder in any other way.

In December of 1988, twenty-year-old Lisa Saunders was dragged from her car in Big Pine Key, the same area where the Brandts lived. She was stabbed and beaten to death. Her remains were found with the heart missing.

On July 16, 1989, the partially clothed body of Sherry Perisho was found in Big Pine Key, near the North Pine Channel Bridge. At the time of her death, Perisho was homeless and was living on a dinghy near the bridge. Her throat had been cut so deeply she was almost decapitated. The body showed extensive mutilation, and her heart had been taken out. The location where her body was found was less than one thousand feet from Brandt's house. A witness from that night saw a man close to where she was found, and the composite drawing matched Brandt. The Monroe County police determined that Brandt had killed Perisho and closed the case in 2006.

Darlene Toler was killed in 1995. Her body was found near a highway wrapped in plastic, and her head and heart were missing. Brandt was a regular driver on this particular highway and kept track of the mileage on his journeys. His records showed that he had traveled the same amount of distance as the distance between Big Pine Key and Miami, where her body was found, on the day she was killed.

Trial

Because Brandt committed suicide, there was never a trial for any of the murders.

Outcome

After the investigation into the murders of Teri and Michelle, it was discovered that Teri kept diaries. Upon reading them, it became clear that she had suspected her husband of being a murderer. This shocked investigators; it was hard to believe a woman would continue living with a man she thought was a killer.

It wasn't clear whether Brandt had intended on killing Michelle or whether the opportunity arose and he took advantage of it.

Two days before the murders of Teri and Michelle and his own suicide, Brandt had visited his father in Ormond Beach. His father told the police investigators that when Brandt was leaving, he hugged his father like he never had before. Perhaps he knew what he was going to do and was saying goodbye. Nobody will ever know.

Trivia

On the back of the Brandts' bedroom door was a rather graphic poster of the female anatomy.

Brandt called Michelle "Victoria Secret."

On his computer, investigators discovered search results for websites that included violent acts toward women, necrophilia, and fantasies about death.

Angela, Brandt's sister, was relieved he had killed himself because she hadn't been able to sleep well while he was alive; now she could relax at night.

BRILEY BROTHERS

James Dyral Briley

Date of birth: June 6, 1956

Aliases/Nicknames: JB

Characteristics: Robbery, gang, suspected zoosadism

Number of victims: 11

Date of murders: 1979

Date of arrest: October 22, 1979

Victim profile: Michael McDuffie; Mary Gowen, 76; Christopher Philips, 17; John Gallaher; Mary Wilfong, 62; Blanche Page, 79; Charles Garner, 59; Harvey Wilkerson; Judy Barton, 23; her son Harvey, 5; Judy's unborn child

Method of murder: Shooting, bludgeoning, stabbing

Location: Richmond, Virginia, USA

Status: Executed by electrocution in Virginia on April 18, 1985.

Linwood Earl Briley

Date of birth: March 26, 1954

Aliases/Nicknames: Nil

Characteristics: Robbery, gang, suspected zoosadism

Number of victims: 12

Date of murders: 1971, 1979

Date of arrest: October 22, 1979

Victim profile: Orline Christian; Michael McDuffie; Mary Gowen, 76; Christopher Philips, 17; John Gallaher; Mary Wilfong, 62; Blanche Page, 79; Charles Garner, 59; Harvey Wilkerson; Judy Barton, 23; her son Harvey, 5; Judy's unborn child

Method of murder: Shooting, bludgeoning, stabbing

Location: Richmond, Virginia, USA

Status: Executed by electrocution in Virginia on October 12, 1984.

Anthony Ray Briley

Date of birth: February 17, 1958

Aliases/Nicknames: Nil

Characteristics: Robbery, gang, zoosadism

Number of victims: 1 - 11

Date of Murders: 1979

Date of arrest: 22 October 1979

Victim profile: Uncertain what killings he was involved in, but charged with one murder

Method of murder: Shooting

Location: Richmond, Virginia, USA

Status: Single life sentence with parole eligibility. To date, all his applications for parole have been denied by the state parole board.

Background

The Briley brothers, Linwood, James and Anthony, lived with their parents in the Highland Park area in Richmond, Virginia. It was a stable home, with no apparent issues with violence or substance abuse. The boys were considered to be helpful to their older neighbors, always offering to mow lawns or fix their cars.

As far as childhood pets go, the brothers had a rather strange collection of exotic animals. These included boa constrictors, tarantulas, and piranhas. There is some suggestion that the three brothers indulged in zoosadism, but this was never confirmed. The boys' father was so unnerved by their behavior, however, that he padlocked his own bedroom door shut at night. Their mother eventually moved out of the home because of her sons' behaviors.

Murders

The first murder was committed by Linwood in 1971, when he was sixteen years old. At home by himself one day, he fired his rifle out of his bedroom window. The bullet struck an elderly neighbor, Orline Christian, and killed her. At first, it was thought she had died of natural causes while hanging out the laundry. But when her family went to view her body, they noticed a small bloodstain under her armpit.

When the medical examiner took a second look, he found the bullet wound under her armpit. Police were notified and went to the scene of the shooting to look for clues. They used a piece of wood to represent her body with a tiny hole cut out for the location of the bullet wound. Using this method, they were able to determine the bullet had come from the Briley home. On searching the home, they found the rifle. Linwood confessed to firing the gun and killing Christian, saying, "I heard she had heart problems, she would have died soon anyway."

Linwood was sentenced to one year in a reform school because of his age. His brother James soon followed suit, also sentenced to reform school after firing a gun at a police officer while being chased.

The Briley Brothers, along with their friend Duncan Meekins, began committing random killings in 1979. The killing spree lasted for seven months, and the whole city was in fear.

On March 12, 1979, Linwood knocked on the door of William and Virginia Bucher. He told them he needed to use their phone because he was having car trouble. He eventually forced his way inside, held the couple at gunpoint, and signaled for Anthony to enter the house. The Buchers were tied up while Linwood and Anthony went from room to room, stealing valuables. As they went, they poured kerosene in each room, and, as they left, they tossed a lit match. Fortunately, the Buchers were able to escape, but they would be the only victims to survive an attack by the Brileys.

Days later, on March 21, they attacked Michael McDuffie in his home. He was assaulted, robbed, and murdered. Then on April 9, the Brileys followed the elderly Mary Gowen, seventy-six, across town to her home. They managed to gain entry to the house and then raped and murdered her. They left the house after robbing it of valuables.

Christopher Philips, seventeen, was seen by the brothers hanging around Linwood's car on July 4. Suspecting he was going to try to steal the car, they surrounded him. Philips was dragged into a yard nearby, and the brothers wrestled him down to the ground. As he screamed for help, Linwood dropped a cinderblock on his head, killing him.

Disc jockey John "Johnny G" Gallaher had been performing at a nightclub in South Richmond with his band on September 14, when he went outside for a break. Unfortunately, the Brileys had been looking for a victim all night, and he literally walked right into their hands. Gallaher was put into his own car's trunk after Linwood assaulted him, and the car was then driven to Mayo Island in the James River. Once there, he was taken out of the trunk and shot in the head; he died instantly. His body, disposed of in the river, was found two days later. Linwood stole a ring from Gallaher.

Mary Wilfong, a sixty-two-year-old nurse, was followed home by the Brileys on September 30. Linwood used a baseball bat to beat her to death before she even made it inside her home. Afterward, the Brileys went into her apartment and robbed it. On October 5, Blanche Page, seventy-nine, and her boarder Charles Garner, fifty-nine, were attacked by the brothers. Garner was killed with a variety of weapons, including knives, scissors, a baseball bat, and a fork. The fork and scissors were left in his back. Page was bludgeoned to death.

The last known murders were committed on the morning of October 19. That very day, James Briley told a judge that he would stay out of trouble while he was on parole. Instead, he led his brothers on the hunt for a victim. Harvey Wilkerson, who had been a friend of the Brileys for a long time, saw them down the street. Instinctively, he closed and locked his door, with his pregnant wife Judy Barton, twenty-three, and her son Harvey, five, inside the home.

The Brileys noticed Wilkerson lock the door, so they went to the house. Wilkerson was frightened of what they would do if he didn't let them in, so he opened the door. Wilkerson and Barton were quickly overpowered, tied up, and gagged with duct tape. Barton was raped and assaulted by Linwood in the kitchen. Then Meekins sexually assaulted her. Barton was dragged into the living room by Linwood, who searched for valuables before leaving the house.

Meekins and the other brothers remained in the house. They put sheets over the victims, and James told Meekins that he had to "get one." Meekins proceeded to shoot Wilkerson in the head, killing him. Barton was then shot and killed by James.

At the time of the murders, police happened to be in the neighborhood and witnessed the Brileys and Meekins running at high speed down the street. The police didn't know where the shots had come from though, and the victims' bodies weren't found until three days later. Having been seen running from the scene, however, the Briley brothers were all arrested soon after the bodies were found.

Trial

Police decided to offer Meekins a plea agreement for turning state's evidence against the brothers. Rather than risk receiving the death penalty, he accepted the offer and gave full details of the murder spree. He received a sentence of life plus eighty years and would be held in a prison far away from the Brileys.

Anthony Briley, the youngest of the brothers, received a life sentence with the possibility of parole. It was determined he had played a limited role in the murders. Linwood and James received multiple life sentences but were faced with capital charges in the cases where they had actually killed the victims. Linwood received a sentence of death for the murder of Gallaher, and James received two death sentences - one for Judy Barton and one for her son, Harvey. The two brothers were sent to Mecklenburg Correctional Center near Boydton to await their execution dates.

Outcome

On May 31, 1984, six inmates escaped from death row at Mecklenburg including Linwood and James. The brothers had said they were keen to kill the guards they had captured by setting them on fire. However, fellow inmate Wilie Lloyd Turner prevented them from carrying out their plan. Linwood was going to rape a female nurse they held captive, but Wilbert Lee Evans, a cop killer, stopped it from happening.

The escapees had planned to run to Canada. Two of them, Willie Jones and Lem Tuggle, made it as far as Vermont before they were captured. The Brileys managed to make it to their uncle's house in Philadelphia. On June 19, the police and FBI tracked them down by putting a wiretap on their uncle's phone; the Brileys were arrested.

The appeals ran out for Linwood and James, and their previous escape didn't help matters. Linwood was executed by electric chair on October 12, 1984, at the Virginia State Penitentiary in Richmond. James met the same fate on April 18, 1985. They were both buried in Bethel, North Carolina, at the Council cemetery.

Their younger brother Anthony is still incarcerated; his parole applications have been denied.

According to officials who were present at James' execution, he didn't make a final statement and just smiled. For his final meal, Briley requested fried shrimp with cocktail sauce and a lemon-lime-flavored soft drink.

Trivia

A pack of bubble gum and trading card set called "The Briley's Card Collection" was released in 1984. There are fourteen cards in the set, and more than six hundred of them were sold.

The creator of the bubble gum cards, Terry Rea, was a commercial artist; he also created T-shirts with the logo "The Brileys' Summer '84 Tour."

"The Ballad of the Briley Brothers," was a song composed by two employees of a Lynchburg radio station. Some of the lyrics included:

Now the death row in Mecklenburg ain't the nicest place for sure;

You won't find it in a travelogue or auto club brochure.

The rooms are small, the food ain't great, and the guards are big and burly.

So Lin and James and four more guests checked out a little bit early.

. . . Well the local folks and the FBI are getting mad at you,

You're never where you're supposed to be, come on, you know it's true.

Linwood Briley continued to claim he was innocent of murder right up until he was executed.

PETER BRYAN

Date of birth: October 4, 1969

Aliases/Nicknames: Nil

Characteristics: Schizophrenia, cannibalism

Number of victims: 3

Date of murders: March 18, 1993, February 17 and April 25, 2004

Date of arrest: February 2004

Victim profile: Nisha Sheth, 20; Brian Cherry, 43; Richard Loudwell, 60

Method of murder: Hitting with a hammer, strangulation

Location: London, England, United Kingdom

Status: Sentenced to closed psychiatric confinement in 1993. Released in 2004. Sentenced to life in prison on March 15, 2005.

Background

Bryan, the youngest of seven siblings, was born in London on October 4, 1969. His parents were immigrants from Barbados. His schooling was unremarkable, as was his childhood. When he was around fifteen, he left school and began to work at a clothing stall. Later on, he went to work at a local soup kitchen, teaching other people how to cook.

Bryan was living in East London in 1987 when he tried to throw another resident from a sixth-floor window. The man escaped after a struggle, and Bryan received a large gash to his head. There had been no provocation by the intended victim before the attack.

Murders

In 1994, Bryan admitted he had murdered a shop assistant, twenty-one-year-old Nisha Sheth. He had beaten her to death in 1993 with a hammer. Bryan was sent to the Rampton Secure Hospital for treatment. By February 2001, the hospital staff thought he had made good progress with his behavior, insight, emotions, and attitude. He was transferred to the John Howard Centre that June.

An application for a Mental Health Review Tribunal was made in 2002, and he was moved again to Riverside Hostel in North London. While there, he could come and go as he pleased and had his own door keys. Psychiatrists noted that his behavior continued to improve. His social worker reported to the Home Office in November 2003 that Bryan no longer presented any major risks to himself or the public.

In January 2004 Bryan was transferred to an open psychiatric ward in Newham General Hospital for his own safety. Allegations had been made that he had indecently assaulted a teenage girl near the hostel. The following month, February, he walked out of the unit and killed his friend, Brian Cherry.

A friend of Cherry arrived at the apartment and let herself in. Upon entering, she noticed a strong disinfectant smell. At that point, Bryan walked into the room shirtless and holding a knife. He told her Cherry was dead. Not believing what she was hearing, she went into the other room to see for herself. Cherry was lying on the floor, naked; one of his arms had been dismembered.

When police found Bryan, his hands, jeans, and shoes were bloodstained, and he was cooking Cherry's brain in a frying pan. Cherry's skull had been struck with at least 24 blows from a hammer and his head had been partially sawn off by Bryan. One arm and both legs had been removed.

Bryan was sent to Broadmoor Hospital. Two months later, he killed a fellow patient. Richard Loudwell, sixty, had been beaten on the head and Bryan had tied a ligature around his neck in an attempt to strangle him. Although he was rescued during the attack, Loudwell died later that day in the hospital. Bryan admitted that he would have eaten his flesh if he hadn't been interrupted.

Bryan told the doctors, "I get these urges you see. I've had these urges ever since I saw him. He's the bottom of the food chain, old and haggard. He looked like he'd had his innings."

Trial

Bryan went to court on March 15, 2005 and pleaded guilty to two manslaughters on the grounds of diminished responsibility. He was committed to Broadmoor Hospital for treatment of his paranoid schizophrenia.

Outcome

Bryan will never be released from Broadmoor because he was given a whole life sentence. The judge said, "You had the urge not only to kill but also to eat the flesh of your victims. You experienced feelings of power and invincibility. Not only that, but you gained sexual excitement from the act of battering your victims to death. The earlier treatment at the hospital did not cure your disease, and there is no reason to believe a hospital order now will do what it failed to achieve back in 1994. It is clear that you can appear calm and cooperative while harboring bizarre psychotic beliefs."

Trivia

"I ate his brain with butter, it was really nice." - *Bryan*

"I was just waiting for my chance to get at him. I wanted to kill him and eat him. I didn't have much time. If I did I'd have tried to cook him and eat him." - *Bryan*

JUDIAS BUENOANO

Date of birth: April 4, 1943

Aliases/Nicknames: Judias Welty, Judy, the Black Widow

Characteristics: Killed to collect insurance money, poisoner

Number of victims: 3

Date of murders: 1971 - 1980

Date of arrest: January 11, 1984

Victim profile: James Goodyear; Bobby Joe Morris; Michael Goodyear

Method of murder: Arsenic poisoning, drowning

Location: Florida, Colorado, USA

Status: Executed by electrocution in Florida on March 30, 1998

Background

Buenoano was born Judias Welty in 1943, in Quanah, Texas. Her father was a farm laborer, and her mother had been described as a member of the Mesquite Apache tribe, which is actually non-existent. Buenoano didn't have a close relationship with her mother, and when she was four years old, her mother died of tuberculosis. Buenoano, along with her younger brother, was sent to live with her grandparents; her two older siblings were put up for adoption.

When her father remarried, he moved to Roswell, New Mexico, and took Buenoano and her brother to live with him and his new wife. According to Buenoano, her father and new stepmother both abused her, and she wasn't happy in Roswell. She claimed she was starved, beaten, and forced to work as a slave for long hours. At the age of fourteen, she attacked her father, stepmother, and her two stepbrothers, which resulted in a prison sentence of two months.

When Buenoano was released from prison, she opted to go to a reform school rather than return to her family. She graduated from Foothills High School in Albuquerque in 1959. In 1960, she started working as a nursing assistant in Roswell, under the name of Anna Schultz. She gave birth to her son Michael the following year and gave him the surname Schultz. The name of the boy's father was never confirmed.

Murders

In 1971, Buenoano married a sergeant in the US Air Force, James Goodyear. When he died on September 16, that same year, his death was first thought to have been the result of natural causes. Later it was discovered Buenoano poisoned him with arsenic so she could claim his life insurance money.

Buenoano moved in with Bobby Joe Morris in 1973, and he died in January of 1978. During his autopsy, analysis of his tissues showed arsenic poisoning. That same year, she legally changed her name to Buenoano.

In 1979, Buenoano's son Michael became severely ill, and he developed paraplegia. Buenoano took him out in a canoe on May 13, 1980, and when the canoe tipped over, Michael was weighed down by the braces on his limbs, and he drowned.

Buenoano moved on to another man, named John Gentry, and by 1983, they were engaged to be married. Later that year, Gentry was seriously injured from an explosion in his car. As investigators started to make inquiries into what caused the explosion, they found out some interesting information about Buenoano. According to friends of the couple, she had been telling them since November 1982 that Gentry had a terminal illness and that she had been giving him vitamin pills. When police had these pills examined, they discovered they contained arsenic and formaldehyde.

This information led investigators to the deaths of Michael and James Goodyear, and Bobby Joe Morris, and the police finally linked all the deaths to Buenoano.

Trial

Buenoano was convicted of killing her own son, Michael, in 1984; she was also found guilty of the attempted murder of Gentry. The following year, she was convicted of killing James Goodyear. For Michael's death, she received a sentence of life imprisonment. The sentence she received for the attempted murder of Gentry was twelve years. For the killing of James Goodyear, she was sentenced to death.

In addition to the murder charges, she was also found guilty of multiple counts of insurance fraud and arson.

Outcome

Buenoano was incarcerated in the death row for women at the Florida Department of Corrections Broward Correctional Institution. Her final appeal was rejected on March 29, 1998, and her death warrant was signed by the governor. She was moved to the death watch area, a twelve by seven-foot cell, and spent her time watching television while waiting for her execution date.

The execution was set to take place on March 30, 1998, at 7:00 a.m. As part of the preparation, her head was shaved so her hair wouldn't catch fire from the electricity that would be pumped through her body.

After she was taken to the death chamber and strapped into the electric chair, the warden asked if she wanted to make a final statement; she declined. She wouldn't look at the witnesses, keeping her eyes shut until the leather mask was placed over her face.

The electrocution cycle lasted thirty-eight seconds, and she was pronounced dead at 7:13 a.m.

Trivia

Her last meal before her execution was asparagus, broccoli, and strawberries, with some hot tea.

During her last day, she was visited by her children and a cousin. She spent most of the day eating chocolates and watching hunting and fishing shows on television.

She was the first woman to be executed in Florida since a slave had been hanged in 1848. She was also the third woman executed since the reinstatement of the death penalty in 1976.

She claimed to be a devout Roman Catholic.

Buenoano had stated that she preferred to be executed than to spend her life in the Broward jail.

She made friends with two other females on death row, and they would see each other during exercise time. They referred to themselves as Las Tres Amigas, which translates to The Three Friends.

She alleged she had been physically and sexually abused by relatives as a child.

HARVEY CARIGNAN

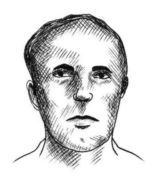

Date of birth: May 18, 1927

Aliases/Nicknames: Harv the Hammer, the Want Ad Killer

Characteristics: Rape

Number of victims: 5 +

Date of murders: 1949, 1972 - 1974

Date of arrest: September 24, 1974

Victim profile: Laura Showalter, 58; Leslie Laura Brock, 19; Kathy Sue Miller, 15; Eileen Hunley; Kathy Schultz

Method of murder: Hitting with a hammer

Location: Alaska, Washington, Minnesota, USA

Status: Sentenced to death in Alaska in 1949. Reversed in 1951. Paroled in 1960. Sentenced the maximum of forty years in prison in Minnesota in 1975.

Background

Carignan narrowly escaped execution long before he went on his murderous and violent rampage. In 1949, he was convicted of murdering a woman in Alaska, and was sentenced to hang. The death sentence was reversed in 1951 and, nine years later, he was released on parole. In 1965, after a number of crimes, he was sentenced in Washington to fifteen years in prison. But he was out again in 1969 after time off for good behavior.

His first marriage occurred after his parole, but it quickly failed. He married again in 1972, but his lewd attentions toward his new teenaged step-daughter caused the young girl to run away from home, and his marriage fell apart.

Murders

In May 1973, Carignan placed an advertisement for employees for a service station he leased, and Kathy Miller responded. Then she went missing. A month later her remains were found by two boys who had been hiking on an Indian reservation near Everett, Washington. Her body was nude and wrapped in plastic. The autopsy revealed she had been bludgeoned to death, and the holes in her skull indicated the weapon had been a hammer.

Because of his previous crimes, detectives were quick to question Carignan. They hounded him, trying to get him to confess, but he wouldn't. The unwanted attention made Carignan move from the area.

On June 20, Carignan was issued a speeding ticket in Solano County, California. Several women had been murdered in that area, but Carignan had never come up as a suspect. From Solano County, Carignan started traveling across the country.

Before he left Solano County, however, Carignan attacked another woman. Marlys Townsend had been waiting at a bus stop when she was knocked unconscious from behind. When she regained consciousness, she found herself in Carignan's car. He tried to force her to masturbate him, but she was able to jump from the car as it sped down the road.

Carignan picked up Jewry Billings, thirteen, on September 9, as she was hitchhiking rides in Minneapolis. Once inside the car, he threatened the young girl with a hammer. He then forced her to perform oral sex on him while he raped her with the handle of his hammer. Though he released her, she felt so humiliated she kept the event to herself for many months.

A year later, Carignan was in a relationship with Eileen Hunley. On August 10, she disappeared. Hunley had previously told friends that she was going to end her relationship with Carignan. Her body was found five weeks later in Sherburne County. Her skull showed severe injuries from hammer blows.

On September 8, Carignan picked up two hitchhikers in Minneapolis. Lisa King and June Lynch, both sixteen years old, were offered money to help him go retrieve another car that had been stranded. As soon as they were out of town, he stopped the car and started to beat Lynch. King escaped to get help, and Carignan took off, leaving Lynch on the side of the road.

Carignan flagged down Gwen Burton on September 14 and offered her a ride. In the car, he ripped her clothes, choked her until she was almost unconscious, and then raped her with his hammer. Finally, he struck her violently in the head with the hammer and left her out in a field to die. Incredibly, she survived and managed to crawl out to the highway to signal for help.

Four days later, Carignan picked up two more girls, Sally Versoi and Diane Flynn. He used the same ruse as before, telling the girls he needed help to fetch another car. As soon as they got into the vehicle, he started making lewd suggestions. When they failed to respond, he assaulted them both. Luckily for them, the car ran out of fuel, and Carignan was forced to stop at a service station. The girls managed to escape.

Two days later, on September 20, eighteen-year-old Kathy Schultz didn't show up for her classes at college, and she was listed as a missing person. Her body was found the following day by hunters, forty miles away from Minneapolis. Like the other victims, her skull had been bashed in by hammer blows.

Police in Minneapolis were starting to communicate with those in Washington and they realized the cases were linked. Those who had survived attacks by Carignan were shown lineups, and they identified Carignan as their abductor and rapist.

Trial

When police searched Carignan's belongings, they found maps of the United States and Canada, with 181 red circles drawn on them. They investigated the areas. Some didn't seem to indicate any crimes; they were simply places where he had either applied for jobs or bought vehicles. Others, however, appeared to link him to a number of unsolved murders.

At his trial for the attempted murder of Gwen Burton, Carignan and his defense team tried to plead insanity, saying he had received messages from God. But this ploy failed, and he was convicted.

Outcome

Carignan received a sentence of forty years for the attempted murder of Burton. The law in Minnesota determined that nobody could be sentenced to more than forty years, so even though he was found guilty of other murders and attacks, he would still only serve the maximum of forty years.

For the assault on Jewry Billings, he received a sentence of thirty years. The murder of Eileen Hunley got him a sentence of forty years. He also received forty years for the murder of Kathy Schultz. In total, his sentences totaled one hundred fifty years in prison.

Trivia

He claimed to be doing God's work by raping and mutilating women.

Carignan applied for parole in 2015, but it was declined.

His next parole hearing is in 2022, and he will be in his nineties.

His family was plagued with tragedy, especially his children. Of his three children, one had died from cancer, one from a gunshot, and the other died from a drug overdose.

MICHAEL BEAR CARSON AND SUZAN CARSON

Michael Bear Carson

Date of birth: 1950

Aliases/Nicknames: James Clifford Carson

Characteristics: Drug use, claimed to be killing witches, homosexuals, and abortionists in the name of Allah

Number of victims: 3

Date of murders: 1981 - 1983

Date of arrest: January 12, 1983

Victim profile: Keryn Barnes, 22; Clark Stephens; John Hillyar

Method of murder: Stabbing with knife, shooting

Location: California, USA

Status: Sentenced to 75 years to life in prison in 1984.

Suzan Carson

Date of birth: September 14, 1941

Aliases/Nicknames: Susan Barnes

Characteristics: Drugs

Number of victims: 3

Date of murders: 1981 - 1983

Date of arrest: January 12, 1983

Victim profile: Keryn Barnes, 22; Clark Stephens; John Hillyar

Method of murder: Stabbing with knife, shooting

Location: California, USA

Status: 75 years to life.

Background

Carson was living in Phoenix, Arizona, in 1977 when his marriage fell apart and his wife left with their daughter Jennifer. Not long afterward, Carson met Susan Barnes and the two started a relationship. Susan had two adolescent sons when they married.

It wasn't long before Carson and his new wife became involved in mysticism and drugs. Carson wrote a letter to his daughter and told her that his new name was Michael Bear, saying that God had given him the name Michael. Susan changed her name to Suzan Bear.

The Carsons spent a year in Europe and returned to the US in 1980. They settled into the Haight-Ashbury area of San Francisco and were still heavily involved in drug use. Carson's first wife became frightened that he would track them down and kidnap their daughter, so she went into hiding and stopped contact with people they knew in common.

Murders

In March of 1981, twenty-two-year-old aspiring actress Keryn Barnes was found dead in the apartment she shared with the Carsons. Her skull had been crushed, and her body had been stabbed thirteen times. She was wrapped in a blanket and hidden in the basement of the apartment. Investigators believed she had been murdered by someone she knew and the Carsons naturally became the main suspects. But the Carsons had fled before her body was even discovered.

The couple went to Grants Pass, Oregon, and hid out in the mountains until the spring of 1982. From there, they moved to Alderpoint, California, where they worked on a marijuana farm. Coworkers later described the couple as anarchists who predicted there would soon be a nuclear apocalypse.

In May of 1982, a worker on the farm, Clark Stephens, was shot and killed by Carson following a dispute. His body was burned and then buried under chicken fertilizer in the nearby woods. Stephens was reported missing two weeks later, and eventually his body was discovered. By then, the Carsons had taken flight again. They were quickly determined to be the main suspects, and when investigators searched their abandoned belongings, they found a manifesto calling for the assassination of President Ronald Reagan.

Michael Carson was apprehended by police in November of 1982, in Los Angeles, after he was seen hitchhiking. Due to police error, he was released before he could be questioned about the Stephen's murder.

In January of 1983, the Carsons were picked up by Jon Charles Hillyar while hitchhiking near Bakersfield. Suzan apparently decided that he was a witch who had to be killed. As Hillyar was driving them along Route 101 in Sonoma County, an argument began which culminated in a physical altercation between Hellyar and the Carsons. The car came to a stop, and the fight carried outside of the vehicle. While Hillyar and Michael were struggling over a gun, Suzan stabbed Hillyar. This was seen by passing motorists who notified the police. The Carsons attempted to flee in Hillyar's car, but after a high-speed chase, they were caught by police.

Trial

The Carsons confessed to the murders of Barnes, Stephens, and Hillyar during a press conference. But before the trial began, they withdrew their confessions and entered not guilty pleas. On June 12, 1984, they were both found guilty of the murder of Barnes and were sentenced to twenty-five years in prison.

The next trial was for the murders of Stephens and Hillyar. Again, they were found guilty. They received sentences of fifty years to life for the murder of Stephens, and seventy-five years to life for the murder of Hillyar.

During an interview with KGO-TV, the *San Francisco Chronicle*, and homicide detectives which lasted for five hours, the Carsons claimed they were vegetarian yoga practitioners and pacifists who had converted to a form of Islam. They stated they were "vegetarian Muslim warriors." Their mission was to kill individuals who they believed were witches. The Carsons stated they had murdered Barnes because they thought she had made a fake conversion to their religion, and they believed she was draining the health and yogic powers from Suzan. They said they had killed Stephens because he had sexually assaulted Suzan, and Hellyar was killed because he had sexually abused Suzan and called her a witch. They have never shown any remorse for the murders.

Outcome

The Carsons had said they had a list of targeted individuals, which included Ronald Reagan, Johnny Carson, and other political figures and celebrities. They were suspects in almost twelve other murders in Europe and the US.

Trivia

The Carsons have been included in several true crime documentaries:

- *Deadly Women* (Season 6, Episode 1, "Hunting Humans")
- *Wicked Attraction* (Season 2, Episode 1, "The Two Bears")
- *The Devil You Know* (Season 2, Episode 2, "A Serial Killer in the Family")
- *Snapped*: "Killer Couples," Season 2 Episode 10.

In a *Criminology* podcast, the murders committed by the Carsons were profiled, and Michael's daughter Jennifer Carson was interviewed.

Jennifer was interviewed in Lisa Ling's show *This Is Life*, and the episode was called "Children of Killers."

The Carsons' murders were featured in the series *Murder Mountain* in 2018.

Jennifer Carson is against the Carsons getting parole.

Suzan created a religion that she called Islam, but was essentially an excuse to justify the Carsons' murderous actions. Her religion stated that murder, anarchy, theft, driving without a license, and drug use was okay, but abortion and homosexuality were punishable by death.

The Carsons got married at Stonehenge, England, at night in the moonlight.

STEVEN DAVID CATLIN

Date of birth: 1944

Aliases/Nicknames: Nil

Characteristics: Poisoner, -parricide, collector of insurance money

Number of victims: 3

Date of murders: 1976, 1984

Date of arrest: December 23, 1985

Victim profile: Joyce Catlin; Martha Catlin; Glenna Kaye Catlin

Method of murder: Poisoning by the herbicide paraquat

Location: California, Nevada, USA

Status: Sentenced to death in California in 1990.

Background

Catlin was adopted by Glenn and Martha Catlin as a baby in 1944, and the first few years of his childhood were spent in Kern County, California. The family moved to Bakersfield in the early 1950s and settled there. Catlin eventually dropped out of school, but he wasn't interested in working for a living. He was arrested at the age of nineteen for forgery, and he spent nine months in a California Youth Authority camp as his sentence.

Catlin married, but it was a violent union, largely due to his use of illegal drugs. He married a second wife in 1966 under a false name, while he was still married to the first one. He was arrested a few months later for stealing a credit card while he was working at a gas station. He was sent to prison for three years.

Upon his release, he divorced the first wife and married the second one again, this time using his real name. This marriage wasn't to last either and, after ten months, they separated. Catlin married his third wife soon after but divorced her after just eight months. His fourth wife was Joyce, and this marriage would end much worse than the others.

Catlin was fascinated with cars and ended up on the pit crew of car racer Glendon Emery. He became infatuated with Emery's stepdaughter and began courting her while still married to Joyce.

Murders

Joyce was admitted to the hospital in April of 1976, with what seemed to be a severe case of the flu.

She started to recover, and then suddenly worsened; she died on May 6. Catlin ordered her body to be cremated without any delay or an autopsy.

Catlin met and married his next wife, Kaye, in May of 1977. He was quite successful at his work in a local garage and was promoted to the supervision of forty employees. But he never seemed to have enough money, most likely due to his extravagant tastes. His father died suddenly on October 28, 1980, from what appeared to be fluid in his lungs, likely due to his pre-existing cancer. Catlin again ordered a quick cremation.

In 1981, it was noticed that there had been a sudden increase in auto parts going missing from the garage, and Catlin's employers ran background checks on the employees. Catlin's previous criminal record, which he hadn't disclosed to them, led the employers to assume he was the thief. He was forced to resign, but they didn't press any charges against him.

His wife Kaye suddenly became ill on February 17, 1984, while in Las Vegas. She was admitted to the hospital with fluid in her lungs, and doctors were unable to diagnose the cause of it. She died on March 14. Meanwhile, Catlin had another fiancée, whom he crossed paths with while visiting the hospital. It is said that his "grief" was overcome by the love of his new fiancée, and probably from the life insurance payments of fifty-seven thousand dollars he had received.

Catlin's third wife noticed the bad luck that seemed to befall those close to Catlin and she reported her suspicions to the local sheriff. Although Joyce had been cremated, the hospital had retained some tissue samples, and the sheriff had these submitted for analysis in November of 1984.

On December 8, Catlin's mother suddenly died after he had visited her. The cause of death was thought to be a stroke and, once again, he tried to have her cremated right away. This time though an autopsy was ordered.

When the tissue samples from his two deceased wives and his mother were analyzed, they were found to contain paraquat, a severely lethal herbicide. Paraquat is so potent that it is banned in the US. Investigators found a bottle of the deadly chemical in Catlin's garage, and his fingerprints were on it.

Trial

Shortly after Catlin married wife number six, he was indicted for the murder of Kaye. The trial began in May of 1986, and he was found guilty. He received a sentence of life imprisonment.

On June 1, 1990, Catlin was also convicted of the murders of Joyce and Martha Catlin. The prosecution had alleged special circumstances, including murder by poison, murder for financial gain, and multiple murder.

Five days later, on June 6, Catlin was sentenced to death.

Outcome

Catlin is still on death row awaiting his execution date.

Trivia

The television movie *Poisoned by Love: The Kern County Murders*, produced in 1993, depicted Catlin's crimes. Harry Hamlin portrayed Catlin in the movie.

GEORGE CHAPMAN

Date of birth: December 14, 1865

Aliases/Nicknames: Seweryn Antonowicz Kłosowski

Characteristics: Poisoner

Number of victims: 3

Date of murders: 1897 - 1902

Date of arrest: October 25, 1902

Victim profile: Mary Spink; Elizabeth Taylor; Maud Marsh

Method of murder: Antimony poisoning

Location: London, England, United Kingdom

Status: Executed by hanging at Wandsworth Prison on April 7, 1903.

Background

Chapman was born in Nagórna, in the Warsaw Governorate of Congress Poland in 1865. At the age of fourteen, he was apprenticed to a surgeon, Moshko Rappaport, in Zwoleń, and his role was to assist in procedures. Then he enrolled at the Warsaw Praga Hospital to complete a course in practical surgery. This was a short course, lasting only about three months, but Chapman continued to work as a doctor's assistant or a nurse until December of 1886.

Chapman moved to England and settled in the East End of London. He became an assistant to a hairdresser sometime in late 1887 or early 1888. After five months, he left and opened his own barbershop.

In 1889, Chapman married a Polish woman, Lucie Badewski, and the couple had two children. Unbeknownst to his new wife, Chapman was still married back in Poland. His first wife made her displeasure known that her husband had married another woman.

Chapman and Lucie moved around to different areas of London before moving to the United States in 1891. They settled in New Jersey, and Chapman began working in a barbershop. The couple fought a lot and, in February of 1892, Chapman attacked his wife while she was pregnant. He told her he had planned to kill her, so she moved back to London.

Eventually, Chapman also returned to London, and the couple reunited for a short while before they decided to end their marriage completely. While working for a hairdresser in 1893, Chapman met

Annie Chapman; after being in a relationship for a while, they moved in together. In 1894, when Annie was pregnant, Chapman brought another woman home to move in with them. Annie left after a few weeks.

Murders

Chapman had a minimum of four mistresses who posed as his wife. The first, Mary Isabella Spink, met Chapman while he was working at a barbershop. Spink's husband had left her and taken their son due to her alcoholism. Spink and Chapman moved in together, and they leased a barbershop in an area of Hastings. The business wasn't successful, and they ended up shifting the shop to a better location. As a way to encourage customers in the door, they began doing "musical shaves," where Chapman would do the shaving while Spink entertained them on the piano.

The couple made a decent income from the barbershop, and Chapman bought a sailboat that he named the Mosquito. He was violent toward Spink, and she was often seen with bruises and marks on her neck.

Despite their initial success, the barbershop eventually failed, and Chapman began managing a pub. He purchased some tartar emetic from a chemist and, while he was working in the pub, poisoned Spink. She died, leaving Chapman £500 in her will.

Soon after Spink's death, Chapman hired Bessie Taylor to work in the pub. They started a relationship, and it wasn't long before Chapman became abusive toward Taylor. At one point, he threatened her with a gun. Not long afterward, she started displaying the same symptoms Spink had suffered. To avoid any possible controversy, Chapman and Taylor moved to Bishop's Stortford, Hertfordshire, where he ran The Grapes Pub.

Taylor underwent an operation, but her condition didn't improve. They moved to London, and Chapman leased the Monument Tavern. In 1901, Taylor died. The pub was losing its lease, so Chapman tried—without success—to burn it down for the insurance money. That same year, he hired Maud Marsh to work as a barmaid, and they quickly entered into a fake marriage. Once again, he was physically abusive. Eventually, he poisoned her, and she died in October of 1902.

A lot of suspicion surrounded Marsh's death, and a police investigation was started. This resulted in the exhumation of Chapman's two previous partners, and it was discovered that all three women had been poisoned.

Trial

Because an indictment for murder at that time could only contain one count, Chapman was charged with the murder of Marsh, the most recent crime. The jury was convinced of his guilt when they were shown the receipt for the purchase of the tartar emetic. On March 19, 1903, he was convicted and sentenced to death, and almost collapsed in court.

When his execution day came around, Chapman was so distraught he had to be half-carried to the gallows. The executioners had to hold him in place. He was hanged at Wandsworth Prison on April 7, 1903.

Outcome

When Chapman was arrested, a detective at Scotland Yard, Frederick Abberline, was convinced they had finally caught Jack the Ripper. He believed Chapman was the Ripper following an interview with Chapman's previous wife, Lucie. She had said Chapman often went out at night for hours on end.

The case for Chapman being the Ripper is mainly due to his history of violence toward women. At one point, he had attempted to strangle Lucie and told her he was planning on cutting off her head.

Chapman had moved to Whitechapel about the same time that the first Ripper murder occurred. The description of the man seen with the fifth victim matched Chapman, and when he moved to the US, the murders stopped.

There are convincing arguments, however, against Chapman being the killer. For one thing, serial killers seldom change their methods. Chapman was a poisoner, and the Ripper mutilated his victims. Also, the Ripper victims seemed to be unknown to the killer, whereas Chapman killed acquaintances.

Trivia

Chapman was featured in "Secrets of Scotland Yard, Poisoner, Publican and Lady Killer" in 1949.

The story of Chapman and his murders was featured in *The Black Museum,* in the 1951 episode called "The Straight Razor."

After he had qualified as a junior surgeon in Poland, he left the country.

JOHN CHRISTIE

Date of birth: April 8, 1899

Aliases/Nicknames: The Rillington Place Strangler

Characteristics: Necrophilia

Number of victims: 8

Date of murders: 1943 - 1953

Date of arrest: March 31, 1953

Victim profile: Ruth Fuerst, 21; Muriel Amelia Eady, 32; Beryl Evans, 20; Beryl's daughter Geraldine, 15 months; Ethel Christie, 54; Kathleen Maloney, 26; Rita Nelson, 24; Hectorina MacLennon, 26

Method of murder: Strangulation

Location: London, England, United Kingdom

Status: Executed by hanging at Pentonville Prison on July 15, 1953.

Background

Christie was one of seven children, and his relationship with his father was troubled. His father showed very little emotion toward his children, especially Christie, and he was quick to dole out punishment for trivial offenses. Christie's older sisters and his mother would sometimes coddle him and other times bully him.

As he grew older, Christie was often described as "queer" and was known to keep to himself. He wasn't a popular child among his peers. His grandfather died in the house in 1911, and Christie later said that seeing his grandfather's body laid out made him feel powerful.

Christie had a lifelong issue with impotence and this led to nicknames such as "Reggie-No-Dick" and "Can't-Do-It- Christie." Later, he was only able to perform sexually with prostitutes.

With World War I breaking out, Christie enlisted in the army on April 12, 1917, and served as an infantryman. His regiment was sent to France in April of 1918, and that June, he was injured during an attack by mustard gas. He later claimed that it was this attack that prevented him from talking loudly, his voice barely above a whisper for the rest of his life. Doctors stated the effect on his voice was more likely a psychological response to the attack rather than an effect of the gas.

Demobilized from the army on October 22, 1919, Christie joined the RAF in December of 1923. He didn't last with the RAF for very long though and was discharged in August of 1924.

Christie married Ethel Simpson on May 10, 1920 and, because his impotence issues continued, he visited prostitutes. The couple moved to Sheffield, but after four years of marriage, they separated. Christie moved to London but became involved in a lot of petty crime, which led to him spending time in and out of prison. After he was released in 1934, he reunited with Ethel, and they moved into 10 Rillington Place.

Murders

The first murder Christie admitted to was the killing of Ruth Fuerst, twenty-one, a munitions worker and part-time prostitute. Christie invited her to his house on August 24, 1943, while his wife was away. They engaged in sex, and then Christie strangled her with rope. At first, he put her body beneath the living room floorboards, but the following night, he buried her in the back garden.

In 1944, Christie was working at a radio factory and met Muriel Amelia Eady. He invited Eady to his home on October 7, 1944, promising her that he had a mixture that would cure her of bronchitis. Christie had set up a jar with a tube and told Eady to inhale the gas. While her back was turned, he inserted another tube into the jar which was attached to coal gas. She quickly fell unconscious; Christie then raped her and strangled her to death. Her body was buried next to Fuerst's in the garden.

Timothy Evans and his wife Beryl moved into the top floor flat at 10 Rillington Place in the Easter of 1948. That October, their daughter Geraldine was born. Evans notified the police in late 1949 that Beryl was dead. During their initial search of Rillington Place, police couldn't find anything, but when they searched again, they found the bodies of Beryl, Geraldine, and a sixteen-week-old fetus. They had been hidden in an outdoor washhouse. The autopsies showed they had been strangled, and Beryl had been assaulted before her death.

Evans told police that Christie had killed his wife during a dodgy abortion operation, but under pressure and continuous questioning, he eventually confessed. There was some suspicion that the confession was fabricated by the police.

Evans went on trial for the murder of his daughter on January 11, 1950, after investigators decided not to prosecute him for the death of his wife. Christie was a witness and told the court how Evans and his wife had many quarrels. Evans was convicted of the murder of Geraldine and sentenced to death. He was hanged on March 9, 1950.

Christie decided to kill Ethel. On the morning of December 14, 1952, he strangled her while she was still in bed. He then made up a variety of stories as to her location. He had been unemployed since December 6 and had sold her wedding ring, her watch, and some furniture to survive. Christie forged Ethel's signature on January 26, 1953 and withdrew all the money from her bank account.

Three more women were murdered by Christie between January 19 and March 6, 1953. Kathleen Maloney, a prostitute, was invited back to Christie's flat and murdered. Rita Nelson had been visiting her sister when she met Christie. She was six months pregnant when he invited her home and killed her.

The third woman, Hectorina MacLennan, was living with her boyfriend in London when she met Christie. They were looking for somewhere to live, and Christie let them stay at Rillington Place. The three would meet up regularly, and sometimes Christie and MacLennan would meet alone. On one particular occasion, Christine convinced her to come back to his flat and, like the other women, he killed her.

Each of the last three victims was raped repeatedly by Christie while they were unconscious and even after they died. Before he buried or disposed of the bodies, Christie would place a vest or piece of material between their legs and wrap their bodies in blankets. He hid the last three victims in an alcove behind the kitchen wall and later covered the area with wallpaper.

Trial

On March 20, 1953, Christie moved out of the flat and sublet it to a couple, which he legally wasn't allowed to do. The landlord forced the new tenants to leave. At the same time, he allowed another tenant to use the kitchen in Christie's flat. On March 24, the tenant tried to insert brackets into the wall and discovered the alcove. He peeled back some of the wallpaper and found the bodies of Maloney, Nelson, and MacLennan. The police were called, and a search began for Christie.

When news of the discovery broke, Christie wandered around London, spending most of his time in cafes. He was seen by a police officer on March 31 near Putney Bridge and was asked to provide identification. All he had though was a few coins and a newspaper clipping about the trial of Timothy Evans.

Christie was arrested. Initially, he only admitted to killing the three women found in the alcove and his wife, Ethel. But when investigators mentioned the bodies in the back garden, he confessed to those killings as well. Later on, he admitted he had killed Beryl Evans, but he staunchly denied killing Geraldine.

Christie went on trial for the murder of Ethel on June 22, 1953. He tried to plead insanity, but a doctor said that although he had a hysterical personality, he was sane. His plea was rejected, and after the jury deliberated for eighty-five minutes, they found him guilty of the murder. Christie lodged no appeal.

Outcome

On July 15, 1953, Christie was hanged at Pentonville Prison. Ironically, he had the same executioner as Evans. After he was prepared to hang, Christie complained that he had an itchy nose, to which the executioner, Albert Pierrepoint responded, "It won't bother you for long."

One of the things police found while searching Christie's flat was a collection of pubic hair he had taken from his victims. The hair only matched up to one of the bodies though (Ethel's), which lead investigators to believe there were more victims they didn't know about. However, no attempts were ever made to try to trace any other possible victims.

After Christie was convicted and stated that he had killed Beryl Evans, a lot of controversy arose surrounding the conviction and execution of timothy Evans. An inquiry was commissioned to determine whether Evans had been innocent and there had been a miscarriage of justice. The result was that Evans was indeed guilty of the murders of his daughter and wife.

But people still weren't convinced. A second inquiry was chaired by Sir Daniel Brabin, a High Court Judge. This time the conclusion was that it was more probable that Evans had killed his wife, but Christie was responsible for the murder of Geraldine. As a result, a posthumous pardon was given to Timothy Evans. This enabled his family to take his remains and rebury them in a private grave.

In January 2003, Evans' half sister and his full sister were granted ex-gratia payments as compensation for the miscarriage of justice.

Christie's home was renamed Ruston Close in 1954 in an attempt to remove the stigma attached to 10 Rillington Place. Later, the house and the street were demolished. A small garden now stands where 10 Rillington Place was.

Trivia

A play by Howard Brenton, *Christie in Love*, opened in September of 1969. It tells the story of Christie's murders and his psychological tendencies toward violence and sadism.

Film

The film, *10 Rillington Place* was released in 1971, and Richard Attenborough played the role of Christie. He said afterward, "I do not like playing the part, but I accepted it at once without seeing the script. I have never felt so totally involved in any part as this. It is a most devastating statement on capital punishment."

For the film, Albert Pierrepoint, who was an executioner, served as a technical advisor for the scene that depicts the execution. He worked under an assumed name. He had to remain anonymous due to the Official Secrets Act which prevented any details of executions from being made public information.

Television

A biographical crime series was commissioned by the BBC in 2016, called *Rillington Place*. Actor Tim Roth played the part of Christie.

Art

Brett Whiteley, an Australian artist living in London, created a series of paintings based on the Christie murders in the 1960s.

Demolition

After Christie was arrested and charged, guards were posted on Rillington Place to stop "trophy hunters" from trying to take souvenirs from the building at number ten. For the movie *10 Rillington*, the house at number 7 was used for interior shots. The guards remained stationed there until the site was demolished.

JOSEPH CHRISTOPHER

Date of birth: July 26, 1955

Aliases/Nicknames: .22-Caliber Killer, Midtown Slasher

Characteristics: Racially motivated attacks

Number of victims: 12

Date of murders: September - December 1980

Date of arrest: January 18, 1981

Victim profile: Glenn Dunn, 14; Harold Green, 32; Emmanuel Thomas, 30; Joseph McCoy; Parler Edwards, 71; Ernest Jones, 40; Luis Rodriguez, 19; Antone Davis, 30; Richard Renner, 20; "John Doe"; Roger Adams, 31; Wendell Barnes, 26

Method of murder: Shooting, stabbing with knife

Location: New York, USA

Status: Sentenced to life in prison on November 14, 1985.

Background

Christopher was born on July 26, 1955, in Buffalo, New York. He was the only son of Nicholas and Therese, and had two older sisters and a younger sister. His father was a hunter and an outdoorsman, and he taught Christopher how to handle and use firearms from a young age.

After school, Christopher began an automotive mechanics program in 1971; he dropped out in early 1974. A variety of odd jobs followed until Christopher gained employment at Canisius College as a maintenance man. Working the night shift, he was caught sleeping at work and was fired in March of 1979. This resulted in Christopher moving back in with his parents.

Christopher had previously been diagnosed as a paranoid schizophrenic, and when he felt his mental health deteriorating in 1978, he tried to get help. However, the psychiatric center told him that because he wasn't a danger to himself or others, he couldn't be admitted. Within fourteen days, Christopher began committing murders.

Murders

Beginning on September 22, 1980, over a period of thirty-six hours, Christopher murdered four black men with a sawed-off rifle. Because of the caliber of the weapon, he was dubbed the .22-Caliber Killer. On October 8 and October 9, he killed two more people, this time bludgeoning them to death and cutting out their hearts.

Christopher enlisted in the US Army a month later and was stationed at Fort Benning. He went on furlough at Christmas, and on December 22, in Manhattan, he killed four more victims. These victims were killed by stabbing, and the media called him the Midtown Slasher. Christopher returned to Buffalo, and on December 29, he stabbed another black man to death. He killed again on December 30, and then returned to his station at Fort Benning.

Back at the Fort, Christopher attacked a fellow soldier, an attack that was considered unprovoked. The victim survived, but Christopher was put in the stockade. He tried to kill himself with a razor but failed. During one of his psychiatric sessions, he claimed he had to kill black people. The police were notified and searched his home, where they found evidence linking him to three murders. In April of 1981, he was indicted for murder and sent back to Buffalo.

Trial

His trial began on May 8, and he pled not guilty to the three murders. Christopher's mother hired lawyers to defend him, but he decided to represent himself. He was found guilty of the murders and received a sentence of sixty years. This ruling was overturned, as the defense had been barred from presenting psychiatric testimony regarding his ability to stand trial.

After further assessments, Christopher was found sane enough to stand trial. He went on trial again in 1985 and was sentenced to life imprisonment.

Outcome

After more than a decade in prison, Christopher died of breast cancer on March 1, 1993. He was just thirty-seven-years-old.

Trivia

Although he wasn't educated, he was described by many as intelligent.

While in prison, Christopher later claimed to have killed thirteen people.

CYNTHIA COFFMAN

Date of birth: January 19, 1962

Aliases/Nicknames: Nil

Characteristics: Kidnapping, rape, robbery

Number of victims: 4

Date of murders: October - November 1986

Date of arrest: November 14, 1986

Victim profile: Sandra Neary, 32; Pamela Simmons, 35; Corinna Dell Novis, 20; Lynel Murrays, 19

Method of murder: Strangulation

Location: California, Arizona, USA

Status: Sentenced to death in San Bernardino County, California, on August 31, 1989.

Background

Born into a devout Catholic family, Coffman became pregnant at the age of seventeen. Because of her family's religious beliefs, abortion was out of the question, so she was forced to get married. The marriage lasted five years before Coffman fled with little more than her car and the clothes she was wearing. She stopped in Page, Arizona, where she worked in a diner. She met a local man and moved in with him after a few weeks. However, they were evicted in the fall of 1985 due to noisy parties.

Coffman and her boyfriend were stopped by the police on May 8, 1986, after running a stop sign. In Coffman's purse, police found a loaded gun and methamphetamine, but she was released, and the charges dropped. Her boyfriend ended up in the county jail for six weeks, and it was then that she met his cellmate, James Gregory Marlow.

Marlow had a history of committing crimes, including armed robberies and home invasions. He had spent time in Folsom Prison and had been nicknamed The Folsom Wolf. His body was adorned with neo-Nazi Aryan Brotherhood tattoos. For Marlow and Coffman, it was love at first sight and, when Marlow was released, they headed to California together.

The couple stayed with Marlow's relatives, living for free, and stealing anything they could find that was worth money. Eventually, they were asked to leave. Other family members started turning them away as well, and they ended up living in the woods.

On July 26, 1986, they were linked to the burglary of cash, a shotgun, and jewelry from a home in Whitley County, Kentucky. A few days later, Coffman and Marlow were married and drifted west to look for more victims to easily rob.

Murders

Sandra Neary, thirty-two, left her home in Costa Mesa, California, on the evening of October 11, 1986, to get some money from a cash machine. She never came back, and her car was found in a local parking lot by police. Her body was found two weeks later, on October 24 by hikers in Corona, Riverside County. She had been strangled.

On October 28, Pamela Simmons, thirty-five, was reported missing in Bullhead City, Arizona. Police found her car near their headquarters; they theorized was that she had been abducted while withdrawing cash from a cash machine.

Corinna Novis, twenty, disappeared on November 7 while running an errand to get cash in Redlands, California. She was snatched in broad daylight in a shopping mall. Then on November 12, Lynel Murrays, a nineteen-year-old psychology student, failed to meet her boyfriend for a date. Her car was still parked outside the dry-cleaning business where she worked. Her body was later found naked and strangled in a Huntington Beach motel room. There was evidence she had been sexually assaulted.

Then, the case started to change for the investigators. A checkbook belonging to Novis was found in a dumpster in Laguna Niguel, inside a fast-food bag along with papers bearing the names of Coffman and Marlow. Stationery was found in a San Bernardino motel room they had stayed at that showed someone had been practicing the signature of Lynel Murrays. When police looked at their criminal records, they issued a statewide alert.

On November 14, 1986, the proprietor of a mountain lodge in Big Bear City, California, called the police after identifying his newest guests as Coffman and Marlow. Police arrived en masse, with one hundred officers, but the lodge was empty. They searched through the nearby woods, and that afternoon, found Coffman and Marlow hiking along a mountain road.

Both fugitives were arrested without a fight. Hours later, Coffman lead police to a vineyard near Fontana, where the body of Novis had been buried in a shallow grave. She had been sodomized before she was strangled.

Trial

Coffman and Marlow were charged with the murder of Novis on November 17. They were held in custody without bail or bond. Fingerprints belonging to both were found in Novis' car, and Coffman had been linked to a pawn shop where Novis' typewriter had been pawned for cash.

It took another thirty-two months before the trial began. By that stage, Coffman and Marlow were blaming each other for the situation they were in. On July 18, 1989, the trial opened in San Bernardino County. They were both found guilty and sentenced to death on August 30.

Outcome

Marlow later claimed Coffman had driven him to commit the murders, but the California Supreme Court upheld the death sentences for them both. The attorneys for both Coffman and Marlow made claims that their trials should have been separate rather than together for a fairer outcome, but the claims were rejected.

According to the judge, there was enough strong evidence to show they were both guilty of the murders, and any small error would have been harmless.

Trivia

Since the death penalty was reinstated in California in 1977, Coffman was the first woman to be sentenced to death.

While in prison, Coffman studies history.

Coffman got a tattoo on her bottom that says "Property of the Folsom Wolf" as a wedding present.

DANIEL CONAHAN

Date of birth: May 11, 1954

Aliases/Nicknames: Hog Trails Killer

Characteristics: Kidnapping, homosexual torture murders, genital amputation

Number of victims: 1 - 6

Date of murders: 1994 - 1996

Date of arrest: July 3, 1996

Victim profile: Transients, hitchhikers, and hustlers

Method of murder: Strangulation

Location: Charlotte County, Florida, USA

Status: Sentenced to death on December 10, 1999.

Background

Shortly after his birth in 1954, Conahan and his family moved from Charlotte, North Carolina to Punta Gorda, Florida. During his high school years, his parents found out he was homosexual and were very displeased about it. They sent him to a psychiatrist to try to "cure" him of it. When he graduated from high school in 1973, he joined the navy. Four years later, he was stationed at Naval Station Great Lakes in Illinois.

In 1978, Conahan nearly faced a court-martial for homosexual solicitation. After his homosexual behavior triggered a large fight a few months later, Conahan was discharged from the Navy.

He stayed in Chicago for thirteen years before moving back to his parents' house in Punta Gorda. Conahan gained his license as a practical nurse in 1995 and began working at the Charlotte Regional Medical Center in Punta Gorda.

Murders

The body of a man was found on February 1, 1994, in Punta Gorda. The victim had been outside for about a month and showed signs of mutilation. The genitals had been removed and discarded, and there were rope burns on the skin. Police were not able to identify the man at the time.

Two years later, on January 1, 1996, a human skull was brought home by a family dog in North Port. More bones were found by police. They were able to determine the genitals had been removed, and the victim was a male. This victim was also never identified.

On March 7, 1996, the mutilated body of another man was found in North Port, and it was estimated he had been dead for ten days. He remained unidentified until 1999, when it was discovered he was John William Melaragno.

In Charlotte County on April 17, 1996, another male skull was found. The woods nearby were searched. Not only did they find the rest of the victim, but they also unearthed another one. The second victim had been killed the day before, after being raped, and was mutilated like the other victims. He was identified as Richard Allen Montgomery. The first victim was later identified as Kenneth Lee Smith. The murders became known as The Hog Trail Killings by the media.

Trial

Conahan came to the attention of police in May of 1996, after witnesses pointed them in his direction. One witness had actually escaped when Conahan's car got stuck on a dirt road. While investigating Conahan, police discovered a report from Fort Myers police in 1994: victim Stanley Burden had been tied to a tree after being propositioned and was nearly strangled.

A search of Conahan's home and property was carried out, and police found evidence linking him to both Burden and murder victim Montgomery. Conahan was arrested on July 3, 1997, for the attempted murder of Burden. He was charged with the murder of Montgomery the following February after the attempted murder charges had been dropped.

Another skeleton was found on May 22, 1997, in Charlotte County. The victim was later identified through DNA as William Charles Patten. He had disappeared in 1993.

When Conahan's trial began on August 9, 1999, he waived his right to a jury trial. The major witness was Stanley Burden. Judge William Blackwell deliberated for twenty-five minutes on August 17, 1999 and found Conahan guilty of the murder and kidnapping of Montgomery. Conahan eventually was sentenced to death.

Outcome

More bodies were found in Charlotte County with similarities to Conahan's other victims. One body was found in 2000, two in 2001, and one in 2002. Then, on March 23, 2007, a further eight skulls and skeletal remains were found in some woods in Fort Myers. Conahan was considered a possible suspect because the location was only one mile from where Stanley Burden had been attacked.

Trivia

There have been a number of items related to Conahan available to buy on murderabilia sites, including his car, razor blade, wristwatch, his playing cards, and some artwork produced by him.

RORY ENRIQUE CONDE

Date of birth: June 14, 1965

Aliases/Nicknames: The Tamiami Trail Strangler

Characteristics: Anal necrophilia

Number of victims: 6

Date of murders: 1994 - 1995

Date of arrest: June 26, 1995

Victim profile: Lazaro Comesana; Rhonda Dunn, 21; Elisa Martinez; Charity Fay Nava; Wanda Cook Crawford; Necole Schneider

Method of murder: Strangulation

Location: Tamiami, Florida, USA

Status: Sentenced to death on March 7, 2000. Pleaded guilty to the murder of five others and was sentenced to five consecutive life terms without parole on April 5, 2001.

Background

Conde started life in Barranquilla, Colombia, and when he was six years old, his mother died of tetanus. Conde's paternal grandmother took over the care of him and his sister Nelly. At the age of twelve, he went to live with his father in Miami. But it wasn't the best situation, with Conde later saying his father was emotionally abusive. There was some suggestion Conde may have also been sexually abused by his father, but this was never confirmed.

Conde married in 1987 when he was twenty-one, and his wife Carla was just fifteen. The marriage produced two children. The marriage wasn't great, with Conde being abusive toward Carla. In 1992, he spent some time in jail due to a fight that occurred between them when Conde brought other females over to the house.

The couple stayed together a bit longer and moved to a condo near the Tamiami Trail. Conde often disappeared at night, and there was no longer any intimacy between him and his wife. Carla eventually left Conde in July of 1994 and went to live at her parents' house with the kids. Conde threatened that if she dated anyone else he would kill her.

Murders

Conde's first known murder took place in 1994. On September 17, Conde was engaging in sex with Lazaro Comesana. When he discovered that Comesana was a cross-dressing prostitute, he killed him. On October 8, he murdered prostitute Elisa Martinez, followed by Charity Nava on November 20. He wrote, "THIRD! I will call Dwight Chan 10. See if you can catch me," across the back and buttocks of Nava. Dwight Chan 10 was a reference to television anchor Dwight Lauderdale.

Three more prostitutes died at Conde's hands, with Wanda Crawford killed on November 25, followed by Necole Schneider on December 17, and Rhonda Dunn on January 12, 1995. Conde strangled his victims and had anal sex with the bodies after they were dead.

Following the murder of Dunn, Miami police had connected all six victims to one suspect by DNA analysis. But they hadn't worked out who the suspect was at that stage.

Then on June 19, 1995, loud banging sounded from Conde's house. Police were called, and inside, they found a woman bound and gagged. The victim, Gloria Maestre, pointed out who had attacked her using photos that were in the house. Police tracked Conde to his grandmother's house in Hialeah, and he was arrested on June 24, 1995.

Trial

Under questioning, Conde confessed that he had killed the six victims, but he blamed his separation from Carla as the catalyst that drove him to kill. Each victim was strangled from behind; he would then have anal sex with the body before they were each dumped near the Tamiami Trail.

Conde was charged with six counts of first-degree murder. He had to face separate trials for each, and the first case was the murder of Dunn. After the jury heard his confession in October 1999, they found him guilty.

Outcome

On March 7, 2000, Conde was sentenced to death for the murder of Dunn. Later he pled guilty to the other murders and received five sentences of life without parole on April 5, 2001.

His appeal to get his death sentence overturned failed, and he was told on September 4, 2003, that the death penalty still stood.

Trivia

The hunt for Conde was the largest in the history of the Metro-Dade police.

John Farrell, chief of the agency's criminal investigation unit, said, "We had 108 investigators on the case at one time and investigated more than 5,000 leads. Conde was lead 4,919."

Conde cried throughout his confession.

The "Tamiami Trail" is the common name given to the last section of Highway 41 going from Tampa to Miami.

ERIC EDGAR COOKE

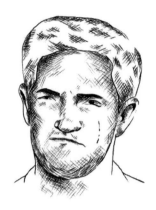

Date of birth: February 25, 1931

Aliases/Nicknames: The Night Caller

Characteristics: Inconsistent, random methods of killing, random victims

Number of victims: 8

Date of murders: 1959, 1963

Date of arrest: September 1, 1963

Victim profile: Jillian Macpherson Brewer; Brian Weir, 29; John Sturkey, 19; George Walmsley, 54; Shirley Martha McLeod, 18; Constance Lucy Madrill, 24; Patricia (Pnena) Vinico Berkman, 33; Rosemary Anderson

Method of murder: Shooting, stabbing with knife, strangulation

Location: Perth, Western Australia, Australia

Status: Executed by hanging at Fremantle Prison on October 26, 1964.

Background

Cooke was born into a troubled and violent family in 1931, in Victoria Park, Perth, Australia. His parents married only because his mother was pregnant with him. His father Vivian was a violent alcoholic who would beat Cooke regularly, especially if the boy tried to protect his mother from his father's rages. Cooke often hid beneath the house or would wander the streets at night to stay away from his father. At times, Cooke was sent to foster homes or orphanages. But he always ended up back home.

As a child, Cooke was admitted to the hospital for numerous injuries, supposedly from being accident-prone. At one point, the doctors suspected he might have suffered some level of brain damage. He suffered from terrible recurrent headaches and spent some time in an asylum. Apparently, he had an operation in 1949 which stopped him from having blackouts, but it is unknown what the surgery was.

Born with a cleft palate and hare lip, Cooke underwent surgical repairs. These procedures were not completely successful, so he was left with a facial deformity, and he tended to mumble when he spoke. This made him the target of bullying at every school he attended.

At the age of fourteen, Cooke left school and went to work for Central Provision stores as a delivery boy. His wages were given to his mother to help support the family. Still accident-prone, Cooke suffered numerous injuries at his future jobs. At the Harris, Scarfe and Sandover factory he was struck in the nose by a winch and ended up in the hospital.

When he was sixteen, Cooke worked in a workshop at Midland Junction as a hammer boy. The injuries he suffered there included burns to his face by steam, an injury to his right hand, and an injury to his left thumb.

By the time he was seventeen, Cooke was committing petty crimes and vandalism most nights. At one point, he burnt down a church after he was rejected following an audition for the choir. He spent eighteen months in jail for the arson. He often broke into homes and stole valuables, then would keep the newspaper articles about his crimes and show them to people to try to impress them.

On May 24, 1949, Cooke was arrested and charged with vandalism, theft, and arson. He had left fingerprints at the crime scenes, which made it easy for the police to link multiple crimes to him. It was a lesson that would change Cooke's modus operandi in future crimes he committed.

Cooke spent three months in the army, but was discharged once his previous criminal record came to light. On October 14, 1953, Cooke married a waitress, Sarah Lavin, nineteen, and they went on to have seven children. Following their marriage, Cooke was arrested for many crimes, including Peeping Tom offenses. In 1955, he was charged with stealing a car and was sentenced to two years. When he was released, having learned from his mistakes, Cooke started wearing women's gloves when he committed a crime to ensure his fingerprints weren't left behind.

Cooke, for unknown reasons, later shifted from petty theft and minor criminal to one who would leave a city in terror.

Murders

On November 25, 1958, Cooke broke into the home of Mollie McLeod, fifteen, in Applecross. He bludgeoned her while she slept. When her parents found her, she was covered in blood and incoherent. The weapon was never identified, nor the motive for the attack.

The following month, on December 27, Kathy Bellis was struck by a stolen car being driven by Cooke. The force of car threw her eighteen meters, but she managed to survive.

The first known murder occurred on January 30, 1959, in South Perth. Cooke broke into the flat of Pnena Berkman. She awakened to the sounds of the break-in to find Cooke standing in her bedroom. A fight ensued, but Cooke overcame her and killed her with a knife.

Several months passed before Cooke committed his next violent attack. On August 8, 1959, Alix Doncon, seventeen, was asleep in bed in her Nedlands flat. When the nursing student woke up, Cooke was in her bedroom. He bashed her in the head, fracturing her skull, and then fled. Though she survived, the injury left her with severe epilepsy.

On December 20, 1959, Jillian Brewer was asleep in her flat in Cottesloe when Cooke broke in. While she was still asleep, Cooke hacked her to death with an axe. Then, using scissors, he mutilated her body.

Another few months passed, and then Cooke struck again. He stole a car in Como, which was easy since the keys had been left in the ignition. As he drove down Munt Street in Bayswater, he came across Glenys Peak who was walking home after a night out. He struck her with the car, throwing her into the dirt on the side of the road. Cooke turned the car around, intending to strike her again, but she was able to escape.

Jill Connell was walking home from work on May 13, 1960. Cooke drove past her as she headed down Daly Street in Belmont, then he turned around. When the car struck her, she hit the windshield, and then landed on the side of the road. Though seriously injured, she managed to survive.

On the night of May 20, 1960, Cooke struck three victims with a vehicle. Cousins Terese Zagami and Maureen Rogers, along with friend Georgina Pitman, were walking along George Street, Queens Park. When Cooke hit them with the car, Terese was able to jump clear, but Maureen and Georgina weren't so lucky. Maureen took the full force of the crash and was left with ongoing medical issues.

Cooke entered a home in Nedlands on March 3, 1962, through an unlocked door. Anne Melvin, twenty-three, was asleep in her bed and woke to find Cooke wrapping a towel around her neck. He tightened the towel long enough that she fell unconscious, but was still alive. Then he tied her arms with stockings. A noise distracted Cooke and, while he was investigating it, Anne regained consciousness. She started screaming, which made Cooke flee the house. It was a lucky escape for Anne.

Peggy Fleury, asleep in a sleepout in Hawkestone Street, Cottesloe, woke to find Cooke in her room on December 29, 1962. He was in the process of removing her clothes when she screamed, and Cooke responded by striking her in the face with his fist and then a flashlight. She carried on screaming and Cooke left. Peggy required surgery to fix the injuries to her face.

January 26, 1963, was a terrifying night, and is known as Cooke's "Australia Day killing spree." First, he broke into a house in Como; while stealing money and valuables, he found a .22 caliber rifle and some ammunition.

A young couple was parked in their car when Cooke approached and opened fire. Though they were both injured, they survived and sped down Napier Street. It was the early hours of January 27. Cooke next walked to nearby Broome Street and climbed up on top of a garage roof which was also used as a balcony. He took aim through a set of open doors and shot his next victim, Brian Weir, in the head. Weir was severely injured with brain damage, and he died as a result of his injuries a few years later. His last years were filled with suffering.

Cooke then started knocking on doors, trying to find more victims. Tragically, two more people were shot and killed. John Sturkey, eighteen, was killed with a gunshot to the head. When George Walmsley, fifty-five, opened his door that night, he was also fatally shot in the head. Over the course of that night, Cooke shot five people, killing three. (This latter number includes Brian Weir, even though he survived for a significant period of time).

Cooke's next murder took place on February 9, 1963. Using a vehicle, he struck Rosemary Anderson in Shenton Park, and she died from her injuries. Her boyfriend, John Button, was arrested soon after under suspicion of killing Anderson. Bizarrely, he confessed and went on trial for her murder.

Lucy Madrill was asleep in her flat in West Perth on February 15, 1963, when she became Cooke's next victim. She was strangled to death with a lamp cord. Cooke didn't leave her body in her bed; instead, he carried and dragged the body approximately twenty-four meters and left it underneath a neighbor's house.

Cooke assaulted Carmel Read on June 15, 1963, while she was in her bed in her flat in Nedlands. The window had been left partially opened, and the opportunistic Cooke entered without difficulty. Carmel awakened when she heard a sound, and Cooke stabbed her with an umbrella. She screamed, and he ran from the home.

Shirley McLeod was babysitting in a Dalkeith house on August 10, 1963, when Cooke entered the home. From the hallway, he shot and killed her while she sat in a chair studying. The parents of the children she was babysitting found her in the same position when they returned home that night.

Cooke was hard to catch because there were no links between the victims, and his methods of killing were varied. Though serial killers normally stick to one method, Cooke used a vehicle, knives, an axe, guns, and other objects to commit murder. His victims were selected randomly, with Cooke taking advantage of whoever crossed his path.

Two suspects were arrested for the murders of Brewer and Anderson. John Button was convicted of killing Anderson, and Darryl Beamish was convicted of killing Brewer. Beamish, originally sentenced to death, was able to have his conviction overturned.

In August of 1963, a rifle was found underneath some bushes on Rookwood Street in Mount Pleasant. Testing of the gun showed it was the weapon used in the murder of Shirley McLeod. To try to catch the killer, police put the gun back where it had been found, but first they made it inoperable using fishing line so it couldn't be fired. Then they waited. Seventeen days later, Cooke went to the scene and tried to collect the gun, at which point he was arrested.

Trial

While under interrogation, Cooke confessed to eight murders and fourteen attempted murders. He went on trial for the murder of John Sturkey, pleading not guilty by reason of insanity. His lawyers claimed Cooke suffered from schizophrenia, but the director of the state mental health services testified that Cooke wasn't insane. Independent psychiatrists were not allowed to examine Cooke by the state. On November 28, 1963, after a trial that lasted just three days, Cooke was convicted of the murder.

He received a death sentence and instructed his lawyers not to appeal the sentence, as he believed he needed to pay for the crimes he had committed. Cooke spent thirteen months in prison, before being taken to the gallows on October 26, 1964. Minutes before he was hanged, he placed his hand on a Bible and swore that he was responsible for the murders of Anderson and Brewer, the crimes two other men had been convicted of.

Outcome

Because of Cooke's gallows confessions, the cases of Anderson and Brewer's murders were looked at again. Darryl Beamish, a deaf-mute, had been convicted of killing Brewer and served fifteen years in prison, even though during that time, Cooke had made his confession. His first appeal was dismissed because the court didn't believe Cooke had been truthful.

John Button, who had been convicted of killing his girlfriend Anderson, fought against his conviction. An appeal lodged with the appeal court showed that Cooke had provided details of the murder that only the suspect could have known, but the court dismissed the appeal. The judges didn't believe Anderson's body could have been thrown over the roof of the Holden EJ (the car Cooke said he was driving), without causing damage to the sun visor.

Button and his supporters didn't give up though. His friends, Bret Christian, who owned a newspaper, and Estelle Blackburn, a journalist, continued to push for a retrial. They reenacted Cooke's claims about the Holden, and proved that what Cooke had said happened was possible. In 2002, Button's conviction was finally quashed by the Court of Criminal Appeal.

This opened the way for Beamish to appeal again and, in 2005, he was also acquitted.

Trivia

Cooke's memory for details surprised police investigators during his confession. He subsequently admitted committing more than two hundred fifty robberies, and could even tell investigators how many coins he stole and what denominations they were.

Cooke was the last person hanged in Western Australia. Buried in Fremantle Cemetery, his body was placed above the remains of Martha Rendell, a child killer who had been hanged in Fremantle Prison in 1909.

The biography *Broken Lives*, about the life of Cooke. was written by Estelle Blackburn. She researched the book for six years. A large point of focus in the book was the impact Cooke's crimes had on the families of his victims. It was the information in the book that led to the exoneration of Beamish and Button.

Randolph Stow's novel, *The Suburbs of Hell*, indicated there was a delayed response to Cooke's murders by the public. It took a while for the full horror of the crimes to be acknowledged.

A biography was written about Randolph Stow by Suzanne Falkiner, and it showed that his sense of humor was triggered when it was learned people in Perth would knock on doors and say, "It's the Nedlands Monster," while crimes were still being committed.

The novel *The Nedlands Monster* was written about Cooke by Tim Winton in 1991. It was later adapted for television in 2011.

Cooke was featured in an episode of *Crime Investigation Australia* In March 2009.

JOHN COOPER

Date of birth: September 3, 1944

Aliases/Nicknames: The Bullseye Killer

Characteristics: Rape, robbery

Number of victims: 4

Date of murders: December 22, 1985, June 29, 1989

Date of arrest: May 13, 2009

Victim profile: Richard Thomas, 58; Richard's sister Helen, 54; Peter Dixon, 51; Peter's wife Gwenda, 52

Method of murder: Shooting

Location: Pembrokeshire, Wales, United Kingdom

Status: Sentenced to life imprisonment on May 26, 2011.

Background

Cooper had a real taste for money, and in the 1970s, he won a small fortune. But it didn't take him long to squander it all on gambling, leaving him without his beloved money. To help him fund the lifestyle he wanted, Cooper turned to violent crime.

Murders

On December 22, 1985, Cooper targeted a home for burglary in Scoveston Park. The three-story farmhouse was home to siblings Richard and Helen Thomas. On entering the home, he killed them both and then set fire to the house, burning it down before he fled.

Cooper appeared on a TV game show on May 28, 1989. During questioning by the host, he commented that he had a hobby of scuba diving and that the ideal place to indulge his hobby was in Pembrokeshire. Footage recorded on that day would later be used to help match him with descriptions from witnesses.

Peter and Gwenda Dixon were on vacation in Pembrokeshire on June 29, 1989, and had gone for a walk along the coastal path. They failed to return from the walk, and their bodies were later found along the path. They had been tied up, and then forced to tell Cooper the PIN number for their bank cards. Afterwards, they were both shot in the face, point-blank, with a sawn-off shotgun. Cooper managed to rob the couple of £300.

Trial

There was a witness to the Dixons' murder, and they provided the police with a sketch of the man they had seen. When shown the footage from the television show, the sketch was a match, but there wasn't enough to arrest him.

Cooper was later charged in 1998 for robbery and burglary on unrelated cases, and he was sentenced to fourteen years in prison. In January of 2009, he was released from prison.

A cold case review of the Dixon murders was undertaken in 2009. There had been significant developments in forensic science by then, including DNA. But it was Cooper's shotgun that was finally identified as the murder weapon. He was arrested in May of 2009.

Cooper went on trial for the double murders in 2011, and in May of that year, he was convicted and sentenced to four life sentences without parole.

He launched an appeal in September of 2011, but it was rejected in November of 2012.

Outcome

When the sentence was handed down to Cooper, High Court judge Mr. Justice John Griffith Williams said: "Life for these murders will mean just that. You are a very dangerous man and a significant risk. You are very predatory and, were it not for advances in DNA techniques, may well have continued to evade capture."

Trivia

A documentary about Cooper was broadcast in the *Real Crime* series in Britain in 2011.

A documentary about the police interview strategy, the forensic techniques, and Cooper's conviction was produced by Welsh television channel S4C on May 24, 2016.

In the *Crime Files* series in Wales, a documentary about the case was broadcast in September 2016 and featured an interview with the detective who had interviewed Cooper.

The documentary *The Gameshow Serial Killer: Police Tapes* about Cooper was broadcast on July 12, 2018.

Another documentary about Cooper appeared as part of the *Murder by the Sea* crime series in January 2019.

RAY AND FAYE COPELAND

Ray Copeland

Date of birth: December 30, 1914

Aliases/Nicknames: Nil

Characteristics: Robbery

Number of victims: 5 +

Date of murders: October 1986 - May 1989

Date of arrest: October 17, 1989

Victim profile: Paul Jason Cowart, 21; John W. Freeman, 27; Jimmie Dale Harvey, 27; Wayne Warner; Dennis Murphy, 27

Method of murder: Shooting (.22 caliber Marlin bolt-action rifle)

Location: Mooresville, Missouri, USA

Status: Sentenced to death, 1991. Died in prison in October of 1993.

Faye Copeland

Date of birth: August 4, 1921

Aliases/Nicknames: Nil

Characteristics: Robbery

Number of victims: 5 +

Date of murders: October 1986 - May 1989

Date of arrest: October 17, 1989

Victim profile: Paul Jason Cowart, 21; John W. Freeman, 27; Jimmie Dale Harvey, 27; Wayne Warner; Dennis Murphy, 27

Method of murder: Shooting (.22 caliber Marlin bolt-action rifle)

Location: Mooresville, Missouri, USA

Status: Sentenced to death on April 27, 1991. Commuted to life in prison in 1999. Died in prison on December 30, 2003.

Background

Ray Copeland was born in 1914, in Oklahoma. Because his family was trying to survive like so many others during the Great Depression, they moved around quite a lot. Ray started his life of petty crime at a fairly young age, which started with stealing pigs from his own father. Before long, he was involved in check fraud and numerous other non-violent crimes. He spent short periods of time in jail.

In 1940, Ray met Faye Wilson, and they quickly married. The couple had several children and money was tight. Because of Ray's criminal reputation, they had to keep moving, which didn't help the finances. After spending more time in jail, he came up with a way to improve his illegal financial methods so he wouldn't get caught.

They settled in Mooresville in 1967, and Faye worked in factories and motels while Ray worked on the farm. Ray had been known since the 1970s for picking up hitchhikers and getting them to work on his farm. Over the years, the neighbors noticed many disheveled looking people coming to the farm to work, and then they would be gone again.

The Crime Stoppers hotline, a means of anonymously reporting crimes, received a call in the late summer of 1989 that lead police to investigate the Copelands and what exactly had been going on at the farm.

Murders

Because Ray was so well-known as a fraud, he would use the drifters and hitchhikers he picked up to help him with his schemes. He would employ them as farmhands and then get them to use his bad checks at the market to buy cattle. Ray would sell the cattle quickly, and the farmhands would disappear. The scam worked for a while, but police soon caught up with Ray and sent him back to jail.

When he was released this time, he made sure his new farmhands couldn't be connected to him like the previous ones. Then, in August of 1989, a former employee of the Copelands, Jack McCormick, called the Crime Stoppers hotline with what seemed to be a fantastical story. He told police that while he had worked on the Copelands' farm, he had seen human bones. Furthermore, Ray had once tried to kill him.

Skeptical at first, the story gained more weight when the police checked on Ray's criminal background. In October of 1989, armed with a search warrant, a team of officers and sniffer dogs went to the Copeland farm. Nothing was found at first, but further searching revealed three bodies of young men in a barn. Then, even more bodies were discovered. Later, it was determined they had all been killed by the same weapon, a .22 caliber Marlin rifle, which was found in the Copeland home. Each man had been shot in the back of the head at close range.

In the house, they found a register with the names of the different farmhands who had worked on the farm. Police used this to help identify the bodies they had found. Next to twelve of the names was an 'X' marked in Faye's handwriting. In addition to the rifle, the register, and the bodies, another piece of shocking evidence found was a handmade quilt Faye had created out of clothing belonging to the dead men.

The known victims were identified as:

Dennis K. Murphy, of Normal, Illinois - killed October 17, 1986
Wayne Warner, of Bloomington, Illinois - killed November 19, 1986
Jimmy Dale Harvey, 27, of Springfield, Missouri - killed October 25, 1988
John W. Freeman, 27, of Tulsa, Oklahoma - killed December 8, 1988
Paul J. Cowart, 21, of Dardanelle, Arkansas - killed May 1, 1989

Trial

The Copelands were charged with five murders: Murphy, Warner, Harvey, Freeman, and Cowart. When Faye went on trial in November of 1990, the defense depicted her as a dutiful wife and mother who had generally been treated badly and beaten by Ray. Her attorney tried to persuade the jury that she was a sufferer of Battered Woman Syndrome. Though the jury acknowledged she was a battered wife, they felt it didn't excuse her involvement in the murders. They found her guilty of four counts of murder and one of manslaughter, and she was given four death sentences and one sentence of life without parole.

Ray went on trial in March of 1991. He was found guilty of five counts of murder and was sentenced to death. When he heard that his wife had also received the death penalty, Ray said, without emotion, "Well, those things happen to some, you know."

Outcome

Ray would never receive the lethal injection. Nature took its course, and he died on October 19, 1993. His body was cremated.

Faye appealed her conviction based on the jury not hearing the evidence of abuse Ray had inflicted upon her. In August of 1999, her death sentence was overturned, and she was sentenced to five terms of life without parole instead.

On August 10, 2002, Faye suffered a stroke; it left her partially paralyzed and unable to speak. A medical parole was granted in September 2002, and she was sent to a nursing home in Chillicothe, Missouri. She subsequently died there, at the age of eighty two.

Trivia

Until her medical parole, Faye had been the oldest female on death row.

The comic book *Family Bones* features the story of the Copelands. It was created by Shawn Granger, a nephew of the Copelands.

David Wiltse wrote a play *Temporary Help* based on the story of the Copelands, and it was performed Off-Broadway in 2004.

The Copeland case has featured in several television series, including *Wicked Attraction*, *Forensic Files*, and *The New Detectives*.

"I begged [Ray] time and time again to please stay out of trouble. We had our home, and everything paid for. We were on Social Security. So why would he turn around and mess all that up just like he has?" — *Faye Copeland*

JUAN VALLEJO CORONA

Date of birth: February 7, 1934

Aliases/Nicknames: The Machete Murderer

Characteristics: Homosexual rape

Number of victims: 25

Date of murders: 1960s - 1971

Date of arrest: May 26, 1971

Victim profile: Sigurd Emil Beiermann; John Raggio Smallwood; Mark Beverly Shields; Joe Carriveau; Raymond Reand Muchache, 47; Kenneth Edward Whiteacre; Melford Everett Sample; Charles Cleveland Fleming; John Joseph Haluka, 52; Warren Jerome Kelley, 61; Donald Dale Smith, 60; William Emery Kamp, 63; Elbert J.T. Riley, 46; Paul Buel Allen, 59; Clarence Hocking, 53; James Wylie Howard, 64; Edward Martin Cupp, 44; Albert Leon Hayes, 58; John Henry Jackson, 64; Lloyd Wallace Wenzel, 60; Joseph J. Maczak, 55; four unidentified victims

Method of murder: Shooting, stabbing, bludgeoning

Location: Yuba City, California, USA

Status: Sentenced to 25 consecutive terms of life imprisonment in January 1973.

Background

In February of 1934, Corona was born in Autlán, an area of Jalisco, Mexico. It was a large family, with ten children and three half-siblings. In 1950, at the age of sixteen, Corona dropped out of school and immigrated illegally across the border to California. He found work on farms, picking fruit and vegetables, and studied the English language at night school.

He moved to Marysville, Yuba City, in May of 1953. His brother Natividad had previously moved there and suggested Corona move there too. There he met his first wife, Gabriella E. Hermosillo, and they married in Reno, Nevada, on October 24, 1953. Corona would later marry another woman, Gloria I. Moreno, in 1959.

A major flood occurred in December of 1955, and it was one of the most destructive in the history of Northern California. A total of seventy-four people were killed in the flood, and the devastation and death toll had a serious effect on Corona's mental health. He believed that he was living in a land of ghosts, thinking everyone else had been killed in the flood.

Corona's brother had him committed to DeWitt State Hospital on January 17, 1956, and he was subsequently diagnosed with schizophrenia. His treatment involved twenty-three electric shock treatments, and three months afterward, he was declared recovered and released. Corona was sent back to Mexico after he got out of the hospital.

Corona came back to the US in 1962, this time legally, with a green card which enabled him to work. He was considered a hard worker despite having a violent temper. He became a licensed labor contractor and was responsible for hiring workers for fruit ranches.

Murders

A farm owner who employed Corona to find field workers noticed a freshly dug hole in his peach orchard on May 19, 1971. The following day the hole had been filled in with dirt. This seemed suspicious to the farmer, so he called the police, who went to the orchard to investigate. There they found the body of a man in the hole; he had been hacked and stabbed to death.

This was just the first body to be found. In one of the graves, two receipts for meat—with Corona's signature on them—were found. In two other graves, bank deposit slips with Corona's name on them were found. Witnesses reported they had seen some of the victims in Corona's truck before they disappeared.

Police entered Corona's home in the early hours of May 26, 1971 and arrested him. Further evidence was found, including knives stained with blood, a pistol, a machete, and clothing with blood on it. They also found a work ledger with a list of thirty-four names and dates. Seven of the known victims' names were in the ledger. Prosecutors later alleged the dates were the dates of the murders.

When the search of the orchard ended on June 4, the bodies of twenty-five male victims had been found. Four of them were unable to be identified. It is possible there were more bodies buried elsewhere.

Victims:

Sigurd Emil Beiermann
John Raggio Smallwood
Mark Beverly Shields
Joe Carriveau
Four unidentified men
Raymond Reand Muchache, forty-seven
Kenneth Edward Whiteacre
Melford Everett Sample
Charles Cleveland Fleming
John Joseph Haluka, fifty-two
Warren Jerome Kelley, sixty-one
Donald Dale Smith, sixty
William Emery Kamp, sixty-three
Elbert J.T. Riley, forty-six
Paul Buel Allen, fifty-nine
Clarence Hocking, fifty-three
James Wylie Howard, sixty-four
Edward Martin Cupp, forty-four
Albert Leon Hayes, fifty-eight
John Henry Jackson, sixty-four
Lloyd Wallace Wenzel, sixty
Joseph J. Maczak, fifty-five

Trial

Initially, Corona received legal aid, and his public defender, Roy Van den Heuvel, asked for a psychological evaluation of Corona's mental state by several psychiatrists. At Corona's arraignment on June 2, he pled not guilty.

Corona received a new defense attorney under legal aid on June 14. Richard Hawk replaced Van den Heuvel and, in return for his representation, he made an agreement with Corona for exclusive literary and dramatic property rights to Corona's life story. As part of the agreement, the attorney-client privilege was waived. Before Hawk even bothered to look at Corona's medical and psychiatric reports, he decided Corona wouldn't plead not guilty by reason of insanity.

On June 18, Corona suffered a mild heart attack. A twenty-five-count murder indictment was returned against him on July 12, by the grand jury.

The trial started on September 11, 1972, in Fairfield, California. It took several weeks to select the jury, and the trial lasted for three months. Colona denied being responsible for the deaths but was never called to testify. After deliberating for forty-five hours, the jury found him guilty of all twenty-five counts of murder. Corona was sentenced to twenty-five terms of life imprisonment without parole.

His sentence started at California Medical Facility because of his heart issues. On December 6, 1973, Corona allegedly bumped into a fellow inmate in a corridor and didn't say "excuse me." As a result, he was stabbed thirty-two times in his cell. Four inmates were charged with the assault, and Corona survived the attack.

Corona's conviction was overturned on May 18, 1978, by the California Court of Appeals, due to the incompetence of his defense attorney during his trial. A new trial was ordered, and this began on February 22, 1982. The defense tried to shift the blame to Corona's brother, who had died several years earlier, but this failed. During this trial, the defense called over fifty witnesses, and Corona also took the stand.

After seven months, the trial came to an end, and Corona was once again convicted of the murders.

Outcome

Corona was sent to Corcoran State Prison in California in 1992. He is housed in the Sensitive Needs Yard due to his dementia.

To date, he has been denied parole eight times. His last parole hearing was in November 2016, and his next eligibility date is in 2022. By then, he will be at least 87.

Trivia

"Yes, I did it, but I am a sick man, and a sick man can't be judged by the same standards as other men." — *Corona*

Corona was once considered the most prolific serial killer in U.S. history that had been identified and captured. But he was overtaken by Dean Corll in 1973, when twenty-eight bodies were recovered.

ANDRE CRAWFORD

Date of birth: March 20, 1962

Aliases/Nicknames: Nil

Characteristics: Rape, necrophilia

Number of victims: 11

Date of murders: 1993 - 1999

Date of arrest: January 28, 2000

Victim profile: Patricia Dunn; Rhonda King; Angel Shatteen; Shaquanta Langley; Sonja Brandon; Nicole Townsend; Cheryl Cross; Tommie Dennis; Sheryl Johnson; Constance Bailey; Evandrey Harris

Method of murder: Strangulation

Location: Chicago, Illinois, USA

Status: Sentenced to life in prison without parole on December 17, 2009.

Background

As an infant, Crawford was put into foster care after he was found living alone. His mother would leave him unattended for long periods of time, and the house was in squalor. Crawford became transient as an adult and would sleep in vacant buildings around Chicago.

Murders

A thirty-seven-year-old woman was found murdered on September 21, 1993, in a vacant factory lot on the 700 block section of West 50th Street. She had suffered blunt trauma to the head. A twenty-four-year-old woman was found murdered on December 21, 1994. Her body was discovered in an abandoned building on the 800 block of West 50th Place.

The body of a thirty-six-year-old woman was found on April 3, 1995, in an empty house on the 5000 block of South Carpenter. On July 23, 1997, the body of a twenty-seven-year-old woman was discovered in a closet in an abandoned house on the 900 block of West 51st Street.

On December 27, 1997, a forty-two-year-old woman was assaulted at knifepoint. A man had approached her from behind while she was walking, placed a knife to her head, and dragged her into an abandoned building on the 5100 block of South Peoria. She was then beaten and raped.

In June of 1998, the dead body of a thirty-one-year-old woman was found murdered in a vacant building on the 5000 block of South May Street. Then on August 13, 1998, a forty-four-year-old woman was found murdered. Her body was found in the kitchen of an abandoned house on the 900 block of West 52nd Street. Her clothes were located in the alley nearby.

On August 13, 1998, a real estate agent discovered the decomposed body of a thirty-two-year-old woman lying on the floor in an attic on the 5200 block of South Marshfield. On December 8, 1998, a thirty-five-year-old woman was found dead in a building on the 1200 block of West 52nd Street, with one leg of her pants down around her ankle and the other leg of her pants off. She had marks on her neck from a rope, and there were injuries to her face; it was believed she had been strangled with a ligature.

On February 2, 1999, a thirty-five-year-old-woman was found killed, her body was discovered on the 1300 block of West 51st Street. A forty-four-year-old woman was found murdered on April 21, 1999. Her body was discovered in a vacant house on the 5000 block of South Justine.

On June 20, 1999, a forty-one-year-old woman was murdered, her body discovered in the attic of an empty building on the 1500 block of West 51st Street.

Many of the victims had been prostitutes or drug addicts. Crawford also had sex with the bodies after death.

DNA evidence was found on every victim. Throughout the killing spree, Crawford had been arrested for other crimes and processed, but his DNA was never taken.

Trial

Crawford was identified as the killer, and his DNA matched the DNA evidence found on several of the victims. These included Patricia Dunn, Rhonda King, Angel Shatteen, Shaquanta Langley, Sonja Brandon, Nicole Townsend, Cheryl Cross, Tommie Dennis, Sheryl Johnson, Constance Bailey, and Evandrey Harris. Crawford was formally charged with their murders.

His lawyers argued against the death sentence, citing Crawford's history of being mistreated and sexually abused as a child. But the State's Attorney disagreed, saying that someone who killed so many women in such a brutal way didn't deserve mercy.

The jury disagreed. After deliberating for ten hours, the jury found him guilty of all murders but— unable to reach a unanimous decision, which is required for a death sentence—did not recommend the death penalty. Instead, he was sentenced to life imprisonment without parole. Crawford showed no emotion as the verdict and sentencing were announced.

Outcome

In 1997, Hubert Geralds Jr. was convicted of six murders of women in the Englewood neighborhood of Chicago. One of those victims was Rhonda King. Geralds was sentenced to death, but in 2000, a motion to vacate the conviction for King's murder was moved because DNA evidence linked her murder to Crawford. Geralds remained on death row for the other five murders.

Crawford was arrested for felony theft in March of 1993. If Illinois had required him to supply a DNA sample at that time, authorities would have been able to match him to the first murder. This might have prevented a further ten murders and attempted murder.

Trivia

According to psychologists, Crawford had been abused by his mother.

According to a neighbor, when Crawford saw "streetwalkers," he said they should get a job and do something with their lives.

Police received a tip by someone stating they had overhead Crawford discussing the murders while on a bus. Supposedly, Crawford had said, "Drug-addicted sex workers need to be strangled and have their heads beaten in."

"I'm glad I got caught. I was like a shark in a pool." *- Crawford.*

JOHN MARTIN CRAWFORD

Date of birth: March 29, 1962

Aliases/Nicknames: The Lady Killer

Characteristics: Rape, torture

Number of victims: 4 +

Date of murders: 1981, 1992

Date of arrest: January 1995

Victim profile: Mary Jane Serloin; Eva Taysup; Shelley Napope; Calinda Waterhen

Method of murder: Stabbing with knife, strangulation

Location: Alberta, Saskatchewan, Canada

Status: Sentenced in 1981 to 10 years' imprisonment for manslaughter. Released on March 23, 1989. Sentenced to three concurrent life sentences in 1996.

Background

Crawford was born into an abusive family, and by the time he was twelve years old, he had become a bully to others. He started sniffing glue and was often overheard talking to himself or to objects. At the age of thirteen, he had sex with an eleven-year-old girl along with some friends, after they paid the girl to do it.

When Crawford was sixteen years old, he began hearing voices, and these voices started to torment him. Three years later, in 1981, Crawford met Mary Jane Serloin, thirty-five, in a bar in Lethbridge, Alberta. Her naked body was discovered on Christmas Day; her breasts had been bitten.

Crawford was apprehended and charged with murder. He pled guilty to manslaughter and was sentenced to ten years in prison. Eight years later, in 1989, he was released and moved in with his mother in Saskatoon, Saskatchewan.

By 1992, Crawford was sniffing glue and injecting drugs every day. He was a heavy alcohol abuser, consuming twenty-four cans of beer and twenty-six ounces of hard liquor a day. He would drive around the run-down parts of town looking for prostitutes nearly every night.

Murders

On May 9, 1992, a complaint was made by a woman named Janet Sylvestre who told the police she had been raped by Crawford. When they found him, he was on a beach and nearly dead from a combination of substance abuse and sunstroke. He remained in custody until his mother paid his bail in June and he was released to her.

Later on that year, Crawford and another former inmate Bill Corrigon picked up sixteen-year-old Shelley Napope. They both raped her then beat her. Afterward, Crawford dragged her into the bushes and stabbed her to death.

On September 20, he raped, tortured, and strangled Eva Taysup. He cut off her arm before he buried her. The following day, he also raped, tortured, and strangled twenty-two-year-old Calinda Waterhen.

Crawford took part in the beating death of a man in October of 1992. For his part, he spent the majority of 1993 in a correctional center for assault.

In 1994, human remains were found by a hunter in the southwest area of Saskatoon. Police identified Crawford as the main suspect and put him under surveillance for four months. Crawford picked up Theresa Kematch, raped and beat her, and left her on the street. Police arrested him immediately.

Trial

Once Crawford was arrested, other women came forward to say they had been raped by him, and in some cases, nearly strangled to death. Bill Corrigan was named as an accomplice by several of the women.

In May of 1996, Crawford was convicted of three counts of murder, though authorities believed he was responsible for several more murders.

Outcome

Crawford was sentenced to three concurrent life sentences. He is serving his time in the Saskatchewan Penitentiary in Prince Albert.

The murder of Janet Sylvestre, which occurred in 1994, remains unsolved.

Trivia

The book *Just Another Indian, A Serial Killer and Canada's Indifference* by Warren Goulding contains the story of Crawford's murders. The book claims the case was "played down" by media due to the victims being Aboriginal.

CHARLES CULLEN

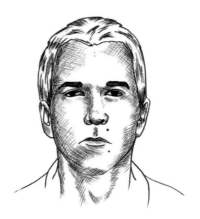

Date of birth: February 22, 1960

Aliases/Nicknames: Nil

Characteristics: Nurse - victims were patients

Number of victims: 29 - 45

Date of murders: 1984 - 2003

Date of arrest: December 14, 2003

Victim profile: John W. Yengo Sr., 72; Lucy Mugavero, 90; Mary Natoli, 85; Helen Dean, 91; LeRoy Sinn, 71; Earl Young, 76; Catherine Dext, 49; Frank Mazzacco, 66; Jesse Eichlin, 81; Ottomar Schramm, 78; Matthew Mattern, 22; Irene Krapf, 79; William Park, 72; Samuel Spangler, 80; Daniel George, 82; Edward O'Toole, 76; Eleanor Stoecker, 60; Joyce E. Mangini, 74; Giacomino J. Toto, 89; John J. Shanagher, 83; Dorthea K. Hoagland, 80; Melvin T. Simcoe, 66; Michael T. Strenko, 21; Florian J. Gall, 68; Pasquale M. Napolitano, 80; Christopher B. Hardgrove, 38; Krishnakant Upadhyay, 70; James R. Strickland, 83; Edward P. Zizik, 73

Method of murder: Medication poisoning

Location: New Jersey, Pennsylvania, USA

Status: Pled guilty to murdering twenty-two people in New Jersey. Sentenced to eleven consecutive life terms on March 1, 2006. Sentenced to seven life sentences in prison for seven murders in Pennsylvania.

Background

Cullen was the youngest of eight children and was born in West Orange, New Jersey. His father died when he was a baby. And when Cullen was nine, he attempted suicide by drinking the chemicals in a chemistry set. This would be the first of many attempts to end his life.

His mother was killed in a car accident in 1977. A year later, Cullen left school and joined the US Navy. He rose to the rank of petty officer third class and served aboard submarine USS Woodrow Wilson. When he started showing signs that he wasn't mentally stable, he was transferred to a supply ship. Over the next few years, he tried to kill himself seven times. He was medically discharged from the Navy in 1984.

Cullen began to study nursing and graduated in 1987. He took on a job in the burn unit at St. Barnabas Medical Center in Livingston and later stated he would fantasize about stealing drugs from the hospital to kill himself with.

Murders

On June 11, 1988, Cullen administered a lethal overdose of medication to a patient. He later admitted to killing several patients at St. Barnabas. He left in January of 1992 when the hospital started investigating the contamination of IV bags, which had led to the deaths of dozens of patients. The investigation later determined Cullen was most likely the culprit.

A month after leaving St. Barnabas, he became employed at Warren Hospital in Phillipsburg. Three elderly women were murdered there by overdoses of digoxin, a heart medication. The following year, his wife divorced him. He later said he wanted to quit nursing in 1993, but he shared custody of his daughters and the child support payments forced him to continue.

Cullen broke into a female coworker's home in March of 1993 but left without disturbing the woman and her son. He started stalking her, and she filed a report with the police about it. He pled guilty to trespassing and was sentenced to a year of probation. He attempted suicide again and took two months off work while he received treatment in psychiatric facilities. He attempted to kill himself two more times before the end of the year and left his job at Warren Hospital.

From there, Cullen began working in the intensive care/cardiac care unit at Hunterdon Medical Center in Flemington. He said he didn't kill anyone for the first two years, but this couldn't be verified as the hospital records had been destroyed. However, between January and September of 1996, he did kill five patients with digoxin overdoses. He left Hunterdon and started working at Morristown Memorial Hospital but was fired due to his poor performance.

Cullen was readmitted to a psychiatric facility but wasn't there for very long. In February of 1998, he was hired by the Liberty Nursing and Rehabilitation Center in Allentown, Pennsylvania. Cullen was accused of giving medications at unscheduled times, and was fired after he was seen going into a patient's room with syringes. During his time at Liberty, he killed one patient, but the death was blamed on another nurse.

Cullen then went to work at Easton Hospital in Pennsylvania. On December 30, 1998, he killed a patient with a digoxin overdose. An internal investigation took place, but nothing pointed directly to Cullen.

Because of the national shortage of nurses at the time, Cullen found no trouble gaining employment as a nurse despite his reputation and record. He started working in the burn unit of Lehigh Valley Hospital in March of 1999. He killed one patient and attempted to kill another before he resigned and moved on to St. Luke's Hospital. While working in the cardiac care unit at St. Luke's over the next three years, Cullen killed at least five patients and tried to kill two others.

On January 11, 2000, Cullen tried to commit suicide by lighting a charcoal grill in his bathtub. He had hoped he would die from carbon monoxide poisoning. However, his neighbors smelled the smoke and called the fire department and the police. He was taken to a psychiatric hospital but released the next day.

Nobody suspected Cullen was responsible for the patient deaths at St. Luke's until vials of medication were found in a disposal bin. An investigation revealed that Cullen had taken the medication. St. Luke's offered him a deal: If he resigned, they would give him a neutral recommendation. The alternative was to be fired. He took the deal and left in June of 2002.

Seven of Cullen's coworkers at St. Luke's alerted the Lehigh County District Attorney that they suspected Cullen had killed patients using drugs. Nine months later, the case was dropped. The investigators hadn't looked into his past and there seemed to be no evidence.

Cullen began employment at the Somerset Medical Center in September of 2002. While working in the critical care unit, he killed at least eight patients. He used digoxin, insulin, and epinephrine, and by mid-2003, had tried to kill at least one more. On June 18, 2003, he tried to kill patient Philip Gregor but failed.

Somerset began noticing clues that Cullen may be doing something very wrong. The computers showed he had been accessing the medical records of patients he wasn't caring for, and the drug dispensing cabinets, which were also computerized, showed strange medication requests. Somerset officials were warned by the executive director of the New Jersey Poison Information and Education System in July of 2003 that an employee was possibly killing patients. But the authorities weren't informed until October, and by then Cullen had killed another five patients.

Cullen's last victim was killed in October of 2003. The patient had died of low blood sugar, which was found to be due to an insulin overdose. The police were notified. Cullen was fired on October 31, 2003, supposedly for lying on his job application form. Meanwhile, another nurse, Amy Loughren, also contacted the police with her suspicions about the deaths and Cullen accessing the drugs. As a result, police decided to keep him under surveillance.

Trial

On December 12, 2003, Cullen was arrested while at a restaurant. He was charged with one count of murder and one of attempted murder. Two days later, he admitted to two other murders at Somerset. Then he confessed he had killed up to forty patients in his nursing career.

At his trial in New Jersey in April 2004, Cullen pled guilty to killing thirteen patients. He also pled guilty to attempting to kill two others. A plea agreement was offered, stating the death penalty wouldn't be sought as long as he cooperated with authorities. He agreed.

A month later, he pleaded guilty to the murders of three more patients. In November of 2004, he pleaded guilty to six more deaths and the attempted murders of three other patients.

Outcome

Cullen was sentenced to eighteen consecutive life sentences on March 2, 2006. He will not be eligible for parole until 2403, so there is no chance of him ever getting out of prison.

On March 10, in the courtroom for a sentencing hearing, Cullen became upset with Judge William H. Platt. He kept repeating, "Your honor, you need to step down," for thirty minutes. The judge had Cullen gagged with cloth and duct tape. He still kept trying to say the same phrase repeatedly. Cullen received another six life sentences.

Trivia

The video *Killer Nurse* from 2008 was based loosely on the story of Cullen.

The film *The Good Nurse* is being scripted, and it is adapted from the nonfiction book *The Good Nurse: A True Story of Medicine, Madness, and Murder*, which contains the story of Cullen.

ANDREW CUNANAN

Date of birth: August 31, 1969

Aliases/Nicknames: Nil

Characteristics: Killing spree

Number of victims: 5

Date of murders: April - July 1997

Date of arrest: Not applicable

Victim profile: Jeffrey Trail; David Madson; Lee Miglin, 72; William Reese, 45; Gianni Versace, 50

Method of murder: Shooting

Location: Minnesota, Illinois, New Jersey, Florida, USA

Status: Committed suicide by shooting himself on July 23, 1997.

Background

Born on August 31, 1969, in California, Cunanan's parents were Modesto Cunanan, a Filipino American and Mary Anne Schillaci, and Italian American. Cunanan was the youngest of four children, and while he was young, his father served in the Navy in the war in Vietnam.

Cunanan was intelligent; his IQ was measured at 142 while he was in school. As a teenager, he became a prolific liar and made up fantastical stories about his life. He was also good at changing his appearance on a whim. He was voted "Least Likely to be Forgotten" in high school.

In 1988, nineteen-year-old Cunanan, who was gay, began having liaisons with older, wealthy men. He frequented the local gay clubs, and when his deeply religious mother found out he was gay, a violent fight took place. Cunanan threw his mother against a wall during the argument, and she ended up with a dislocated shoulder.

Cunanan met Gianni Versace, the famous fashion designer, in 1990 while in San Francisco. Sometime later, Cunanan entered into a relationship with older wealthy man Norman Blachford. He was housed and financially supported by Blachford until they broke up in 1996. To finance his lifestyle, Cunanan went back to selling drugs, and he also was a regular user.

In April of 1997, Cunanan told friends he was going to Minneapolis to visit and ex-lover, David Madson, and their mutual acquaintance, Jeff Trail. Both of these men had previously distanced themselves from Cunanan. Madson was an architect; Trail, a former officer in the Navy, was a manager of a propane delivery company.

Cunanan arrived at Madson's apartment on April 25. Two days later, one of the three men would be dead.

Murders

On April 27, 1997, an argument broke out between Cunanan and Trail, with neighbors reporting loud voices. Trail was beaten up to thirty times with a claw hammer by Cunanan, with most of the strikes hitting him in the face and head. It's believed he then forced Madson at gunpoint to help him roll up the body of Trail in a large rug. For the next two days, they stayed in the apartment with the decomposing body and made no attempts to clean up the blood spatter. After the two days, they left.

Madson was the next to die. He was shot once in the back, once in the cheek, and the fatal shot entered through his eye and exited the back of his head. There was no sign of any struggle. His body was discovered by fishermen on the shore of Rush Lake, Minnesota, on May 3.

From there, Cunanan traveled to Chicago. On May 4, he tied up the hands and feet of Lee Miglin, a seventy-two-year-old real estate developer. At some point during the attack, he wrapped the man's head in masking tape and left small holes so he could still breathe. Cunanan then stabbed him more than twenty times with a screwdriver and pruning shears. Next, he used a hacksaw to cut his throat. The body was later found underneath a car in his garage.

Cunanan stole Miglin's car, and five days later, located his next victim in Pennsville, New Jersey. In the Finn's Point National Cemetery, he took forty-five-year-old William Reese, the caretaker, back to the man's office at gunpoint. He forced Reese down to his hands and knees and shot him in the back of the head, using the same gun that had killed Madson.

The next murder would be the one that garnered international media attention. On July 15, Gianni Versace was trying to open his front gates when he was approached by Cunanan. He shot Versace twice in the head and then ran, leaving the designer in a pool of blood on the sidewalk. Versace was rushed to the nearby Ryder Trauma Center and was pronounced dead.

When police responded to the shooting of Versace, they located the car Cunanan had stolen from Reese parked in a garage nearby. Inside the vehicle were newspaper reports of Cunanan's murders, his clothes, and a passport.

Trial

Cunanan was holed up in a houseboat at Miami Beach and knew the police were close to finding him. So, on July 23, Cunanan shot himself through the mouth, ending his life. When officers arrived at the scene, they found Cunanan lying faceup on the bed, wearing only boxer shorts. The .40 caliber handgun was lying on his stomach. It was the weapon he had used to commit the other murders.

Outcome

Cunanan was cremated, and his ashes were interred at the Holy Cross Catholic Cemetary in San Diego. The motive behind all of the murders remains unknown. Although the media suggested he had committed the murders because he found out he was HIV positive, the autopsy showed that he was actually HIV negative.

He left no suicide note, and there were very few belongings on the houseboat.

Trivia

Films

In the film *The Versace Murder*, released in 1998, actor Shane Perdue portrayed Cunanan.

In the 2013 made-for-television film, *House of Versace*, actor Luke Morrison portrayed Cunanan.

The Man Who Killed Versace would have featured Freddie Prinze Jr. in the lead role, with William Friedkin directing. But the film was never made.

In the 2009 film *Murder in Fashion a.k.a. Fashion Victim*, actor Jonathan Trent played the role of Cunanan.

Music

Rock band Modest Mouse created a song "Pistol (A. Cunanan, Miami, FL. 1996)" and released it on their album 'Strangers to Ourselves' in 2015.

In the song "Bad Boyz" released by rapper Shyne, Cunanan is mentioned in the lyrics.

Television

"The Assassination of Gianni Versace: American Crime Story" was created for television, and was first screened on January 17, 2018. Darren Criss played Cunanan and received a Golden Globe for "Best Actor - Miniseries, or Television Film" and an Emmy Award for "Outstanding Lead Actor in a Limited Series or Movie."

An episode of *Mugshots* on Court TV featured Cunanan, and was called "Andrew Cunanan - The Versace Killer."

The True Crime series, *Six Degrees of Murder*, featured Cunanan's murders in the episode "The Body in the Rug."

DEATH ANGELS

Date of birth: N/A

Aliases/Nicknames: Zebra Murders

Characteristics: Rape, dismemberment, disorganized mission-oriented

Number of victims: 15

Date of murders: 1973 - 1974

Date of arrest: 1974

Victim profile: Quita Hague, 28; Frances Rose, 28; Saleem Erakat, 53; Paul Dancik, 26; Marietta DiGirolamo, 31; Ilario Bertuccio, 81; John Doe; Tana Smith, 32; Vincent Wollin, 69; John Bambic, 84; Jane Holly, 45; Thomas Rainwater, 19

Method of murder: Shooting, dismemberment

Location: California, USA

Status: Life imprisonment.

Background

The Death Angels were a group of Black Muslim males who committed a slew of murders in San Francisco, California. Between the group members, they murdered at least fifteen people and tried to kill a further eight. All of the victims were white. Some investigators believe they may actually be responsible for up to seventy-three murders.

The case was called the Zebra Murders, named after the special police radio band that was assigned to the investigation. Four men were arrested in 1974 and went on trial for the murders.

Murders

Richard Hague and his wife Quita were taking a walk near their home on Telegraph Hill on October 19, 1973. The couple was abducted by a group of black men and forced into a van, where Quita was fondled by two of the captors. She was then attacked with a machete and almost beheaded. Richard was also hacked with the machete and left on the roadside. Miraculously, he survived; Quita did not.

On October 29, Frances Rose was driving up to the gate of the University of California Extension when a man blocked her path. He demanded she give him a ride and then opened fire, shooting her repeatedly.

Robert Stoeckmann was assaulted on November 9, but was able to get the gun away from his attacker. An arrest was later made, and Leroy Doctor was convicted of assault with a deadly weapon.

Grocery store owner Saleem Erakat was attacked and tied up, then shot dead in the restroom of his store on November 25. On December 11, Paul Dancik was shot in the chest three times while getting ready to use a payphone.

Two days later, the mayor of San Francisco, Art Agnos, was at a meeting in Potrero Hill, a relatively black neighborhood. Afterward, while talking to two women on the sidewalk, he was shot twice in the back. Although he was seriously injured, he managed to survive.

The same night, December 13, Marietta DiGirolamo was shoved into a doorway by a man while she was walking along Divisadero Street. He shot her twice in the chest, the force of the gunshots spinning her around; she was then shot in the back. She died at the scene.

A female college student was shot near her apartment on December 20. Two men were involved in the shooting. Though she lived, her spine was damaged. Later that night, Ilario Bertuccio, a janitor, was shot while walking home from work. Four bullets struck his chest and shoulder, and he died almost instantly.

Two more victims were shot and killed within a few minutes of each other on December 22. Neal Moynihan was walking near the Civic Center when a man walked ahead of him, turned, and shot him in the heart, neck, and face. Six minutes later, Mildred Hosler was walking to her bus stop and was shot four times—likely by the same man. On December 24, an unidentified man was shot and killed.

After a brief break, the Death Angels started killing again on January 29, 1974. While walking to a fabric store, Tana Smith was shot. Vincent Wollin was shot while walking home, and John Bambic was shot while collecting bottles and cans. The next victim, housewife Jane Holly, was killed in a laundromat, and Roxanne McMillian was shot while carrying items to her apartment from her car. The only victim that survived that night was McMillian, but she would spend the rest of her life in a wheelchair.

On April 1, 1974, Thomas Rainwater and Linda Story, Salvation Army Cadets, were shot while walking to the Mayfair Market. Rainwater died, but Story survived. Police were on the scene within seconds but were unable to apprehend the shooter. They quickly linked the attacks to other Zebra Murders by the weapon used.

Thirteen days later, two more victims were shot. Ward Anderson and Terry White were waiting at a bus stop when a black man approached and shot them. Luckily, they both survived.

On the night of April 16, Nelson T. Shields IV was in the process of picking up a rug in the Ingleside district. He opened the back of his vehicle to make room for the rug and was shot multiple times. A witness saw a black man run away from the crime scene. Again, the shell casings found at the scene matched the weapon used in other Zebra Murders.

Trial

A reward of thirty thousand dollars was offered for information leading to the capture of those behind the Zebra Murders. An employee of the Black Self-Help Moving and Storage Company, Anthony Harris, called police after sketches were broadcast of the suspects. He told police he was one of the men in the sketches and agreed to meet them at a parking lot. Harris was able to give police a lot of details about the murders because he said he had been present at a lot of them. He denied he had killed any of the victims.

Harris told police about the existence of the Death Angels. He also spoke of a murder that didn't make the papers, that of a homeless man who had been hacked up and dumped into the bay. Police believed him because they had found the butchered torso of a man on December 24, washed up in the Ocean Beach district.

The names, dates, locations, and other details of the suspects were given by Harris and warrants were issued. Harris was given immunity for his help in breaking the case, and new identities were given to him, his girlfriend, and her child.

Predawn simultaneous raids took place on May 1, 1974, resulting in the arrests of Larry Craig Green and JCX Simon. Other suspects were arrested at the Black Self-Help Moving and Storage facility. Seven men were arrested in total, but four were released due to lack of evidence.

All of their attorneys were paid for by the Nation of Islam, with the exception of Jessie Lee Cooks, who had pleaded guilty.

On March 3, 1975, the trial began. With the testimony of Harris and the weapon evidence, the prosecutors were able to show that the men on the stand were guilty.

Outcome

With the testimony of one hundred eight witnesses and eight thousand pages of transcripts, it became the longest criminal trial in California history. Four men—Larry Green, JCX Simon, Manuel Moore, and Jessie Lee Cooks—were found guilty. Each of the men received a life sentence.

Trivia

JCX Simon was found unconscious in his cell on March 12, 2015. He died, and the cause of death was not released.

The group's ideology and their MO were very similar to that of John Allen Muhammad, a spree killer.

BANDALI DEBS

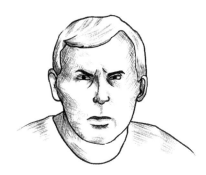

Date of birth: July 18, 1953

Aliases/Nicknames: Nil

Characteristics: Robbery

Number of victims: 3

Date of murders: June 17, 1997, August 16, 1998

Date of arrest: September 24, 2001

Victim profile: Kristy Mary Harty, 18; Sergeant Gary Silk, 21; Senior Constable Rodney Miller, 28

Method of murder: Shooting

Location: Victoria, Australia

Status: Sentenced to two consecutive terms of life imprisonment with no minimum term in February 2003. Sentenced to a third consecutive term of life imprisonment in May 2007.

Background

Little has been reported on the background life of Debs other than he was from Narre Warren, in southeast Melbourne, Australia. He worked as a tiler and was the father of five children.

Murders

On April 22, 1995, Donna Ann Hicks' naked body was found on a roadside in Minchinbury, west Sydney. She had been killed by a gunshot to the head. She had been working on the Great Western Highway as a prostitute before she died.

Kristy Mary Harty was working as a prostitute on June 17, 1997, along the Princes Highway. She met Debs, and they drove to a secluded bush track in Upper Beaconsfield. After they had unprotected sex, Debs fatally shot her in the back of the head.

On the night of August 16, 1998, Victoria Police Officers Sergeant Gary Silk and Senior Constable Rodney Miller were staking out the Silky Emperor Restaurant in Moorabbin. At around midnight, both men were shot at close range. Both were killed, and the murders became known as the Silk-Miller murders or the Moorabbin Police Murders.

Broken vehicle glass was found at the scene, and when it was tested, it matched a late model Hyundai hatchback. After much investigation, the results were narrowed down to a specific make and model. The vehicle was registered to the daughter of Debs.

Trial

Debs was arrested along with an accomplice named Jason Roberts. Both were charged with the murders of Silk and Miller, along with thirteen charges of armed robbery from previous crimes. In February of 2003, Debs was sentenced to two terms of life imprisonment for the murders of the police officers. Roberts received two terms of life with a minimum term of thirty-five years.

Outcome

Debs was convicted in May of 2007 for the murder of Kristy Mary Harty and received another life sentence. In court, Justice Kaye stated:

"Your murder of Ms. Harty was entirely senseless, needless, and wanton. The evidence discloses beyond any doubt that this was not a case of a sexual encounter in which, in the heat of the moment, feelings or passions may have led to a spontaneous and irrational act of violence. Rather, and quite to the contrary, this was, most clearly, a callous, craven and senseless murder in cold blood of an entirely innocent, defenseless and vulnerable young woman. The evidence leads to the inevitable conclusion that you murdered Kristy Harty for no other reason than for the sheer sake of it."

Trivia

Since 1999, the Australian Rules football clubs St. Kilda and Hawthorn have played for the Blue Ribbon Cup, which is dedicated to officers who have died on duty. The Silk-Miller medal is presented to the best player on the day.

Prison life

Debs has studied psychology, computer training, and life skills while in prison, and works as a carpet cleaner inside the prison.

Media

In the television movie *Underbelly Files: Tell Them Lucifer Was Here*, the role of Debs is played by actor Greg Stone.

THOMAS DILLON

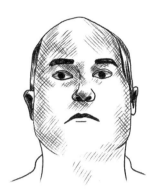

Date of birth: July 9, 1950

Aliases/Nicknames: Nil

Characteristics: Sniper, shot outdoorsmen in random, motiveless attacks

Number of victims: 5 - 11

Date of murders: 1989 - 1992

Date of arrest: November 27, 1992

Victim profile: Donald Welling, 35; Jamie Paxton, 21; Kevin Loring, 30; Claude Hawkins, 49; Gary Bradley, 44

Method of murder: Shooting

Location: Ohio, Indiana, Michigan, USA

Status: Pled guilty to five counts of murder in Ohio and was sentenced to life in prison with no chance of parole for 165 years on July 12, 1993.

Background

Dillon was a draftsman for a municipal water department, the Canton Ohio Waterworks. He was married with a son. Those who knew him considered him to be mild-mannered, but he liked to pretend he was something he was not. Dillon drove the back roads of southeastern Ohio pretending he had cured AIDS, was a winning Super Bowl quarterback, or a scientist who had cured AIDS.

Dillon often drove for hundreds of miles and sometimes imagined himself as a Special Forces soldier, hunting for enemies. Between the late 1980s and early 1990s, Dillon's soldier fantasy crossed over into reality.

Murders

On April 1, 1989, Dillon committed his first murder near a quiet community, New Philadelphia. While out jogging, Donald Welling, thirty-five, was shot and killed. Dillon later claimed he committed this murder because a voice in his head told him to.

Jamie Paxton, twenty-one, was out hunting near St. Clairsville, Ohio when he was shot and killed. Then on November 28, 1990, Kevin Loring, thirty, was murdered while he was out hunting in

Muskingum County. On March 14, 1992, Claude Hawkins, forty-nine, was fishing in Coshocton County when he was murdered.

Gary Bradley, forty-four, met the same fate while fishing in April of 1992. This murder occurred near Noble County. All of the victims, except for Loring, were killed on weekends. Two were killed on a Saturday and two on a Sunday. Investigators believed they had all been shot from a nearby road, and a high-powered rifle was used to fire the fatal shots.

During 1992, a friend of Dillon's reported him to police after hearing the press release the task force put out regarding the murders. Next, an attempted murder occurred. Larry Oller was fired at while hunting in Tuscarawas County, but the shooter missed him.

On November 27, 1992, Dillon was arrested for owning a suppressor and was placed under probation. At this time, police announced that he was their main suspect in the murders and asked for anyone to come forward who had engaged in firearms transactions with Dillon.

A gun dealer brought a gun to the police on December 4, saying Dillon had sold it to him on April 6. It was a Swedish Mauser rifle, and ballistic testing suggested it was the same rifle used to kill Bradley and Hawkins. Now that they had enough evidence, Dillon was indicted on two charges of murder for Bradley and Hawkins.

Trial

Dillon admitted committing the murders, but only after the prosecution removed the death penalty from the case. Dillon went to court on July 12, 1993 and pled guilty to five murders. He received five consecutive sentences of thirty years to life.

Outcome

Dillon's wife tried to sell the story to Hollywood, which led to the passing of the Paxton Bill. This prevented murderers or their relatives from profiting from their crimes.

On October 21, 2011, Dillon died following an illness that had lasted three weeks. He was sixty-one years old.

Trivia

"I have major problems," he said at the time. "I'm crazy. I want to kill. I want to kill."

In an episode of *The FBI Files* called "Human Prey," it is shown how a letter sent to a local newspaper provided a vital clue to Dillon's capture.

In *Crime Stores*, the episode "The Silent Sniper" is about the murders committed by Dillon.

WESTLEY ALLAN DODD

Date of birth: July 3, 1961

Aliases/Nicknames: Nil

Characteristics: Kidnapping, rape, child molestation

Number of victims: 3

Date of murders: September 4, October 29, 1989

Date of arrest: November 13, 1989

Victim profile: William Neer, 10; Cole Neer, 11; Lee Iseli, 4

Method of murder: Stabbing with knife

Location: Clark County, Washington, USA

Status: Executed by hanging in Washington on January 5, 1993.

Background

Dodd was one of three children born to parents Jim and Carol. He later claimed that though there was no abuse or neglect, he never heard his parents tell him they loved him. When he was thirteen, he started indecently exposing himself to children, and by the time he reached high school, he had graduated to molestation. He started with younger cousins then kids he was babysitting.

On his fifteenth birthday, Dodd's father tried to commit suicide after an argument with his wife. Not long afterward, Dodd was arrested for indecent exposure, but he was released with the recommendation he get some counseling.

Dodd attempted to kidnap two little girls in August of 1981; though the girls reported him, the police did nothing about it. The next month, Dodd enlisted with the Navy and was sent to the submarine base in Bangor, Washington.

Dodd started molesting the children who lived on the base and, at one point, offered fifty dollars to some boys to play strip poker in a motel room. He was arrested for this and, even though he told police he had planned to molest the boys, the police released him without charge. Soon after, he was caught after exposing himself to a boy and the Navy discharged him. As a result of the indecent exposure, he spent nineteen days in jail and had to have court-ordered counseling.

Dodd was arrested again in May of 1984, for molesting a boy, but received only a suspended sentence. He carried on abusing children, including those of his neighbor, who resisted telling the police because she thought it would be too traumatic for her children.

In 1987, Dodd tried to lure a boy into a vacant building. Instead, the boy went to the police. Once again, Dodd got off lightly, spending only 118 days in jail. He then moved to Canada, and over the next few years he was arrested many times for child molestation. Each time, he received only a short sentence. By now, he had amassed over fifty victims; all of them were male and under the age of twelve.

Over the years, Dodd's fantasies started to include a lot of violence, and he wrote about wanting to "cannibalize the genitals of his victims and perform experimental surgeries to turn them into obedient zombies."

Murders

On September 4, 1989, two brothers, Cole and William Neer, were lured to a secluded area by Dodd, where they were forced to take their clothes off then tied to a tree. Dodd performed sexual acts on both boys, then stabbed them repeatedly and fled. When the boys were discovered, Cole was already dead; William died on the way to the hospital. Cole was eleven, and William was ten.

Dodd moved on to Portland, Oregon, and continued to try to lure children. He met Lee Iseli, four, and his brother Justin, nine, at a park on October 29. After Justin left, Dodd told Lee he would drive him home. Instead, he took Lee to his apartment and made him take off his clothes. Dodd tied the small boy to the bed and molested him while taking photographs. He continued to molest the poor child all night, keeping notes in his diary of what he was doing. The next morning, Lee was strangled to death. Dodd hung his body in the closet and took another photograph.

The boy's body was then placed into trash bags and thrown into bushes near Vancouver Lake. The clothes belonging to Lee were burned, except for the underwear, which Dodd kept as a souvenir. The body was found a few days later, and a manhunt was underway to catch the killer. During this time, Dodd kept a very low profile.

On November 13, Dodd kidnapped a six-year-old boy from the bathroom at the New Liberty Theater in Camas, Washington. The boy started fighting and crying, and employees of the theater became suspicious. Outside, Dodd released the boy and drove away, but his car broke down just a short distance up the road. The boyfriend of the boy's mother, aware that this was the man who had just tried to abduct the boy, offered to help Dodd to stall him. He then put him into a headlock and dragged him back to the theater where they awaited police.

The task force investigating the murder of Lee was notified and, over the next three days, Dodd was interrogated. He eventually admitted to committing the three murders. When police searched his room, they found a homemade torture rack, newspaper articles about his murders, Lee's underwear, and photographs of Lee and other children in underwear advertisements. Also found was his diary, with all the details of his crimes.

Trial

Dodd was charged with three counts of first-degree murder and kidnapping of another victim. He initially pleaded not guilty, but later changed his plea to guilty.

Excerpts of Dodd's diary were read aloud during his trial, and the court was shown the photographs of Lee. Though no witnesses or evidence were brought forward by the defense team, they suggested that Dodd was insane. Dodd later said that if he had spoken to defend himself, it would have been pointless. He said the system had failed repeatedly, and if it would bring peace to the victims' families, he was willing to die, preferably by hanging.

In 1990, Dodd was sentenced to death.

Outcome

Dodd refused to appeal his sentence and therefore spent less than four years in prison before his execution. He stated in one court brief, "I must be executed before I have an opportunity to escape or kill someone else. If I do escape, I promise you I will kill and rape again, and I will enjoy every minute of it."

While on trial, he wrote a booklet on how to protect children from people like himself.

Dodd was given the choice of hanging or lethal injection, and he chose to hang. His reason was, "because that's the way Lee Iseli died."

His last words were recorded as follows:

"I have confessed all my sins," he told a reporter in his interview. "I believe what the Bible teaches: I'll go to Heaven. I have doubts, but I'd really like to believe that I would be able to go up to the three little boys and give them a hug and tell them how sorry I was and be able to love them with a real true love and have no desire to hurt them in any way."

On January 5, 1993, Dodd was executed at 12:05 a.m. at Washington State Penitentiary. He was cremated after an autopsy and his family received his ashes.

Trivia

In the novel *The Information* written by Martin Amis, there are similarities between a character and the story of Dodd. In the book, a reference to a newspaper article describes "the trial, and conviction, of a child murderer in Washington State." The description of the killer in the book matches the description of Dodd. The description of the murders in the book is also the same as Dodd's.

In the Netflix series *Real Detective*, the episode "Malice" is about Dodd and how his arrest and conviction affected the detective involved in the case.

In the 2002 film *Insomnia*, there is a reference to a character "Wayne Dobbs," who is a child killer. The circumstance of the murder in the film is similar to the killing of Lee Iseli.

RONALD DOMINIQUE

Date of birth: January 9, 1964

Aliases/Nicknames: The Bayou Serial Killer

Characteristics: Rape

Number of victims: 23 +

Date of murders: 1997 - 2006

Date of arrest: December 1, 2006

Victim profile: Kenneth Randolph, 20; Michael Barnett, 21; Leon Lirette, 22; August Watkins, 31; Kurt Cunningham ,23; Alonzo Hogan, 28; Chris Deville , 40; Wayne Smith, 17; Nicholas Pellegrin, 21; David Mitchell, 19; Gary Pierre, 20; Larry Ranson, 38; Oliver LeBanks, 27; Joseph Brown, 16; Bruce Williams, 18; Manuel Reed, 21; Angel Mejia, 34; Mitchell Johnson, 34; Michael Vincent, 23; Anoka Jones, 26; Datrell Woods, 19; Larry Matthews, 46; Christopher Sutterfield, 27

Method of murder: Strangulation, suffocation

Location: Louisiana, USA

Status: Pled guilty to eight murders. Sentenced to eight life sentences in prison on September 23, 2008.

Background

Dominique lived in Thibodaux, a small bayou community between Baton Rouge and New Orleans, for much of his childhood and youth. At high school, he was a member of the glee club, and former classmates later said he was ridiculed for being gay even though he wouldn't admit to it.

There seemed to be two different Dominiques as he grew older. One was very helpful to his neighbors in the trailer parks he lived in. The other liked to cross-dress and go to the local gay club, where he performed terrible impersonations of Patti LaBelle. It seemed that he didn't fit anywhere, and many said he wasn't that well-liked.

Dominique was arrested and charged with a number of crimes from assault, to drunk driving, to rape. On February 10, 2002, he was arrested for slapping a woman during a Mardi Gras parade. Instead of going on trial, he was required to attend an offender's program.

He was summoned to court on May 19, 2000, for disturbing the peace, and was released after he pled guilty and paid a fine.

On August 25, 1996, Dominique was arrested on charges of forcible rape. His bond was set at one hundred thousand dollars. A young man, partially nude, had escaped from Dominique's home screaming, saying that Dominique had tried to kill him. But when it was time to go to court, the victim could not be found; without his testimony, the case was discontinued indefinitely.

Dominique was charged with driving while intoxicated and speeding on May 15, 1994. Then on June 12, 1995, he was charged with telephone harassment and paid a fine.

The forcible rape charge spooked Dominique, and he was tired of going back and forth to jail, so he had to come up with a way to carry on indulging in his perverted pleasures without getting caught.

Murders

Dominique developed what he thought was a foolproof plan to not get caught. He had quite a smooth manner about him and would persuade men to come back to his trailer and have sex for money. But, once they were there, they had to agree to let Dominique tie them up. Some of the victims he targeted were heterosexual, so he would promise them sex with his "wife," who of course didn't exist. He told them she was shy and liked her men to be tied up. Once they were bound, they couldn't escape.

He would then rape the men and kill them, either by strangulation or smothering. Their bodies were dumped in six different areas in Southern Louisiana.

The case finally broke when a man told his parole officer that a man had offered him money to have sex with his wife, but the condition was that he had to be tied up. The man went to Dominique's trailer, got scared, and was able to escape.

Due to the number of male bodies that had been found recently, investigators took the man's story seriously. They were able to locate Dominique's trailer and, when they approached him, he voluntarily gave them a sample of is DNA. This linked him—without a doubt—to two of the murders, and he was charged.

Trial

Eventually, Dominique was charged and convicted of eight murders. He pled guilty and bowed his head as the names of his victims were read by the judge.

"The lives of eight young men were taken from these families by the actions of the defendant," Assistant District Attorney Mark Rhodes said before sentencing.

"He knew nothing about them or their families, and he callously killed the victims and left a lifetime of pain as their legacy."

Outcome

Dominique was sentenced to eight consecutive life sentences. He is serving his sentence at the Louisiana State Penitentiary.

Trivia

Dominique may have been responsible for up to twenty-three murders.

When Dominique was arrested, he claimed he had a heart condition, and he walked with the assistance of a cane. However, many believe this was a ruse by Dominique to show he was too weak to have committed the murders.

THE DOODLER

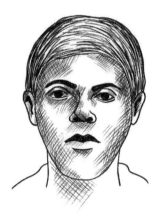

Date of birth: Unknown

Aliases/Nicknames: The Black Doodler

Characteristics: Gay victims, sketched victims before murder

Number of victims: 5 - 14

Date of murders: January 1974 - September 1975

Date of arrest: Not apprehended

Victim profile: Gerald Cavanaugh, 49; Joseph "Jae" Stevens, 27; Klaus Christmann; Frederick Capin, 32; Harald Gullberg, 66; others not named

Method of murder: Stabbing

Location: California, USA

Status: Unknown.

Background

The Doodler was a serial killer who has remained unidentified. Between January of 1974 and September of 1975, it is believed The Doodler killed fourteen men and committed a further three assaults. The victims were from the gay community of San Francisco. He was given the nickname "the Doodler" because he had a habit of sketching his victims before he killed them.

Murders

The Doodler's main method of murder was to stab the victim in the front and the back of their body. Police believed the victims had been killed in or near the locations their bodies were found.

Gerald Cavanaugh

Gerald Earl Cavanaugh is believed to be the Doodler's first victim. He had been stabbed to death. Cavanaugh's body was found on January 24, 1974, on Ocean Beach in San Francisco, in the early hours of the morning. It was determined that he had been conscious at the time of his death, and self-defense wounds showed he had tried to fight off his killer. He initially was unidentified, being temporarily referred to as "John Doe #7" by the medical examiner.

Joseph "Jae" Stevens

Joseph Stevens was discovered by a woman walking along Spreckels Lake, San Francisco, on June 25, 1974. Investigators believed Stevens had traveled to the lake with his killer, possibly willingly.

Klaus Christmann

Klaus Christmann was discovered by a woman walking her dog on July 7, 1974. His death had been more violent than the previous killings, with his body suffering more stab wounds than the other victims. The killer had also slashed his throat multiple times.

Frederick Capin

The body of Frederick Elmer Capin was discovered on May 12, 1975, in San Francisco. He had been stabbed and died from stab wounds to his aorta. Investigators found evidence (marks in the sand) that his body had been moved or dragged a distance of about twenty feet.

Harald Gullberg

Harald Gullberg's body was discovered in a decomposed state on June 4, 1975, about two weeks after he had been killed, in Lincoln Park. It is believed Gullberg was the last victim of the killer. During the time he was unidentified, he was known as "John Doe #81."

Trial

A suspect was questioned by police, but they couldn't proceed with charges because the surviving victims didn't want everyone to know they were gay, which would have come out in a trial. One of the survivors was a diplomat, and another was a well-known entertainer. Police strongly believed that their suspect was The Doodler, but there wasn't enough evidence. He has never been named publicly.

Outcome

As of May 2018, the case of The Doodler is still open and ongoing. With advances in DNA technology, progress could be made by re-examining the evidence. Police offered a one hundred-thousand-dollar reward in February of 2019 for information that would lead to the arrest of the killer.

Trivia

At the time of the murders, activist Harvey Milk expressed his empathy for the victims who wouldn't speak with police, stating: "I understand their position. I respect the pressure society has put on them."

It was believed that only about 25 percent of gay men in the San Francisco area were actually open about their sexuality, and they were least likely to come forward for fear of damaging their relationships with their family and friends, and their work lives.

Media

A TV drama series is set to be made about the Doodler, which was announced on February 19, 2019. Ryan J. Brown is the writer of the series and UK film company Ugly Duckling Films is producing it.

JOHN DUFFY AND DAVID MULCAHY

John Duffy

Date of birth: 1956

Aliases/Nicknames: The Railway Killer, the Railway Rapist

Characteristics: Serial rape

Number of victims: 3

Date of murders: 1985 - 1986

Date of arrest: November 23, 1986

Victim profile: Alison Day, 19; Maartje Tamboezer, 15; Anne Lock, 29

Method of murder: Strangulation

Location: North London, England, United Kingdom

Status: Convicted of two murders and four rapes. Sentenced to life in prison (minimum thirty years) in February 1988.

David Mulcahy

Date of birth: 1959

Aliases/Nicknames: The Railway Killer, the Railway Rapist

Characteristics: Serial rape

Number of victims: 3

Date of murders: 1985 - 1986

Date of arrest: February 3, 1999

Victim profile: Alison Day, 19; Maartje Tamboezer, 15; Anne Lock, 29

Method of murder: Strangulation

Location: North London, England, United Kingdom

Status: Sentenced to three life sentences, with a thirty-year recommendation, on February 1, 2001.

Background

Duffy and Mulcahy first met at secondary school in North London and became fairly inseparable. Mulcahy was a lot taller than Duffy and mentally stronger, while Duffy never got any taller than five foot, four inches. Mulcahy nicknamed him "the midget."

In 1976, they went on a shooting spree with an air rifle and shot four people. They were convicted of causing actual bodily harm. It wasn't long after this that Mulcahy suggested they should commit a rape together. Both had strong feelings of sexual inadequacy. Duffy had a low sperm count and was unable to have children, and Mulcahy had issues with maintaining an erection.

In October of 1982, they located their first victim, a twenty-year-old walking home from a party. They stifled her screams with sticking plaster and dragged her into a nearby garden. She was stripped of her clothing, blindfolded, and then raped by both men. She reported they had threatened her with a knife.

The two men attempted to rape another woman in March of 1983. A restaurant manager was walking by the railway station when the men grabbed her. She put up an admirable fight, biting Mulcahy's hand, and they eventually let her go without raping her.

A social worker from America was attacked on January 20, 1984, on Barnes Common. Duffy and Mulcahy had been decorating Duffy's parents' house when they came across the victim. She was stripped and raped.

The next victim was grabbed from the West Hampstead railway station on June 3, 1984. They dragged her across the train tracks and raped her.

On July 8, they seized a young woman but were interrupted when a neighbor heard the commotion and called the police. The victim had been gagged and had tape on her wrists, and this would later provide evidence against Mulcahy.

Two Danish au pairs were attacked on July 15 as they walked on Hampstead Heath. Both were raped.

Three months later, Duffy and Mulcahy were found in possession of stolen building materials and arrested. They managed to get away with just receiving fines.

A German au pair was attacked by the men on January 26, 1985. She was gagged and blindfolded with her own scarf under a canal bridge at Brent Cross. She was stripped naked and raped. January 30, four days later, the men came across a teenage girl on Hampstead Heath. Duffy later said that Mulcahy was becoming very violent, so he broke off the attack in case Mulcahy killed the young girl.

Another failed attempt occurred on February 2, when a French au pair screamed and struggled when they tried to attack her. Then, on March 1, they raped a twenty-five-year-old woman on Hampstead Heath. But the sexual excitement was no longer enough to satisfy Mulcahy.

Murders

On December 29, 1985, Duffy and Mulcahy targeted Alison Day, nineteen. Day was on her way to meet up with her fiancé at his work when they grabbed her at the Hackney Wick railway station and dragged her to playing fields nearby. Both men raped her and, as she tried to escape, she either fell— or was pushed—by Mulcahy into the freezing canal. Duffy said he pulled her out, and Mulcahy proceeded to rape her again. Then he ripped a piece of fabric from her blouse and throttled her. They weighted her coat pockets down with stones and threw her back into the canal. Seventeen days later she was found.

Maartje Tamboezer, fifteen, fell into the hands of Duffy and Mulcahy on April 17, 1986. They had strung a length of fishing line across a path, and she was knocked off her bicycle as she rode along it. They walked her across fields, and Duffy raped her. All of a sudden, Mulcahy lost his temper and became really aggressive. He punched the girl, and she crumpled to the ground. While she was unconscious, Mulcahy took her belt and wrapped it around her throat, telling Duffy that because he had killed the last one, it was now Duffy's turn. Duffy twisted the belt until she was dead. They both left the scene, but Mulcahy went back. He set her body on fire and stuffed burning material into her vagina in an attempt to destroy any forensic evidence.

Anne Lock, twenty-nine and recently married, was grabbed by Duffy and Mulcahy as she got off a train at Brookmans Park on May 18, 1986. Duffy raped her, then Mulcahy gave him the car keys and told him to collect the car. When Mulcahy joined him in the car, he said he had taken care of it, and she wouldn't be able to identify them. Her body was found two months later, a mile from her home; her own sock had been used to suffocate her.

Another rapist appeared on the scene on August 6, 1996. Ted Biggs, a bedding shop salesman, was committing rapes at night. Operation Loudwater was launched by police to track down Biggs. Coincidentally, one of the Operation Loudwater officers met up with DC John Haye in a pub, who had been the exhibits officer in the Duffy inquiry. They quickly realized that the cases were very similar.

Duffy had started to commit rapes by himself and was arrested while following a woman in a park. Police questioned him about the other rapes and murders, and he was subsequently charged. Police were aware that he hadn't acted alone, but Duffy wouldn't give up Mulcahy.

Trial

Duffy's trial began in February of 1988; he was found guilty of two murders and four rapes. He received a minimum sentence of thirty years, and later the Home Secretary extended it to a whole life sentence. But the European Court of Human Rights removed the ability of politicians to reset sentences, so it was reverted back to thirty years.

In 1997, Duffy finally implicated Mulcahy. This led to police tracking Mulcahy for several months. When DNA testing was done, the results implicated Mulcahy in the rapes and murders. Mulcahy went on trial in 2000 and Duffy was a witness against him. It was the first time a prisoner of Duffy's category had given evidence against an accomplice.

The trial lasted for fourteen days, and the evidence put forward by the prosecution showed Mulcahy was the chief perpetrator.

Outcome

Mulcahy was found guilty of three murders and seven rapes. He was given three life sentences, with the recommendation of thirty years.

Duffy was further convicted of seventeen more rapes. He was sentenced to twelve more years. It is expected that neither Duffy nor Mulcahy will ever be released from prison. They are still the prime suspects in many sex attacks that date back to the 1970s, and authorities also believe Mulcahy committed sexual attacks after Duffy was imprisoned.

Trivia

There were claims in a newspaper that Duffy received a payment of twenty thousand pounds for providing information on his accomplice.

There has been talk that Mulcahy is a loan shark in prison and is feared.

The case of Duffy and Mulcahy is the focus of *Witness of Truth: The Railway Murders*, a documentary that premiered on television in 2001.

Mulcahy was assaulted in jail in 2008, which resulted in him needing ten stitches. Convict Dean Winfield froze a can of carrots, put the can in a sock, and struck Mulcahy in the head.

PETER DUPAS

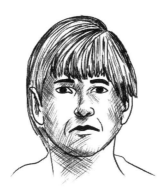

Date of birth: July 6, 1953

Aliases/Nicknames: Nil

Characteristics: Rape, Mutilation

Number of victims: 3 - 6

Date of murders: 1997 - 1999

Date of arrest: April 22, 1999

Victim profile: Margaret Josephine Maher, 40; Mersina Halvagis, 25; Nicole Amanda Patterson, 28

Method of murder: Stabbing with knife

Location: Melbourne, Victoria, Australia

Status: Sentenced to life imprisonment with no possibility of parole on August 22, 2000. Sentenced to a second term of life imprisonment on August 16, 2004. Sentenced to his third life sentence with no minimum term on August 17, 2007.

Background

When Dupas was fifteen, he visited his neighbor on October 3, 1968, and asked to borrow a knife so he could peel some vegetables. He proceeded to stab the woman in the neck, face, and hand. He was apprehended and told police he didn't know why he had attacked her. He spent two weeks in a psychiatric hospital and was given eighteen months' probation.

In October 1969, Dupas allegedly broke into a mortuary at the Austin Hospital. Two elderly female bodies had been horribly mutilated using the pathologist's knife. There was a strange-looking wound on the thigh of one of the bodies which matched a wound Dupas later inflicted on another victim.

Dupas attacked a woman in her home and was sentenced to nine years in prison (with a minimum of five years) on July 25, 1974. He had broken into her home, threatened her at knifepoint, tied her up, and raped her. He also had threatened to hurt her baby if she didn't obey him during the attack.

Dupas was released from prison in 1979. Two months later, he attacked another four women over a period of ten days. He was sentenced to five years in prison on February 28, 1980. He served the five years and was released in February of 1985. Just a month later, he raped a young woman on a beach. He received another twelve years in prison but was out again after seven years.

Two years later, Dupas was arrested again. In January of 1994, he had followed a woman at Lake Eppalock and held her at knifepoint in a toilet block. Luckily, her friends noticed and chased him off. As he drove away, he crashed his car and police arrested him. He pled guilty on August 18, 1994, and received a sentence of three years and nine months. He was released in September of 1996 and moved to Pascoe Vale, a suburb of Melbourne.

Murders

Nicole Amanda Patterson, twenty-eight, was a psychotherapist and youth counselor and used her home in Northcote as her office. On the day of her murder, neighbors reported hearing screaming, and that afternoon, her boyfriend was unable to get in contact with her. Her body was found on April 19, 1999, by a friend. She had been horribly mutilated. She was naked from the waist down, and small pieces of tape were attached to her body. Most disturbing of all, her breasts had been cut off and taken away by Dupas. She had suffered a total of twenty-seven stab wounds to her chest and her back.

On October 4, 1997, Margaret Josephine Maher, forty, was working as a prostitute; she was last seen alive at the Safeway supermarket in Broadmeadows at 12:20 a.m. That afternoon, a man collecting cans found her body under a cardboard box. She had been stabbed in the wrist and had bruising to her neck. There was blunt force trauma to her face, and she had lacerations on her arm. One of her breasts had been cut off and placed in her mouth.

The next murder victim, twenty-five-year-old Mersina Halvagis, was killed on November 1, 1997, while at Fawkner Cemetery. She had been visiting the grave of her grandmother. She was meant to meet her fiancé later that day, and when she didn't show up, the alarm was sounded. In the early hours of November 5, her body was found in an empty plot three graves away from her grandmother's. She suffered eighty-seven stab wounds in the neck, breasts, and knees.

While police were investigating the murder of Patterson, they noted a new client called "Malcolm" was listed in her diary, along with a telephone number. The number was traced to a student at La Trobe University, who explained Dupas had offered him work in exchange for the use of the phone.

Dupas was arrested on April 22, 1999, and charged with the murder of Patterson.

Trial

Dupas had made several calls to Patterson over a period of six weeks before he attacked her. When police searched his home, they found newspaper articles about Patterson's murder, clothing stained with blood, a ski mask, PVC tape, and an advertisement for Patterson's psychotherapy services.

On trial, it took the jury less than three hours to convict Dupas. He was sentenced on August 22, 2000, to life imprisonment without parole.

Dupas appealed his conviction in August of 2001, but the appeal was dismissed.

He went on trial for the murder of Maher in 2004. During the trial, the similarities between the murders of Patterson and Maher, especially the breast removal, showed the same man had committed both crimes. The jury wasn't told of Dupas receiving a life sentence for Patterson's murder. It took them less than a day to convict him.

On July 25, 2005, Dupas went to court to appeal his conviction for the murder of Maher. The appeal was dismissed.

Dupas was charged with the murder of Halvagis on September 11, 2006. This came about after it was revealed Dupas had confessed to the crime while gardening in prison in 2002, but it didn't come to light until much later. The Victorian Director of Public Prosecutions requested the case go directly to trial rather than go through the committal hearing process. Dupas appeared in court by video link on September 26, 2006. He pled not guilty.

The trial lasted twenty-two days, and on August 9, 2007, Dupas was found guilty of the murder of Halvagis. He received his third life sentence.

On September 17, 2009, his appeal against the conviction was upheld, with the court ruling the directions of the judge in the original trial were inadequate. A second trial for the murder of Halvagis began on October 26, 2010. Dupas was convicted again on November 19, 2010.

Outcome

Dupas is suspected of the following murders:

Helen McMahon

McMahon, forty-seven, was discovered on a beach on February 13, 1985. She had been beaten to death. At first, it was believed Dupas couldn't have killed her because he was in prison. It was later discovered he was on pre-release leave and living in the area at the time of the murder.

Renita Brunton

Brunton, thirty-one, was killed in Sunbury, Victoria, in 1993.

Kathleen Downes

Downes, ninety-five, was stabbed to death on December 31, 1997. She was living in the Brunswick Lodge nursing home, and investigations revealed Dupas had called the home before the murder. He was subsequently charged with her murder in February of 2018.

While he has been in prison, Dupas has attempted to kill himself several times. Although he is described as a model prisoner by prison staff, they also say he is a monster when released.

Trivia

Dupas and Grace McConnell, a mental health nurse at the prison, developed a relationship and later married in 1987 at Castlemaine Gaol. She was sixteen years older than Dupas.

She described their marriage during the inquest into the murder of Mersina Halvagis:

"He insisted that he was in love with me .... and that with my help he could come out of himself and become a normal person. I agreed (to marry Dupas), not out of particular love for this man but from a sense of responsibility to help him become a useful member of the community. In my mind, our relationship was mother and son. Our sex life was very basic, almost non-existent. I would go along with it out of a sense of responsibility ... It got to the stage where I could not bear him touching me."

She divorced him in the mid-1990s, describing him as "lazy, self-obsessed, needy and a snob."

The story of Dupas' crimes was featured on an episode of *Crimes That Shook Australia* in 2014.

PAUL DUROUSSEAU

Date of birth: August 11, 1970

Aliases/Nicknames: The Jacksonville Serial Killer

Characteristics: Rape

Number of victims: 7

Date of murders: 1997 - 2003

Date of arrest: February 6, 2003

Victim profile: Tracy Habersham, 26; Tyresa Mack, 24; Nicole L. Williams, 18; Nikia Kilpatrick, 19 (six months pregnant); Shawanda Denise McCalister, 20 (pregnant); Jovanna Jefferson, 17; Surita Cohen, 19

Method of murder: Strangulation

Location: Florida, Georgia, USA

Status: Sentenced to death in Florida on December 13, 2007.

Background

Durousseau was born in Texas but moved to Los Angeles to live with his mother's family after his father left. His first job after graduating high school was as a security guard. As an adult, his first criminal offenses occurred on December 18, 1991, and January 21, 1992, when he was arrested for carrying a concealed firearm.

In November of 1992, he enlisted in the army and was stationed in Germany. He met a woman called Natoca while there, and they married in 1995. They were transferred to Fort Benning, Georgia in 1996. A year later, on March 13, Durousseau was arrested for the abduction and rape of a young woman, but by August, those charges were dropped. In January of 1999, he was dishonorably discharged from the army after he was court-martialed and found guilty of being in possession of stolen goods.

The Durousseaus moved to Jacksonville, Florida, and had two children, both girls. Durousseau had trouble keeping jobs, and he regularly fought with his wife about the financial strain. Once, after he had slapped his wife, police advised her to file for a restraining order. Between September and October of 2001, Durousseau spent forty-eight days in jail for domestic battery against his wife.

Despite his criminal history, he was still able to get jobs, including that of a school bus driver and animal control worker and, in 2003, a taxi driver.

Murders

Within a month of Durousseau being acquitted of the rape charge, the body of Tracy Habersham, twenty-six, was found on September 7, 1997, in Fort Benning. Habersham had last been seen leaving a party and had been missing for forty-eight hours before her body was found. Although Durousseau was not considered a suspect at the time, DNA evidence would later link him to the murder.

Tyresa Mack, twenty-four, was raped and murdered in 1999. Durousseau was seen leaving her home with a television, yet he wasn't identified. Then in 2001, he was arrested for the rape of a young woman in Jacksonville and spent thirty days in jail. On December 19, 2002, the body of Nicole L. Williams, eighteen, was discovered at the bottom of a ditch. She was wrapped in a blue blanket and had been missing for two days.

Family members of Nikia Kilpatrick, nineteen, had not heard from her for a number of days, and on January 1, 2003, they went to check on her. Entering her apartment, they found her body in the bedroom. Her two children, two years old and eleven months old, were alive but malnourished, as Nikia had been dead for two days. She had been raped then strangled to death with a cord. At the time of her death, she was six months pregnant.

Another pregnant woman was raped and strangled to death eight days later. Shawanda Denise McCalister, twenty, was found dead in her apartment. The scene was almost identical to Kilpatrick's crime scene. McCalister was killed on the same day that Durousseau started working as a taxi driver.

The bodies of the next two victims were found near each other in a ditch beside a construction site in Jacksonville. Jovanna Jefferson, seventeen, and Surita Cohen, nineteen, were killed approximately ten days apart, with Jefferson having been murdered around January 20. Witnesses reported they had seen both victims with a taxi driver before they disappeared, and the description matched Durousseau.

Trial

Police began making links between the murders and Durousseau, and several pieces of evidence could be traced back to him. These included DNA, fibers, cell phone records, and taxi records. Fibers from the blanket Nicole Williams was wrapped in were found in Durousseau's house. DNA from some of the crime scenes matched Durousseau's DNA. Police also found jewelry that had belonged to Surita and Jovanna in Durousseau's car, and the girls' cell phone records showed they had both called the taxi company, specifically Durousseau, before they disappeared. A surveillance tape from a bank showed Durousseau's taxi in the background while Shawanda withdrew money.

The investigator's case against Durousseau was very strong, given the amount of evidence against him. On June 17, 2003, he was charged with five counts of first-degree murder. He was also charged with two counts of child abuse for leaving Nikia's young children alone in the apartment after he killed their mother.

Durousseau was found guilty of all charges.

Outcome

Durousseau was initially sentenced to death on December 13, 2007. But in January of 2017, the sentence was overturned and commuted to life imprisonment on the grounds that the jury had not made a unanimous decision. There had been a 10-2 split, which made the decision by the jury unconstitutional in capital sentencing.

Trivia

The case was featured on *Crime Stories: The Killer Cabbie* on television in 2012.

Initially, it was reported that the taxi company hadn't run a background check on him. However, this was actually the responsibility of the City of Jacksonville, and it was the city who issued his taxi permit.

Often, he would ask women when they were planning on making films with him.

He was described as a "lewd womanizer" by friends and neighbors.

A witness claimed they had seen him hitting on a young girl who was only about thirteen or fourteen years old.

VOLKER ECKERT

Date of birth: July 1, 1959

Aliases/Nicknames: Brummi Killer

Characteristics: Mutilation, paraphilia, photographed victims

Number of victims: 6 - 19

Date of murders: 1974 - 2006

Date of arrest: November 17, 2006

Victim profile: Women (mostly prostitutes)

Method of murder: Strangulation

Location: France, Spain, Germany

Status: Committed suicide in his cell in Bayreuth, Germany, on July 2, 2007.

Background

Eckert started killing at the young age of fourteen, but this wouldn't be discovered until decades later. His first murder took place in 1974, when Eckert went to the home of his classmate and neighbor Silvia Unterdorfel, also fourteen. Using his hands and a ligature, he strangled her to death and then staged the scene to make it appear she had committed suicide by hanging from the doorknob. He then went home and masturbated.

This was only the beginning, and though it was some years before he killed again, he wasn't going to stop.

Murders

In 1987, Eckert attacked two women, nearly killing them. As a result, he was charged with two counts of attempted murder and was sentenced to twelve years in prison. He was released in 1994 and began working as a truck driver. This involved Eckert traveling to several European countries; his home base was in Hof.

His known victims were:

June 25, 2001 - a Kenyan prostitute was killed near Chermignac, near the city of Bordeaux in western France.

October 9, 2001 - a twenty-four-year-old prostitute was killed in Maçanet de la Selva.
March 1, 2005 - a Russian prostitute was killed in Sant Sadurní d'Osormort, in the Catalonia region of northeastern Spain.
October 2, 2006 - a twenty-eight-year-old Polish prostitute was killed at Reims, France.
November 2, 2006 - a twenty-year-old Bulgarian prostitute was killed in Hostalric, in Catalonia, Spain

The majority of the murder victims were strangled, and Eckert performed amateur postmortems on the bodies before photographing them. He would sometimes dress the bodies or cut off their hair, which he kept as a "trophy" in his truck cab or his apartment.

Eckert is believed to be responsible for a further seven murders in Europe:

April 1987 - an eighteen-year-old was killed in Plauen, East Germany.
August 2002 - a twenty-three-year-old prostitute from Sierra Leone was killed in Troyes, France.
September 5, 2004 - a twenty-five-year-old Ghanaian prostitute was killed in Rezzato, Italy.

There were also four women in the Czech Republic and another one in France.

Trial

Following the murder of the Bulgarian prostitute on November 2, 2006, surveillance camera footage captured Eckert's truck parked next to the corpse. This was reported to the Spanish police, and they identified Eckert by his truck. He was detained by German police a few weeks later on November 17, 2006, in Wesseling near Cologne.

While he was being interrogated, Eckert confessed to six murders. These included five prostitutes in France and Spain and the young girl he killed as a teenager. However, he would never make it to trial.

Outcome

On July 2, 2007, in the middle of the legal proceedings, Eckert committed suicide. He was found dead in his cell. Following his death, further evidence was found that suggested Eckert had killed nine women, and possibly another four. Five months after Eckert's death, in December of 2007, the investigation was ended and the file closed.

Trivia

The first time Eckert got into trouble with the law was when he was thirteen, in 1973. He had stolen his mother's car and disappeared for several weeks before he was arrested following a police chase. He spent eighteen months in prison.

At the age of ten, he became obsessed with hair, and he started touching wigs and dolls' hair and masturbating at the same time. He later moved on to an obsession with human hair.

EDWARD EDWARDS

Date of birth: June 14, 1933

Aliases/Nicknames: Nil

Characteristics: Rape, insurance money

Number of victims: 5

Date of murders: 1977, 1980, 1996

Date of arrest: July 30, 2009

Victim profile: Billy Lavaco, 21; Judy Straub, 18; Tim Hack, 19; Kelly Drew, 19; Dannie Boy Edwards, 25

Method of murder: Shooting, strangulation

Location: Ohio, Wisconsin, USA

Status: Sentenced to death in Ohio on March 8, 2011. Sentenced to life in prison in Wisconsin. Died in prison on April 7, 2011.

Background

Born in Akron, Ohio, Edwards spent most of his childhood an orphan following the suicide of his mother, of which he was a witness. He claimed that he was physically and emotionally abused while in an orphanage, and he blamed this as contributing to his criminal behavior. He spent time in juvenile detention and was released to join the US Marines. However, he went AWOL and was dishonorably discharged.

Throughout his twenties and thirties, Edwards traveled around doing odd jobs, even selling vacuum cleaners at one point. But most of his adult life was spent in Louisville, Kentucky. He continued to commit crimes and was in and out of jail.

Edwards escaped from jail in 1955, and roamed the country, financing his travels by robbing gas stations. He later said he didn't disguise himself because he wanted to be famous. In 1961, he was added to the FBI's Ten Most Wanted list. He was returned to prison, in Leavenworth, and was paroled in 1967.

Edwards married and claimed he was reformed; he even became a motivational speaker on the subject. He appeared on two television shows and wrote an autobiography in 1972, *The Metamorphosis of a Criminal: The True Life Story of Ed Edwards*. He didn't stay reformed though, and by 1982, he had gone back to his criminal ways.

Murders

William Lavaco, twenty-one, and his girlfriend, Judy Straub, eighteen, went missing sometime in 1977. Their bodies were discovered on August 8, 1977, in Norton, Ohio. They had both been shot in the neck at point-blank range with a shotgun.

In 1980, Edwards found work as a handyman at a reception hall in Jefferson County, Wisconsin. Around August 9, Timothy Hack, nineteen, and his girlfriend Kelly Drew, also nineteen, disappeared. The last location they had been seen was at Edwards' place of work. Authorities became suspicious of Edwards, but he fled the state and was on the run for two years. The body of Drew was found on October 19; she had been strangled to death. The next day, Hack's body was found; he had been stabbed.

Edwards drifted to Pennsylvania in 1982 and was arrested after burning down a rental house. He was sent to prison for two years but wasn't charged with the murders of Drew and Hack. He was released, and little is known about what he got up to in the early 1990s. But in 1996, Edwards decided to kill for financial gain.

Edwards' foster son, Danny Boy Edwards, twenty-five, had an insurance policy worth two hundred fifty thousand dollars. Danny Boy, a solider, was persuaded by Edwards to go AWOL. Edwards took him to the woods near his home in Burton, Ohio, and shot him twice in the face. He buried Danny Boy in a shallow grave, which was later discovered by a hunter. Although he was questioned over the murder, he was never charged.

In 2009, police were able to trace Edwards back to the murders of Drew and Hack. He was arrested on July 30.

Trial

After his arrest, Edwards confessed to the murders of Danny Boy, Lavaco, and Straub. He agreed on June 9, 2010, to plead guilty to all of the murders but Danny Boy's. During his trial, he suffered many health issues, including diabetes, and for a while, he needed an oxygen mask. The trial was lengthy, and Edwards was found guilty of the murders of Lavaco and Straub. He was sentenced to life in prison. For Danny Boy's murder, he was sentenced to death on March 8, 2011.

Edwards wasn't concerned about the death sentence and had previously said he welcomed it.

Outcome

Edwards died from natural causes on April 7, a month after he had been sentenced for the murder of Danny Boy. He was seventy-seven years old. At that point, he had been suffering from diabetes, heart disease, and leukemia.

There was some speculation that Edwards was responsible for other murders, but these have never been confirmed, and his official body count stays at five.

Some investigators noticed that Edwards had lived in the same area as the infamous Zodiac Killer's murders in the late 1960s. At the time, he would have closely matched the description of the killer, but others have disputed that theory. His daughter later said that when he watched news reports on the Zodiac's murders, he would sometimes shout out, "That's not how it happened!"

Trivia

The book *It's Me, Edward Wayne Edwards, the Serial Killer You Never Heard Of* was published by John A. Cameron, a former cold case investigator, and a police detective.

A six-part documentary series was created called *It Was Him: The Many Murders of Ed Edwards*. The work was about Wayne Wolfe, the grandson of Edwards, and John A. Cameron looking at unsolved murders and trying to establish a link with Edwards. The series premiered on April 16,

2018.

A documentary was broadcast in March 2017 about the murders of Kelly Drew and Tim Hack.

A documentary, *People Magazine Investigates - My Father, The Serial Killer* was broadcast in January of 2018. It revealed how the daughter of Edwards had discovered her father was the killer and how she had informed the authorities, which led to his arrest.

MACK RAY EDWARDS

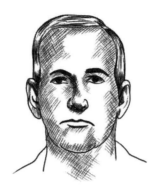

Date of birth: 1919

Aliases/Nicknames: Nil

Characteristics: Rape

Number of victims: 6 +

Date of murders: 1953 - 1970

Date of arrest: March 5, 1970 - Surrendered

Victim profile: Stella Darlene Nolan, 8; Gary Rochet, 16; Donald Allen Todd, 13; Don Baker, 13; Brenda Howell, 11; Roger Madison, 16

Method of murder: Shooting

Location: Los Angeles County, California, USA

Status: Sentenced to death in 1971. Committed suicide by hanging himself in his cell in San Quentin on October 30, 1971.

Background

Born in Arkansas, Edwards moved to Los Angeles County in 1941. He became a heavy equipment operator and worked on freeways. On March 6, 1970, he walked into the Los Angeles Police Department's Foothill station and stated he wanted to "clear his conscience." He proceeded to tell a detective that he had killed six children over two decades.

Murders

From 1953 to 1956, Edwards murdered three children. He also claimed to have killed three more in 1968 and 1969. Edwards said he had disposed of one of the victims underneath the Ventura Freeway, and another underneath the Santa Ana Freeway. Three of his victims were:

Stella Darlene Nolan, aged eight. Stella, of Compton, California, had disappeared on June 20, 1953.
Gary Rochet, sixteen. His body was found on November 26, 1968, after he had been shot to death. He was from Granada Hills, California.
Donald Allen Todd, thirteen. Donald, of Pacoima, California, disappeared on May 16, 1969.

Two of the other murders Edwards had confessed to were Donald Lee Baker, fifteen, and Brenda Jo Howell, twelve, who went missing together on August 6, 1956. Howell was the sister of his wife.

Roger Dale Madison, fifteen, of Sylmar, California, disappeared on December 16, 1968. Because the bodies of these victims were never found, Edwards wasn't charged with their murders.

Edwards, along with a teenage male accomplice, kidnapped three girls in 1970 from their home in Sylmar, California. The girls managed to escape, and because they had once been neighbors of Edwards, they could identify him. This is what prompted Edwards to go to the police and confess to the murders.

Trial

There is little information about his trial, other than he was charged with three murders. He pled guilty to all three and received the death penalty.

Outcome

While in prison, Edwards tried to commit suicide at least twice before finally succeeding. On October 30, 1971, he hung himself in his cell using a television cord. Before he died, a letter was smuggled out of the prison in which he recanted most of his confession. He said in the letter he was taking the blame for a man he called "Billy the cripple." Police dismissed the letter as an invention of Edwards' mind.

In March of 2007, Edwards was being investigated as a possible suspect in the disappearance of Thomas Eldon Bowman, eight, of Redondo Beach. Bowman went missing in Pasadena on March 23, 1957. The likeness between Edwards and the sketch of the abductor was quite strong. Edwards had also written a letter to his wife that states he had left Thomas Bowman out of his confession.

Edwards is also considered a suspect in the disappearance of Bruce Kremen, six, who went missing from a YMCA camp on July 12, 1960, in Angeles National Forest. Likewise, he has been considered a suspect in the disappearance of Karen Lynn Tompkins, eleven, who went missing on August 18, 1961, and Dorothy Gale Brown, eleven, who disappeared on July 3, 1962. Brown's body was later recovered from the ocean at Newport Beach; she had been molested before she was drowned.

There is also a possible link between Edwards and the disappearance of Ramona Price, seven, in August of 1961.

Trivia

In the drama *The Shield*, the last episode has a reference to Edwards. The detective in the program is interviewing a teenager who he believes is a serial killer, and he makes the point that the killers who don't have a "catchy" nickname are easily forgotten by the public.

BEVAN SPENCER VON EINEM

Date of birth: 1945

Aliases/Nicknames: Nil

Characteristics: Child sex offender, rape, torture

Number of victims: 1 - 5

Date of murders: 1979 - 1983

Date of arrest: November 3, 1983

Victim profile: Richard Kelvin, 15; boys and young men

Method of murder: Torture, massive blood loss (captive for five weeks)

Location: Adelaide, South Australia, Australia

Status: Sentenced to life with a non-parole period of 36 years, 1984.

Background

On the night of May 10, 1972, two gay men were thrown into the River Torrens by a group of men who were believed to be police officers. This was a popular area where gay men would meet in secret since homosexual acts were illegal at that time in South Australia. One of the victims was Dr. George Duncan, who had only been in Australia for a few weeks. He drowned, while the other man, Roger James, managed to crawl to the road despite having a broken leg. Einem, who happened to be driving past, rescued James and drove him to the hospital.

It was suspected that the officers responsible for throwing the men into the river were senior members of Vice Squad. At the Coroner's Inquiry, the officers were asked to give evidence, but they wouldn't answer any questions. James refused to identify the men who had attacked him that night. Because of their refusal to answer questions, the three officers were suspended and later resigned from duty.

This was Einem's first brush with the law, only this time, he was one the right side of it. Ten years or so later, he would wind up on the very wrong side of the law.

Murders

Richard Dallas Kelvin, fifteen, was abducted in the early evening of June 5, 1983. He was only sixty meters from his home, had just seen a friend off at a nearby bus stop, and was on his way home for dinner. Despite a wide search, the offer of rewards for information, and extensive media coverage, Kelvin wasn't found. His father was a popular and longtime news presenter, so Kelvin's disappearance was broadcast more than most other disappearances.

Seven weeks after his disappearance, on July 24, 1983, Kelvin's body was found beside a dirt airstrip near One Tree Hill, in the Adelaide Hills. He hadn't been concealed and was fully dressed in the same clothes he was wearing when he disappeared. His body had been washed and posed in the fetal position.

Kelvin's cause of death was massive blood loss due to a horrendous anal injury, likely caused by a blunt object with a tapered neck being inserted into his anus. His body also showed injuries and bruising to the head, back, and right buttock. In his bloodstream were traces of alcohol and five drugs, all hypnotics—Mandrax, Amytal, Noctec, Rohypnol, and Valium.

Mandrax wasn't readily available in 1983 due to regulations, so the police began to search for prescriptions for it. They discovered one issued to Einem, whose name was familiar to police. Einem had previously been questioned about the deaths of three young men and an alleged sexual assault of another.

Einem was questioned about Kelvin's murder four days after the body was found. Einem claimed he had been in bed with the flu on the night Kelvin was abducted and knew nothing about it. His home was searched, and a bottle of Mandrax was found which Einem said he used to help him sleep. Though he said there were no other drugs in the house, police found a bottle of Noctec. Fibers from his carpets, as well as hair and blood samples, were taken by police without Einem putting up a fight.

Following the initial questioning, three factors made police more suspicious that Einem was the culprit.

First, when they knocked on his door and asked if they could ask him a few questions, Einem said he wouldn't answer anything without speaking to his lawyer. This made it seem as though he had something to hide.

Second, instead of denying involvement in Kelvin's murder, he instead said he wouldn't commit this sort of act because it would be "unethical." This was a strange thing to say, especially for someone claiming innocence.

Third, when Einem was asked about drugs, he admitted he had the Mandrax but said there were no other drugs in his possession. When police found the Noctec, he became nervous and said he rarely used them.

Despite all of this, Einem was allowed to leave the country to visit the United Kingdom and the Soviet Union during August and September of 1983. While he was away, the case against him strengthened, and fibers found on Kelvin's clothing matched those taken from Einem's home. Also, hairs found on Kelvin's body matched those belonging to Einem.

Police tried to find a man who had previously told police that Einem was involved in the murder of Alan Barnes in 1970. The injuries Barnes suffered were very similar to those inflicted on Kelvin. The man, known as "Mr. B" to keep his identity protected, was eventually located. He told police how he and Einem used to pick up male hitchhikers and give them alcohol laced with hypnotic drugs. They would then take them to Einem's previous home in Adelaide, abuse them all night, and then set them free the next day. Mr. B also provided information that Kelvin was at Einem's home around the time he died. Armed with all of this information, police arrested Einem on November 3, 1983, and charged him with murder.

Einem was the prime suspect in the murders of four other young men that had taken place between 1979 and 1982. The victims were:

June 1979: Alan Barnes
August 1979: Neil Muir

August 1981: Peter Stogneff

February 1982: Mark Langley

An inquest regarding the deaths of these four men was requested. The results revealed major similarities between their murders and Kelvin's—especially the murders of Langley and Barnes.

On September 15, 1989, Einem was arrested and charged with the murder of Barnes. Then, on November 10, 1989, he was charged with Langley's murder as well. There wasn't enough evidence to charge him with the other two murders.

Trial

On February 20, 1984, the committal hearing to determine if there was enough evidence to go to trial took place. Einem changed his story to refute the forensic evidence the prosecution had produced, saying he had actually been in contact with Kelvin the night he disappeared. Einem portrayed the encounter as innocent, though—a man and a troubled or confused young man having an innocent conversation about life at Einem's house. He also said he hugged Kelvin, and they had sat on his bed for a while and played with Einem's harp. Two hours later, he dropped Kelvin off in the city and gave him money for a taxi home.

This new statement contradicted Einem's initial claim that he was home in bed with the flu the night Kelvin disappeared. Also, the number of fibers and hairs on Kelvin far exceeded the number that would have been present after just two hours in Einem's company and a brief hug. Therefore, Einem was ordered to stand trial.

Einem's trial began on October 15, 1984, and the jury retired to consider their verdict on November 5, 1984. They returned after seven and a half hours, finding Einem guilty of Kelvin's murder. He received an automatic life sentence with a non-parole period of twenty-four years. The Attorney-General of South Australia appealed the non-parole period right away and, on March 29, 1985, it was increased to thirty-six years.

On March 5, 1990, the committal hearing to decide if Einem should stand trial for the murders of Langley and Barnes took place. Einem pled not guilty to both murders. He was ordered to stand trial on May 11, 1990. The defense appealed the decision, however, launching an abuse of process action in the Supreme Court of South Australia. They stated the media interest would prevent Einem from getting a fair trial. On June 19, 1990, proceedings began, and on December 17, 1990, the findings were released; Einem was ordered to stand trial. There were concerns, however, with the majority of the prosecution's evidence.

On December 19, 1990, the pre-trial hearing began. After the findings of the appeal, it was decided to have Einem tried separately for the murders of Langley and Barnes. It was ruled that evidence related to the Kelvin case was inadmissible. On December 21, the charge for the murder of Langley was withdrawn. The prosecution tried to carry on with the trial for the murder of Barnes, but that was also withdrawn on February 1, 1991.

Outcome

Einem has certainly not been a model prisoner throughout his incarceration. Some of his misbehaviors and news reports include:

- On January 29, 2006, news media reported that Einem was being investigated for allegedly raping an inmate several times at Yatala Labour Prison.

- It was reported on October 29, 2006, that Einem had been selling hand-painted greeting cards to prison officers for twenty dollars each.

- On November 12, 2006, it was reported by the *Sunday Mail* newspaper that Einem was getting special treatment from some of the officials at Yatala Labour Prison. He was receiving home-cooked meals and the use of a phone.

- On November 26, 2006, it was revealed than Einem had been prescribed Cialis by a prison doctor in 2003. This drug is predominantly used to treat erectile dysfunction.

- February 4, 2007, the ABC reported that Einem had been charged with commercial dealings during his incarceration, including selling hand-painted greeting cards.

- On June 14, 2007, it was reported that he had been charged with creating and possessing child pornography. Police alleged he had written three fictional stories that described sexual acts between a man and a child. His lawyer stated he would be cleared by an analysis of his handwriting.

- On July 27, 2007, Einem was transferred from the maximum-security B-Division of Yatala Labour Prison to Port Augusta Prison.

- On August 11, 2007, it was reported by *The Australian* that detectives were asking for information that could establish the identity of a young man shown in the Seven Network's news archive that showed police searching a stormwater drain following the disappearance of the Beaumont children. The man bore a striking resemblance to Einem when he was young.

- On August 13, 2007, the Seven Network broadcasted a follow-up story that the man in their archived film and a young Einem matched the police sketch of the suspect seen with the Beaumont children at the beach on the day of their disappearance.

- On November 1, 2007, a report by the ABC said that Einem was now eligible for parole after twenty-four years behind bars. South Australian Premier Mike Rann, however, vowed to push new legislation that would ensure Einem would never get parole.

- On December 7, 2007, the ABC reported that Einem had been granted a further adjournment before answering charges of possessing child pornography.

- On January 25, 2008, *The Advertiser* reported that Einem would not answer to charges of possessing child pornography for at least another two months.

- On March 28, 2008, it was reported by the ABC that the fingerprints found on the child pornography in Einem's cell did not match, and neither did the handwriting. Einem's lawyer Sam Abbott said he expected the most serious charge of producing the material to be dropped. Einem had been excused from attending his court hearings so that he could avoid an "unpleasant" three-hour drive with other inmates.

- On March 30, 2008, it was announced that key suspects in "The Family" murders were going to be DNA tested as part of a new investigation into the murders. Einem had been the only member of "The Family" convicted, and police were now reviewing the case.

- On April 13, 2008, it was announced that fresh investigations into the unsolved murders would involve questioning transvestites who may have information that could aid the inquiry. Some had been associates of Einem and could possibly have important information.

- On April 27, 2008, it was reported that police were traveling overseas to interview a number of key witnesses as part of their new inquiry into the murders.

- On May 4, 2008, it was reported that a chiropractor from Adelaide who had left Australia while under investigation for his involvement in "The Family" murders was now being sought in Europe. He had been an associate of Einem.

- On June 6, 2008, it was announced that one charge of producing child pornography had been dropped. Einem still faced charges of possession.

- On September 18, 2008, it was announced that the allegations that Einem had written stories of child pornography in prison were dropped.

- On October 28, 2008, it was reported that police were hoping one of the four suspects in the murders would come forward to help solve the case. The state government had doubled the reward to one million dollars. This was announced just a few days after Einem was interviewed by Major Crime detectives.

- On May 27, 2009, Einem pled guilty to possessing child pornography – the first time he had ever confessed to a crime.

- On June 24, 2009, Einem was sentenced to a further three months for the possession of child pornography.

Trivia

The main witness in Einem's case claimed he had received intimidating phone calls to try to dissuade him from talking to the authorities. It was suggested that someone wanted him to stay quiet, and there were rumors Einem was protected by "The Family," who was an influential group.

Connection with the Beaumont Children

One of the most famous unsolved mysteries in Australia is the disappearance of the Beaumont children from Glenalg Beach on January 26, 1966. A witness later claimed that before victim Barnes was kidnapped, Einem stated he had abducted the Beaumont children, "connected them up," and "did some brilliant surgery on them," during which one of the children had died. He further stated he had dumped the bodies at Myponga or Moana, south of Adelaide.

As it turns out, Einem was in Adelaide when the children went missing, and he resembles the witness description. He would often go to Glenalg Beach to "perv" on children.

SCOTT ERSKINE

Date of birth: December 22, 1962

Aliases/Nicknames: Nil

Characteristics: Rape

Number of victims: 3 +

Date of murders: June 23, 1989, March 27, 1993

Date of arrest: Linked to the crimes in 2001, while incarcerated at Wasco State Prison

Victim profile: Renee Baker, 26; Jonathan Sellers, 9; Charlie Keever, 13

Method of murder: Strangulation

Location: California, Florida, USA

Status: Sentenced to death on September 1, 2004.

Background

Erskine suffered a head injury when he was five years old, after running out in front of traffic and getting struck by a vehicle. He was in a coma for sixty hours, and though it seemed he recovered physically, he regularly complained of headaches. After the accident, he told his mother he had blackouts and couldn't remember what he was doing.

When he was ten, Erskine began molesting his younger sister, who was only six at the time. He would force her to perform oral sex, and soon after, he also began to abuse her friends. The little girls were told they would be killed if they told anyone about it.

During his teens, Erskine spent time in a juvenile detention facility, and when he was fifteen years old, he escaped. That same day, he raped a thirteen-year-old girl at knifepoint; the next morning, he assaulted a female jogger with a knife.

In 1980, Erskine was on his way to an interview to become a camp counselor when he came across a fourteen-year-old boy. He attempted to rape the boy and beat him unconscious. Erskine begged the judge not to send him to an adult prison, and his mother pleaded for him to be sent to a mental health institution. The judge ignored both their requests, sending Erskine to adult prison for four years. He was released in 1984.

Erskine met a woman at a bus stop in 1993 and invited her back to his home. She was held hostage by Erskine for several days, during which time he raped and sodomized her repeatedly. Eventually, he let her go and was promptly arrested. He was sentenced to seventy years in prison, was required to register as a sex offender, and had to provide a sample of his DNA.

Murders

In March of 2001, the cold case investigation into the unsolved murders of two young boys in 1993 was reexamined. Jonathan Sellers, nine, and Charlie Keever, thirteen, had disappeared while out riding their bicycles. Two days later, their bodies were found in the brush along the Otay River bank in Palm City. They were both naked from the waist down and had been gagged and bound with tape. Both of the boys had been molested before they were killed.

Swabs from Keever's mouth contained semen; it was determined that because the boy wasn't physically mature enough to produce sperm, it must have come from whoever had killed him. A DNA sample was extracted and entered into CODIS. It came back as a match to Erskine.

Because he was already in prison, it was easy for the police to charge Erskine with the two murders. While waiting for his trial, his DNA was also matched to another unsolved murder. Renee Baker, twenty-six, was killed on June 23, 1989. In 2003, Erskine was charged with her murder. He admitted he had raped her, broken her neck, and left her near the Intracoastal Waterway bank, where she drowned.

Trial

The trial for the murders of Sellers and Keever began in September of 2003. Photos from the crime scene were shown to the jurors to emphasize just how horrific these murders were. The photographs of Sellers showed him naked below the waist, his arms and legs tied with rope. A gag was in his mouth, and there were obvious signs of sexual assault on his genitals. The young boy had a noose tied around his neck.

The photographs of Keever showed he was also tied and gagged and naked from the waist down. There were extensive bite marks on his genitals, and he too had a noose tied around his neck. The pathologist testified that Keever had been alive when his genitals were savaged. DNA from Erskine was also found on cigarette butts near the boys' bodies.

The defense did not deny Erskine had murdered the boys but tried to get the jury to focus on the head injury Erskine suffered as a young child. The public defender stated the injury to Erskine's brain left him with a diminished capacity for understanding right and wrong. Instead of a death penalty, they argued that it would be more appropriate for him to be sentenced to life without parole.

On October 1, 2003, Erskine was found guilty of the murders, but the jury struggled to agree on the sentence. The majority of the jurors voted for the death penalty, but one was against it. Since the vote had to be unanimous, a mistrial was declared on the penalty phase.

A second jury was established to determine the sentencing, and this time, they all voted for the death penalty. The sentence was affirmed by the judge on September 1, 2004.

Also in 2004, Erskine pleaded guilty to the murder of Renee Baker. For this crime, he received a sentence of life in prison.

Outcome

Following an appeal to have Erskine's sentence changed from death to life, the California Supreme Court decided in May 2019 to uphold the death penalty. All of the arguments put forward by Erskine's appellate attorney were rejected.

He remains on death row awaiting his execution.

Trivia

Erskine was put into "special classes" in high school that dealt with children who were emotionally disturbed.

Randy Baker stated, after Erskine's conviction for his sister's murder, "I'd like to get a hold of a gun and kill him. He didn't get what he deserves for my sister, but he got what he deserved for those two little boys in California."

RICHARD EVONITZ

Date of birth: July 29, 1963

Aliases/Nicknames: Nil

Characteristics: Kidnapping, rape

Number of victims: 3 +

Date of murders: 1996 - 2002

Date of arrest: Committed suicide before an arrest could be made

Victim profile: Sofia Silva, 16; Kristin Lisk, 15; Kati Lisk, 12

Method of murder: Strangulation

Location: Virginia, South Carolina, California, Florida, USA

Status: He was surrounded by police when he shot and killed himself on June 27, 2002.

Background

Evonitz was the eldest of three children born to parents Joseph and Tess. When he was young, he was often referred to as Marc instead of Richard to avoid confusing him with an uncle who had the same name. At the age of sixteen, he graduated from high school and worked for a while before joining the Navy. Evonitz served for eight years as a sonar technician in the Navy. During this time he received a Good Conduct Medal, and he was honorably discharged when he left the Navy.

In January of 1987, while he was still with the Navy, he exposed himself and masturbated in front of a fifteen-year-old girl in Orange Park, Florida. A month later, when his ship returned to port, he was arrested and sentenced to three years of probation.

Evonitz worked steadily for companies that sold grinding equipment and compressors. In 1988, he married Bonnie Lou Gower. The marriage ended in 1996 and, following the divorce, Evonitz struggled financially. He filed for bankruptcy in 1997. A failed business resulted in the foreclosure on his home in 1999.

Evonitz's second marriage took place in 1999 when he wed Hope Marie Crowley. He worked at an air compressor company in South Carolina until the day he was surrounded by police.

Murders

Sofia Silva, sixteen, was abducted by Evonitz on September 9, 1996, from her yard in Spotsylvania County. A month later her body was found in a creek in King George County.

On May 1, 1997, sisters Kristin, fifteen, and Kati Lisk, twelve, were abducted from their yard close to the Spotsylvania Courthouse. Their bodies were discovered five days later in the South Anna River, Hanover County.

Fifteen-year-old Kara Robinson was abducted on June 24, 2002, from the front yard of her friend's house in Columbia, South Carolina. Evonitz took her back to his apartment, tied her to his bed, and raped her. When he fell asleep, she managed to escape and went to the police. She was able to identify Evonitz. When Evonitz woke and discovered she had gone, he fled and was surrounded by police in Sarasota, Florida.

Trial

Police surrounded Evonitz near the waterfront in Sarasota on June 27, 2002. They urged Evonitz to surrender peacefully, but he had a pistol in his hand. A police dog was released and bit Evonitz several times. At this point, he shot himself and died.

Outcome

While searching Evonitz's apartment after his death, investigators unearthed clues that this wasn't the first time he had attacked girls. A footlocker contained newspaper articles about the Silva and Lisk murders, as well as items that would be considered trophies of the murders.

In late August, forensic tests confirmed that Evonitz had murdered Silva and the Lisk sisters. Fibers from his apartment matched those found on the girls' bodies. A handprint belonging to Kristin Lisk was found in the trunk of Evonitz's car. Samples of DNA were also a match.

Police believe Evonitz may also have been responsible for the death of Alicia Reynolds in 1996, in Culpeper, Virginia. The footlocker in Evonitz's apartment held a note with handwritten directions to the dump site of Reynolds' body.

Trivia

A reward of one hundred fifty thousand dollars was given to the girl who escaped and identified Evonitz to police. The reward had been offered for solving the murders of the Lisk sisters and Silva.

After his wife moved out of their house, Evonitz was unable to pay his bills. His mortgage payment was $859 a month, plus he had other obligations including a student loan. His wages were twenty-one hundred dollars per month as a parts salesman at Walter Grinders.

While Evonitz was on the run from police, he started to call his relatives and utter cryptic confessions.

RAYMOND FERNANDEZ AND MARTHA BECK

Raymond Fernandez

Date of birth: December 17, 1914

Aliases/Nicknames: The Lonely Hearts Killer

Characteristics: Robbery

Number of victims: 5 - 17 +

Date of murders: 1947 - 1949

Date of arrest: February 28, 1949

Victim profile: Jane Lucilla Thompson; Myrtle Young; Janet Fay, 66; Delphine Downing, 41; Delphine's two-year-old daughter Rainelle

Method of murder: Overdose of drugs, strangulation, shooting, drowning

Location: Spain, Illinois, New York, Michigan, USA

Status: Executed by electrocution at Sing Sing prison in New York on March 8, 1951.

Martha Beck

Date of birth: May 6, 1919

Aliases/Nicknames: The Lonely Hearts Killer

Characteristics: Robbery

Number of victims: 4 +

Date of murders: 1948 - 1949

Date of arrest: February 28, 1949

Victim profile: Myrtle Young; Janet Fay, 66; Delphine Downing, 41; Delphine's two-year-old daughter Rainelle

Method of murder: Overdose of drugs, strangulation, shooting, drowning

Location: Illinois, New York, Michigan, USA

Status: Executed by electrocution at Sing Sing prison in New York on March 8, 1951.

Background

Raymond Fernandez

Fernandez was born in Hawaii on December 17, 1914, to Spanish parents. When he was around three years old, the family moved to Connecticut in the US. Fernandez was a frail child, and his father had hoped for a stronger son.

In 1932, Fernandez moved to Spain to work for an uncle on his farm. When he was twenty years old, he met and married Encarnacion Robles. When World War II broke out, Fernandez joined Spain's Merchant Marine, and then the British Intelligence, where he was a well respected spy for the British government.

When the war ended, he decided to return to America and boarded a freighter ship. One day, as he was heading up to the deck, a steel hatch cover fell and struck him on the head. It left a severe indentation on his skull. When the ship docked in December of 1945, he was admitted to the hospital. He remained there until March of 1946.

After the accident, his personality changed; Fernandez became moody, distant, and he angered quickly. The injury had occurred in the frontal lobe region of his brain, an area that is known to affect reasoning and logic. Fernandez decided to move to Alabama and traveled there by ship. Upon arriving, he stole a lot of clothing and items from the storeroom on the ship and was arrested at customs. He received a one-year prison sentence. While there, Fernandez's Haitian cellmate introduced him to voodoo.

In 1946, Fernandez was released from prison and went to live with his sister in Brooklyn. He suffered bad headaches and would lock himself away in his room for days. He began writing letters to "lonely hearts" clubs and would the seduce women who responded. After he gained their trust, he would rob them of their jewelry, money, and checks; then he would disappear.

Martha Beck

Born in Milton, Florida, Beck suffered from a problem with her glands that resulted in her experiencing early puberty and made her obese. She later claimed she had been raped by her brother, and that her mother had beaten her when she told her what had happened. Her mother had allegedly claimed it was Martha's fault her brother had raped her. Not surprisingly, Beck ran away from home when she was a teenager.

Beck still managed to finish school and she studied to be a nurse. Due to her weight, however, she had difficulty finding nursing work. Beck worked as an undertaker's assistant for a while, then quit and moved to California. She eventually gained work as a nurse in an Army hospital. Sexually promiscuous, she became pregnant, and after the baby's father refused to marry her, she moved to Florida.

Beck told people in Florida that the father was killed during the war, which garnered her much sympathy. The story even made it into the local newspaper. She gave birth to a girl and soon was pregnant again by Alfred Beck, a bus driver. They married, but the union lasted only six months; she later gave birth to a boy.

Beck started working at the Pensacola Hospital for Children in 1946. Wanting a relationship, she placed a lonely hearts ad in 1947. Fernandez answered the ad. They met when Fernandez visited for a brief time. Beck went around telling everyone they were going to get married, and when he returned to New York City, she busied herself with making wedding plans.

Beck got fired from her job, so she packed up everything and went to New York to be with Fernandez. Her children, whom she left behind, were sent to the Salvation Army. Fernandez told Beck his schemes, of gaining the trust of women and then robbing them, and she was ready and willing to help him. Often she would pose as his sister. Their victims would feel secure with another woman in the house and would agree to stay with them.

An extremely jealous woman, Beck would do whatever she could to stop Fernandez from having sex with the women. Her violent temper was regularly unleashed.

Murders

In 1949, Janet Fay, sixty-six, became engaged to Fernandez and went to stay with him at his apartment in Long Island. Beck caught them in bed together and used a hammer to smash Fay in the head. She was still alive, so Fernandez finished the job and strangled her to death. Fay's family knew she had gone to visit Fernandez and were suspicious when they couldn't contact her. Worried they would get caught, Fernandez and Beck fled.

They traveled to Byron Center Road in Wyoming Township, Michigan. There they met Delphine Downing, a widow, and her two-year-old daughter. Downing became agitated on February 28 and was given sleeping pills to calm her down. When her daughter saw her mother in a drug-induced stupor, she began crying, which angered Beck. She choked the poor child but didn't kill her.

Fernandez thought Downing would be suspicious when she saw the bruises on her daughter's neck, so he shot her and killed her. For several days, they stayed in the house until the crying of the young girl enraged Beck, and she drowned her in a basin of water. The bodies were buried in the basement. When neighbors reported they had disappeared, the police arrived and arrested Fernandez and Beck on March 1, 1949.

Trial

Once arrested, Fernandez confessed to the murders almost immediately. He later tried to retract his confession, saying he only made it to try to protect Beck. Police attributed seventeen murders to the pair, but they denied being responsible.

When the trial for the murder of Janet Fay began, the stories of sexual perversity caused a sensation. The newspapers weren't kind when describing Beck's appearance, and she wrote to the editors to complain. Fernandez and Beck were found guilty of Fay's murder, and both were sentenced to death.

Outcome

Fernandez and Beck were executed on March 8, 1951, by electric chair. Fernandez was the first to die; being a weak man, he had to be carried to the electric chair. Beck, weighing two hundred pounds, was too big to sit in the chair, so she had to be wedged in.

Trivia

Though Fernandez and Beck had a rocky relationship with many arguments, they loved each other. This is shown in their last statements:

"I wanna shout it out; I love Martha! What do the public know about love?" - *Raymond Fernandez.*

"My story is a love story. But only those tortured by love can know what I mean. I am not unfeeling, stupid or moronic. I am a woman who had a great love and always will have it. Imprisonment in the Death House has only strengthened my feeling for Raymond." - *Martha Beck.*

MICHEL FOURNIRET

Date of birth: April 4, 1942

Aliases/Nicknames: The Ogre of the Ardennes, the Virgin Hunter

Characteristics: Kidnapping, rape

Number of victims: 10 +

Date of murders: 1987 - 2001

Date of arrest: June 2003

Victim profile: An unidentified man; Isabelle Laville, 17; Fabienne Leroy, 20; Jeanne-Marie Desramault, 22; Elisabeth Brichet, 12; Natacha Danais, 13; Farida Hellegouarch; Céline Saison, 18; Manyana Thumpong, 18; an unidentified 16-year-old girl

Method of murder: Strangulation

Location: France, Belgium

Status: Sentenced to life in prison on May 28, 2008.

Background

Fourniret was born near the Belgium border in France in 1942. His mother was the daughter of a farmer, and his father was a metal worker. Fourniret was quiet and intelligent as a child and enjoyed classical music and playing chess. As an adult, he had trouble holding on to a job and worked in a variety of roles, including a supervisor at a school and a forestry worker.

In 1966, he was arrested for molesting a child, and his first marriage ended. He married again and fathered three children. But when he was arrested again for the rape of minors, his second marriage also came to an end.

While Fourniret was in custody waiting for his trial to begin, he placed an advertisement in a Catholic magazine for a pen pal. Nurse and mother, Monique Olivier, replied to the advertisement and the two began communicating. Olivier had been in a number of relationships where she was physically abused. During her correspondence with Fourniret, she promised that she would help him "hunt virgins" if he agreed to help her kill her ex-husband.

When Fourniret was released from prison in 1987 for good behavior, Olivier was waiting at the prison gates. Just two months later, their killing spree began.

Murders

In separate vehicles, Fourniret and Olivier drove to Auxerre on December 11, 1987. They had seen a young girl the day before and decided to target her. Olivier stopped beside the girl, Isabelle Laville, seventeen, and asked her to get into the car and help her with directions; the girl agreed. As they drove down the road, Fourniret stood next to his car, which he pretended had broken down. Just as they had planned, Olivier pulled over and offered him a lift. Inside the car, Fourniret used a piece of rope to choke Laville; then Olivier sedated her with Rohypnol. They took Laville back to their home, where she was raped and strangled by Fourniret. They discarded her body in an abandoned well, where it remained until July 11, 2006.

While he had been in prison, Fourniret met bank robber Jean-Pierre Hellegouarch. In March of 1988, his wife, Farida Hammiche, contacted Fourniret and asked him to help her locate the loot that had been stolen by members of the Gang des postiches and buried in a cemetery in Fontenay-en-Parisis. Fourniret agreed.

As payment for his help, Hammiche gave Fourniret a share of the loot worth five hundred thousand francs. On April 12, Hammiche was lured out of her home by Fourniret and Olivier, strangled, and buried in Clairefontaine-en-Yvelines. The couple then broke into her house and stole her share of the loot.

Using the money, they bought a château called the Château du Sautou in Donchery. Olivier became pregnant, but this didn't stop them from carrying on with the murders. They drove to a supermarket on August 3, and met Fabienne Leroy, twenty, in the car park. Olivier pretended to be ill, and they asked Leroy to get in the car and help them find a doctor's office. Once she was inside the car, they drove to a forest near a military camp. Olivier was told by Fourniret to check to see if Leroy's hymen was intact, but she refused. Fourniret raped Leroy anyway and then shot her in the chest, killing her.

The next victim was Jeanne-Marie Desramault, twenty-one. Fourniret had met the young woman on a train in January of 1989; she said she was staying at a convent. Nothing happened at this point, but when they met again on March 18, she was invited to the couple's house in Floing; Desramault accepted. Fourniret promised he would take her home after the visit. Once they arrived at the house, Desramault was asked if she was a virgin. She told Fourniret she wasn't and that she had a boyfriend, which enraged him. Fourniret tried to rape her, but she fought back, so the couple used bandages to gag her before Fourniret strangled her to death. She was buried in the garden of their château.

On December 20, Fourniret, Olivier, and their infant son drove across the border to Saint-Servais, Namur. Fourniret noticed Elisabeth Brichet, twelve, walking to a friend's house. They waited outside until Brichet left to walk back home, at which point they asked her to get in the car and help them find a doctor for their son. Instead, they drove back to Floing. As Fourniret undressed Brichet, he noticed she was menstruating, so he made Olivier clean her. The following day, they went to the château. Fourniret tried to suffocate her using a plastic bag, but this failed, so he strangled her. The body was buried in the garden near their previous victim, Desramault.

On November 21, 1990, Fourniret and Olivier drove to a shopping center in Rezé, near the western coast of France. Natacha Danais, thirteen, was walking home when they saw her. She was lured into their van, under the ruse of needing directions. They drove her to a secluded place and stabbed her in the chest twice with a screwdriver. Then she was strangled, and her body left on the beach. Later, it was determined she had been raped after her death.

In the early 1990s, the family moved to Belgium. On May 16, 2000, Fourniret picked up Céline Saison, eighteen, who was walking home after school. He drove her back to Belgium and blackmailed her into having sex. Then Fourniret strangled her using a rope and left her body in a forest. Her remains were found on July 22.

Fourniret traveled back to France on May 5, 2001, and came across Thai girl Mananya Thumpong, thirteen. They had met previously, so when he invited her to come home with him to play with his son, she agreed. Fourniret drove her to Nollevaux, Paliseul, and strangled her to death. He left her body in a forest, where it was almost completely devoured by animals. Her bones were found on March 1, 2002.

Trial

On June 26, 2003, Fourniret was arrested at his home in Sart-Custinne, Belgium. He had attempted to kidnap a young girl but failed, which led police to his doorstep. Both Fourniret and Olivier were extensively questioned, but they would not confess to any crimes. A year later, however, Olivier admitted to police that Fourniret had killed several people since 1987.

The trial began on March 27, 2008, and ended a day later. Fourniret was found guilty of seven murders, those where the bodies had been located. He was sentenced to life imprisonment without the possibility of parole. For her role in the crimes, Olivier was sentenced to life with a minimum period of twenty-eight years. The couple was also ordered to pay moral compensation to the victims' families to the amount of 1.5 million euros.

No appeals were lodged by either Fourniret or Olivier.

On November 16, 2018, Fourniret and Olivier were convicted of murdering Farida Hammiche. Olivier received another twenty years in prison, and Fourniret was given another life sentence.

Outcome

Fourniret and Olivier divorced while in prison on July 2, 2010.

Fourniret made a confession in February 2018 that he had killed two more women.

Trivia

Fourniret saw his raping of virgins to be a "sport."

The French Minister at the time, Rachida Dati, wanted the attitude toward preventative custody and parole under supervision to be more relaxed. Changing the law would allow cases like Fourniret's to be positively impacted, as the supervision would have picked up on his activities much sooner.

Fourniret claimed he had experienced sex with his mother multiple times when he was a young man. He believed that this incest caused him emotional trauma, which led to him committing the crimes.

According to Fourniret, he became obsessed with virginity after his first marriage. His wife had apparently lied, having claimed she was a virgin when in fact that she was not. He, however, claimed to be a virgin at the time of the wedding, despite his admission about having sexual relations with his mother.

Fourniret's daughter, Marie- Hélène, couldn't cope with her father's crimes and committed suicide in 2006.

KENDALL FRANCOIS

Date of birth: July 26, 1971

Aliases/Nicknames: The Poughkeepsie Killer

Characteristics: Hid the bodies in the house that he shared with his parents, prostitutes

Number of victims: 8

Date of murders: 1996 - 1998

Date of arrest: September 1, 1998

Victim profile: Wendy Meyers, 30; Gina Barone, 29; Catherine Marsh, 31; Kathleen Hurley, 47; Mary Healey Giaccone, 29; Michelle Eason, 27; Sandra Jean French, 51; Catina Newmaster, 25

Method of murder: Strangulation

Location: Poughkeepsie, New York, USA

Status: Sentenced to 8 consecutive life sentences on August 11, 2000.

Background

Francois grew up in Poughkeepsie, and by the time he was in high school, he stood six foot four inches ; he played on the school football team until he graduated. In 1990, he joined the Army, and his basic training took place at Fort Sill in Oklahoma.

Francois started taking college classes in liberal arts in 1993, at the Dutchess County Community College. He continued his studies on and off and finished in 1998. He undertook a variety of jobs including that of a monitor at Arlington Middle School from 1996-1997. Complaints were made by some of the teachers at the school regarding the way Francois behaved toward female students. He was often seen touching their hair and was sometimes overheard telling them jokes with sexual overtones. The students nicknamed him "Stinky." Despite the complaints, he had a clean employment record at the school.

Murders

Wendy Meyers, thirty, was reported missing in October of 1996, in Ulster County, New York. The last time she had been seen was at the Valley Rest Motel in a small town called Highland, south of Kingston. She was white with a slim build, short brown hair, and hazel eyes.

160

In December of the same year, Gina Barone, twenty-nine, was reported missing by her mother. She had last been seen on November 29, on a street corner in Poughkeepsie, and it appeared she had been involved in an argument with a man. Barone was of small build and had brown hair.

The following month, January of 1997, Kathleen Hurley, forty-seven, went missing. She was last seen walking along the main street in downtown Poughkeepsie. Like the other missing girls, Hurley was white with a small build and had brown hair.

At the time, prostitutes in the area had reported Francois to the police as someone who was rough during sex. While investigating the murders, they placed Francois' home under surveillance.

Another young woman was reported missing by her mother in March of 1997. Catherine Marsh was last seen on November 11, 1996. She was white with a small build and brown hair, and she had blue eyes. The police decided to call in the FBI for assistance, but FBI were unable to create a profile of a suspect without a crime scene.

Mary Healey Giaccone was reported missing by the police in November of 1997. They had been trying to locate her since her mother had died in October. During the search, they discovered that she had last been seen in February of 1997.

Then on June 12, 1998, fifty-one-year-old Sandra Jean French went missing. Her car was found three blocks away from the home of Francois. A few months later, in August, Catina Newmaster went missing. She was known to frequent the same places and streets as the other missing women, and her physical description was very similar.

On September 1, 1998, Francois abducted a prostitute and took her back to his home. While he was in the process of strangling her, she managed to break free and run from his house. She fled to a nearby gas station. Police officers happened to pull in at the same time, and another woman, Deborah Lownsdale, approached them and said that the woman who was currently walking away had just said she was assaulted. The officers caught up with her, and she confirmed she had been attacked. They transported her to the police station, and she filed a complaint against Francois.

That afternoon, police went to Francois's house to discuss the complaint. He agreed to accompany them to the police station for questioning. Francois, after several hours of questioning, eventually said he was responsible for the disappearances of the women.

He was formally arrested and charged with the murder of Newmaster. With a search warrant in hand, officers went to Francois's house to look for evidence. What they found were several bodies.

Trial

Francois appeared in court on September 9 and entered a plea of not guilty. The following month, on October 13, he was charged with a further eight counts of first-degree murder, eight counts of second-degree murder, and an attempted assault.

Faced with the possibility of the death penalty, Francois pleaded guilty to all charges on December 23. With the guilty plea, he would avoid a trial by jury and thus remove the possibility of a death sentence.

Outcome

Francois was sentenced to life in prison without parole on August 11, 2000. He was incarcerated in Attica Correctional Facility.

Trivia

Francois kept the dead bodies of his victims in his basement and attic. Once they decomposed, he took the skulls and put them in a plastic "kiddie pool" in his attic.

It was suggested that the skulls were his trophies, and that is why he removed them.

In 1995, Francois was diagnosed with HIV, which he thought he had caught from Wendy Myers, who was his first victim.

FRANKFORD SLASHER

Date of birth: Unknown

Aliases/Nicknames: Frankford Slasher

Characteristics: Sexual assault

Number of victims: 8 - 9

Date of murders: August 19, 1985 - September 6, 1990

Date of arrest: Never apprehended

Victim profile: Helen Patent, 52; Anna Carroll, 68; Susan Olszef, 64; Jeanne Durkin, 28; Catherine M. Jones, 29; Margaret Vaughan, 66; Theresa Sciortino, 30; Carol Dowd, 46; Michelle Dehner, 30

Method of murder: Stabbing

Location: Frankford, Pennsylvania

Status: Unknown.

Background

The Frankford Slasher operated in the neighborhood of Frankford, Philadelphia, between 1985 and 1990. There were nine alleged victims. Though Leonard Christopher was convicted of one of the murders, he did not match the description of the killer given by witnesses. Most of the women who were murdered had been seen with a white, middle-aged man before they died. Christopher was black.

Murders

The first victim linked to the Frankford Slasher was Helen Patent, fifty-two, who was killed on August 19, 1985. Her body was discovered a week later, with her top pulled up over her breasts, and her legs spread open; she was naked from the waist down. The medical examination showed she had been stabbed forty-seven times.

On January 3, 1986, Anna Carroll, sixty-eight, was found with a knife still embedded in her body; she too was naked from the waist down. Christmas Day, 1986, brought the next victim. Susan Olszef, sixty-four, was murdered in her home. It was later discovered that these three victims were all regular customers at Goldie's, or Golden Bar as it was also known.

Jeanne Durkin, twenty-eight, was a homeless woman who slept on the street near Goldie's. She was killed on January 8, 1987, and her body left underneath a truck. Durkin was sexually assaulted before she was stabbed a total of seventy-four times. Unlike the others, she was wrapped in a large coat. Soon after, Catherine M. Jones, twenty-nine, was killed. Most don't consider her as a Slasher victim though, because she wasn't sexually assaulted or stabbed to death. On November 11, 1988, the body of Margaret Vaughan, sixty-six, was found in the apartment building she had been evicted from. She had been stabbed to death.

Theresa Sciortino, thirty, was found dead on January 19, 1989, in her home. Apart from a pair of socks, her body was naked, and she had been butchered. Witnesses had seen her and previous victim Vaughan with a white, middle-aged man before they were killed. A sketch was done, but no tips came through. Then, on April 29, 1990, forty-six-year-old Carol Dowd was found behind a store. She had been stabbed thirty-six times, and one of her nipples had been cut off.

The last suspected victim of the Frankford Slasher was Michelle Dehner, thirty, also known as Michelle Martin. She was killed in her apartment on September 6, 1990. Before she was stabbed to death, she had been sexually assaulted.

Trial

Leonard Christopher was questioned after the murder of Carol Dowd. He was working at the store her body was found behind, and when investigators spoke to local prostitutes, two of them put him at the scene. They also saw a large knife tucked into his belt around the same time. Police arrested Christopher and charged him with Dowd's murder. He had allegedly said to his boss that maybe he had killed her.

Christopher was convicted on December 12, 1990.

Outcome

Despite similarities between the crimes, there was never any evidence to suggest that Christopher was responsible for the other eight murders. After Dehner's death and his arrest, however, there were no further murders attributed to the Frankford Slasher. This led many to believe Christopher was responsible for all of the murders.

The biggest discrepancy is Christopher's appearance; he didn't match the description of the man seen with two of the victims before they were killed. However, it is well known that witness testimony is often unreliable. Skin color is usually undisputed testimony though, as it's often the main feature remembered by witnesses.

The true identity of the Frankford Slasher has never been uncovered. There were no strong leads or clues to point to a suspect. To date, the eight murders remain unsolved.

Trivia

"I was railroaded. I didn't kill Carol Dowd. I did not even know Carol Dowd. I was implicated by prostitutes… that the police put up." - *Leonard Christopher*

JOSEPH PAUL FRANKLIN

Date of birth: April 13, 1950

Aliases/Nicknames: James Clayton Vaughn Jr., the Racist Killer

Characteristics: Former Klansman and neo-Nazi, racially motivated serial killer

Number of victims: 15 +

Date of murders: 1977 - 1980

Date of arrest: September 25, 1980

Victim profile: Gerald Gordon, 42; Bryant Tatum; Harold McIver; Darrell Lane, 14; Dante Evans Brown, 13; Arthur Smothers, 22; Kathleen Mikula, 16; Nancy Santomero, 19; Vicki Durian, 26; Ted Fields; David Martin; Alphonse Manning Jr.; Toni Schwenn; Johnny Brookshire, 22; Raymond Taylor; Jesse Taylor, 42; Marian Vera Bressette, 31; Mercedes Masters, 15; Lawrence Reese, 22; Leo Thomas Watkins, 19; Rebecca Bergstorm

Method of murder: Shooting

Location: Wisconsin, Missouri, Tennessee, Georgia, Virginia, Indiana, Ohio, Pennsylvania, West Virginia, Utah, USA

Status: Sentenced to death in Missouri on February 27, 1997. Executed by lethal injection in Missouri on November 20, 2013.

Background

Born James Clayton Vaughn Jr., Franklin had a troubled home life. His father was an abusive alcoholic who would beat the children and their mother, and he was put in jail twice for public intoxication. His mother was strict and a perfectionist. It was claimed by Franklin that they never had enough to eat and that his mother didn't care about her children. Franklin also said this affected his emotional development, and he was ten years behind other people his own age in maturity.

While in high school, Franklin developed a keen interest in Christianity, then Nazism. Later, he would hold memberships with both the Ku Klux Klan and the National Socialist White People's Party. Franklin dropped out of high school following an accident that greatly impaired his vision. He legally changed his name to Joseph Paul Franklin to honor Paul Joseph Goebbels and Benjamin Franklin. After reading *Mein Kampf* by Adolph Hitler, he felt inspired to begin a race war.

Franklin was able to avoid conscription to the military during the Vietnam War because of his impaired eyesight. In 1968, he married. Soon after the wedding, however, his personality changed.

According to his wife, he began to beat her, thus becoming the father he had hated so much. Other times, his wife found him crying for no apparent reason.

Over the next few years, Franklin was involved in some racial incidents; he was also periodically arrested for carrying a concealed weapon. After his mother's death in 1972, he moved to Atlanta, and this is when he gained membership with the two white supremacy factions.

Between the years 1977 and 1980, it is believed he traveled across the South and Midwest. It is claimed he used eighteen different pseudonyms and regularly changed his cars. He even dyed his hair so much that it almost fell out. While he was traveling across the country, Franklin murdered thirteen people in a one-man war against the minorities.

Murders

On July 29, 1977, Franklin destroyed the Beth Shalom Synagogue in Chattanooga, Tennessee, by firebombing it. Luckily there weren't enough people attending that night, and the attendees left early.

The following month, on August 7, interracial couple Alphonse Manning Jr. and Toni Schwenn were shot in a parking lot at East Towne Mall in Madison, Wisconsin. Then, on October 8, 1977, Franklin hid near the Brith Sholom Kneseth Israel synagogue and waited for the people inside to exit. As they did, Franklin opened fire, killing Gerald Gordon and wounding William Ash and Steven Goldman.

Larry Flynt, the *Hustler* magazine publisher, and his lawyer, Gene Reeves were shot in Lawrenceville, Georgia, on March 6, 1978. Franklin later confessed to this shooting—one of the most famous of all time—and said he had carried it out because an edition of *Hustler* had displayed interracial sex.

The next attack occurred on July 29, 1978. Hiding near a Pizza Hut in Chattanooga, Tennessee, Franklin opened fire on another interracial couple. Bryant Tatum, a black man, was killed; Nancy Hilton, a white woman, survived despite being shot with a 12-gauge shotgun.

The following year, on July 12, 1979, Franklin fired through a window of a Taco Bell and killed Harold McIver, the manager, who was a black man. Franklin later confessed to this murder but wasn't charged. His reasoning behind the murder was that McIver had been in close contact with white women.

Franklin shot Vernon Jordan, a civil rights activist and Urban League president, on May 29, 1980, after he saw him with a white woman in Fort Wayne, Indiana. Jordan survived the shooting. Franklin denied this shooting and was acquitted, but he later admitted his responsibility.

Cousins Dante Evans Brown and Darrell Lane were shot and killed on June 8, 1980. Franklin had been waiting to shoot an interracial couple but shot the teenage boys instead. Days later, on June 15, Franklin laid in wait at the Washing Street Bridge for his victims to come along. He shot Arthur Smothers and Kathleen Mikula as they walked across it, killing them both. Smothers was a black man and Mikula a white woman.

Hitchhikers Vicki Durian and Nancy Santomero were shot and killed by Franklin on June 25, 1980, in Pocahontas County, West Virginia. He decided to murder the girls after one of them told Franklin she had a boyfriend who was black.

The last two murders occurred in Salt Lake City, Utah, on August 20, 1980. Two black men, David Martin, and Ted Fields were shot and killed by Franklin near Liberty Park.

When Franklin was traveling through Kentucky, he was detained regarding the transportation of a firearm in his vehicle. Evidence was found in his vehicle that made investigators suspicious he was the sniper responsible for the killings across the country. The fact that he had racist tattoos didn't help him either. But Franklin fled the interrogation. When authorities found he had a habit of going to blood banks, they put out a nationwide alert. A call was made to the FBI in October of 1980 by an employee of a blood bank, and Franklin was arrested on October 28, in Lakeland.

166

Trial

During the judgment phase of the trial for the murder of Gerald Gordon, Franklin tried to escape. He was found guilty of the murder and sentenced to death. A psychiatrist who had interviewed Franklin over a period of time before the trial believed he was unfit to stand trial due to paranoid schizophrenia, but this was denied. Larry Flynt called for clemency for Franklin, saying, "that a government that forbids killing among its citizens should not be in the business of killing people itself."

Outcome

Following his sentencing, Franklin was held at the Potosi Correctional Center near Mineral Point, Missouri, on death row. When the time came for his execution, an export ban on the drugs used for lethal injections led to the announcement that a new method of using a single drug would be used instead.

This new method raised numerous concerns. As a result, a stay of execution was granted to Franklin the day before it was meant to be carried out. Another stay was granted that night because Franklin had claimed he was mentally incompetent to be executed. The appeals court overturned both stays, and his final appeals were rejected.

On November 20, 2013, Franklin was executed. It took ten minutes for him to die, and it was the first time the single-drug injection was used instead of the usual three-drug method. According to media witnesses, there were no signs shown by Franklin that he was in pain. Once the injection was administered, he blinked a few times and then breathed heavily a few times before swallowing hard. Finally, his chest stopped heaving, and he was dead.

Franklin gave no final statement before his execution.

Trivia

Franklin thought that killing Larry Flynt would have been his big trophy killing, since Flynt was the famous publisher of *Hustler* magazine.

"I saw that interracial couple he had, photographed there, having sex in an issue of *Hustler*, that featured several photos of a black man with a white woman. It just made me sick. I think whites marry with whites, blacks with blacks, Indians with Indians. Orientals with Orientals. I threw the magazine down and thought, I'm gonna kill that guy." - *Franklin*

Media

The novel *Hunter* was written by William L. Pierce, (pseudonym Andrew MacDonald) who is a white supremacist. It presents the story of fictional character Oscar Yeagar, and Yeagar's crimes are very similar to Franklin's. Pierce dedicated the book to Franklin.

LEONARD FRASER

Date of birth: June 27, 1951

Aliases/Nicknames: The Rockhampton Rapist

Characteristics: Rape

Number of victims: 4 +

Date of murders: 1998 - 1999

Date of arrest: April 22, 1999

Victim profile: Sylvia Benedetti, 19; Beverly Leggo, 36; Julie Turner, 39; Keyra Steinhardt, 9

Method of murder: Strangulation

Location: Rockhampton, Queensland, Australia

Status: Sentenced to life imprisonment on June 13, 2003. Died in prison on January 1, 2007.

Background

Fraser was born in 1951 in Ingham, North Queensland, Australia. His childhood and family life were considered normal; when he was six years old, the family moved to Mount Druitt in Sydney. At the age of fourteen, despite being functionally illiterate, Fraser left school. Everything went downhill from there.

At fifteen, Fraser was sent to the Gosford Boys Home for twelve months for stealing. Not long after he was released, he was convicted of assault, driving without a license, car theft, and offensive behavior. He was placed on a bond for two years. Then he served twelve months of hard labor.

In 1974, Fraser began attacking and raping women. He was caught following a failed attempt to rape a woman, and during questioning, he admitted to two other rapes and also two attempted rapes. He was then interviewed by a court psychiatrist who thought Fraser was beyond help. According to the psychiatrist, Fraser had an unfathomable belief that the women he raped wanted him to have sex with him and that they enjoyed it. Fraser had no impulse control and no conscience; nothing would stop him from doing whatever he wanted. Fraser was sentenced to twenty-two years for the rapes and was given a parole period of seven years, as per the law at the time. The judge felt he should never be released, but, unfortunately, he was. Fraser was paroled in 1981, moved to Mackay, and found work with the railways.

In 1982, Fraser forced his way into the home of a woman with the intention of raping her. But, for some bizarre reason, he let her call her husband, and Fraser explained to her how easy it would be for her to be raped by someone. For this crime, he was sentenced to two months in jail.

After he was released, Fraser became involved with a woman who had a young child, and he stayed out of trouble for the next two years. The couple also had a child of their own during this time. But Fraser's behavior deteriorated again and, in 1985, he brutally raped a young woman he had been stalking for several days. He was quickly arrested and, given his record, sentenced to twelve years' imprisonment.

While Fraser was in prison, he was nicknamed Lenny the Loon by the other inmates. His behavior was often chaotic and unpredictable. He was made to serve the full twelve years of his sentence, and he was released again in 1997.

Fraser moved in with a woman who had written him letters while he was in prison. Although she had a terminal illness, it wasn't long before their relationship became sexual. The woman eventually left, due to his violent streak, and moved to Brisbane for medical treatment. But he followed her. It is alleged that he raped her in the hospital chapel, but he was never charged. The woman died from her illness six months later.

Toward the end of 1998, Fraser was living with Cristine Wright, nineteen, an intellectually handicapped woman in Rockhampton. The beginning of the next year, another woman moved into the house along with her eleven-year-old daughter. They left soon after, following accusations Fraser had assaulted the daughter. Shortly afterward, Fraser was kicked out of the house when the landlady claimed she had seen him having sex with a dog.

Murders

On April 22, 1999, Fraser followed Keyra Steinhardt, nine, home after school. He attacked her while she was walked through a vacant lot, striking her on the head before raping her and then killing her. A woman had seen the attack but waited twenty minutes before she called the police. Keyra couldn't be saved, but Fraser was arrested quickly. It took police two weeks to get the location of Keyra's body from him. When they found her body, it was apparent her throat had been cut, but little else could be determined due to extensive decomposition.

Trial

On November 20, 2000, Fraser was found guilty of the murder of Keyra Steinhardt. It was obvious to the judge that there was no prospect of successful rehabilitation for Fraser. As a result, he was given an indefinite life sentence with no possibility of parole.

Outcome

Fraser later confessed to three other murders between September 1998 and April 1999. He was able to show police where the bodies were, and he received more time added to his life sentence. This was unfortunate instance where the courts had tried to have Fraser locked up for a long time. However, because of the Australian legal system, he kept getting released. A number of rapes and murders could have been prevented if only he had been kept behind bars. When police searched through his home and belongings, they found a number of items from the victims he had kept as trophies. Among them, they also found three ponytails, all belonging to different women. They were unable to trace the hair to his known victims.

In all, Fraser was tried and convicted of four murders. These included Beverley Leggo, Sylvia Benedetti, and Julie Turner.

On December 26, 2006, Fraser complained of chest pains and was taken to the secure wing of Princess Alexandra Hospital in Woolloongabba. Fraser died on January 1, 2007, from a heart attack.

Trivia

The crimes committed by Fraser were featured on an episode of *Crime Investigation Australia*. The episode is called "The Predator: Leonard John Fraser."

The hair discovered in Fraser's home could not be matched to any of his victims, nor to any of the persons missing in Australia.

GERALD AND CHARLENE GALLEGO

Gerald Gallego

Date of birth: July 17, 1946

Aliases/Nicknames: Sex Slave Killer, Stephen Feil

Characteristics: Rape

Number of victims: 10

Date of murders: September 10, 1978 - November 2, 1980

Date of arrest: November 17, 1980

Victim profile: Rhonda Scheffler, 17; Kippi Vaught, 16; Brenda Judd, 14; Sandra Colley, 13; Stacey Redican; Karen Chipman Twiggs; Linda Aguilar, 21, and unborn child; Virginia Mochel, 34; Craig Miller, 22; Mary Elizabeth Sowers, 21

Method of murder: Shooting, beating, ligature strangulation

Location: California, Oregon, Nevada, USA

Status: Sentenced to death in Nevada and California. Died of rectal cancer on July 18, 2002, at the Nevada prison system's medical center.

Charlene Gallego

Date of birth: October 10, 1956

Aliases/Nicknames: Mary Martinez

Characteristics: Sex Slave Killer

Number of victims: 10

Date of murders: September 10, 1978 - November 2, 1980

Date of arrest: November 17, 1980

Victim profile: Rhonda Scheffler, 17; Kippi Vaught, 16; Brenda Judd, 14; Sandra Colley, 13; Stacey Redican; Karen Chipman Twiggs; Linda Aguilar, 21, and unborn child; Virginia Mochel, 34; Craig Miller, 22; Mary Elizabeth Sowers, 21

Method of murder: Shooting, beating, ligature strangulation

Location: California, Oregon, Nevada, USA

Status: 16 years and 8 months, has now been released.

Background

Gerald Gallego

Gerald was born in 1946. During his younger years, his mother had many boyfriends who were physically abusive toward him. His mother became a prostitute, and some of her clients would also abuse Gerald. Often, he was left dirty and hungry and would plead with his mother for a hug. His father had no part in his life.

Gerald married several times, but none of the marriages worked, especially once the wives ran out of money. Once the money was gone, so was Gerald. At one point, he started to sexually abuse his daughter.

Charlene Gallego

Charlene Adelle Williams was born in 1956 near Sacramento, California. Her father was the vice president of a supermarket chain, and he and his wife regularly traveled for business. At one point, Charlene's mother was badly hurt in a car accident. Unable to travel anymore, Charlene took on the role of going on business trips with her father.

When Charlene was younger, she was described as well-spoken and intelligent, but things changed in high school. At that time, she began using drugs and bragged about having a black man as a lover. She married young, to a wealthy, heroin-addicted husband, used a lot of drugs, and her appearance suffered. Eventually, the marriage came to an end.

The next man Charlene married was a soldier. Charlene called him a "mother's boy" and became bored with him. They divorced, and Charlene then became involved with a married man. That dalliance came to an end when Charlene asked if they could have a threesome with the man's wife. Afterwards, Charlene tried to commit suicide. Not long after, Gerald came into her life.

At first, they had a really good sex life. Charlene wanted a dominant man who would take charge, and she saw that in Gerald. A week after they met, they moved into a house together. It soon became apparent to Charlene that Gerald was more interested in his own sexual satisfaction than anything else. Something about him fascinated her, and she began to share his indecent fantasies.

After a few months of living together, Gerald brought home a teenage girl. Gerald and Charlene had a threesome with the sixteen-year-old. But Gerald would not allow the two women to touch each other; they were only allowed to touch him. Later, he caught them in bed together and was so angered, he threw the girl out the window. Then he hit Charlene.

Gerald began abstaining from sex with Charlene, telling her he was impotent. More likely, it was because he didn't like the way she wasn't dependent on him for sexual satisfaction.

Murders

Charlene became jealous of Gerald working as a bartender. She feared he was sleeping with the customers and thought this was why he wasn't having sex with her. They stayed together anyway, and after a year, Gerald said he needed a pair of love slaves. He asked Charlene to get the girls for him. Some believe she agreed to this because she saw Gerald's word as law. Others think she agreed to it because she desired women and fantasized about being in control of a girl that was tied up.

On September 11, 1978, Charlene approached Rhonda Scheffler, seventeen, and Kippi Vaught, sixteen, at a mall in Sacramento. She somehow managed to lure them to their van. Once inside, Gerald used a gun to threaten them and tie them up. They drove to Baxter, where both girls were raped by Gerald and executed.

Brenda Judd, fourteen, and Sandra Colley, thirteen, had gone to the Washoe County Fair in Reno, Nevada on June 24, 1979. They were on their way home when Charlene stopped them. She asked the girls if they wanted to make some money by helping her distribute advertising leaflets, and they both agreed. She led them to the van, saying they needed to get more leaflets. Once inside, Gerald appeared and with a gun in his hand and tied the girls up. They then drove to a hardware store, where Gerald purchased a shovel and a hammer. At one point, Gerald told Charlene to take over driving, and he got into the back with the girls. He took his time assaulting them, while Charlene drove into the Nevada hills. When they stopped, Gerald took each girl away from the van. One at a time, he killed them with the hammer. He used the shovel to bury the bodies.

Two seventeen-year-olds, Stacey Redican and Karen Chipman Twiggs, disappeared from a mall in Sacramento. Charlene approached the girls and offered them free drugs and a ride. They accepted and got in the van. Gerald pointed his gun at them and told Charlene to start driving. As they traveled on the I-80 Highway, Gerald got into the back of the van and raped both girls repeatedly. They ended the trip at Limerick Canyon near Lovelock. Once again, he walked each girl away and killed them with a hammer.

Gerald and Charlene had begun living under false names, the Feils. They went on a vacation to Oregon, and on June 7, 1980, they spotted their next victim. Linda Aguilar, twenty-one, was pregnant and walking alongside the highway. Gerald asked if she needed a ride, and she accepted. As Charlene drove, Gerald sexually assaulted Linda. They came to a stop in the woods a while later. Gerald took Linda away, smashed her in the head with a rock, and then strangled her to death.

When Linda's body was found, her boyfriend became the main suspect in her death. Despite a witness placing Linda getting into a van, the police felt the circumstantial evidence was enough. After all, he had physically assaulted her in the past. It looked as though he was going to be charged with her murder.

By now Gerald had become very bold, but he had also become impatient. On July 16, 1980, after they had consumed a substantial amount of alcohol, Gerald and Charlene went to a local bar, the Sail Inn, where they continued to drink. After the bar closed, Gerald told Charlene he wasn't ready to go home. When bartender Virginia Mochel came out, Gerald forced her at gunpoint into the van. This time though, the couple went back to their home. While Gerald raped Virginia, Charlene sat and watched television. After a while, Gerald told Charlene to get in the van and drive. As they traveled along the road, Gerald strangled Virginia to death. They left her body near Clarksburg.

During the investigation into her murder, customers of the Sail Inn reported that two strangers had come into the bar the night she disappeared. They said the man's name was Stephen and his girlfriend's name was Charlene. The police managed to make a link to Gerald and went to question him at his workplace. Gerald said he had been at the Inn, but he didn't know what had happened to Virginia. Charlene, when questioned, made similar statements, though she said she and her boyfriend had been fishing that day. Detectives were suspicious when she mentioned this because Virginia's hands had been bound with fishing line. However, they had nothing else to go on, and the Gallego's were not arrested.

By September, the level of violence Gerald inflicted on Charlene had intensified, and she left him and moved back in with her parents. For a while, Gerald saw a previous girlfriend, but by November, he and Charlene were back together. On November 1, they borrowed a car so they could have a night out. They both got drunk, and Gerald told Charlene that he wanted to get more love slaves.

Charlene once again agreed, and she drove around shopping centers, with Gerald on the lookout for another victim. During the early hours of November 2, Gerald found his targets—a college-age man and woman.

The victims were Craig Miller and Mary Elizabeth Sowers. Gerald walked up to them with a gun, and to avoid being attacked by the drunken man, they agreed to go with him and Charlene. Before they left the scene, a friend of Craig's leaned into the car window and asked Craig and Mary what they were doing. At this point, Charlene started shouting and quickly drove off. Suspicious of her behavior, the friend took down the license plate number.

Gerald and Charlene drove into El Dorado County, where Gerald told Charlene to stop the car. Craig was ordered to get out of the car, and Gerald shot him three times in the head, killing him. They then drove back to Gerald's apartment with Mary still in the car. Inside the apartment, Charlene sat and watched television while Gerald raped Mary in the bedroom. When he was finished, they got back into the car and headed back out to the country. There, he shot and killed Mary.

The following morning, Gerald and Charlene went back to the home of Charlene's parents, where they were shocked to see the police. Gerald disappeared, and Charlene was left to deal with the police and their questioning. She initially told them they had used Gerald's red Triumph car when they went out, but the detectives pointed out that the Triumph had been parked outside the house all night. She then said they had been so drunk she couldn't remember what car they had used the night before.

Spooked, Gerald decided they had to move Craig's body, which had been left out in the open where it could easily be found. What Gerald was unaware of, was that the body had already been found. When he and Charlene returned to the scene to shift the body, it was gone. So they decided to make a run for it. They headed to Reno, and then caught a bus to Salt Lake City.

Evidence was mounting against Gerald and Charlene. Craig's friend identified Gerald as the man he had last seen with Craig and Mary. Police were then told by Charles Williams that the man they knew as Stephen Feil was, in fact, Gerald Gallego. Furthermore, the bullets recovered from Craig's body matched the ones found in the ceiling of the bar Gerald had worked at.

Charlene contacted her parents asking for money, and they obliged by wiring it to her. The couple moved to Denver, and then to Omaha, Nebraska. Charlene called her parents again, and they reluctantly said they would send her money again. The FBI, however, knew what was happening. When Gerald and Charlene arrived at the Western Union office in Omaha to collect the money, they were arrested instead.

Trial

To ensure she got a better sentence in California, Charlene agreed to plead guilty to the murders of Craig and Mary in exchange for testifying against Gerald. As a result, Charlene was sentenced to sixteen years and eight months in prison. For the charges in Nevada, she also made a deal and pleaded guilty to the second-degree murder of Karen Twiggs and Stacy Redican, and she received another sixteen years and eight months. Prosecutors in Oregon made the decision not to put Charlene on trial and dropped the charges in that state.

Gerald decided to represent himself at his first trial, which was an utter disaster. First, he deferred from making an opening statement until after the prosecution had made their opening statement. Then he decided to cross-examine one of the prosecutor's strongest witnesses, Mercedes Williams, whom he had borrowed the vehicle from the night Craig and Mary were killed. And when Charlene took the stand, he cross-examined her for six days.

Charlene testified that she had gone along with Gerald's plans because she was frightened of him. In response, Gerald brought into evidence a love note she had written him after their arrest. According to Gerald, she was a drug addict, and during his cross-examination, he managed to get her to admit she had had a lesbian affair while in jail.

Next, Gerald put himself on the stand. During questioning, the prosecution called him out on numerous inconsistencies. When it was time to make his closing statement, Gerald admitted the prosecution case had been stronger but asked the jury to believe him on faith. Of course, they didn't, and on June 21, 1983, Gerald received the death penalty.

Gerald was then put on trial in Nevada for the murders of Karen Twiggs, Stacy Redican, Sandra Colley, and Brenda Judd. The bodies of Judd and Colley hadn't been found, so the case was stronger case for Twiggs and Redican. While helping the prosecution, Charlene even showed them a ball of rope in Gerald's car that matched the rope used on Twiggs and Redican.

This trial started on May 23, 1984. Gary Marr, the public defender, was handling his case this time. His main goal was to discredit Charlene. After she detailed the murders of Twiggs and Redican, however, the jury was convinced of Gerald guilt. He was again sentenced to die.

Outcome

In March of 2002, Gerald was shifted from death row the prison system's regional medical center because of his deteriorating health. He died on July 18, 2002, from rectal cancer that had metastasized to his lungs and liver. . He made no final statements and had no visitors before he died.

Charlene was released from prison in July of 1997. Though she agreed to register as a felon once she had settled somewhere, she did not tell the authorities where she was going. She had given birth to a son while she was in prison, and Mercedes Williams ended up raising the child. According to Williams, Charlene had left California at the time of her release and wouldn't be back.

Trivia

Gerald is one of only a few criminals in America to be sentenced to death in two states at the same time.

In a somewhat bizarre coincidence, Gerald's birth father, who had nothing to do with him throughout his life, was executed for killing two police officers.

MICHAEL GARGIULO

Date of birth: February 15, 1976

Aliases/Nicknames: Hollywood Ripper, Chiller Killer

Characteristics: Overkill

Number of victims: 3 - 10

Date of murders: August 14, 1993, 2001- 2008

Date of arrest: June 6, 2008

Victim profile: Tricia Pacaccio, 18; Ashley Ellerin, 22; Maria Bruno

Method of murder: Stabbing

Location: Illinois, California, USA

Status: Awaiting trial.

Background

Gargiulo was raised in a suburb of Chicago and was a member of his high school football team. He went on to have a variety of jobs including plumber, air conditioning repairer, and bar doorman. He is married, and a father.

Around 1997, Gargiulo moved to Los Angeles, and in 1999, he was working the door of the Rainbow Bar & Grill on the Sunset Strip. He had trained in martial arts and boxing, and nobody knew he was leading a double life.

Gargiulo thought of himself as a forensic science expert and was very fond of a book that explained which parts of the body would be the most effective to stab. The "boy next door killer" was stalking and watching potential victims in his neighborhood, and in 1993, he had gone from a voyeur to a murderer.

Murders

On the morning of August 14, 1993, the body of Tricia Pacaccio, eighteen, was found by her father on the back doorstep of her home. She had been stabbed forty-seven times, and Gargiulo happened to be her neighbor. This is the first murder attributed to Gargiulo, and it wasn't the last.

Ashley Ellerin was stabbed to death in her home in Hollywood on February 21, 2001. Her neck had been cut so deeply that the only thing keeping her head attached to her body was the spinal cord.

There were severe cuts and stab wounds to her chest, stomach, and back, some of which were as deep as six inches. A stab wound to her head was made so forcefully that the blade had gone through the skull and removed a chunk of it. Ellerin happened to be dating actor Ashton Kutcher at the time of her death.

Gargiulo allegedly killed Maria Bruno, his neighbor in El Monte, California, on December 1, 2005, by stabbing her seventeen times. He then allegedly attacked another neighbor, in Santa Monica, on April 28, 2008. Michelle Murphy fought back and was able to survive. Gargiulo also left his blood at the scene, and his DNA was extracted.

Trial

On June 6, 2008, Gargiulo was arrested by the Santa Monica Police Department. He was charged with the murder of Ellerin and Bruno. The charge of first-degree murder for the death of Tricia Pacaccio was made against Gargiulo on July 7, 2011, in Cook County. In total, he received three charges of murder and one of attempted murder.

Although he has yet to be linked to any other murders, a statement Gargiulo made while in jail led investigators to believe that there could be more victims. Gargiulo said that just because his DNA was present and ten women had been killed, didn't mean he had murdered them.

The trial for the murders of Ellerin and Bruno and the attempted murder of Murphy began on May 2, 2019. The Deputy District Attorney Dan Akemon said in his opening statement, "His hobby was plotting the perfect opportunity to attack women with a knife in and around their homes."

There is a list of almost two hundred and fifty potential witnesses that could be called during the trial, including Ashton Kutcher, who has just recently given his testimony.

Outcome

The trial is ongoing, and Gargiulo also faces a second trial for the murder of Pacaccio. There has been a strong media buzz around the case because of Kutcher's involvement and testimony.

If Gargiulo is found guilty, he will likely receive the maximum penalty of life in prison without the possibility of parole.

Trivia

Ellerin and Kutcher were meant to go on their first date the night of her murder. They were going to attend a Grammy event. Kutcher was late picking her up, and when she didn't respond to his knock at the door, he figured she was angry with him, so he left, thinking she had probably already gone out. He did notice, however, that there was a red stain on the carpet, but he thought it might have been red wine that had been spilled.

CARLTON GARY

Date of birth: September 24, 1950

Aliases/Nicknames: The Stocking Strangler

Characteristics: Rape

Number of victims: 7 +

Date of murders: 1975 - 1978

Date of arrest: May 3, 1984

Victim profile: Ferne Jackson, 60; Jean Dimenstein, 71; Florence Scheible, 89; Martha Thurmond, 69; Kathleen Woodruff, 74; Mildred Borom, 78; Janet Cofer, 61,

Method of murder: Strangulation, often with stockings

Location: New York, Georgia, USA

Status: Sentenced to death in Georgia on August 27, 1986. Executed on March 15, 2018.

Background

Gary was born in Columbus, Georgia, on September 24, 1950. From the time of his birth, his father wanted nothing to do with him, and he never provided any form of financial support to Gary's mother. Gary did meet his father when he was twelve years old, but the man was never in his life. His mother was very poor, and they moved frequently as a result. There often was not enough food, and Gary was malnourished during a large portion of his childhood. He had two aunts who worked for wealthy elderly women, and his mother often left him in their care.

When he was in elementary school, Gary had an accident in the playground where he was knocked unconscious and suffered serious trauma to his head. In his teens, he began using drugs and became a heavy drug abuser. When Gary was between fourteen and eighteen years of age, he committed multiple crimes, including assault, arson, and robbery and was arrested a number of times.

Gary later married and had two children. He moved to Albany, New York in 1970, where he planned to become a famous singer. But he carried on committing crimes instead.

Murders

Not long after Gary had moved to Albany in May of 1970, Marion Brewer, an elderly woman, was attacked and robbed while in her hotel room. Then, two months later, Nellie Farmer, eighty-five, was attacked in her apartment. She was robbed and then strangled to death.

Gary next attempted to attack another elderly woman, but this failed, and he was soon arrested. When his fingerprints were checked, they matched one that had been left at the murder scene of Farmer. He admitted he had been involved in the robbery of Farmer but that another man, John Lee Mitchell, had actually killed her. He testified in court against Mitchell and, despite there being no other evidence linking Mitchell to the crime, he was charged with the murder. For his part in the robbery, Gary was sentenced to time in the Onondaga County Correctional Institution.

In 1975, Gary was paroled, and he went to live in Syracuse, New York. Soon after, two elderly women were attacked. Both were raped then strangled; only one of them survived. The survivor wasn't able to identify Gary, however, because it had been dark. Only four days separated these two attacks.

Although Gary wasn't charged with any of the attacks, he returned to prison for robbery and parole violation. He managed to escape on August 22, 1977, after sawing through the bars of his cell. Gary went back to Columbus, Georgia.

A month later, on September 16, 1977, Ferne Jackson, sixty, was beaten, raped, and strangled with a nylon stocking at her home in Columbus. Just nine days later, Jean Dimenstein, seventy-one, was raped and strangled to death, followed by Florence Scheible on October 21, and then Martha Thurmond on October 23. Just five days later, Kathleen Woodruff, seventy-four, was strangled to death after being raped.

On February 12, 1978, Ruth Schwab triggered the alarm beside her bed when she was attacked, and Gary fled from her home. Rather than call it quits, Gary went to another house two blocks away and raped Mildred Borom, seventy-eight, before he strangled her to death. The last known victim was Janet Cofer, sixty-one, who was killed in the same manner on April 20, 1978.

An announcement was made by police that the suspect was believed to be an African-American man. Then, William Henry Hance, who called himself the "Chairman of the Forces of Evil," stated that he was going to murder black women if the Stocking Strangler wasn't caught. It turned out he was just trying to cover up his own murders by blaming white vigilantes. Hance was arrested on April 4, but when Cofer was murdered while he was in custody, it became clear that he wasn't the Stocking Strangler.

Gary was arrested for robbery in December of 1978, in Gaffney, South Carolina. He confessed to the robbery and was sentenced to twenty-one years. But, he escaped in 1983 and spent a year at large before he was caught again. During this time, evidence related to a gun that had been traced to Gary, as well as a fingerprint match, made police realize that Gary was the serial killer they had been hunting.

Trial

On May 5, 1984, Gary was indicted for the seven murders. The jury found him guilty of three murders. The District Attorney maintained throughout the trial that only one man was guilty of all seven murders, and he used the details from the other cases to show a pattern of behavior demonstrated by Gary.

Gary was sentenced to death.

Outcome

Gary's last appeal was denied on December 1, 2009. His execution date was set for December 16. A stay of execution was requested on December 15, but this was denied. Then, just hours before he was set to die, the Georgia Supreme Court halted the execution to determine if DNA tests should be done to confirm his guilt or innocence. Following the hearing, a new execution date was set for March 15, 2018.

The execution went ahead on this date, and Gary was put to death by lethal injection. He did not make a final statement and was declared dead at 10:33 p.m.

Trivia

The night before his execution, Gary declined a special meal and said he wanted to have the same as the other prisoners. He received what is called "the institutional tray," which consisted of a hot dog, grilled hamburger, coleslaw, beans, and a soda.

SEAN VINCENT GILLIS

Date of birth: June 24, 1962

Aliases/Nicknames: Nil

Characteristics: Rape, mutilation

Number of victims: 8

Date of murders: 1994 - 2004

Date of arrest: April 29, 2004

Victim profile: Katherine Hall, 29; Johnnie Mae Williams, 45; Donna Bennett Johnston, 43; Ann Bryan, 81; Hardee Schmidt, 52; Joyce Williams, 36; Lillian Robinson, 52; Marilyn Nevils, 38

Method of murder: Strangulation, stabbing with knife

Location: Baton Rouge, Louisiana, USA

Status: Sentenced to life in prison in August 2007.

Background

Gillis was born to parents Norman and Yvonne on June 24, 1962. An alcoholic, Norman also had issues with mental illness, and at one point held a gun to Gillis's head; eventually, Norman left the family and spent time in and out of mental institutions. Despite the ups and downs with his father, and being raised by his mother alone, Gillis had a fairly normal childhood. Beginning when he was about ten years old, however, neighbors often described Gillis as a bully toward other children.

As an adult, Gillis was not fond of working; he preferred to stay home and watch pornography on the computer. He was particularly fond of videos and photographs that showed rape, killing, and dismemberment of females. He became so interested in computers that he went to community college and got a certificate in the field.

His mother moved to Atlanta, Georgia in 1992 when she was offered a better job. Gillis didn't want to go with her, and witnesses would later observe him yelling and screaming at the sky, cursing his mother for leaving him. At one point, he was apprehended while peeping into the windows of a female neighbor. He told officers he was looking for his cat.

Gillis met Terri Lemoine two years later, and they began dating. They moved in together in 1995, and though she came to realize Gillis had an addiction to watching and looking at pornography on the computer, she claimed she was unaware of the depraved material he was actually looking at.

From the time he was seventeen years old, Gillis had come into contact with the police on many occasions, but it was always for minor issues. These included possession of marijuana, traffic citations, driving under the influence, and contempt of court. There was nothing to suggest he would become a violent and sadistic killer.

Murders

In March of 1994, Gillis entered the retirement home where Ann Bryan, eighty-one, lived, in Baton Rouge. His plan was to rape her, but she screamed when he tried to touch her. To shut her up, he slit her throat. Then he stabbed her fifty times. This was Gillis' first murder.

On January 4, 1999, Gillis lured prostitute Katherine Hall into his car, under the pretense of wanting oral sex. Instead, he tried to strangle her with a zip tie. When she struggled and tried to get out of the car, he stabbed her to death. Then he undressed Hall and mutilated her body.

Four months later, he saw Hardee Schmidt jogging in Baton Rouge and began to stalk her. He did this for three weeks before deciding to take action. First, he struck her with his car, which knocked her into a ditch on the roadside. Gillis placed a zip tie around her neck, tightening it without strangling her, and transported her to an isolated place. Then he raped her and killed her. He left her body in the back of a truck for two days before dumping it.

Joyce Williams was the next victim. Gillis killed her on November 12, and then mutilated her at his home. Gillis engaged in cannibalism with the body, eating her nipples after he had cut them off. Her body was dumped, and wouldn't be found until 2000.

Three more victims were murdered between 2000 and 2003. His final victim, Donna Johnston, forty-three, was killed on February 26, 2004. Johnston was raped and horrifically mutilated, with one arm dismembered and a nipple removed. She had been strangled to death, and Gillis ate her nipple. He took multiple photographs of her body before he dumped it.

At that time, another serial killer, Derrick Todd Lee, was active in the area. A task force was created on March 3 to look into some of the murders; it was found that several of the murders couldn't be linked to Lee. Authorities now knew there was another serial killer in action.

At the site where Johnston's body was found, tire tracks were discovered, and they were matched to a particular model of vehicle. Owners of that model were interviewed by police, and their DNA samples were taken. Gillis was one of those questioned, and he had his DNA swabbed. When a match came back to hairs found on two of the victims, Gillis was arrested.

The day of his arrest, he confessed to the murders he had committed, and police undertook a search of his home. There they found newspaper clippings about the murder of Carrie Yoder, Lee's final victim. Gillis also had a file on his computer called "DTL," the initials of Lee, and in the file were news stories and information about the murders Lee had committed.

Investigators also found photographs of Johnston's mutilated corpse, including ones of her body in the trunk of his vehicle. Photographs of other victims were found as well.

Gillis was charged with the murders of Katherine Hall and Johnnie Williams, killed in October of 2003, and Donna Johnston.

Trial

On July 21, 2008, Gillis went on trial for the murders of Hall, Williams, and Johnston. He was found guilty and, after the jury had deadlocked during the penalty stage, he was given a life sentence. He had also pleaded guilty the year before to second-degree murder for the killing of Joyce Williams. On February 17, 2009, Gillis pleaded guilty to the murder of Marilyn Nevils and received another life sentence.

Outcome

Gillis was incarcerated at the Louisiana State Penitentiary. Because of his life sentences, and the fact that there is no parole period, he will never be released and will spend the rest of his life behind bars.

Trivia

In letters between Gillis and a longtime friend of Johnston's, Tammie Purpera, Gillis explained her murder with some level of remorse:

"She was so drunk it only took about a minute and a half to succumb to unconsciousness and then death. Honestly, her last words were I can't breathe. I still puzzle over the post mortem dismemberment and cutting. There must be something deep in my subconscious that really needs that kind of macabre action."

Gillis claimed it was stress that drove him to kill.

He says he is "pure evil" and "beyond sorry" for committing the murders.

In the series *The Devil You Know*, the story of Gillis is featured in an episode titled "A Twisted Mind."

His story was also told in the series *Dead of Night*, in the episode called "The Graveyard Shift."

Gillis used to lie on his front lawn and bark at the moon. This frightened his neighbors, so they avoided him.

DAVID ALAN GORE AND FRED WATERFIELD

David Alan Gore

Date of birth: August 21, 1953

Aliases/Nicknames: The Killing Cousins

Characteristics: Alcoholic, kidnapping, rape

Number of victims: 6

Date of murders: 1981, 1983

Date of arrest: July 26, 1983

Victim profile: Hisang Huang Ling, 48; Ying Hua Ling, 17; Judy Kay Daley, 35; Angelica Lavallee, 14; Barbara Ann Byer, 14; Lynn Elliott, 17

Method of murder: Shooting, strangulation

Location: Florida, USA

Status: Sentenced to death on March 16, 1984. Resentenced December 8, 1992. Executed by lethal injection on April 12, 2012.

Fred Waterfield

Date of birth: September 29, 1952

Aliases/Nicknames: The Killing Cousins

Characteristics: Kidnapping, rape

Number of victims: 6

Date of murders: 1981, 1983

Date of arrest: July 26, 1983

Victim profile: Hisang Huang Ling, 48; Ying Hua Ling, 17; Judy Kay Daley, 35; Angelica Lavallee, 14; Barbara Ann Byer, 14; Lynn Elliott, 17

Method of murder: Shooting, strangulation

Location: Florida, USA

Status: Life imprisonment.

Background

David Gore

Born in Florida in 1953, Gore later developed two obsessions: women and firearms. His first job was as an attendant at a gas station, but he was fired when his boss discovered a hole had been drilled into the women's bathroom so Gore could spy on them.

As an auxiliary sheriff's deputy, Gore would sometimes use his badge when committing his crimes. He also worked at a citrus grove as a caretaker, and this secluded area provided him with a place to later rape and kill his victims.

Fred Waterfield

Born in 1952, Waterfield grew up in New Jersey. He played football at high school, but little else is known about his childhood and youth. He was a bad-tempered individual, and though he was popular and was always surrounded by people, his temper drove friends away. Waterfield also enjoyed violent sex, and when he and his cousin Gore talked, they discovered they both had thought about the same thing - rape and murder.

Murders

On February 19, 1981, Gore used his police badge to lure Ying Hua Ling, seventeen, into his truck. The two men then drove the girl to her house, where they found her mother, Hsiang Huang Ling, forty-eight. They kidnapped both mother and daughter, and while Hsiang was tied to a tree, slowly choking to death, they raped her daughter. Once the women were dead, their bodies were dismembered and placed into oil drums, which Gore and Waterfield then buried.

The next victim was Judith Daley, thirty-five. On July 15, 1981, while her car was parked at the beach, Gore disabled the vehicle so it wouldn't start. He then offered her a ride to a telephone, so she could call for assistance. Instead, Gore drove to a secluded spot where Waterfield was waiting. They both raped Daley and, after she had been killed, her body was dumped in a swampy area.

The following week, Gore tried to kidnap a teenage girl but failed, despite showing her his badge. A complaint was made to the police by the girl's father, and his badge was taken away from him. Within days, Gore was seen hiding in the back seat of a woman's car by police. They found he was carrying a pistol, handcuffs, and a police scanner. Gore was charged and convicted of armed trespassing. He received a sentence of five years but was out again in March of 1983.

Two months after his release, Gore and Waterfield found their next targets. Angelica Lavallee, fourteen, and Barbara Ann Byer, fourteen, were hitchhiking when the killing cousins came upon them. The girls were kidnapped, raped, and killed, and both bodies were dismembered.

On July 26, 1983, Gore and Waterfield picked up two more hitchhikers who were on their way to Wabasso Beach. Lynn Elliott, seventeen, and Regan Martin, fourteen, students of Vero Beach High School, were taken to a house that was owned by Gore's parents. On their way there though, Waterfield had seen his sister, which unsettled him, and he left, leaving Gore alone with the two girls. Gore tied both of the girls up and put them in separate rooms. As he raped Martin, Elliott managed to escape, despite having her hands tied behind her back. The naked girl ran down the driveway and slipped, allowing Gore to catch up with her. She fought constantly as he tried to drag her back into the house, so Gore shot her twice in the head.

A boy riding past on his bicycle witnessed the whole incident. He immediately notified the police, and they swooped into the area. A standoff lasting ninety minutes ensued until Gore finally gave up. Martin, still in the house, was located in the attic with electrical cords binding her legs, handcuffs on her wrists, and completely naked.

During Gore's interrogation, he admitted he had killed five victims and was quick to implicate his cousin, Waterfield, who was promptly arrested.

Trial

A grand jury charged Gore with first-degree murder, two counts of sexual battery, and two counts of kidnapping, on August 10, 1983. A petition to move his trial from Vero Beach to St. Petersburg, Florida was granted on January 6, 1984.

On March 16, 1984, Gore was convicted of murder and received the death penalty.

Waterfield was tried and convicted in January of 1985 for the murders of Byer and Lavallee and was sentenced to two life sentences to be served consecutively.

Gore's death sentence had been handed down after the jury voted 11-1. Normally, the vote has to be unanimous. Following an appeal, the Supreme Court announced on August 22, 1985, that the conviction and the death penalty would stand.

Further appeals were lodged, but the death sentence for Gore continued to be upheld.

Outcome

On April 12, 2012, Gore was executed by lethal injection. His final statement was as follows:

"I would like to say to Mr. and Mrs. Elliott that I am truly sorry for my part in the death of your daughter. I wish above all else my death could bring her back. I am not the same man today that I was 28 years ago. When I accepted Jesus Christ as my Savior, I become a New Creature in Christ, and I know God has truly forgiven me for my past sins. I am able to face today because I know Christ lives in me. The Apostle Paul said 'for to die is to gain.' So I do not fear today but truly look forward to spending eternity with Christ. Mr. and Mrs. Elliott, I have prayed for you both and pray y'all can find the peace that only Christ can give. Last, I just want to say I have had a tremendous amount of remorse and pray you and your family can forgive me. God bless all of y'all".

Waterfield remains in prison, still claiming he is innocent. He has a lot of supporters, including his family, who believe he should not have been found guilty, and that it is a terrible injustice that he is in prison.

Was Waterfield really an innocent man in all of this? A lot of information is available on Gore, and he features predominantly in any literature that has been written about the murders. But there are some who believe that the real leader of the two was actually Waterfield. He was the one, after all, who could draw people to him, whereas Gore was always in the background. Why would this be any different when it came to their crimes? This is certainly something to ponder.

Trivia

For his last meal before his execution, Gore chose fried chicken, french fries, and butter pecan ice cream.

"All of a sudden I realized I had just done something that separated me from the human race and it was something that could never be undone, I realized from that point on I could never be like normal people." *- Gore*

"You constantly think about getting caught, but the rush is worth the risk." *- Gore*

MARK GOUDEAU

Date of birth: September 6, 1964

Aliases/Nicknames: The Baseline Killer

Characteristics: Rape, robbery

Number of victims: 9

Date of murders: 2005 - 2006

Date of arrest: September 7, 2006

Victim profile: Georgia Thompson, 19; Tina Washington, 39; Romelia Vargas, 38; Mirna Palma-Roman, 34; Liliana Sanchez-Cabrera, 20; Chao Chou, 23; Kristin Nicole Gibbons, 26; Sophia Nunez, Carmen Miranda, 37

Method of murder: Shooting

Location: Phoenix, Arizona, USA

Status: Sentenced to 438 years in prison on December 14, 2007. Sentenced to death in 2011.

Background

Goudeau was born in Phoenix, Arizona in 1964, the twelfth child in a family of thirteen children. His father Willie was an attendant at a car dealer lot, and his mother Alberta was a maid. Willie was a strict parent, and some of the siblings claimed he was a verbally abusive alcoholic. Others say the home was a peaceful one, so the stories are conflicting. Willie and Alberta later divorced, and the children stayed with Alberta. When Goudeau was twelve years old, Alberta died. Goudeau was good at sports in high school and played for the school football team. Due to a lack of credits, he never graduated from high school.

Goudeau was first arrested in 1982, along with one of his brothers, for the rape of a young woman. However, no charges were filed. In 1987, he was charged with trespassing, and the following year, he was charged with driving under the influence of alcohol.

In August of 1989, Goudeau kidnapped a woman, raped and bludgeoned her, and was arrested and charged. He claimed he had only engaged in oral sex with the woman, and that two others had raped and assaulted her. He received a sentence of fifteen years for the abduction, and because he had also been charged with a robbery that occurred in 1990, he received another sentence of twenty-one years.

Goudeau served thirteen years in prison and was released on parole in 2004. Married by now to Wendy Carr, he moved to an area that would later become the Baseline Killer crime location. Goudeau was very well-liked by his neighbors, despite them knowing he had been in prison. He began working for a construction company, and a year after his prison release, the Baseline Killer crimes started.

Murders

Goudeau didn't commit murders right away; a number of violent sexual attacks and robberies led up to the killings. On August 6, 2005, he forced three teenagers, one of them a boy, behind a church near Baseline Road and sexually molested the two girls. Several days later, on August 14, he robbed and sexually assaulted another victim.

The first murder occurred on September 8, 2005, and was quickly followed on September 15 by a sexual assault. Five days later, on September 20, Goudeau approached two sisters as they walked home from a park. One of the women was pregnant, and Goudeau sexually assaulted one sister while pushing the gun into the pregnant woman's belly.

A robbery was committed on September 28. That same night, Goudeau committed a second robbery and also sexually assaulted the victim.

There were no further crimes committed by Goudeau until November 3, 2005; once again, he struck twice in the same night. The first crime he committed was a robbery. He walked into a store and held the staff at gunpoint, demanding money. He left the store with seven hundred twenty dollars. Within ten minutes of leaving the store, he came across a woman who was putting items into a donation receptacle in a parking lot across the road. He abducted her and forced her into her own car. He then sexually assaulted her and ordered her to drive to the next corner to drop him off.

A few days later, on November 7, Goudeau committed three robberies. At Las Brasas, a Mexican restaurant, he held four people at gunpoint, demanding their money. Then he went to the Little Caesar's Pizza restaurant next door and robbed the three people who were inside. After leaving Little Caesar's, he robbed three people on the street. He fired a bullet into the air as he fled the scene.

A month passed. Then, on December 12, Goudeau attacked Tina Washington, thirty-nine, as she was walking home from work. She was killed by a gunshot to the head, and a witness saw a man with a gun standing over her body behind a restaurant. The next day, Goudeau robbed a woman at 4:00 p.m. on E. South Mountain Avenue in Phoenix.

The next homicide occurred on February 20, 2006. Goudeau shot and killed Romelia Vargas, thirty-eight, and Mirna Palma-Roman, thirty-four. Their bodies were found inside their food truck. Police didn't initially link these murders to the Baseline Killer, believing instead that the killings were related to drugs. They were officially linked to the Baseline Killer in July of 2006.

On March 15, 2006, two more victims were shot and killed. Liliana Sanchez-Cabrera, twenty, and Chao Chou were both employees at Yoshi's Restaurant and were on their way home together when Goudeau attacked. The body of Sanchez-Cabrera was found in another restaurant's parking lot, and Chou's body was found a mile away.

A businessman saw bloodstains on the gravel of a parking lot on March 29, 2006 and notified police. They searched, but found nothing. A week later, while investigating a terrible odor in the area, the businessman found the decomposed body of Kristin Nicole Gibbons. She had been killed by a gunshot to the head.

A woman was abducted on May 1, 2006, by a man in a Halloween mask. He held her at gunpoint as he sexually assaulted her.

On June 29, 2006, Carmen Miranda, thirty-seven, was at a self-serve carwash and using her mobile phone when she was abducted. Her body was found behind a nearby barbershop; she had been shot in the head. This time, the crime was captured on closed-circuit television.

In August of 2006, while Goudeau was on parole, information was given to the police about Goudeau as a possible suspect. The Northeast Parole Office suggested that Goudeau matched the identikit sketch of the Baseline Killer. This resulted in police searching Goudeau's home, where they found a toy gun and a ski mask. They subsequently found further items that linked him to the Baseline Killer crimes.

Trial

On September 4, 2006, Goudeau was arrested for the attack on the sisters in Phoenix after DNA testing matched him to the crime. His trial took place in September of 2007, and he faced nineteen charges related to the attack on the sisters. He was found guilty, and on December 14, 2007, he was sentenced to four hundred thirty-eight years in prison.

Following his trial for the murders, Goudeau was given a death sentence.

Outcome

A story was published in April of 2009 that revealed the Phoenix Police Department had been in possession of Goudeau's DNA before he went on his murder and robbery spree. It just hadn't been analyzed.

His DNA had actually been on file since 2004.

Goudeau is still on death row awaiting his execution.

Trivia

Goudeau was known to wear disguises, including ski masks and Halloween masks. He would often pretend he was a homeless person or a drug addict.

His wife, Wendy Carr, claimed police had arrested the wrong man: "My husband is innocent. This is a huge miscarriage of justice. And they have an innocent man in prison. This is all a mistake. He shouldn't be in prison for something he didn't do."

GWENDOLYN GRAHAM AND CATHERINE MAY WOOD

Gwendolyn Graham

Date of birth: August 6, 1963

Aliases/Nicknames: The Lethal Lovers

Characteristics: Nurse's aide - killed patients in a lover's pact with another woman

Number of victims: 5

Date of murders: January - April 1987

Date of arrest: December 1988

Victim profile: Belle Burkhard, 74; Marguerite Chambers, 60; Edith Cook, 97; Myrtle Luce, 95; Mae Mason, 79

Method of murder: Smothering

Location: Kent County, Michigan, USA

Status: Sentenced to life in prison without parole on November 3, 1989.

Catherine May Wood

Date of birth: March 7, 1962

Aliases/Nicknames: The Lethal Lovers

Characteristics: Nurse's aide - killed patients in a lover's pact with another woman

Number of victims: 1 - 5

Date of murders: January - April 1987

Date of arrest: December 1988

Victim profile: Belle Burkhard, 74; Marguerite Chambers, 60; Edith Cook, 97; Myrtle Luce, 95; Mae Mason, 79

Method of murder: Smothering

Location: Kent County, Michigan, USA

Status: Pled guilty. Sentenced to 20 to 40 years in prison in September 1989.

Background

In 1984, Wood was overweight and depressed, and she had no maternal affection toward her young child. Her home was neglected, and her marriage had suffered. She once had told her husband she had wondered what it would be like to stab somebody.

Wood demanded a divorce in 1986 and started a series of relationships with other women. At the same time, Graham started working at the Alpine Manor Nursing Home alongside Wood. Before long, they became lovers. They moved in together and managed to arrange their work schedules so they could work the same shifts.

Wood and Graham started to experiment sexually, and they indulged in bondage and sexual asphyxia. They would determine who would be the submissive partner in their sexual exploits by playing word games, with the loser taking on the submissive role. At one point, the idea of murdering patients was discussed while they were playing a word game. The women called it the "Murder Game," and they decided to use the initials of their victims to spell out "murder." When they talked about committing murder, both women found it sexually stimulating.

Murders

According to Wood, Graham entered the room of a woman with Alzheimer's disease in January of 1987 and smothered her using a washcloth. Wood stayed outside the room and acted as a lookout, ready to signal to Graham if anyone came along. The female patient, weakened by illness, was unable to fight back. There was no autopsy performed as the death appeared to the doctors to be natural.

Wood later claimed that Graham used murder to relieve her tension and that both of them felt that murder (a secret between them) would prevent the other from leaving.

Four more patients were killed by Graham over the next few months. They ranged in age from sixty-five to ninety-seven, and all were incapacitated by Alzheimer's disease. Wood and Graham found it difficult to carry out their initial plan of using their victims' initials to spell murder, so instead, they began counting each kill as a "day." This came from a poem Wood gave to Graham, which ended with, "You'll be mine forever and five days."

The relationship between Wood and Graham ended when Graham started seeing a nursing aide who also worked at the nursing home. Graham and the aide moved to Texas, and she began working at a hospital where her role involved the care of infants.

In 1988, Wood's ex-husband went to the police and told them the details of the murders given to him by Wood. She was subsequently brought into custody and questioned intensively over a number of interviews. She eventually leaked snippets of information about the murders, blaming Graham as the actual mastermind of the plan and naming her the killer.

For the investigation, two of the victims were exhumed and reexamined, but there was no evidence of homicide detected. Other victims had been cremated. Based on the information given to police about the murders, however, the medical examiner listed the deaths as homicides anyway.

The police issued warrants for Wood and Graham, and on December 4, 1988, Wood was arrested in Walker. Graham was then arrested in Tyler, Texas. Both women were charged with two murders.

Trial

Wood was able to plea bargain to get a reduced sentence during the trial; she continued to claim it was Graham who had planned the murders and carried them out while Wood was just a lookout. Graham stated she was innocent, and that the murders were a "mind game" devised by Wood. Even though there was no physical evidence, Graham's girlfriend testified that she had admitted killing five patients.

On November 3, 1989, Graham was found guilty of five counts of murder and one charge of conspiracy to commit murder. She was sentenced to five life terms in prison.

Because of her plea bargain, Wood was convicted of one count of second-degree murder and one of conspiracy to commit second-degree murder. On each count, she received a sentence of twenty years and was first eligible for parole in March of 2005.

Outcome

On December 18, 2018, Wood said she would stay incarcerated until an appeal regarding her parole was settled. She stated, "I can just stay right here until the appeal is done. That doesn't need to be made a decision. I have no problem with that."

She further said there was no point in setting her free because if the appeal didn't go in her favor, she would have to go back to prison anyway.

Trivia

The true crime book *Forever and Five Days* by Lowell Cauffiel was based on the case.

In two episodes of *The Serial Killers*, both Graham and Wood were interviewed about their crimes and their relationship.

Graham and Wood were featured on an episode of *Snapped: Killer Couples*.

A highly adapted version of their crimes was told in *American Horror Story*, the television series. They were depicted as Bridget and Miranda Jane.

On October 5, 2008, Wood posted two photographs of herself along with her physical attributes (six foot, two hundred eighty pounds, 44-38-48) on cowtowninfo.com (formerly jailbabes.com). She also included the following advertisement for a pen pal:

Teach me! I've been incarcerated for two decades. I go to the parole board soon, and I need someone who's kind and patient to teach me about the exciting new things in the world. I'm looking for a friend, male or female, to teach me everything I forgot. Are you honest? I am honest and non-judgmental. We can talk about anything and everything. I've never done drugs, and I don't smoke. I like to play and have fun. Do you have time for a good friend?

HARRISON GRAHAM

Date of birth: October 9, 1958

Aliases/Nicknames: Marty

Characteristics: Drug abuser, low mentality, necrophilia

Number of victims: 7

Date of murders: 1986 - 1987

Date of arrest: August 17, 1987 - Surrendered

Victim profile: Cynthia Brooks, 27; Valerie Jamison, 25; Mary Jeter Mathis, 36; Barbara Mahoney, 22; Robin DeShazor, 29; Sandra Garvin, 33; Patricia Franklin, 24

Method of murder: Strangulation

Location: Philadelphia, Pennsylvania, USA

Status: Sentenced to life imprisonment, followed by six electrocutions (to prevent parole) in May 1988. Deemed incompetent to be executed on December 20, 2003.

Background

As a young child, trouble at home drove Graham out onto the streets, where he felt more loved than he had with his family. He became a prostitute, and his pimp was also his lover. Graham began using drugs, and would later allegedly sell drugs to boost his finances. At one point, when Graham was a teenager, his mother had some sort of spiritual awakening, and she dragged him back from the streets, preaching to him about the immoral facets of his lifestyle.

As an adult, Graham was well-liked by his neighbors who described him as easygoing. The women in his building weren't afraid of him at all, and Graham had done some handyman work for some of them, they were that comfortable with him.

Up until the summer of 1987, those around Graham had no inkling of who he really was, and what he did behind closed doors.

Murders

Residents at Graham's apartment complex started to complain about a foul smell in the summer of 1987. Police responded and made a horrific discovery behind a door that had been nailed shut by Graham. The decomposing bodies of female victims were hidden behind the door.

An officer who was the first to respond to the complaint commented that he could smell death the minute he entered the building. Following the smell, he went upstairs to a third-floor apartment. Inside, the front room contained moldy newspapers, food containers, a high pile of filthy clothing, and dried feces. Someone had drawn a naked woman on one of the walls, and there were words written in what looked like blood.

When the officer reached the door that had been nailed shut, he could see a body through the keyhole. At first, he thought it was a live person, and he demanded they open the door. When there was no sign of movement, he called for backup. The door was pried open and on a mattress was the body of a black woman, bloated and decomposing. Beside the mattress was another body, a second female.

At first, they weren't sure if the women had died from drug overdoses or if they had been murdered. As officers continued to search through the disgusting apartment, a third body was found, this time in a skeletal condition. Clearly, whatever had been happening in this apartment had been going on for quite a while.

A fourth body was found wrapped in sheets, which essentially mummified the corpse. Then, between two mattresses, police found a fifth body. The body was so badly decomposed that it was impossible to identify whether it had been a male or a female. A sixth body was found in a closet amongst the garbage.

Because of the weather and temperatures that day, authorities decided to call off the search for the night and start again the next morning. On August 10, investigators began searching the area outside of the building. On top of the building, a leg and a foot were found. Five days later, when the search had broadened to another apartment complex down the street, a body was found in the basement, wrapped similarly to one that had been found in the apartment.

Police were quick to identify Graham as the number one suspect, as the bodies had been found in his apartment. His photograph was published in newspapers, and everyone was on the search for him. On August 17, Graham's mother received a phone call from him, asking her to meet him and bring him some food. Instead, she convinced him to turn himself in. The police were notified of his location, and they arrested him on a street corner where he was waiting for them.

Trial

While Graham was being interrogated, he wrote a confession that was ten pages long. However, his public defender, Joel S. Moldovsky, claimed during the arraignment that Graham was suffering from mental illness. Moldovsky wasn't convinced that Graham was capable of making his confession. Also, despite Graham's mother being present during the interrogation, he claimed Graham wasn't told he could have an attorney present.

Graham was assessed by a psychiatrist who cited his IQ was only sixty-three, which is usually indicative of mental incompetence. When added to Graham's substance abuse issues, the laws of Philadelphia meant Graham was incapable. According to the psychiatrist, Graham suffered from psychosis, chronic paranoia, auditory hallucinations, and blackouts because of the drug abuse. It was also found by a psychologist that Graham was incompetent in basic academics, including telling the time.

Moldovsky continued to argue Graham was mentally unwell and claimed he suffered from multiple personality disorder. According to Moldovsky, Graham would regularly speak in a second and third personality. One of his personalities, "Marty," was the easygoing handyman, popular with his neighbors, who liked his mother, was religious, and a heterosexual. "Junior," another personality, was like a child and would be seen carrying around his Cookie Monster stuffed toy. A third personality, "Frank," hated women. It was Frank who killed the women and engaged in necrophilia.

Before the judge ruled on the mental health claim, a witness named Paula was brought in. She claimed she had been living with Graham on and off for three years. According to Paula, Graham often strangled her during sex. She said he had bragged to her about killing Robin DeShazor and having sex with her corpse. Paula said she was so frightened he would do the same to her she couldn't leave him. After all, she said, Graham told her he had killed DeShazor because she had tried to leave him.

But there were discrepancies between Paula's claims and the actual facts of DeShazor's murder. She hadn't been strangled, as Paula stated Graham had told her. She was beaten to death. Also, there was no history of Graham ever having a long-term relationship with anyone.

Graham told the judge on March 8 that he wasn't the killer and that someone else had done it. He waived his right to a jury trial and left his fate in the hands of the judge. Graham was found guilty of all counts of first-degree murder and abuse of a corpse. Graham showed no reaction when he heard the verdict, but asked that he get his Cookie Monster back.

In May, the judge ruled that he would sentence Graham to six death sentences. However, he would sentence Graham to serve life in prison first, which meant he would not be executed. Graham was also sentenced to a further six sentences of seven to fourteen years to be served consecutively.

Outcome

In 1994, the Supreme Court conducted a routine review and decided Graham's sentence was illegal and unethical. A ruling was made that Graham's sentence of life be overturned, and the death sentence be implemented. An execution date of December 7, 1998 was set. Ironically, the same judge who originally sentenced Graham was then responsible for deciding whether the execution should go ahead or not, and he granted a stay.

After a number of appeals, the Supreme Court banned mentally retarded inmates from being executed after 2002. At first, Graham didn't meet the mental retardation criteria as set out in the ban. Although his IQ was below seventy, he was a functioning adult. However, he was saved by the criteria created by the American Psychiatric Association that stated if mental illness began before a person was eighteen years old, then an execution could not take place.

Graham still resides in prison and will be not released. He has been described as being "nonviolent" throughout his incarceration. He attained a religious minister's certificate while in prison and continues to practice his faith.

Trivia

Graham took his Cookie Monster stuffed toy, a water bottle, and some clothing when he left the apartment.

He would often go for long walks and occasionally played basketball with the neighborhood kids. Then he would entertain the kids with his Cookie Monster toy.

He was described as a loner by neighbors, and they said he would go a bit crazy after drinking alcohol.

Graham was seen talking to his Cookie Monster toy all the time.

Following Graham's guilty conviction, Moldovsky later told reporters, "I assume he knows he was found guilty, but I'm not sure."

RICKY LEE GREEN

Date of birth: December 27, 1960

Aliases/Nicknames: Nil

Characteristics: Bisexual, rape, sexual mutilation

Number of victims: 4 - 12

Date of murders: 1985 - 1986

Date of arrest: April 27, 1989

Victim profile: Jeffrey Davis, 16; Steven Fefferman, 28; Sandra Bailey, 27; Betty Jo Monroe, 28

Method of murder: Stabbing with a knife, beating with a hammer

Location: Tarrant County, Texas, USA

Status: Executed by lethal injection in Texas on October 9, 1997.

Background

As a young child, Green was abused by both his father and his grandfather throughout his childhood. When he was six years old, his father made him run from the house while he shot at him with a BB gun. No matter how fast Green ran, he was always struck by the small metal BB's. His father would then tell him he should learn to run faster so he wouldn't get hit.

Green was also subjected to other abuse, including sexual, verbal, and physical abuse. He was constantly told by his father that he was no good and "never would be." Every time Green was sent to stay with his grandfather, he was sodomized. As a young boy, Green couldn't understand why his family would hurt him if they were meant to love him.

Green got married to Mary Francis on February 18, 1984. To Green, Mary was the closest thing to family he had ever had. But the relationship was based entirely on sex, so it wasn't surprising that the marriage began to fail after just two months. Green believed his wife was sleeping with other men and became extremely unhappy. He began drinking alcohol a lot and would drive around town to escape reality at home.

One evening after drinking heavily for a long period of time, Green pulled a knife on Mary when she returned home from work. He raped her, and when Green passed out, Mary grabbed her things and left. She never returned.

Green wasn't alone for long. Within a few weeks he met Sharon Dollar, and their first night together was a binge of alcohol and sex. Sharon asked Green to move in with her after just three days together, and he agreed. Green was happy with Sharon, but his consumption of alcohol continued to increase.

One night, after Sharon had pricked his penis with a needle and sucked away the blood, Green discovered she had a real taste for blood. It wasn't long before the two embarked on a killing spree to satisfy their wants and needs.

Murders

Sharon was out of town when Green met a teenager, Jeffrey Davis, and asked him if he wanted to hang out together. Davis agreed, and they started the evening by driving around town. At one point, Green pulled over to urinate, and when he returned to the car, Davis was masturbating. Davis asked if Green wanted to touch him, which angered Green, and he beat him. They drove around some more, and the more Davis complained, the more Green beat him.

Finally, they pulled into a secluded area, at which point Green dragged Davis out of the car. He started viciously beating him. Using a knife, he then cut off Davis's penis and threw it into a lake. After mutilating the body, he disposed of it in another secluded area nearby.

In 1980, Green was driving when he saw a woman hitchhiking, and he pulled over and offered her a ride. She told him her name was Montana, and Green asked her if she wanted to go back to his house so she could take a shower. She agreed.

While Montana was in the shower, Green opened the shower curtain and asked if he could join her. She agreed, and they proceeded to have sex. This carried over into the bedroom until Green said he had to pick up Sharon from work.

Sharon was surprised to see another woman in the car, and when they returned home, Green suggested they have a threesome. At first, Montana agreed, but she changed her mind when she saw Sharon naked. By then it was too late—they were going to have sex together whether she wanted to or not. The couple tied Montana to the bed, and when they got tired of her kicking and screaming, they dragged her into the bathroom, where Green attempted to sodomize her.

Sharon retrieved a knife from the kitchen, went back to the bathroom, and plunged the knife into Montana's body. Green went to the bedroom to get his pocketknife, and when he got back to the bathroom, Montana was trying to stand up. Green stabbed her over and over, then left the room to retrieve a hammer. He came back and struck her in the head three or four times. Sharon wanted a turn, so she too struck Montana in the head with the hammer.

When Montana was finally dead, Green began to fondle Sharon's breast, which excited her. They had sex amid the blood on the floor, then cleaned up and put Montana's body into the trunk of their car. They drove to a secluded spot and dumped the body.

Green then met Sandra Bailey at a club, and little did the woman know she was to be the next victim of this dreadful couple. Green convinced Bailey to go back to his house. When they got there, and she saw he had a wife, Bailey tried to leave. Instead of letting her leave, they tied her up and carried out the same scenario they had with Montana. This time though, the sex afterward was not as powerful as when they had killed Montana. They dumped Bailey's body in an area similar to where they had dumped Montana.

The last known victim was Steven Fefferman, whom Green met in a parking lot that was frequented by gay men. This time, Green agreed to go back to Fefferman's home. As soon as they arrived, Fefferman began to fondle Green, and then excused himself to have a shower. Upon his return to the bedroom, Green asked if they could take turns tying each other up. Green tied up Fefferman and then pulled out a knife. Green began to tell Fefferman that he hated homosexuals; then he stabbed Fefferman over and over again.

Fefferman was still alive, so Green went and got a large knife from the kitchen. He stabbed Fefferman in the throat, and then cut him open from his sternum to his scrotum. Remarkably, Fefferman was still alive, gasping for air, trying to breathe. Last, Green cut off Fefferman's penis and shoved it into his mouth. When he was dead, Green robbed him of some money and went home.

After the murders, Green and Sharon's marriage started to derail. They were both regularly indulging in drugs and alcohol, and after a few years, Sharon left.

Trial

On the night of April 27, 1989, police surrounded Green's home and arrested him for the murder of Fefferman. Although Green knew he would be caught one day, he never thought it would be because Sharon had turned him in.

The trial had to be shifted to Austin, Texas, because the media attention the case had garnered in Fort Worth, Texas affected Green's chance of a fair trial.

During the trial, Marc Barta, the prosecuting attorney said, "With confessions, bloodstained knives and photographs, the likelihood of an acquittal was minimal."

Some of the jurors had such an unpleasant reaction to the horrific nature of the evidence that they had to leave the room for a period of time. One of the female jurors had to excuse herself so she could vomit. The evidence was so disturbing they struggled to get through it. After the trial, some members of the jury sought psychiatric care because they were traumatized by the evidence they had seen.

Green was convicted for the murder of Fefferman, and also for three other murders. For her part, Sharon received ten years' probation.

Outcome

Green was sentenced to death for the murder of Fefferman, and he was given three life sentences for the other murders.

In October of 1997, Green was executed by lethal injection. It took seven minutes for him to die following the administration of lethal drugs.

Trivia

Quote: "They all deserved it. They were kind of the dregs of society."

Green's last statement:

"I want to thank the Lord for giving me this opportunity to get to know Him. He has shown me a lot, and He has changed me in the past two months. I have been in prison 8 1/2 years and on death row for 7, and I have not gotten into any trouble. I feel like I am not a threat to society anymore. I feel like my punishment is over, but my friends are now being punished. I thank the Lord for all He has done for me. I do want to tell the …"

But he didn't finish his statement as the drugs had taken effect.

Green believed that he was doing the country a favor by killing "whores and homosexuals."

VAUGHN GREENWOOD

Date of birth: 1944

Aliases/Nicknames: The Skid Row Slasher

Characteristics: Bodies found bearing signs of ritualistic abuse - cups of blood next to bodies

Number of victims: 11

Date of murders: 1964, 1974 - 1975

Date of arrest: February 2, 1975

Victim profile: David Russell; Benjamin Hornberg, 67; Charles Jackson, 46; Moses Yakanac, 47; Arthur Dahlstedt, 54; David Perez, 42; Casimir Strawinski, 58; Robert Shannahan, 46; Samuel Suarez, 49; George Frias, 45; Clyde Hays, 34

Method of murder: Stabbing with a knife, slashed throats

Location: Los Angeles, California, USA

Status: Sentenced to 32 years to life in prison on January 19, 1977.

Background

Referred to as one of the "Skid Row Slayers" of Southern California, Greenwood began killing in 1964. He stopped for about a decade, however, before embarking on another murder spree in Los Angeles. Greenwood committed nine murders in Los Angeles over a brief period of two months.

His victims were posed after death, and salt was sprinkled around their bodies. Cups of their blood were found nearby, and strange markings were made around the wounds inflicted by the killer. To try to solve the case, police used every resource possible, including psychiatric profiles and sketches. The case was eventually solved by accident, and it was discovered the profiles were well off the mark.

Murder

The first known victim was killed on November 13, 1964. A transient man, David Russell, was discovered on the steps of a library with multiple stab wounds and a cut throat. The next day, Benjamin Hornberg, sixty-seven, was murdered in the restroom of a budget hotel, with stab wounds to his head and upper body and his throat slashed.

The killing stopped for ten years, until December 1, 1974, when Charles Jackson, forty-six, was murdered. Jackson was a drifter and an alcoholic, and he was killed in the same spot that David Russell had been killed a decade before. The next killing took place on December 8, when Eskimo Moses Yakanac, forty-seven, was stabbed to death in an alley in Skid Row.

Three days after Yakanac was killed, Arthur Dahlstedt, fifty-four, was murdered outside an abandoned building. On December 22, the body of David Perez, forty-two, was found in some bushes next to the Los Angeles Public Library. There was a break of a week or two, and then Casimir Strawinski, fifty-eight, was found murdered in his hotel room on January 9.

On January 17, a hotel maid found the body of Robert Shannahan, forty-six, in his hotel room. He had been dead for several days, and there was a bayonet stuck in his chest. The last known victim of the Skid Row Slasher was Samuel Suarez, forty-nine, who was found dead in a room in a seedy hotel.

Greenwood moved to Hollywood for an unknown reason and on January 29, 1975, George Frias, forty-five, was stabbed to death in his apartment. Just two days later, Clyde Hays, thirty-four, was found dead in his Hollywood home with the same injuries and mutilations that had been present on the other victims.

On February 2, the Hollywood home of William Graham was invaded by a prowler, who proceeded to attack Graham with a hatchet. Another man in the house, Kenneth Richer, intervened, attacking the intruder, and they both fell through a window. The intruder, Greenwood, fled; he next tried to break into the home of actor Burt Reynolds. As he left, he dropped a letter, addressed to himself, in the driveway of the home.

Greenwood was arrested and charged with burglary and assault. As part of their investigation, they searched his home and discovered a pair of cufflinks. These had belonged to George Frias, one of Greenwood's victims. From there, the investigation progressed into a murder investigation, and on January 23, 1976, Greenwood was charged with eleven counts of murder.

Trial

Before his trial for the murders, Greenwood was convicted of assault for the attack on William Graham and Kenneth Richer. He was sentenced to thirty-two years to life for the assaults.

His trial for the murders ended on December 30, 1976. Greenwood was convicted of nine counts of first-degree murder. The jury was unable to come to a decision regarding the murders of David Russell and Charles Jackson.

Outcome

Greenwood was sentenced to life imprisonment on January 19, 1977. The judge presiding over the case recommended that Greenwood never be released, saying, "His presence in any community would constitute a menace."

He continues to serve his sentence.

Trivia

Greenwood would take the shoes from his victims and place them pointing toward their body.

Initially, police believed the suspect was a white male, in his late twenties or early thirties, who stood six feet tall and weighed around one hundred ninety pounds. They also thought he would have long blond hair and have some kind of physical deformity. In reality, Greenwood was black and had no deformities.

Greenwood has never explained why he posed the bodies the way he did or the meaning behind the strange rituals he performed, including the placement of the shoes.

BELLE GUNNESS

Date of birth: November 11, 1859

Aliases/Nicknames: Brynhild Paulsdatter Størseth, Lady Bluebeard

Characteristics: Insurance money, robbery

Number of victims: 13 - 42

Date of murders: 1880s - 1908

Date of arrest: Never apprehended.

Victim profile: Men and children

Method of murder: Strychnine poisoning, bludgeoning

Location: Illinois, Indiana, USA

Status: On April 28, 1908, the bodies of Gunness' children were found in their home, along with a headless adult female corpse, after a fire. The corpse was not positively identified. Gunness was never located, and her death was never confirmed.

Background

Gunness was born in Selbu, Norway in 1859, the youngest of eight children. There have been some conflicting stories about her childhood and youth, but there is one story that has remained constant throughout the years. Apparently, while in her youth, Gunness attended a dance while she was pregnant. The story is that a man attacked her at the dance and kicked her in the belly, causing her to suffer a miscarriage. The attacker came from a wealthy family and wasn't prosecuted for the assault. However, he died not long after he had attacked Gunness.

A year after the assault, Gunness began working on a large farm and remained there for three years. Then she used her wages to follow her sister to America in 1881. It was then that she changed her name to Belle, to fit in with the American lifestyle.

Gunness married Mads Ditlev Anton Sorenson in 1884, in Chicago. Two years later they opened a store selling confectionery, but it wasn't successful, and within a year, the store burned down. The couple received an insurance payout and used the money to purchase another house.

Despite conflicting information, it is believed Gunness bore four children to Sorenson. The oldest was Caroline, followed by Axel, Myrtle, and Lucy. Both Caroline and Axel died as babies, supposedly from acute colitis, the symptoms of which include fever, diarrhea, nausea, and abdominal cramping. The children's lives were insured, and after their deaths, the claims were paid out.

On July 30, 1900, Sorenson died. This particular day was the only day when two life insurance policies on Sorenson overlapped. The initial report from the doctor who saw Sorenson after his death was that he had died from strychnine poisoning. The family doctor, however, said he had been treating Sorenson for heart problems, and he had, therefore, died of heart failure. Sorenson's death wasn't considered suspicious, so no autopsy was performed.

The day after the funeral, Gunness put in a claim for the insurance money. Sorenson's family believed she had poisoned him for the money. Nonetheless, Gunness was paid the insurance claim of eighty-five hundred dollars. With this money, she purchased a farm near La Porte, Indiana.

Before she moved to the farm, she met up with an old acquaintance, Peter Gunness, who had only recently become a widower. On April 1, 1902, they married. A week later, Peter's baby daughter died while alone in the house with Gunness. It wasn't long before Peter met the same fate.

Murders

In December of 1902, Belle claimed Peter had been reaching for his slippers near the stove and was scalded with brine. A piece of a sausage grinding machine allegedly fell and struck him on the head, causing a fatal injury. From his death, Gunness netted three thousand dollars. But, when the district coroner reviewed the death, he declared Peter had been murdered.

While investigating the case, Jennie Olsen, fourteen, who lived with the Gunnesses, was heard telling a friend at school that "My mama killed my papa. She hit him with a meat cleaver, and he died. Don't tell a soul." She was brought before the coroner's jury to answer questions about the statement, but she denied ever saying it.

Gunness, who was pregnant at the time, managed to convince the coroner she was innocent. In May of 1903, she delivered a baby boy, whom she named Phillip. Three years later, Belle told her neighbors that Jennie had gone away to college. It wasn't until much later, after her body was found buried on the farm, that the truth would be known about the young girl's disappearance.

A man named Ray Lamphere was hired in 1907 to help Gunness run the farm. Around this time, Gunness placed an advertisement in the matrimonial columns of all the daily newspapers in Chicago and those in larger cities, looking for a husband. She received a lot of responses by letter, and many suitors came to the farm but never left.

John Moe was one who replied, and he traveled to the farm from Minnesota. As part of the arrangement with Gunness, he brought one thousand dollars to help pay off her mortgage. Within a week of stepping foot on the farm, he disappeared.

The next suitor was George Anderson from Takio, Missouri. While they were having dinner one night, Gunness and Anderson came to an agreement that he would pay off her mortgage if they decided to get married. That night, while he was in bed, he woke and saw Gunness standing beside the bed with a strange look on her face. It frightened him, and he fled, going back to Missouri.

Elderly widower Ole B. Budsberg arrived from Iola, Wisconsin, and he was last seen alive at the local bank in La Porte on April 6, 1907. He had been mortgaging his own farm back in Wisconsin, to the value of several thousand dollars. After he disappeared, his sons contacted Gunness, but she replied that she had never seen their father and didn't know where he was.

Throughout that year, several other men came to the farm and were never seen or heard from again. In December, Andrew Helgelien from Aberdeen, South Dakota, wrote to Belle in response to her advertisement. She replied, and he traveled to her farm in January of 1908. He had withdrawn his savings, twenty-nine hundred dollars, and within days of his arrival, he and Gunness were seen depositing the check at the bank in La Porte. A few days later, he disappeared, and Gunness was seen on two occasions depositing money into her account.

Meanwhile, Ray Lamphere, the hired hand, had fallen in love with Gunness and did whatever she asked. His jealousy of the different men coming to the farm became a problem and Gunness fired him on February 3, 1908. Shortly after, she went to the courthouse and declared Lamphere was a menace to the public and was not in his right mind. A sanity hearing was arranged, at which he was found to be sane. A few days later, she went to the sheriff and said Lamphere was a threat to her family, and as a result, he was arrested for trespassing.

The brother of Andrew Helgelien, Asle Helgelien, began asking questions about his brother's disappearance. Gunness knew she was in trouble, and she began to set the scene for her own escape. She went to see her lawyer and said she was fearful of her life and that of her children. Lamphere, she claimed, had threatened to kill her and burn down her house. She made out a will, leaving her estate to her children. Then she went to the bank and paid off her mortgage. However, she never went back to the police to tell them the threat was "escalating."

On April 28, 1908, early in the morning, Lamphere's replacement farmhand, Joe Maxson, woke to the smell of smoke in his bedroom on the second floor of Gunness' house. Upon opening the door, he was greeted with flames and screamed out the names of Gunness and her children to escape. Nobody replied. He jumped from the window and raced to get help. But, by the time help arrived, it was too late. The farmhouse was reduced to ruins.

Inside the house were four bodies - the children and a woman. The head of the female body was missing, so it could not be determined if the body belonged to Gunness. The bodies of the children were still in their beds. The sheriff immediately sought out Lamphere, believing he was responsible for the fire after the claims Gunness had made.

Lamphere denied having anything to do with the fire, but a witness said he had seen him running from the house just before it burst into flames. Lamphere was promptly arrested and charged with murder and arson.

The female body found in the fire concerned many, including neighbors of Gunness. Those who saw the body said it could not be her. Even her old friends said it wasn't the body of Gunness. When measurements were taken, the remains belonged to a woman who was five feet three inches and around one hundred fifty pounds. Gunness had been a huge woman, standing six feet tall and weighing more than two hundred pounds.

When the stomach contents of the body were examined, it showed lethal amounts of strychnine. Later, a piece of dental bridgework was found in the ruins, and these teeth were identified as being the ones made for Gunness. Because of this, the coroner concluded that the female body was that of Gunness after all.

Maxson, the hired hand, then went to the sheriff with information regarding specific chores Gunness had asked him to do. He said he was told to bring loads of dirt to a large area where the hogs were fed. He told the sheriff there were several deep depressions in the ground that Gunness had covered by dirt. Gunness told him they contained rubbish.

On May 3, 1908, authorities—digging at the farm in response to Maxson's claims—unearthed the remains of Jennie Olsen. The bodies of two children, unidentified, were found soon after. Then, Andrew Helgelien's remains were found. As the digging continued, more and more bodies were found in the hog's pen. These were:

- Ole B. Budsberg, disappeared May of 1907.

- Thomas Lindboe, from Chicago, worked as a hired man for Gunness.

- Henry Gurholdt of Scandinavia, Wisconsin - a watch corresponding to one belonging to Gurholdt was found with a body.

- Olaf Svenherud, from Chicago.

- John Moe of Elbow Lake, Minnesota.

- Olaf Lindbloom, age thirty-five, from Wisconsin.

Other possible victims included:

- William Mingay, from New York City, who left there on April 1, 1904.

- Herman Konitzer, of Chicago, who went missing in January of 1906.

- Charles Edman of New Carlisle, Indiana.

- George Berry of Tuscola, Illinois.

- Christie Hilkven of Dovre, Barron County, Wisconsin, sold his farm and went to La Porte in 1906.

- Chares Neiburg, twenty-eight, an immigrant from Scandinavia who resided in Philadelphia, told friends he was going to visit Gunness in June of 1906, but he never came back. He took five hundred dollars in cash with him.

- John H. McJunkin, of Coraopolis, had been writing to a woman in La Porte and left his wife in December of 1906.

- Olaf Jensen, a Norwegian immigrant, living in Carroll, Indiana, wrote to relatives in 1906 saying he was going to La Porte to marry a wealthy widow.

- Henry Bizge of La Porte went missing in June of 1906, and his hired man Edward Canary of Pink Lake Ill also disappeared in 1906.

- Bert Chase of Mishawaka, Indiana sold his butchery store and told associates about a wealthy widow he was going to visit. His brother received a telegram that was supposedly from South Dakota stating he had been killed in a train accident. The telegram was found to be fake when investigated.

- Tonnes Peterson Lien of Rushford, Minnesota, went missing on April 2, 1907.

- A gold ring engraved "S.B. May 28, 1907" was found in the house ruins after the fire.

- George Bradley of Tuscola, Illinois, was believed to have traveled to La Porte to meet a widow and three children in October of 1907.

- T.J. Tiefland of Minneapolis was believed to have visited Gunness in 1907.

- Frank Riedinger, a farmer of Waukesha, Wisconsin, went to Indiana in 1907 to marry but never returned.

- Emil Tell, from Kansas City, Missouri, was supposed to have traveled to La Porte in 1907.

- Lee Porter of Bartonville, Oklahoma left his wife and told his brother he was going to La Porte to marry a wealthy widow.

- John E. Hunter left Duquesne, Pennsylvania, on November 25, 1907, after telling his children he was traveling to North Indiana to marry a wealthy woman.

- George Williams of Wapawallopen and Ludwig Stoll of Mount Yeager also left their homes to marry a woman in the West.

- Abraham Phillips, a railway worker of Burlington, West Virginia, left in 1907 to marry a wealthy widow in North Indiana. A railway wristwatch was found in the ruins of the house.

- Benjamin Carling of Chicago, Illinois, was last seen 1907 after telling his wife that he was going to La Porte to meet with a rich widow about an investment. He took one thousand dollars from an insurance company and borrowed money from several investors as well before he left. In June of 1908, his remains were identified by his wife after they were found in the Pauper's Cemetery in La Port.

- Aug. Gunderson of Green Lake, Wisconsin.
- Ole Oleson of Battle Creek, Michigan.
- Lindner Nikkelsen of Huron, South Dakota.
- Andrew Anderson of Lawrence, Kansas.
- Johann Sorensen of St. Joseph, Missouri.
- A possible victim was a man named Hinkley.

Reported unnamed victims were:

- Mrs. H. Whitzer's daughter of Toledo, Ohio, who had disappeared while attending Indiana University near La Porte in 1902.
- An unidentified man and woman are alleged to have disappeared in September of 1906, on the same night Jennie Olsen went missing. Gunness told neighbors the couple was a Los Angeles "professor" and his wife and they had taken Jennie with them to California.
- Miss Jennie Graham's brother of Waukesha, Wisconsin, who had gone to marry a rich widow in La Porte and disappeared.
- A hired man from Ohio, age fifty, is alleged to have disappeared, and Gunness was found to have his horse and buggy.
- An unidentified man from Montana told people he was going to sell his horse and buggy to Gunness. The horse and buggy were found with several others at the farm, but the man was never seen or heard from again.

Many of the bodies and remains found on the farm couldn't be identified, and because of the methods used to unearth them, the exact number of victims is unknown. The figure was believed to be twelve. The remains of seven of her victims were buried together in two coffins in unmarked graves in the pauper's section of Pine Lake Cemetery, La Porte. The bodies of Jennie Olsen and Andrew Helgelien were buried in nearby Patton Cemetery, near the grave of Peter Gunness.

Trial

During Lamphere's trial for the murder and arson, the defense argued he was not guilty because the female body in the burned-out house was not that of Gunness. A jeweler testified that despite gold jewelry melting in the heat of the fire, the gold in the dental bridgework had remained intact. When a test was done of similar dental work placed in a blacksmith's forge, it was found that the real teeth crumbled, the porcelain teeth were pitted, and the gold melted more so than the dental work found in the remains of the fire.

Maxson and another witness claimed they had seen a police officer take the dental bridgework out of his pocket and plant it at the scene. Lamphere was therefore found guilty of arson but not guilty of the murders. He was sentenced on November 26, 1908, to twenty years in prison. He didn't serve his full sentence, however, as he died on December 30, 1909, of tuberculosis.

As he lay on his deathbed, Lamphere allegedly told the reverend who was comforting him that although he hadn't killed anyone, he had helped Gunness bury the bodies. He said she would charm the suitor with a good meal, and then drug his coffee. Once he was in a state of stupor, Gunness would strike the man in the head with a meat chopper. Other times, she would wait until the man went to bed and then chloroform him while he slept. She used various methods of disposing of the bodies, including chopping them into pieces and feeding them to her hogs.

Lamphere also stated that the corpse of the woman found in the burned ruins of the farmhouse was a woman Gunness had lured to the farm by pretending she was going to be hired as a housekeeper. She then drugged the woman and bashed her in the head. Gunness attached weights to the head and threw it into the deeper area of the swamp. Then, Gunness killed her children using chloroform and smothering. Lamphere admitted he had helped Gunness escape, but she had not met him at the agreed part of the road. Instead, he believed she had escaped across the fields and into the woods.

According to Lamphere, Gunness had murdered forty-two men.

Outcome

Sightings of Gunness were reported for decades across the United States. She was reportedly seen by acquaintances in San Francisco, Los Angeles, Chicago, and New York. In 1931, it was reported Gunness was living in Mississippi and owned a lot of property.

The woman Gunness killed and used to fake her own death in the fire was never identified.

The police arrested a woman called Esther Carlson in Los Angeles in 1931 for poisoning a man for money. Based on photographs of Carlson, two people who had known Gunness claimed they were the same woman. However, the identification wasn't proven, and the answers died with Carlson while she was awaiting her trial.

The headless body was exhumed on November 5, 2007, by a team of forensic anthropologists and students from the University of Indianapolis. The descendants of Gunness's sister had given permission. The exhumation was done to try to identify who the headless body belonged too. Using an envelope found at Gunness' farmhouse, they had hoped they could extract DNA from the envelope flap and compare it to the headless body. Unfortunately, it was not successful, as the amount of DNA obtained was not enough.

Trivia

While Gunness was living in Chicago, she ran a "baby farm" out of her home. A baby farm was meant to be a foster care system. During this time, twenty-one babies disappeared; nobody has ever uncovered what happened to them. They could have been sold or murdered.

Gunness' Advertisement:

Personal - comely widow who owns a large farm in one of the finest districts in La Porte County, Indiana, desires to make the acquaintance of a gentleman equally well provided, with view of joining fortunes. No replies by letter considered unless sender is willing to follow answer with personal visit. Triflers need not apply.

FRITZ HAARMANN

Date of birth: October 25, 1879

Aliases/Nicknames: The Butcher of Hannover

Characteristics: Homosexual; - dismemberment; - rumor was that Haarmann would also sell human meat from his victims as canned pork on the black market, although there was never physical evidence to confirm this.

Number of victims: 27 +

Date of murders: 1918 - 1924

Date of arrest: June 23, 1924

Victim profile: Friedel Rothe, 17; Fritz Franke, 17; Wilhelm Schulze, 17; Roland Huch, 16; Hans Sonnenfeld, 19; Ernst Ehrenberg, 13; Heinrich Struß, 18; Paul Bronischewski, 17; Richard Gräf, 17; Wilhelm Erdner, 16; Hermann Wolf, 15; Heinz Brinkmann, 13; Adolf Hannappel, 17; Adolf Hennies, 19; Ernst Spiecker, 17; Heinrich Koch, 20; Willi Senger, 19; Hermann Speighert, 16; Hermann Bock, 22; Alfred Hogrefe, 16; Wilhelm Apel, 16; Robert Witzel, 18; Heinz Martin, 14; Fritz Wittig, 17; Friedrich Abeling, 10; Freidrich Koch, 16; Erich de Vries, 17

Method of murder: Strangulation, biting through the throat

Location: Hannover, Lower Saxony, Germany

Status: Executed by guillotine on April 15, 1925.

Background

Haarmann was described as a quiet child who had few friends, and from a very early age, his behavior was quite effeminate. Instead of playing boy's games, he preferred to play with dolls, and thanks to his close relationship with his mother, he was passionate about cooking and needlework. His mother spoiled him and mollycoddled him, and at school, his academic prowess was below average. When Haarmann was around eight years old, he was apparently molested by a teacher, but he never discussed this in later life.

Following school, Haarmann worked briefly as an apprentice locksmith. In April of 1895, at the age of fifteen, he enrolled in a military academy. At first, he adapted well to military life, but after five months of service, he started periodically suffering lapses of consciousness. Initially these episodes were believed to be due to anxiety, but in October 1895, they were diagnosed as being similar to epilepsy. He discharged himself from the military a month later and went back to Hanover to work in his father's cigar factory.

The first known sex offenses committed by Haarmann occurred when he was sixteen. Each of the victims was a young boy. Haarmann's first arrest was in July of 1896. He was arrested for committing sexual offenses against boys several times, and he was placed in a mental institution to be evaluated. He was determined to be "incurably deranged" and unfit to stand trial for these offenses. Haarmann was therefore committed to the mental institution indefinitely from May 28, 1897.

Haarmann escaped the facility seven months later and fled to Switzerland. In Zurich, he worked in a shipyard as a handyman, but he went back to Hanover in April of 1899. He met a woman, Erna Loewert, early in 1900, and after their engagement, she became pregnant. In October of that year, Haarmann was notified he had to perform compulsory military service.

Haarmann's superiors in the military described him as an exemplary soldier and an excellent marksman, but in October of 1901, his unconscious spells returned. He spent four months in the hospital until he was deemed unsuitable to continue his military service. He was officially discharged on July 28, 1902. Haarmann returned to Hanover to live with Loewert.

After working with his father for a while, Haarmann and Loewert opened their own fishmonger business. While Loewert worked in the business, Haarmann worked as an insurance salesman.He was classified disabled in 1904, however, and deemed unable to work. That same year, Loewert ended their engagement.

Over the next ten years or so, Haarmann committed numerous crimes and was known as a burglar, con artist, and petty thief. From early 1905, he was sent to prison to serve short sentences for larceny, assault, and embezzlement. He ended up spending most of his time between 1905 and 1912 in jail. He was arrested again in late 1913 for burglary. When his home was searched, property was discovered that linked him to many other burglaries. This resulted in a sentence of five years in prison.

Murders

It will never be known exactly how many victims were killed by Haarmann. During his interrogation, he made several inconsistent statements about how many people he killed, and when he started his murderous acts. He originally claimed to have killed "thirty or forty," and then later claimed it was more like fifty to seventy. The first known victim was killed in September of 1918, but it wasn't until 1923 - 1924 that the tally rose dramatically.

It was during the year 1922, shortly after his spree began, that Haarmann would meet his friend, homosexual lover and later accomplice, Hans Grans, with whom he established a serious and very complicated relationship. The two argued often, but Grans knew how to manipulate Fritz in a way that nobody else could and would play an important part in most if not all of the murders that were committed by the Butcher of Hannover.

In a curious twist of events, Fritz Haarmann claimed that Hans Grans had possessed the power to save him from becoming the murderer he eventually turned into, but that his lover had never "loved him enough" to stop it from happening. It is not known if this was really true or simply a way of transferring guilt and responsibility to somebody else.

Either way, Haarmann's line of murders took place as follows:

September 27, 1918:
Friedel Rothe, seventeen, had run away from home and met Haarmann in a café. When he was questioned later on, Haarmann said Rothe had been buried in a cemetery.

February 12, 1923:
Fritz Franke, seventeen. A pianist, originally from Berlin, Franke met Haarmann in the waiting room of Hanover Station. After Haarmann's arrest, it was discovered that Franke's personal items had been given to Grans by Haarmann.

March 20, 1923:
Wilhelm Schulze, seventeen. An apprentice writer, he told his friend he was going to run away from home. His clothes were found in the possession of Haarmann's landlady. His possessions were formally identified at Haarmann's trial.

May 23, 1923:
Roland Huch, sixteen. He vanished from Hanover station after running away from home. Some of his clothing was traced to a lifeguard who later said Haarmann had given them to him.

c. May 31, 1923:
Hans Sonnenfeld, nineteen. A runaway from the suburb of Limmer, he was known to have hung out with friends at Hanover station. His coat and tie were found in Haarmann's apartment.

June 25, 1923:
Ernst Ehrenberg, thirteen. The first known victim, he was killed at Haarmann's Rote Reihe home. Ehrenberg was Haarmann's neighbor's son. He went on an errand for his parents and never came back.

August 24, 1923:
Heinrich Struß, eighteen. From the suburb of Egestorf, Struß had last been seen at a cinema in Hanover. His violin case was found in Haarmann's possession.

September 24, 1923:
Paul Bronischewski, seventeen. He disappeared as he traveled from the city of Bochum to his home, after visiting his uncle in Groß Garz. Haarmann had offered him some work when he got off the train.

September 30, 1923:
Richard Gräf, seventeen. He vanished after telling his family he had gotten a job through a detective from Hanover. His coat was pawned by Haarmann's landlady.

October 12, 1923:
Wilhelm Erdner, sixteen. He disappeared as he was riding his bicycle to work. Haarmann sold Erdner's bicycle on October 20.

October 24, 1923:
Hermann Wolf, fifteen. He was last seen in the vicinity of Hanover station by his brother. The buckle of his belt was found in Haarmann's apartment. Haarmann denied he killed Wolf at his trial. Haarmann was acquitted of this murder.

October 27, 1923:
Heinz Brinkmann, thirteen. He missed his train home to Clausthal and disappeared. A witness later testified to seeing Haarmann and Grans talking with Brinkmann in the waiting rooms at Hanover station.

November 10, 1923:
Adolf Hannappel, seventeen. Unlike most of the other murders, Haarmann readily confessed to killing Hannappel. Hannappel was seen sitting in the waiting rooms at Hanover station by a number of witnesses, and they all later testified they had seen Haarmann approach Hannappel. Haarmann claimed he had committed this murder upon the urging of Hans Grans.

December 6, 1923:
Adolf Hennies, nineteen. He disappeared in Hanover while looking for work. Grans was in possession of his coat. Haarmann claimed Grans and another acquaintance were responsible for this murder, although he dismembered Hennies's body. Haarmann was acquitted of this murder.

January 5, 1924:

Ernst Spiecker, seventeen. He was last seen on his way to court to appear as a witness for a trial. Grans was wearing Spiecker's shirt at the time of his arrest.

January 15, 1924:

Heinrich Koch, twenty. Haarmann claimed he couldn't recognize a photo of Koch, but Koch was known to be an acquaintance of Haarmann. Koch's personal possessions and clothing were given to the son of Haarmann's landlady.

February 2, 1924:

Willi Senger, nineteen. He had been an acquaintance of Haarmann prior to his murder. Haarmann denied any involvement in Senger's disappearance, but police established Haarmann regularly wore Senger's coat after he had disappeared.

February 8, 1924:

Hermann Speichert, sixteen. An apprentice electrician from Linden-Limmer, his clothes were sold by the son of Haarmann's landlady. Grans was given his geometry kit.

c. April 1, 1924:

Hermann Bock, twenty-two. He was a laborer from the town of Uelzen, who had known Haarmann since 1921. He was last seen walking toward Haarmann's apartment by his friends. Haarmann was wearing his suit when he was arrested but was still acquitted of his murder.

April 8, 1924:

Alfred Hogrefe, sixteen. He ran away from home on April 2, after a family argument. He was seen multiple times with Haarmann at Hanover station in the days before his murder. All of his clothes were traced to Haarmann, Grans, or Haarmann's landlady.

April 17, 1924:

Wilhelm Apel, sixteen. He vanished on his way to work from the Hanover-Leinhausen station. He was persuaded to go to Haarmann's apartment. Most of his clothes were later sold by Haarmann's landlady.

April 26, 1924:

Robert Witzel, eighteen. He was last seen visiting a traveling circus. Witzel's skull was found on May 20. The rest of his remains were thrown into the Leine River.

May 9, 1924:

Heinz Martin, fourteen. He was an apprentice locksmith from the city of Chemnitz. His leather cap, shirt, and cardigan were found in Haarmann's apartment. It is believed that he vanished from Hanover station while he was looking for work.

May 26, 1924:

Fritz Wittig, seventeen. He was a traveling salesman from the town of Kassel. Haarmann claimed he hadn't wanted to kill Wittig but was persuaded to "take the boy" by Grans, who wanted Wittig's suit.

May 26, 1924:

Friedrich Abeling, twen. Abeling had been playing truant from school when he disappeared. His skull was discovered in the Leine River on June 13, 1924.

June 5, 1924:

Friedrich Koch, sixteen. He disappeared on his way to college. Koch was last seen by two friends in the company of Haarmann.

June 14, 1924:

Erich de Vries, seventeen. He vanished after telling his parents he was going for a swim in the Ohe River. After his arrest, Haarmann led police to de Vries's skeletal remains, which he had discarded in a lake at the entrance to the Herrenhausen Gardens.

Trial

Haarmann was observed prowling around Hanover station by undercover police officers on the night of June 22. Before long, the officers witnessed Haarmann arguing with Karl Fromm, a fifteen-year-old boy. Haarmann approached the officers and demanded they arrest Fromm for traveling with forged documents. When he was arrested, Fromm stated he had been living with Haarmann for a few days and had been raped repeatedly by him. The following morning Haarmann was arrested and charged with sexual assault.

The arrest led to Haarmann's apartment being searched. Police found heavy bloodstaining on the walls, bedding, and floors in the apartment. Haarmann tried to explain this away by saying it was a result of selling contraband meat.

Upon further investigation, a number of Haarmann's prior neighbors spoke of the teenage boys they saw visiting him at his various homes since 1920. Two witnesses claimed they had followed Haarmann one evening in the spring of 1924 to the Leine River, and saw him toss a sack into the water.

Numerous items of clothing and personal effects belonging to missing boy Witzel were found on June 29. His skull had been found on May 20, in a garden. When a friend of Witzel told police he had seen his friend with Haarmann the day before his disappearance, police confronted Haarmann. At first, he tried to talk his way out of it, but, when Witzel's jacket was found in the possession of Haarmann's landlady, he broke down.

Haarmann went on to confess to the rape, murder, and dismemberment of multiple young men, claiming he suffered a "rabid sexual passion." He stated he didn't set out to kill the men, but would be overcome by an irresistible urge to bite through their Adam's apple. All of the victims were dismembered before being disposed of. Regarding this act, Haarmann said he found it very unpleasant, and that after his first murder and dismemberment, he had been ill for eight days. However, the urge to commit the murder was far stronger than the horror he felt at cutting up the body.

Before beginning to dismember each body, he would have a strong black coffee, then cover the face of the victim with a cloth. Next, he would take out the intestines and put them in a bucket. He used a towel to soak up the blood in the abdominal cavity. After that, he performed three cuts between the ribs and the shoulder, and then he would "take hold of the ribs and push until the bones around the shoulders broke."

The lungs, heart, and kidneys were removed and cut up before being placed in the bucket with the intestines. Then he would dismember the arms and legs. The flesh would be removed from the limbs and torso and disposed of either in the river or down the toilet. The last part of the body removed was the head, after which he would cut off all the flesh from the skull. The skull would be wrapped in rags and placed face down on straw, and Haarmann would strike it repeatedly with an axe to splinter the bone. The brain would then be removed and placed into a bucket, and all of the remains would go into the river.

Haarmann claimed to have killed somewhere between fifty and seventy victims, but police could only connect him with twenty-seven. He was therefore charged with twenty-seven murders. He claimed Grans had insisted he kill some of the victims, so on July 8, Grans was arrested on charges of being an accessory.

The trial of both men started on December 4, 1924. In fourteen of the twenty-seven cases Haarmann was charged in, he admitted his guilt. He said he wasn't sure about the identification of the other thirteen cases. Grans pled not guilty to the charge of being an accessory in several of the cases.

During the two-week trial, one hundred ninety witnesses were called to testify. Some of these witnesses were parents of the victims who were brought before the court to identify their son's property. Haarmann was found guilty of twenty-four out of twenty-seven murders on December 19,

1924. He was sentenced to death by beheading. When the sentence was read out, Haarmann stated, *"I accept the verdict fully and freely. I [shall] go to the decapitating block joyfully and happily. Condemn me to death. I ask only for justice. I am not mad. Make it short; make it soon. Deliver me from this life, which is a torment. I will not petition for mercy, nor will I appeal. I want to pass just one more merry night in my cell, with coffee, cheese, and cigars, after which I will curse my father and go to my execution as if it were a wedding."*

Grans was found guilty of incitement to murder and was also sentenced to die by beheading. He was also given a sentence of twelve years for being an accessory in one case. He collapsed on return to his cell. Grans lodged an appeal against his sentence, but this was rejected in February of 1925. Haarmann made no appeal, saying his death would atone for his crimes. Haarmann also said that if he was freed, he would most likely murder again.

Outcome

Haarmann was taken to the guillotine at six o'clock in the morning on April 15, 1925, and subsequently beheaded. As per the tradition in Germany, he was unaware of his execution date until the night before. Haarmann, according to witnesses to the execution, looked pale and nervous, but he seemed to maintain a sense of "bravado." Just before the execution, he spoke the following:

"I am guilty, gentlemen, but, hard though it may be, I want to die as a man."

Parts of Haarmann's brain were kept for forensic analysis, and on examination of the tissue, traces of meningitis were found. His head was preserved in formaldehyde and was in the care of the Göttingen medical school from 1925 until 2014, after which it was cremated.

Trivia

The film *M*, released in 1931, was the first film to be inspired by Haarmann. It was directed by Fritz Lang, and the main character was portrayed by Peter Lorre.

A film based directly on the Haarmann case, *The Tenderness of the Wolves*, was released in 1973.

Der Totmacher, which translates to "The Deathmaker," was the most recent film based on the crimes of Haarmann. It was released in 1995 and focuses on the psychiatric examinations of Haarmann.

Cyrus: Mind of a Serial Killer (2010) was a film based loosely on Haarmann.

"Often, after I had killed, I pleaded to be put away in a military asylum, but not a madhouse. If [Hans] Grans had really loved me he would have been able to save me. Believe me, I'm not ill — it's only that I occasionally have funny turns. I want to be beheaded. It'll only take a moment, then I'll be at peace."

*"I never intended to hurt those youngsters, but I knew that if I got going something would happen and that made me cry... I would throw myself on top of those boys and bite through the Adam's apple, throttling them at the same time." - **Haarmann***

His last words were, "I repent, but I do not fear death."

JOHN GEORGE HAIGH

Date of birth: July 24, 1909

Aliases/Nicknames: The Acid Bath Murderer

Characteristics: Robbery

Number of victims: 6

Date of murders: 1944 - 1949

Date of arrest: February 26, 1949

Victim profile: William Donald McSwan; Donald McSwan; Amy McSwan; Dr. Archibald Henderson, 52; Rosalie Henderson, 41; Olive Henrietta Robarts Durand-Deacon, 69

Method of murder: Beating with a blunt instrument, shooting

Location: London, England, United Kingdom

Status: Executed by hanging at Wandsworth prison on August 10, 1949.

Background

Haigh was born in Stamford, Lincolnshire, and grew up in Outwood, West Riding of Yorkshire. His parents were members of the conservative protestant sect, the Plymouth Brethren. Haigh later claimed he had suffered from religious nightmares on a recurring basis throughout his childhood.

When Haigh finished school, he started working for a motor engineering firm as an apprentice. After a year, however, he moved on. He shifted into office work, in advertising and insurance, and when he was twenty-one, he was fired on suspicion of theft.

Haigh married Beatrice "Betty" Hamer on July 6, 1934. The marriage didn't last, and the same year of the wedding, Haigh was sent to prison for fraud. Betty gave birth to their daughter while he was in prison, and the baby was given up for adoption. Betty separated from Haigh, and his family ostracized him from then onward.

In 1936, Haigh moved to London and found work as a chauffeur for William McSwann, a wealthy man who owned amusement arcades. As part of his job, Haigh performed maintenance on the machines. Before long, Haigh went back to his criminal activities. Opening offices in Chancery Lane, London, Guildford in Surrey, and Hastings, Sussex, he claimed to be a solicitor by the name of William Cato Adamson. His main business was selling fraudulent stock shares. His ruse was discovered when someone noticed he had spelled "Guildford" incorrectly on his letterhead. He was convicted of fraud and sentenced to four years in prison.

He continued to practice fraud after his release, resulting in more sentences behind bars. It was during his imprisonment that he had a revelation: If he disposed of his victims, he wouldn't be arrested. Haigh learned of murderer Georges-Alexandre Sarret who used sulphuric acid to dispose of his victims' bodies. While in prison, Haigh began experimenting with acid and field mice and concluded it took only half an hour for the mouse to dissolve. Now he had a plan, and upon his release in 1943, he began to set it into action.

Murders

Not long after his release in 1943, Haigh crossed paths with William McSwann again, at which point McSwann introduced Haigh to his parents, Donald and Amy McSwann. William was working for his parents, collecting rent on their properties, and Haigh was jealous of the lifestyle he was leading. William disappeared on September 6, 1944, and Haigh later admitted he had lured him into a basement and struck him over the head. He had then placed the body into a forty-gallon drum and filled it with sulphuric acid. When he returned two days later, the remains had turned into sludge, and he poured it down a manhole.

Haigh contacted William's parents and said he had gone off to Scotland to hide from the military service draft. Then he took over William's house and started to collect the rents for his parents. But Haigh wanted it all for himself. Meanwhile, William's parents began questioning why they hadn't heard from their son. Haigh lured them to the property on Gloucester Road on July 2, 1945, saying William had returned for a surprise visit. He then killed them both and disposed of their bodies.

Haigh stole William's pension checks and sold the properties belonging to the McSwann's. With a profit of around eight thousand pounds, he moved into the Onslow Court Hotel. By summer of 1947, Haigh, a gambler, was running low on funds, so he found another couple to kill and steal from. Dr. Archibald Henderson and his wife Rose were selling their home, and Haigh pretended to be interested in it. He told the couple he could play the piano for their housewarming party, and while he was there, he stole a gun belonging to Archibald.

Then he rented a small workshop in Crawley, Sussex, and shifted the drums and acid to there from the Gloucester Road property. He drove Archibald to the workshop on February 12, 1948, on the pretense of showing him an invention, and shot him in the head with his own gun. Next, he lured Rose to the workshop by saying Archibald had become ill. Then he shot and killed her as well. Their bodies were placed in the drums and filled with acid. He forged a letter and sold their possessions for another eight thousand pounds.

The last victim of Haigh was Olive Durand-Deacon, a wealthy widow who also lived in the Onslow Court Hotel. He had told her he was an engineer, and she explained that she had an idea about creating artificial fingernails. He brought her to the workshop to discuss this on February 18, 1949. As soon as they were inside the building, he shot her in the back of the neck. He stripped her of her Persian lamb coat and valuables and put her into a drum of acid. Two days later, a friend reported her missing.

Because of his extensive criminal record, detectives set about searching Haigh's workshop. They found his attaché case which held a dry cleaner's receipt for the Persian coat. There were also documents pertaining to the McSwanns and the Hendersons.

While he was being questioned, Haigh asked Detective Inspector Albert Webb, "Tell me, frankly, what are the chances of anybody being released from Broadmoor?" to which the inspector said he couldn't discuss that. Haigh then responded, "Well, if I told you the truth, you would not believe me. It sounds too fantastic to believe."

Haigh then confessed that he had killed the McSwanns, the Hendersons, Durand-Deacon, and three other victims. One was allegedly a young man called Max, the second was a woman from Hammersmith, and the third was a girl from Eastbourne. But these three murders couldn't be identified.

Trial

When charged with the murders, Haigh pled insanity. He said he had experienced dreams as a young boy that were dominated by blood. After a car accident in March of 1944, the dream recurred. He explained, "I saw before me a forest of crucifixes which gradually turned into trees. At first, there appeared to be dew or rain, dripping from the branches, but as I approached, I realized it was blood. The whole forest began to writhe and the trees, dark and erect, to ooze blood... A man went from [sic] each tree catching the blood... When the cup was full, he approached me. 'Drink,' he said, but I was unable to move."

The jury was urged to reject the insanity defense by the prosecution because Haigh had acted with "malice aforethought." The defense called witnesses to testify regarding his mental state. One of these witnesses was Dr. Henry Yellowlees, who stated, "The absolute callous, cheerful, bland and almost friendly indifference of the accused to the crimes which he freely admits having committed is unique in my experience."

It became obvious during the trial that the reason Haigh had destroyed the bodies was that he had misunderstood what "corpus delicti" really meant. He had believed that if a body couldn't be found, it would be impossible to be convicted of murder. But even though the bodies were no longer present, there was enough forensic evidence to convict him of all murder charges.

The jury only took a matter of minutes to come to a decision. Haigh was found guilty and sentenced to death.

Outcome

Just before he was to be executed, Haigh was offered a brandy, and he replied, "Make it a large one, old boy." He was taken to the gallows and hanged by executioner Albert Pierrepoint on August 10, 1949.

Trivia

Haigh claimed he would often drink a cup full of his victim's blood.

The Haigh case was dramatized in the episode "The Jar of Acid" on the 1951 radio series *The Black Museum*.

The book *Hide My Eyes*, written by Margery Allingham in 1958, is similar to the Haigh case.

Alfred Hitchcock's unfinished project, *Kaleidoscope*, was inspired by Haigh.

In the television drama *A Is for Acid*, actor Martin Clunes played the role of Haigh.

Haigh's waxwork was exhibited for a time in the Chamber of Horrors at Madame Tussaud's Museum in London.

The play *Under a Red Moon*, written by Michael Slade, although fictional, is based on the examination of Haigh by a psychiatrist before he went on trial.

The play *WAX*, written by Michael Punter, describes a fictional meeting between a female artist from Madame Tussaud's and Haigh. Her job in the play is to create his waxwork for the Chamber of Horrors while he is on death row.

In music

The song "Acid Bath Vampire" by the band Macabre was written about Haigh. It is featured on their *Murder Metal* album.

Another song about Haigh was written by the band Church of Misery, and is called "Make Them Die Slowly (John George Haigh)." It is on their album, *And Then There Were None...*

"When I discovered there were easier ways of making a living than to work long hours in an office, I did not ask myself whether I was doing right or wrong. That seemed to me to be irrelevant. I merely said, 'This is what I wish to do.' And as the means lay within my power that was what I decided."
— *Haigh*

Forensics

Despite the efficiency of acid, not everything had been destroyed. Technicians who were tasked with removing the body parts and objects from the sludge had to cover their arms in Vaseline as a way to protect against the acid should it leech through their gloves.

They found the following items:

1. Twenty-eight pounds of human body fat

2. Three gallstones

3. Part of a left foot, not completely destroyed

4. Eighteen pieces of human bone

5. Upper and lower dentures, still intact

6. The handle of a red plastic bag

7. A lipstick container

While his trial was ongoing, Silvester Bolam, the editor of the *Daily Mirror*, described Haigh as a murderer and was sent to prison for contempt of court.

ARCHIBALD HALL

Date of birth: July 17, 1924

Aliases/Nicknames: Roy Fontaine, Monster Butler, Killer Butler

Characteristics: Jewel thief, accomplice

Number of victims: 5

Date of murders: 1977 - 1978

Date of arrest: January 16, 1978

Victim profile: David Wright; Walter Scott-Elliot; Dorothy Scott-Elliot; Mary Coggle; his half-brother Donald

Method of murder: Shooting, suffocation, beating with a spade and other objects

Location: United Kingdom

Status: Sentenced to life imprisonment, 1978. Died in Kingston Prison in Portsmouth, aged 78, on September 16, 2002.

Background

From the age of fifteen, Hall started stealing. Before long, he had progressed to breaking into houses and robbing them. His first jail sentence was for attempting to sell jewelry he had stolen while in Scotland. While he was incarcerated, he learned the etiquette of the upper class and took voice lessons to weaken his Scottish accent.

After his release, he started to use the name Roy Fontaine. He worked as a butler, but still couldn't keep out of trouble, and went back and forth to prison on burglary charges. Hall returned to Scotland in 1975 and worked as a butler to a wealthy widow, Margaret "Peggy" Hudson. At first, he had planned to rob her of her valuables, but he decided he liked his job and his employer too much.

In 1977, an acquaintance from prison, David Wright, began working on the estate as a gamekeeper. One night, Hall discovered Wright had stolen some of Hudson's jewelry, and the two men got into a fight. Wright threatened to tell Hudson about Hall's criminal history if he told her about the robbery. Unfortunately for Wright, Hall didn't take too kindly to threats.

Murders

Hall's solution to Wright's threat was to trick him into going rabbit hunting with him. As soon as

217

they were out in the fields, he shot and killed Wright. His body was buried next to a stream. Despite his attempts to hide his past, Hudson found out about it, and Hall left his employment with her and moved back to London.

Hall continued to steal and became involved in racketeering in London. He gained employment as a butler to elderly couple Walter Scott-Elliot and his wife, Dorothy. A former member of parliament, Scott-Elliot was wealthy and from an upper-class Scottish family. Hall planned to rob them of their wealth and retire. But, while discussing his plans with accomplice Michael Kitto, Dorothy walked in and overheard what they were saying. Kitto quickly placed a pillow over her face and suffocated her.

Hall and Kitto drugged Scott-Elliot and drove to Scotland, with the assistance of housekeeper Mary Coggle. They buried Dorothy's body in Braco, Perthshire. Then, they beat Scott-Elliot with a shovel and strangled him to death. His body was buried near Tomich, Invernesshire, in a wooded area.

Housekeeper Coggle began to wear clothing and jewelry that belonged to Dorothy, which was problematic because it drew too much attention. Hall and Kitto told her to get rid of the fur coat she had taken from Dorothy, but she refused. Hall and Kitto then beat her to death with a metal fire poker and left her body out in the open, in a stream near Middlebie, Dumfriesshire. Her body was discovered on December 25, 1977 by a shepherd.

The last known victim of Hall and Kitto was Hall's half-brother, Donald, who had recently been released from prison after serving a sentence for being a pedophile. Hall hated Donald, and when they found him at Hall's holiday home in Cumbria, a plan was put into place to get rid of him. Hall and Kitto told Donald their next robbery was going to involve tying up the victim, and they asked if they could practice on him. Donald agreed, and once he was tied up, they incapacitated him with chloroform. Finally, they drowned him in the bath.

What the two men did next ultimately led to their downfall. They placed Donald's body in the trunk of the car and drove to Scotland to dispose of the body. Before they left, Hall instructed Kitto to change the license plate on the car because the current plate contained three nines, which Hall thought was unlucky. It was winter, and because of the dangers on the road, Hall and Kitto decided to stay at the Blenheim House Hotel for the night.

The hotelier was suspicious of Hall and Kitto and was worried they wouldn't be able to pay for their stay. Because of this, he called the police to check them out. When the police looked at the vehicle, they realized the plate and the tax disc numbers weren't a match. Hall and Kitto were taken into custody for questioning. The car was taken to the police station, at which point they discovered the dead body in the trunk.

Kitto was arrested, and Hall made his escape through a bathroom window. He didn't get far though and was recaptured at a roadblock. Further investigation of the registration number of the car revealed a link between the car and a suspicious antique dealer, whom Hall and Kitto had once offered to sell china and silver at low prices. The car was then traced to the Scott-Elliots, and when the apartment was checked, blood spatter was found. Another link was made to the murder of Coggle, who was listed as the housekeeper for the Scott-Elliots. Evidence had been discovered that three men and a woman had stayed a night at a hotel in Scotland, but the next night, only two men returned - Hall and Kitto.

Although he tried to commit suicide while in custody, Hall eventually told the police where the bodies of the victims were buried. After the bodies were located, both Hall and Kitto were charged with five counts of murder.

Trial

At his trial, Hall was convicted of four murders, as it had been decided to keep the murder of Dorothy Scott-Elliot on file. He was sentenced to life imprisonment. In the Scotland judicial system, it was recommended Hall serve a minimum of fifteen years. But in England, the judge recommended he never be released.

Kitto was given life imprisonment for three of the murders. There was no recommended minimum for Kitto in Scotland, and in England, the minimum was set at fifteen years. During his trial, police had given evidence that Hall had actually planned to kill him as well.

Outcome

Over the years, each home secretary that has come into office has placed Hall on the list of dangerous prisoners who should serve a whole life sentence. A letter was sent to *The Observer* newspaper in 1995 by Hall, in which he requested the right to die. During his incarceration, he made many suicide attempts without success.

In 2002, Hall died of a stroke at seventy-eight years of age. At that point, he was one of the oldest of the seventy thousand prisoners in prisons in England, and the oldest to be serving a whole life sentence.

Trivia

Hall published his autobiography, *A Perfect Gentleman*, in 1999.

Film

A movie about Hall was in the process of being filmed when it was canceled due to a lack of funds in 2011. It was going to be called *Monster Butler*. The cancellation left a lot of the crew without pay.

Hall once said that there was "a side of me when aroused, that is cold and completely heartless."

WILLIAM HENRY HANCE

Date of birth: November 10, 1951

Aliases/Nicknames: Chairman of the Forces of Evil

Characteristics: Sent five letters to the Chief of Police and one to the local newspaper

Number of victims: 4

Date of murders: 1977 - 1978

Date of arrest: April 4, 1978

Victim profile: Karen Hickman, 24; Gail Jackson (AKA Brenda Gail Faison), 21; Irene Thirkield, 32; an unnamed female victim

Method of murder: Beating with a jack handle

Location: Georgia, USA

Status: Executed by electrocution in Georgia on March 31, 1994.

Background

A series of murders occurred in Columbus, Georgia in 1978, where elderly white women were strangled to death. Two black prostitutes were also found murdered near Fort Benning. There seemed to be no identifiable link between the victims until a letter arrived on the desk of the local police chief. It was written on United States Army stationery and was handwritten.

In the letter, there was a claim that a gang of seven white men was holding a black woman hostage. It said the gang would kill the woman if the Stocking Strangler wasn't caught. At the time, it was believed that the Stocking Strangler was a black man. The seven men wished to be known as the Forces of Evil and requested communication with the police chief via radio or television messages.

More letters arrived, and the final letter contained a ransom demand of ten thousand dollars for the safe return of the hostage. Phone calls were made to the chief as well. Little did the police know, the whole thing was a hoax to divert the attention away from the real strangler.

Murders

The alleged hostage was Gail Jackson, and she had been killed five weeks before the first letter was even sent. In early April of 1978, her body was discovered. The body of Irene Thirkield was found soon after, at a rifle range at Fort Benning. Meanwhile, the police were still receiving letters and phone calls about the supposed hostage.

On September 16, 1977, the body of Karen Hickman was found at Fort Benning. She had been beaten before being run over by a car, and her body was nude. With no leads or clues, the murder of Hickman was pushed aside due to another serial killer case, Carlton Gary.

The FBI was brought in to help catch the strangler. Profiler Robert K. Ressler created a profile that was the opposite of what police had believed about the killer. Ressler's profile determined there was only one man, not a gang of seven; he was white, single, not well-educated, and was probably in the lower ranks of the military at Fort Benning.

Tapes of the phone calls sent to police were reviewed by an officer. On April 4, he recognized the voice as belonging to William Hance, a twenty-six-year-old private in the army. Police began searching for Hance, focusing on the local bars near the fort. It didn't take them long to find him, and he was promptly arrested. On April 5, he was charged with murder and attempted extortion. He confessed right away to the murders but later recanted.

Trial

When Hance was shown the evidence against him, including handwriting analysis, voice recordings, and shoe prints found at the murder scenes, he confessed to killing Jackson, Hickman, and a third woman whom he had killed in September of 1977. Hickman was an army private who often dated black soldiers. Because she was military, Hance was tried by court-martial. He was convicted of her murder.

He was also tried and convicted in a military court for the murder of Thirkield. During this court-martial he received a life sentence, but this was reversed by the jurors because they deemed he lacked the mental capacity to premeditate the murder. For the murder of Hickman, he received life at hard labor. In 1980, the convictions were set aside, and he wasn't retried by the military court system.

On December 16, 1978, he was tried in a civilian court for the murder of Brenda Faison. He was convicted and sentenced to death, and given an additional five years for the extortion charge.

Outcome

On March 31, 1994, Hance was executed by electric chair. The death penalty had been reinstated in 1976, and Hance was the two hundred thirty-first inmate to be executed and the eighteenth in Georgia. In the hours leading up to his execution, it was decided by the Supreme Court not to consider an appeal.

Trivia

Before he was executed, Hance made a seven-minute statement. Part of it was, "Why are you executing an innocent man? Why? Why? Why?"

CHARLES RAY HATCHER

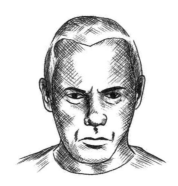

Date of birth: July 16, 1929

Aliases/Nicknames: Crazy Charlie, Albert Aire, Richard Clark, Richard Mark Clark, Richard Martin Clark, Richard Lee Grady, Richard Harris, Carl L. Kalebough, Earl L. Kalebough, Doris Mullins, Hobart Prater, Albert Ralph Price, Richard Lee Price, Ronald Springer, Charles Marvin Tidwell, Doris Mullins Travis, Dwayne Lee Wilfong

Characteristics: Child molester

Number of victims: 2 - 16

Date of murders: 1969 - 1982

Date of arrest: August 3, 1982

Victim profile: Eric Christgen, 4; Michelle Steele, 11; William Freeman, 12; James Churchill, 28

Method of murder: Strangulation, stabbing with knife

Location: Missouri, Illinois, California, USA

Status: Sentenced to 50 years to life in prison without parole in Missouri, 1984. Committed suicide by hanging himself in his cell on December 7, 1984.

Background

Hatcher was convicted of auto theft in 1947 in St. Joseph, after stealing a logging truck from the Iowa–Missouri Walnut Company, the company he had been employed by for two weeks. He received a two-year suspended sentence.

In 1948, he was convicted of auto theft again for stealing a 1937 Buick in St. Joseph. This time, Hatcher was sentenced to two years in prison.

Hatcher was released from prison on June 8, 1949, after serving a little more than half of his time. In the space of a few months, he was back behind bars for check forgery.

Hatcher escaped from prison on March 18, 1951, and attempted to commit a robbery, but was apprehended and given an extra two years' imprisonment.

Hatcher served his extra time and was released from prison on July 14, 1954. But then he stole a 1951 Ford in Orrick and was sentenced to another four years in prison. Hatcher tried to escape from the Ray County Jail in Richmond before he was sentenced, and was given an extra two years.

Hatcher was released from prison on March 18, 1959, after serving his sixth sentence. Within months, he was back in trouble, but this time, it was a violent crime. On June 26, Hatcher attempted to kidnap Steven Pellham, a sixteen-year-old newspaper deliverer, by threatening him with a butcher knife. He was unsuccessful, and Pellham reported the crime. Hatcher was arrested for the incident when the police stopped him in a stolen vehicle.

Hatcher was sentenced to five years in prison for the attempted abduction and auto theft under the Habitual Criminal Act. While waiting for his transport to prison, he tried to break out of the Buchanan County Jail but failed. Upon his arrival at the Missouri State Penitentiary, he claimed he was the most notorious criminal in northwest Missouri since Jesse James.

On August 27th, 1969, Hatcher confessed to abducting William Freeman, aged twelve, in Antioch, California. He stated he had told Freeman to come with him to a creek where he then strangled the boy.

Days later, on August 29, six-year-old Gilbert Martinez was reported missing in San Francisco. According to the six year old girl he had been playing with, Martinez walked away with a man who offered him ice cream. A man walking his dog came across them as Martinez was sexually assaulted and beaten. Police were quickly on the scene and arrested the assailant, who said he was Albert Ralph Price. His identification, however, had the name Hobert Prater. Martinez was lucky to survive the assault. The Federal Bureau of Investigation later identified the attacker as Charles R. Hatcher.

Hatcher, under the name of Price, was charged with kidnapping and assault with attempt to commit sodomy. The judge ordered him to be evaluated for competency to determine if he was fit to stand trial. A psychological evaluation was ordered when Hatcher was unresponsive during the preliminary evaluations. He faked having delusions and claimed he could hear voices; he also faked many suicide attempts to avoid going to prison.

In December of 1970, he was taken back and forth between the courts and the mental hospital on several occasions. One of the psychiatrists treating him diagnosed him as having a passive-aggressive personality with paraphilia and pedophilia. The hospital staff believed Hatcher was making up—or at least exaggerating—the symptoms of his alleged mental disorders. Two psychiatrists examined him in January of 1971. One of the doctors found him to be sane, yet recommended he undergo vigorous treatment in a secure hospital. The second psychiatrist found him insane and incompetent to stand trial and returned him to the hospital.

On May 24, 1971, Hatcher went on trial and pled not guilty by reason of insanity. This time he was taken to a different mental hospital for evaluation, and he was again determined not fit to stand trial. Hatcher escaped from the hospital on June 2. A week later he was caught in Colusa, California and arrested for suspected auto theft under the name of Richard Lee Grady. Hatcher was sent back to the California State Hospital for another mental evaluation. In April of 1972, hospital staff determined his treatment had not been a success and that he was a danger to the other patients, and he was then transferred to the prison state hospital in Vacaville.

In August of 1972, Hatcher was transferred to San Quentin State Prison for his trial, three years after he committed the crime. He was ordered to be given two final assessments, with one declaring him competent to stand trial and the other finding him to be sane at the time he committed the crime.

Hatcher was subsequently convicted of the abduction and molestation of Martinez in December of 1972. A month later, he was determined to be a "mentally disordered sexual offender" and was committed to the California State Hospital. On March 28, 1973, security guards discovered Hatcher hiding near the hospital's main courtyard with two bedsheets stuffed into his pants, and he admitted he was trying to escape. Hatcher was returned to court for sentencing after doctors deemed him still a threat to society. Hatcher was sentenced to one year to life in April and sent to a medium-security prison in Vacaville.

In May of 1973, a psychologist determined Hatcher was a "manipulative institutionalized sociopath." He attempted to kill himself that June by cutting his wrists after learning he would be transferred to a maximum-security prison. He was diagnosed with paranoid schizophrenia, and his transfer was canceled.

In August of 1975, at Hatcher's parole review, guards reported good behavior. In June of 1976, the parole board found Hatcher had improved dramatically and set a parole date of December 25, 1978. Because of the passage of a bill giving inmates credit for time spent in jails and mental hospitals, Hatcher's parole was modified to a date in January of 1977. He was released on May 20, 1977, to a halfway house in San Francisco.

Hatcher was arrested again under the name Richard Clark in Omaha, Nebraska for sexually assaulting a sixteen-year-old boy on September 4, 1978. He was sent to the Douglas County Mental Hospital and released in January of 1979.

On May 3, 1979, he was arrested for assault and attempted murder after he tried to stab Thomas Morton, aged seven. He was sent to a mental health facility, Norfolk Regional Center, after the charges were dropped. A year later, in May of 1980, Hatcher was released from the facility but was sent back two months later for another assault. He escaped in September.

Hatcher was arrested in Lincoln, Nebraska on October 9, 1980, under the name Richard Clark, for the attempted sodomy and assault of a seventeen-year-old boy. He was sent to a mental health hospital and was released after just twenty-one days. Then on January 13, 1981, Hatcher was arrested as Richard Clark in Des Moines, Iowa after a knife fight. After spending time in different mental health facilities, Hatcher was released to a Davenport Salvation Army shelter in April.

Murders

On July 2, 1961, Jerry Tharrington, twenty-six, a prison inmate, was found raped and stabbed to death on the floor of the loading dock at the prison. He had been stabbed multiple times in the back. The only person missing from the kitchen crew at the time he was murdered was Hatcher. There wasn't enough evidence to charge Hatcher with the murder, but he was sent to solitary confinement. While in confinement, Hatcher wrote a note stating he needed psychiatric treatment, but the psychologist at the prison believed it was a ploy for Hatcher to get out of solitary. Hatcher was refused any treatment and sent back to the general population section of the prison. Remarkably, he was released following a shortening of his sentence and was back on the streets on August 24, 1963.

The body of Eric Christgen, four, was discovered beside the Missouri River after he had gone missing on May 26, 1978. The boy had been abused sexually and suffocated to death. The next known victim was Michelle Steele, eleven. She had disappeared from St. Joseph on July 29, 1982, just like Christgen before her. Her nude body was found on the bank of the Missouri River the following day. She had been beaten before being strangled to death. The next day, as Hatcher tried to check himself into the St. Joseph State Hospital, he was arrested for her murder.

Trial

While Hatcher was awaiting trial, he made a confession that he had killed fifteen other children since 1969. William Freeman, twelve, was the first, and he had gone missing in August of 1969. It was the day before Hatcher was charged with another child molestation in San Francisco. For another murder, Hatcher drew a map for police that would lead them to the remains of James Churchill. He had been murdered and buried on the grounds of the Rock Island Army Arsenal near Davenport. He also confessed to killing Eric Christgen.

In October of 1983, Hatcher was convicted of murdering Christgen and was given a sentence of life with no parole for fifty years. The following year he went on trial for the murder of Steele. Hatcher requested the jury give him a death sentence, but they refused, and on December 3, 1984, he received another life sentence.

Four days later, Hatcher committed suicide by hanging himself in his cell.

Outcome

While investigating the murder of Christgen, police had interviewed over one hundred potential suspects, including those known to be pedophiles. One of these men was Melvin Reynolds, twenty-five, who had a history of being sexually abused and had limited intelligence. Over a number of months, Reynolds was questioned several times and each time he cooperated. He was given two polygraph tests and interrogation under hypnosis, with no clear admission of guilt.

Reynolds was questioned again in December of 1978 under the influence of amobarbital - the supposed truth serum - and made a comment that made police more interested in him as a suspect. In February of 1979, Reynolds underwent a further fourteen hours of interrogation. In the end, Reynolds stated, "I'll say so if you want me to."

Over the next few weeks, Reynolds was allegedly fed details about the crime to bolster his admission. He was charged and subsequently convicted of second-degree murder and sentenced to life. When Hatcher confessed to these murders four years later, Reynolds was released.

Trivia

Hatcher told investigators that William Freeman had been either his sixth or seventh victim.

Hatcher was questioned while under the influence of truth serum on December 2, 1982, during which he claimed he was told by demons and voices to "sacrifice the maiden." However, doctors decided he was making this up to try to make excuses for what he had done.

DALE HAUSNER AND SAMUEL DIETEMAN

Dale Hausner

Date of birth: February 4, 1973

Aliases/Nicknames: The Serial Shooter

Characteristics: Drive-by shootings targeting random pedestrians

Number of victims: 8

Date of murders: May 2005 - July 2006

Date of arrest: August 3, 2006

Victim profile: David Estrada, 20; Nathaniel Shoffner; Jose Ortis, 44; Marco Carillo; Claudia Gutierrez-Cruz, 20; Robin Blasnek, 22

Method of murder: Shooting

Location: Phoenix, Arizona, USA

Status: Sentenced to six death penalties on March 27, 2009. Committed suicide by overdosing on amitriptyline in prison on June 19, 2013.

Samuel Dieteman

Date of birth: October 17, 1975

Aliases/Nicknames: The Serial Shooter

Characteristics: Drive-by shootings targeting random pedestrians

Number of victims: 8

Date of murders: May 2005 - July 2006

Date of arrest: August 3, 2006

Victim profile: David Estrada, 20; Nathaniel Shoffner; Jose Ortis, 44; Marco Carillo; Claudia Gutierrez-Cruz, 20; Robin Blasnek, 22

Method of murder: Shooting

Location: Phoenix, Arizona, USA

Status: Life without parole.

Background

There is not a lot of information available about the early lives of either Hausner or Dieteman. Hausner had worked as a custodian at Phoenix Sky Harbor International Airport since 1999 and was also a boxing photojournalist for RingSports and Fightnews.com. Dieteman, with a history of drunk driving and petty theft charges, had returned to Arizona after living in Minnesota.

In 1994, Hausner lost his two sons following a car accident. The car had crashed into a creek, and both boys had drowned. Hausner became very depressed by the tragedy, and his marriage came to an end. He began drinking and joyriding with his brother Jeff. In early 2006, Jeff introduced him to Dieteman at a bar.

Dieteman was a father of two girls. His wife had left him in 2001 and, according to his family, this led to his drug addiction. He lost his apartment and lived with his mother and stepfather for a while but was eventually thrown out because of his alcohol consumption. He moved in with Hausner, and they set up a little money-making scheme. Dieteman would steal CDs and alcohol that Hausner then sold to his coworkers. They also liked to set fires, usually to trees or trash piles, and they often beat up transients.

Murders

All of the victims of their drive-by shootings were random pedestrians innocently going about their business. The men would drive around at night until they found someone to shoot at. Their weapons of choice were a .22 rifle and a .410-gauge shotgun. In one case though, the victim, Timothy Davenport, was stabbed to death. Most of the victims were shot in Phoenix, with some of the crimes taking place in nearby cities. The details of the shootings are as follows:

Victims Killed:

David Estrada, twenty. Estrada was shot to death on June 29.
Nathaniel Shoffner, forty-four. He was murdered on November 11 while trying to protect a dog from being shot.
Jose Ortiz, forty-four. He was murdered on December 12.
Marco Carillo, twenty-eight. Carillo was murdered four days after Christmas, on December 29.
Claudia Gutierrez-Cruz, twenty. Gutierrez-Cruz was shot and killed by Dieteman on May 2, 2006 as Hausner drove.
Robin Blasnek, twenty-two. Blasnek was killed by Hausner on July 30, 2006.

Victims Injured:

Tony Mendez, thirty-nine. Mendez was shot on May 17, 2005.
Reginald Remillard. He was shot on May 24, 2005.
Barbara Whitner. -She was shot on December 29, 2005.
Timmy Tordai. He was shot in the neck on December 29, 2005.
Clarissa Rowley, twenty-one. Rowley was shot on December 30, 2005.
Kibili Tambadu. Hausner shot Tambadu in the back on May 2, 2006.
Timothy Davenport. - He was stabbed in the back and slashed in the face on May 17, 2006, by Dieteman.
James Hodge. Hodge was shot on May 30, 2006, but survived.
Miguel Rodriguez. Rodriguez was shot in the side of his body on May 31, 2006.
Daryl Davies. Davies was shot in the side on May 31, 2006.
Paul Patrick. Patrick was shot on June 8, 2006.
Elizabeth Clark. She was shot in the left hip on June 11, 2006.
Frederic Cena. Cena was shot on June 20, 2006.
Tony Long. Long was shot in the torso on June 20, 2006.
Diane Bein. Bein was shot on July 1, 2006.

Jeremy Ortiz. Ortiz was shot on July 1, 2006.

Joseph Roberts. Roberts was shot on July 3, 2006.

David Perez. Perez was shot on July 7, 2006.

Ashley Armenta. Armenta was shot in the back of the head on July 8, 2006.

Garry Begay. Begay was also shot on July 8, 2006.

Michael Cordrey. Cordrey was shot on July 11, 2006.

Raul Garcia. Garcia was shot on July 22, 2006.

Hausner and Dieteman were first identified as possible suspects by police on July 31, 2006, following tips they had received. Ron Horton, a friend of Dieteman, provided the most information but, unfortunately, he died before the case went to trial. He told police that Dieteman had admitted he was involved in the shootings. The confession was made while Dieteman was drunk.

Due to the information they received, police attained a court order to place listening devices in the apartment of Hausner and Dieteman. Subsequently, they were recorded making statements about the shootings, including details that hadn't been made public.

Both men were arrested on August 3, 2006, and the following morning the announcement was made public that two men were in custody for the serial shootings. Police also stated they had linked them to two arson fires at Wal-Mart stores on June 8, which resulted in up to ten million dollars in damage.

Trial

Hausner was charged with eighty-seven crimes, including:

- Eight murders
- Nineteen attempted murders
- Multiple aggravated assaults
- Drive-by shootings
- Firearms charges
- Cruelty to animals
- Arson

Hausner was found guilty of six murders and eighty charges overall on March 13, 2009. On March 27, he was sentenced to six death penalties. Hausner had instructed his lawyers not to argue against the death sentences stating that if he was put to death, the families of the victims could heal. However, he never actually admitted he was guilty of any of the crimes. A mandatory appeal was lodged. Following this, Hausner waived all future appeals.

Before he was sentenced, Hausner had spoken to the jury for half an hour, during which time he apologized to several people, including members of his family. He said he had ruined the family name. He compared himself to Charles Manson, saying, "When you think of Manson, 50 years from now you'll think of Hausner."

Dieteman pled guilty to two murders and conspiracy to commit some of the other murders. As a result, he received a sentence of life without parole.

Outcome

On June 19, 2013, Hausner was discovered unconscious in his cell. Later that day, he was pronounced deceased. The medical examiner determined his cause of death was an antidepressant overdose.

Trivia

"My favorite thing is, you know when somebody is walking away, you know, it gives me, you know, a couple of extra seconds to aim. I don't have to worry about them looking I get too paranoid of somebody walking toward me and while I'm trying to aim they're frickin' gonna see me, or not... not so much see me but see the gun stickin' out wrong or somethin' and be able to give a description."
— *Dieteman*

A letter to a neighbor in an adjacent cell was emotional:

"I wish we would have known each other on the streets," Hausner wrote. "That would have been so much fun. Imagine all we could have done together. You are like a crazy little brother to me. ... You are smart, funny, and a little insane. But then, so am I.

"Since I have been here, I have tried to make this place better for you. I hope when you look at our friendship, you will remember the fun and laughs we have shared. Remember that I was your friend and that I was always there for you. When you speak of me to others, please tell them I was your friend.

"Thinking about this place, the only thing I will miss is you. (And maybe the pizza.)"

Hausner included a poem with the letter:

"Death is only the beginning.
In Death I find hope,
the hope of better times,
of no memories,
of forgiveness, gotten and given.
In Death, I can see my kids,
I can tell them that I am sorry
and that I love them.
No more pain, guilt or shame.
In Death, I will be able to
Breathe Again.
Death is welcomed, is needed
is longed for.
Death is only the beginning."
He signed it, "An original poem by Dale S. Hausner."

WILLIAM HEIRENS

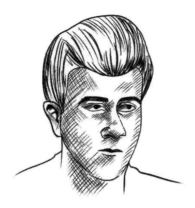

Date of birth: November 15, 1928

Aliases/Nicknames: The Lipstick Killer

Characteristics: Juvenile, robbery, kidnapping

Number of victims: 3

Date of murders: June 1945 - January 1946

Date of arrest: June 26, 1946

Victim profile: Josephine Ross, 45; Francis Brown, 34; Suzanne Degnan, 6

Method of murder: Stabbing with knife, strangulation

Location: Chicago, Illinois, USA

Status: Sentenced to life in prison on September 5, 1946

Background

Heirens and his family lived in Lincolnwood, Chicago, and the family was poor. His parents fought often and to escape the shouting, Heirens would wander the streets. He began stealing at a young age, but only for fun and to release tension. He didn't sell anything he stole, keeping everything. When he was thirteen, the police caught him carrying a loaded gun. During the search of his home, they located a storage shed on a building roof nearby that was full of Heirens's loot. After admitting he had committed eleven burglaries, Heirens was sent to a school for wayward boys, where he stayed for several months.

Shortly after he was released, he was again picked up by police for theft. This resulted in a sentence of three years at the St. Bede Academy, which was run by Benedictine Monks. Heirens excelled in his schoolwork at the academy and did so well that he applied to the special learning program at the University of Chicago. He was accepted and, bypassing high school, he began classes in the fall of 1945 at the age of sixteen.

Because his parents couldn't pay for his tuition or boarding fees, Heirens worked most evenings as an usher. It didn't stop him from stealing, though, and his burglarizing continued. The same year that Heirens entered university, dead bodies began to turn up.

Murders

On June 5, 1945, the dead body of Josephine Ross, forty-five, was found in her Chicago apartment. She had been stabbed multiple times, and her head had been wrapped up in a dress. It was presumed she had interrupted an intruder, which prompted her murder. In her hand were some dark hairs, showing she had tried to fight back. Nothing was taken. A man was seen hanging around the apartment prior to her death, but he was never located.

Frances Brown was found dead on December 10, 1945, also in her apartment in Chicago. A cleaning woman had heard a loud radio coming from the apartment and entered through the partially open door. Brown had been shot in the head and brutally stabbed, a knife sticking out of her neck. Again, police thought she might have interrupted a burglary, but no valuables were missing. However, a message had been written on the wall in lipstick:

For heavens
Sake catch me
Before I kill more
I cannot control myself

On the doorjamb, a fingerprint in blood was discovered. A man had been seen leaving the apartment building, but that wasn't confirmed. Days after the killing, the police announced they thought the killer was a woman, though this wasn't explained in detail.

The next murder occurred on January 7, 1946. Suzanne Degnan was reported missing from her home. A ladder was outside the six-year-old's bedroom window, along with a ransom note. Multiple phone calls ensued, demanding a ransom payment, but no real conversation took place between the caller and the police.

An anonymous tip was given to police, which led them to the little girl's remains. Her head was found in a sewer a block away from her home. Her right leg was in a catch basin, and her torso was discovered in a storm drain. The other leg was found in another drain. A month later, her arms were found in another sewer. In the laundry tubs of a nearby apartment, blood was found. Hundreds of people were questioned, and on several occasions police announced they had the killer, but each time, the person was released.

The mystery surrounding the ransom calls was later solved. Teenager Theodore Campbell told police that another teenager, Vincent Costello had killed Suzanne Degnan. But, when both were put through polygraph tests, the results showed they had no knowledge of the murder. Later, they admitted they had overheard police officers discussing the case and came up with the idea of asking for a ransom.

Heirens was arrested for burglary on June 26, 1946, after he was witnessed breaking into an apartment. As police approached he ran, and the janitor of the building gave chase, blocking him from leaving the building. But when Heirens pointed a gun at him, the janitor had to give up and let him go. Heirens ran to a building nearby to hide but was seen by a resident who notified police. As Heirens tried to escape down a staircase, two police officers approached one at each end of the staircase. Heirens waved his gun at them, but after two misfires, he charged at them instead. While he scuffled with the officers, another officer dropped flowerpots on his head from above, the third one knocking him out.

Later, Heirens claimed police interrogated him for six days straight, around the clock. He said he had been beaten by police and was refused food or drink. He claimed he was unable to see his parents for four days and was refused access to a lawyer for six days.

During a conversation with Captain Michael Ahern, with the state's attorney William Tuohy and a stenographer present, Heirens made an indirect confession. He claimed he had an alter ego, George Murman, who was responsible for all the crimes. Authorities weren't convinced and suspected he was trying to lay the groundwork for pleading insanity.

Trial

The defense attorneys for Heirens thought that he was guilty, and believed their job was to save him from execution. The prosecuting attorney, Tuohy on the other hand, was uncertain he could get a conviction. A plea bargain was offered. Heirens was pressured by his lawyers to take the plea, which meant he would only serve one life sentence if he confessed to the murders.

Heirens signed a confession, along with his parents. The agreement was to make the confession official on July 30. However, when officials gathered to hear the confession, Heirens seemed bewildered and provided noncommittal answers to any questions.

The plea offer was withdrawn and changed to three life terms to run consecutively. Tuohy threatened Heirens that if he went to trial, he would pursue the death penalty. Heirens agreed to the new deal. On August 7, 1946, Heirens took responsibility for the murders. On September 4, he admitted his guilt regarding the murder and burglary charges. The same night, he tried to hang himself but was found before it was too late.

The following day, Heirens was sentenced to the three life terms.

Outcome

While incarcerated, Heirens learned some trades, including television and radio repair, and he had his own repair shop at the prison for a while. On February 6, 1972, Heirens was the first prisoner in Illinois to earn a college degree. For five years he managed the garment factory at the prison, overseeing three hundred fifty inmates. He later transferred to Vienna Prison and set up an educational program. He assisted prisoners with their General Educational Development diplomas.

In 1984, the Seventh District U.S. Court of Appeals ruled that it was unconstitutional to refuse parole to inmates convicted prior to 1973 on deterrence grounds. It was ordered that Heirens be released immediately. However, with the support of some prominent politicians, the ruling was reversed.

Heirens developed diabetes, which affected his legs to the point that he had to use a wheelchair. It also affected his eyesight. On February 26, 2012, he was taken to a medical center with complications from his diabetes. He died on March 5, 2012, at the age of 83.

Trivia

Until his death, Heirens had been the longest-serving prisoner in the history of Illinois.

The film *While the City Sleeps* (1956) was based on Heirens' case.

Following his arrest, Heirens' parents and his brother changed their name legally to "Hill."

Not long after his conviction, his parents got a divorce.

LOREN HERZOG AND WESLEY SHERMANTINE

Loren Herzog

Date of birth: 1966

Aliases/Nicknames: The Speed Freak Killers

Characteristics: Thrill killer

Number of victims: 4 +

Date of murders: 1984 - 1999

Date of arrest: March 17, 1999

Victim profile: Paul Cavanaugh, 31; Howard King, 35; Chevy Wheeler, 16; Cyndi Vanderheiden, 25

Method of murder: Shooting, stabbing with knife

Location: California, Utah, USA

Status: Sentenced to 78 years in prison in California in 2001. Resentenced to 14 years in prison on November 24, 2004. Released on parole in September 2010.

Wesley Shermantine

Date of birth: February 24, 1966

Aliases/Nicknames: The Speed Freak Killers

Characteristics: Thrill killer, drugs

Number of victims: 4 - 24

Date of murders: 1984 - 1999

Date of arrest: March 17, 1999

Victim profile: Paul Cavanaugh, 31; Howard King, 35; Chevy Wheeler, 16; Cyndi Vanderheiden, 25

Method of murder: Shooting, stabbing with knife

Location: California, Utah, USA

Status: Sentenced to death in California on May 16, 2001.

Background

Herzog and Shermantine grew up together in Linden, California. Linden was a small town with less than two thousand residents, and it was well known amongst the community that both Herzog and Shermantine were users of methamphetamine. They frequented the local bar, the Linden Inn, which was owned by the father of Cyndi Vanderheiden. On November 14, 1998, she went missing after she left the bar with Herzog and Shermantine.

Murders

Throughout the investigation into Vanderheiden's disappearance, Shermantine was the main suspect. His car was repossessed in January of 1999, which enabled police to search it. Blood was found in the car, and it was identified as belonging to Vanderheiden. Herzog was brought in for extensive questioning. He said that he and Shermantine had met Vanderheiden in a cemetery near her home after they had left the bar. As they drove back to Linden, Shermantine pulled out a knife and ordered her to perform oral sex. He then stopped the car, raped her, and slashed her throat.

Herzog was accused of murdering Henry Howell, who was shot dead on the highway in September of 1984. Howell's head and teeth had been bashed in before he was shot. According to Herzog, they had passed Howell parked on the highway, and Shermantine pulled the car over. He robbed Howell and killed him. Herzog further told police that the murder of Robin Armtrout, who was found stabbed multiple times on the bank of Potter Creek, was also the work of Shermantine.

He further detailed the murder of Chevelle "Chevy" Wheeler, sixteen, who had disappeared in 1985 while playing truant from school. She had been seen in a car with Shermantine headed into the mountains. Investigators located Shermantine's cabin in the mountains and found blood which DNA revealed belonged to Wheeler.

Trial

Herzog was charged on March 23, 1999, with five counts of murder, including the kidnapping and murder of Vanderheiden.

Shermantine's trial began on November 22, 2000, in Santa Clara. He was charged with four murders, but prosecutors told the court that they believed he might have killed as many as twenty more. The jury was told that, over the years, Shermantine had told acquaintances and family members he had "made people disappear." He had told Herzog he had killed twenty-two people in California, Utah, and Nevada, and that killing people was like a sport.

During both trials, the two men insisted it was the other who had committed the murders. Shermantine hinted that he might know where the bodies were, and Herzog had carried out the killings. However, Herzog's attorney called this a desperate ploy to deflect blame. Herzog stated he had only watched Shermantine kill the victims.

Shermantine was found guilty of four murders - Vanderheiden, Howard King, Paul Cavanaugh, and Chevelle "Chevy" Wheeler. He was sentenced to death.

In 2001, Herzog was found guilty of three murders - Vanderheiden, King, and Cavanaugh. He was also convicted of accessory to murder for the Howell charge. He received a sentence of seventy-eight years. In August of 2004, Herzog's convictions were overturned on appeal, citing his confessions had been coerced. A retrial was ordered for the Vanderheiden case, but a plea bargain was reached instead. He ended up with a sentence of fourteen years, with credit for the six years he had already served. In the end, he served eleven years before being paroled.

Outcome

There was huge opposition to Herzog being paroled, so the California Department of Corrections paroled him to a trailer outside the front gate of High Desert State Prison in Susanville, California, in September of 2010.

In January of 2012, Herzog committed suicide inside the trailer by hanging. He had been told, shortly before his death, that Shermantine was planning on disclosing the location of the missing bodies.

Shermantine sent his sister letters in February of 2010, identifying an abandoned well where the bodies could be found. She gave the letters to the authorities, but when they spoke to the property owner, he said the wells had been sealed before the victims had disappeared, so no action was taken.

However, in February of 2012, a map was drawn by Shermantine that lead police to the same location. This time they searched and discovered over one thousand human bone fragments. On March 30, the identity of the remains was announced. They belonged to two teenage girls, Kimberly Ann Billy, nineteen, and Joann Hobson, sixteen. The girls had disappeared on December 11, 1984. There was also an unidentified victim in the well and the remains of a fetus.

Trivia

The case was profiled on an episode of *American Justice*. The episode was called "Vanished" and was broadcast in September of 2002. Because of the date of the production, newer facts weren't included in the program.

There was an episode of *On the Case with Paula Zahn* that featured the case, which was called "Where Evil Lies." It was broadcast in 2015 and included updated information, including Herzog's suicide.

"I really want to believe in Leonard, but I have these doubts he'll come through, which is a shame because I've been holding the best for last."
— **Shermantine, on revealing their burial sites**

A tattoo in black ink that read "Made And Fueled by Hate and Restrained By Reality" ran down the length of Herzog's left leg to his foot. A tattoo on his right foot read, "Made The Devil Do It."

Herzog's parole agent asked prison officials to check on him in January of 2012, at which point they found Herzog hanging by a rope he had made from a bedsheet. The "rope" had been tied to a ladder behind his trailer.

Herzog left behind a suicide note that said, "Tell my family I love them."

More tattoos were discovered during Herzog's autopsy, including one on his left foot that translated to "Trace of the Devastation." There was also a black-and-green tattoo that covered his arms depicting flames, the grim reaper, skulls, webs, skeletons, a panther, and Satan. On his chest were skulls encasing his wife's nickname, "Sugar," and the name, "Sara." Another tattoo on either side of his abdomen showed two revolvers.

JOHANN OTTO HOCH

Date of birth: 1855

Aliases/Nicknames: The Bluebeard Murderer, John Schmidt, Jacob Huff, CA Calford, William Frederick Bessing, Henry F. Hartman, Martiz Dotz, Martin Dose, Albert Buschberg, Jacob Erdorf, John Healy, Carl Schmidt, Count Otto van Kern, Dr. GL Hart, Leo Prager, Harry Bartells

Characteristics: Poisoner

Number of victims: 15 +

Date of murders: 1890 - 1905

Date of arrest: January 30, 1905

Victim profile: Marie Walcker, and many other wives

Method of murder: Arsenic poisoning

Location: Chicago, Illinois, USA

Status: Sentenced to death on June 23, 1905. Executed by hanging on February 23, 1906

Background

Born John Schmidt in Germany, Hoch immigrated to America in the 1890s as a young man. He dropped his surname and used a number of pseudonyms so he could marry a string of women. He would often take the last name of his recent victim. Hoch robbed all of the women and would either just leave or murder them with arsenic. In total, he married fifty-five women between 1890 and 1905. The exact number of murders is unknown, with police only able to confirm fifteen. Some, however, believe the number to be as high as twenty-five to fifty. Throughout this time, Hoch had only one legal wife - Christine Ramb. They had three children before he left them in 1887.

Murders

There were so many wives and murders, that information on each is scant. The following crimeline details as much information as available:

Crimeline

1881, Austria: Hoch married Annie Hoch.

1883, New York: Hoch arrived in New York with Annie, who was now an invalid. She died several years later.

1888, New York: After arriving from Wurttemberg, Hoch allegedly married a servant girl who "died" before the end of two months of marriage. 1892, Chicago: Mrs. Hoyle Hoch died.

1892, Chicago: In May, he rented a flat under the name C.A. Meyer and had a new wife who reportedly died after three weeks.

1892, Chicago: In June, Hoch rented a flat under the name H. Irick and had a new wife who reportedly died a month later.

1893, Milwaukee: He married Lena Schmitz under the name "Dr. James." Schmitz later died.

1893, Milwaukee: Hoch married Lena Schmitz' sister Clara who died.

1894, Chicago: Hoch rented a flat under a new alias and had a new wife who reportedly died after two months.

1895, Chicago: Under the name "C.A. Calford," Hoch was arrested and charged with having eloped by Mrs. Janet Spencer. He had married and abandoned her, taking off with a few hundred dollars of her money. Hoch was identified as the abductor of Hulda Stevans and was involved in a robbery of diamonds.

1895, April: Hoch married Karoline/Caroline (Miller) under the name Jacob Huff. She died on June 15, 1895. He faked his own death, changed his surname to HOCH, and moved to Chicago.

1895, July 5: Hoch arrived in Chicago.

1895, July 15: Hoch purchased a saloon in Chicago.

1895, August 5: He married Mrs. Maria Steimbucher of Chicago under the name "Jacob Hoch." She died four months later. Hoch sold her property for four thousand dollars. She made a declaration before she died that she has been poisoned, but nobody took any notice.

1895, November: Hoch married Mary Rankin of Chicago. The following day, Hoch disappeared with her money. Allegedly, around 1895, Hoch went back to Germany under the name Schmidt. But a warrant was out for his arrest for him being bankrupt, and owing three thousand marks, so he fled.

1896, April: Under the name "Jacob Erdorf," he married Maria Hartzfield of Chicago. After four months, Hoch disappeared with six hundred dollars of her money.

1896, September 22: He married widow Barbara Brossett of San Francisco under the name "Schmitt." He disappeared two days later with $1,465 of her money. She was so devastated, she died soon after.

1896: Hoch proposed to Mrs. H. Tannert (a landlady) of San Francisco, but she refused him.

1896, November: Hoch married Clara Bartel of Cincinnati Ohio. Three months later, she died.

1896: Mrs. Henry Bartel died in Baltimore; Bartel was known to be a Hoch alias. It is alleged that Hoch married twice more in Baltimore to Mrs. Nannie Klenke-Schultz and Mrs. Henriette Brooks-Schultz. An unidentified Boston woman married to a "Louis/Charles Bartels" came to Baltimore and seized his furniture.

1897, January: He married Julia Dose of Hamilton Ohio-in Cincinnati. Hoch disappeared the same day as the wedding with seven hundred dollars of her money.

1897, July 20: Hoch married in Cincinnati under the name "Henry F. Hartman."

1897, December 6: Hoch married a woman in Williamsburg, New York and disappeared with two hundred dollars of her money.

1898, January 16: Under the name "William Frederick Bessing," Hoch married Mrs. Winnie Westphal in Jersey City. Soon after, he disappeared with nine hundred dollars of her money.

1898, Buffalo, New York: Mrs. Wilhelmina Hoch died.

1898, March, Chicago: Hoch appeared under the alias "Martiz Dotz" with a wife who died in June of 1898.

1898, June: "Adolf Hoch," also known as "Martin Dose," was arrested in Chicago for selling furniture that was already mortgaged. He received one year in jail.

1899, Milwaukee: Hoch married an unnamed sister of Mrs. J.H. Schwartz-Marue. His wife died, and Hoch disappeared with twelve hundred dollars.

1899, Norfolk: Mrs. Hoch died suddenly.

1900: Hoch claimed he was married to Mary Hendrickson.

1900: Under the name "Albert Buschberg," Hoch married Mary Schultz of Argos, Indiana. Schultz, her fifteen-year-old daughter Nettie, and two thousand dollars "disappeared."

1900: A "Jacob Hoch" married Anna Scheffries of Chicago.

1900, December 12: Hoch, a.k.a. "John Healy," married Amelia Hohn of Chicago. He abandoned her after stealing one hundred dollars of her money.

1901, January: Hoch, a.k.a. "Carl Schmidt," married in Columbus, Ohio. He abandoned his wife after two weeks and took her money.

1901: He marries Mrs. Loughken-Hoch in San Francisco. She died, "suddenly."

1901, November: Hoch married Anna Goehrke and soon deserted her.

1902, April 8: Hoch married Mrs. Mary Becker of St Louis. She died in 1903.

1902, May: Hoch, a.k.a. "Count Otto van Kern," married Mrs. Hulda Nagel. She was persuaded to convert her real estate into cash. While she was shopping, her trunk containing three thousand dollars was robbed. "Kern" disappeared.

1903 June 18: Hoch, a.k.a. "Dr. G.L.Hart," tried to poison Mabel Leichmann, his wife of three days. Hoch fled with three hundred dollars worth of diamonds and two hundred dollars of her money.

1903, Dayton Ohio: Hoch married Mrs. Annie Dodd, then deserted her.

1903 Dayton Ohio: Hoch married Mrs. Regina Miller Curtis, then deserted her.

1903, Milwaukee: Hoch courted Ida Zazuil, but left her after a quarrel.

1903, December: Hoch used a marriage license for Zazuil and married Mrs. T.O'Conner of Milwaukee. He then abandoned her, absconding with two hundred dollars of her money.

1904, January 2: Under the name "John Jacob Adolf Schmidt," he married Mrs. Anna Hendrickson of Chicago in Hammond, Indiana, and then disappeared on January 20 with five hundred dollars of her money.

1904, June: Hoch married Lena Hoch of Milwaukee. She died three weeks later, leaving Hoch fifteen hundred dollars.

1904, October 8: Hoch, a.k.a. "Leo Prager," married Bertha Dolder of Chicago. He disappeared after buying twelve hundred dollars' worth of rugs from the thirty-five hundred dollars she had given him for furniture.

1904, October 20: Hoch, a.k.a. "John Schmidt," married Caroline Streicher of Philadelphia. Hoch disappeared on October 31, 1904.

1904, November 9: Hoch appeared in Chicago.

1904, November 16: Hoch leased a cottage in Chicago, under the alias "Joseph Hoch," from November 16, 1904, to January 1, 1905. He purchased one hundred twenty dollars' worth of furniture.

1904, December 10: Hoch married Marie Walcker of Chicago. She sold her candy store for seventy-five dollars and gave Hoch her life savings of three hundred fifty dollars.

1904, December 20: Marie Walcker-Hoch became ill.

1905, January 12: Marie Walcker-Hoch died.

1905, January 15: Hoch married Marie's sister Mrs. Fischer in Joliet, Ill; she gave Hoch seven hundred fifty dollars. Hoch left after Mrs. Fischer's sister denounced him as a swindler and a murderer. Hoch had married Fischer under the alias of John "Hock." It is alleged he married, swindled, and deserted Anna Frederickson in 1904.

1905, January 30: Hoch, under the name "Harry Bartells," proposed to his landlady Mrs. Catherine Kimmerle of New York City. She refused the proposal and Hoch was arrested. Hoch claimed he was "John Joseph Adolf Hoch."

1905, February 1: Two indictments were made against Hoch for bigamy. The alleged number of wives he had were twenty-nine.

1905, February 5: Five more alleged wives of Hoch identified him. At the time of his arrest in New York, 1905, it was alleged Hoch had married and killed (or simply left) a number of women in Vienna, London, England, Paris, and France.

In addition to the above, it is alleged that Hoch was involved with:

Mrs. John Hicks of Wheeling WV (died)
Mrs. Emma Rencke of Chicago
Mrs. Palinka of Batavia, Illinois
Mrs. Fink of Aurora
Natalie Irgang
Hulda Stevens
Schwartzman of Milwaukee
Justina Loeffler, of Elkhart Indiana, who "disappeared" in Chicago in 1903.
Mrs. Lena Hoch died in Milwaukee in 1897
Mrs. Hoch died in 1897
Mrs. Hoch died in 1898-both sisters of Mrs. J.H.H. Schwartzman of Milwaukee
Allegedly, Hoch married twice in Cincinnati, Ohio under the alias of "Henry Bartel" and "Fred Doess."

Trial

The only murder Hoch stood trial for was that of Marie Walcker, which took place on May 19, 1905. On June 23, he was sentenced to death.

Throughout his trial, Hoch whistled, hummed tunes, and twirled his thumbs. He seemed to enjoy his time in the limelight. When his sentence was handed down to him, he told the court, "It's all over with Johann. It serves me right."

Outcome

On June 23, 1905, Cora Wilson of Chicago advanced money to Hoch so he could appeal his sentence to the Illinois Supreme Court. His execution date was set for August 25, 1905. This was delayed until the next sitting of the Supreme Court, and on December 16, the Court refused to intervene.

On February 23, 1906, Hoch was taken to the gallows to face his execution. He stated, "I am done with this world. I have done with everybody." As the trap was sprung, a newsman said, "Mr. Hoch, but the question remains: What have you done with everybody?"

Following his death, several cemeteries refused to bury Hoch. He was therefore buried in a potter's field next to the Cook County Farm at Dunning.

Trivia

To make women fall in love with him, Hoch had a set of rules he claimed to live by. He shared these with the world in the *Chicago Sun* newspaper shortly before his execution:

6 WAYS TO WIN A WOMAN TOLD BY "BLUEBEARD" HOCH

- Nine out of every ten women can be won by flattery
- Never let a woman know her own shortcomings
- Always appear to a woman to be the anxious one
- Women like to be told pleasant things about themselves
- When you make love, be ardent and earnest
- The average man can fool the average woman if he will only let her have her own way at the start

Hoch received a number of marriage proposals while in prison waiting for his execution.

Hoch informed authorities that he would put up a fight if he was taken from the holding cell before 1:30 p.m. because his execution was scheduled for 2:00 p.m. At exactly 1:30 p.m., he was taken to the execution chamber. The minister stated after his death that Hoch denied he was a murderer but admitted his swindling and bigamy.

MICHAEL HUGHES

Date of birth: 1957

Aliases/Nicknames: Southside Slayer

Characteristics: Rape

Number of victims: 8

Date of murders: 1986 - 1993

Date of arrest: December 1993

Victim profile: Yvonne Coleman, 15; Verna Williams, 15; Deanna Wilson, 30; Teresa Ballard, 16; Brenda Bradley, 38; Deborah Jackson, 32; Terri Myles, 33; Jamie Harrington, 29

Method of murder: Strangulation

Location: Los Angeles County, California, USA

Status: Sentenced to life in prison without parole in 1998. Then sentenced to death.

Background

As a teenager, Hughes moved to Los Angeles, and in 1974, he joined the Navy as a machinist. When he left the Navy, he spent some time in jail for theft and perjury. He was married for a brief period, and he went from job to job, with any money he made spent on drugs.

When Hughes committed his first murder in 1986, he was working in the aerospace industry in Long Beach. He was living with his mother and his sister at the time. This murder was only the first of many to come.

Murders

In January of 1986, Yvonne Coleman, fifteen, had skipped school to hang out with her boyfriend. She was on her way back home when she was raped and murdered. Her body was found by a barbecue pit a few blocks away from where Hughes was living. In her mouth and throat, the medical examiner found grass.

The nude body of Verna Williams was found five months later on the grounds of an elementary school. She had been strangled to death. In August of 1990, Hughes, who was now married, raped and strangled Deanna Wilson in her garage while her young child was asleep in a room nearby.

241

Hughes was known to have gone to a motel half a mile away from the scene.

In June of 1993, the body of Deborah Jackson was found in a trash bin. Hughes was working within two blocks of the location. Teresa Ballard, twenty-six, was found dead in Jesse Owens County Park on September 23, 1992.

Later that year, Hughes was arrested for the murder of a woman who was found tied to a shopping cart. He was in the process of trying to dispose of the body when he was discovered.

Trial

Hughes was charged with the murders of Teresa Ballard, Brenda Bradley, Terri Myles, and Jamie Harrington. He was convicted in 1998 and sentenced to life without parole.

On July 3, 2008, Hughes was charged with sexually assaulting and strangling to death two women and two teenage girls between 1986 and 1993. He was linked to the victims through DNA samples. The case of Deanna Wilson was later dropped, but prosecutors still used it to show that Hughes had a pattern.

Outcome

In November of 2011, Hughes was convicted of the murders of Coleman, Williams, and McKinley. In June of 2012 he was sentenced to death. Hughes made a motion to reduce his sentence, but it was denied. He is still waiting on death row at San Quentin State Prison for his execution date.

Trivia

The victims' bodies were all found in public places, often naked, and posed in a manner that would shock whoever found them.

Hughes was physically abused as a child and at one point, witnessed his mother performing a forced abortion on his sister.

There were at least five serial killers operating in the South Los Angeles area in the early 1980s. The majority of the victims targeted were African-American women. Their bodies were often dumped in parks, vacant buildings, or alleys.

COLIN IRELAND

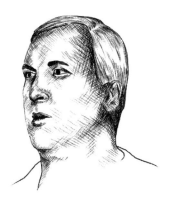

Date of birth: March 16, 1954

Aliases/Nicknames: The Gay Slayer

Characteristics: Gay men

Number of victims: 5

Date of murders: March-June 1993

Date of arrest: July 19, 1993 - surrendered

Victim profile: Peter Walker, 45; Christopher Dunn, 37; Perry Bradley, III, 35; Andrew Collier, 33; Emanuel Spiteri, 41

Method of murder: Strangulation

Location: London, England, United Kingdom

Status: Sentenced to life in prison on December 20, 1993.

Background

Ireland was born and raised in poverty. In his teens, he was arrested and charged with theft and was sent to Borstal. While there, he set fire to the belongings of another boy. When he was seventeen, he was charged and convicted of robbery and was returned to Borstal.

He later joined the army, the Foreign Legion, and became an escape and evasion specialist. When he left, he took on a variety of manual jobs. He was convicted of car theft, two burglaries, and criminal damage in December of 1975 and received an eighteen-month prison sentence. He was charged with extortion in 1977 and went back to prison for another eighteen months. Then, in 1980, he was convicted of robbery and sent to prison for two years. He received a conviction for attempted deception in 1981.

Ireland married in 1982, and the couple had a daughter. In 1985, he was convicted of "going equipped to cheat" and sentenced to six months. The couple divorced in 1987, after his wife discovered he had been unfaithful. Ireland married again in 1989, but he was violent and stole from his wife, and they separated in the early 1990s. Ireland became homeless and lived in a hostel for a while before moving into a flat. He started visiting the Coleherne, a gay pub in Earl's Court, London. It was here that he met his victims.

Murders

Ireland met Peter Walker, forty-five, a choreographer who enjoyed sadomasochism, and they went back to Walker's flat. Once there, Ireland tied him up and placed a plastic bag over his head, suffocating him. He then placed two teddy bears in an erotic position on the body. Walker's two dogs were left locked in another room. The following day, when nothing was reported on the news, Ireland called a journalist and told him about the dogs and that he had murdered Walker. He said he wanted to become a famous serial killer.

The next victim was Christopher Dunn, thirty-seven. When he was found, he was naked and in a harness. At first, it was thought his death might have been due to an accident during an erotic activity. Ireland next met businessman Perry Bradley, III, thirty-five, at the Coleherne pub. They went back to Bradley's flat and Ireland suggested he tie Bradley up; Bradley wasn't keen. To get him to comply, Ireland said he couldn't perform without elements of bondage. Bradley eventually gave in, and Ireland tied him up and placed a noose around his neck. He demanded Bradley give him his PIN number so he could steal his money. Ireland then told Bradley to go to sleep. Once he had fallen asleep, Ireland thought of leaving but, concerned about being identified, he decided to strangle his victim with the noose. He put a doll on top of the body before he left the flat.

By now, Ireland was angry that there had been no publicity about the three murders. He went out and met Andrew Collier, a thirty-three-year-old housing warden, and they went back to Collier's home. Shortly after they entered, there was a loud disturbance outside, and both men went to look out the window. Ireland grabbed hold of a metal bar that ran across the window, but he forgot to wipe his fingerprints off, which would later prove vital for the investigation. He tied Collier up on the bed and demanded his bank details, but Collier refused. Ireland responded by killing Collier's cat and then strangling him with a noose. He then placed a condom on Collier's penis and placed the cat's mouth over it, with the tail of the cat in Collier's mouth. While looking through Collier's belongings, he was angry to discover Collier was HIV positive. He made a phone call to the police asking why they hadn't linked the murders and left the house the next morning.

The last victim was Emanuel Spiteri, a Maltese chef whom he met at the Coleherne pub. Once they arrived at Spiteri's home, Spiteri was persuaded to let Ireland tie him up and cuff him. Ireland tried to get the PIN number out of him, but he refused. Ireland strangled the chef with a noose. He went through his usual process of cleaning the scene, then set fire to the flat and left. Later, he phoned the police and told them to look for a body at the scene of a fire. He also told them he probably wouldn't kill again.

Police investigations showed that Spiteri had left the pub and traveled home with a man by train, and security video captured them on the platform at the train station. It was broadcast, and Ireland recognized himself. He told police he was the man at the station but not the killer, claiming he had left Spiteri at his flat with someone else. But, a fingerprint found in Collier's flat belonged to Ireland, and he was arrested and charged.

Trial

Ireland was charged with the murders of Collier and Spiteri, and he confessed to the other three murders while he was waiting to go on trial. He stated he had no vendetta against homosexuals; he picked them because he thought they were easy targets. He would pretend to be gay to lure them in. He robbed them because he had no job and needed money.

At his trial on December 20, 1993, Ireland pled guilty to all charges. He was sentenced to life imprisonment for each murder.

Outcome

On December 22, 2006, Ireland was one of thirty-five prisoners serving life sentences who were on the Home Office's list of those who were unlikely to ever be released.

On February 21, 2012, Ireland died while still incarcerated. A spokeswoman said, "He is presumed to have died from natural causes; a post-mortem will follow." A postmortem later showed his death was due to pulmonary fibrosis and a fractured hip he had suffered earlier that month.

Trivia

An episode of *Voice of a Serial Killer* on television depicted Ireland's crimes. It was broadcast in 2017.

Ireland decided to become a serial killer as a New Year resolution.

Ireland carried a "Murder Kit" which contained a change of clothes, gloves, knives, and cords, so he was always prepared.

Signature

Ireland would always leave toys in obscene positions close to the victims' bodies, a behavior which became known as his signature.

LESLIE IRVIN

Date of birth: April 2, 1924

Aliases/Nicknames: The Mad Dog Killer

Characteristics: Robbery

Number of victims: 6

Date of murders: December 2, 1954 - March 28, 1955

Date of arrest: April 8, 1955

Victim profile: Mary Holland, 33; Wesley Kerr, 29; Wilhelmina Sailer, 47; Farmer Goebel Duncan, their son, Raymond, and daughter-in-law, Elizabeth

Method of murder: Shooting

Location: Indiana, Kentucky, USA

Status: Sentenced to death. Commuted to life. Died in prison on November 9, 1983.

Background

Irvin was described as sensitive by classmates at school. He didn't like his name, thinking it was a girl's name, and begged the other children to call him Les or Bud. He would often cry himself to sleep for no apparent reason. During high school, he began lighting fires, but none of the blazes created much damage. When asked why he had lit the fires, he said he guessed he was just looking for some excitement.

There was a general friendliness about Irvin that drew people to him. He was intelligent and renowned by those who knew him for his exceptional knowledge of baseball stats. He often spent time in a local bar and played shuffleboard with off-duty police officers.

Murders

Irvin's killing spree began on December 2, 1954, and finished on March 28, 1955. The crimes took place in Vanderburgh and Posey counties in Indiana and Henderson County in Kentucky.

The first victim, Mary Holland, was at work when she was shot in the head at close range. She was three months pregnant at the time of her death. Her husband found her body wedged behind a toilet in the back of the store she worked in; the police had difficulty getting her body free. Her purse was on the floor, and the money was missing. An open bottle of whiskey sat on the counter.

Three weeks later, on December 23, Wesley Kerr was at work at the Standard Oil Station just before midnight when he called his wife. At some point after the phone call, Kerr was shot in the back of the head, and the cash register was emptied. His body was found in the bathroom. Tragically, he had survived fighting in two wars only to be shot and killed at work.

On March 21, 1955, Wilhelmina Sailer was killed in her home and robbed. Her seven-year-old son came home from school and found her dead on the floor, a gunshot wound in her head. Five minutes later, her husband came home. He noticed her purse was open and empty.

Goebel Duncan and Raymond Duncan, father and son, were found on March 28, 1955, their bodies lying face down in stagnant water beside a country road. Their belts had been used to tie their hands behind their backs, and both had been shot in the head. When police went to the house to inform them of the deaths, they found Maple Elizabeth Duncan murdered. She was sprawled on a bed with a bullet hole in her head. Her toddler daughter was sitting beside her unharmed and told the police her mommy was asleep.

But they weren't the only ones in the house. Police heard a moan coming from another room, and inside was Mamie Duncan. Though she had been shot in the head, she was miraculously still alive. She was left permanently blind and had no memory of what had happened that day.

Irvin's car was seen at the Duncan property just before the murders took place. Acting on this tip, police arrested him on April 8. They later found weapons and some of the robbed items in his possession. By April 15, Irvin had confessed to twenty-four burglaries. He was charged with four murders, and he admitted to two others.

Trial

The first trial was for the Kerr murder. There was a lot of pretrial publicity, Irvin he was granted a move to Gibson County. But this was still too close to home, and several more motions to move were lodged, all of which failed. By the time his trial started, at least eight jurors already believed he was guilty.

Irvin was led into the courtroom on what looked like a chain dog leash. From then onward, he was referred to as "Mad Dog." Even the prosecutor called him Mad Dog during his closing statement. Irvin was found guilty of the charges and sentenced to death.

On January 20, 1956, Irvin escaped from jail after making keys using paperback covers, tin foil, and glue. He was apprehended again on February 9, 1956.

Irvin appeared before the United States Supreme Court on a Sixth Amendment claim regarding the pretrial publicity and impartial jury. His conviction was reversed, and a retrial was ordered.

Outcome

The new trial came to an end on June 13, 1962, and once again he was found guilty of the murder of Kerr. He received a life sentence. On November 9, 1983, Irvin died of lung cancer.

Trivia

While incarcerated, Irvin became a talented leather craftsman, creating billfolds, purses, belts, and other items that were then sold in the prison store.

His conviction was the first to be overturned by the Supreme Court due to prejudicial media attention and an impartial jury.

PHILLIP CARL JABLONSKI

Date of birth: January 3, 1946

Aliases/Nicknames: Nil

Characteristics: Rape, necrophilia, mutilation

Number of victims: 5

Date of murders: 1978, 1991

Date of arrest: April 28, 1991

Victim profile: Melinda Kimball; Fathyma Vann, 38; Spadoni Jablonski, 46; Eva Peterson, 72; Margie Rogers, 58

Method of murder: Shooting, stabbing with knife

Location: California, Utah, USA

Status: Sentenced to death in California in 1994.

Background

Jablonski and his first wife, Alice McGowan, met while they were in high school. In 1966, he enlisted with the Army and was deployed overseas. When he returned in 1968, he and Alice married. Jablonski became sexually violent with Alice, and he once put a pillow over her face and tried to suffocate her. He would often strangle her until she passed out. Not surprisingly, Alice left him.

Jablonski started dating Jane Sanders after meeting her in November of 1968. Though he actually raped her on their first date, she never reported it. Jane became pregnant, and they moved to California in July of 1969. By now, Jablonski was out of the military. The violence continued. On one occasion, when Jane wanted him to stop during sex, Jablonski threatened to shoot her if she didn't continue. Then he struck her with the butt of a gun, and she passed out. He continued having sex with her while she was unconscious. Jane left him in 1972.

Later that year, Jablonski raped a woman he knew at knifepoint. Her young child was in the same room at the time. The child managed to escape and went to a neighbor who called the police. Jablonski was convicted of the rape.

Jablonski met Linda Kimball in February of 1977, and they were living together by August. They had a daughter together in December. Linda's mother, who lived nearby, was awakened by Jablonski on the night of July 6, 1978. He said he had planned to rape her but couldn't go through with it because her face reminded him of Linda. She fled the house and went to a neighbor's house but didn't notify the police. Linda left him a few days later, taking their daughter with her.

Murders

Linda went back to Jablonski's apartment on the morning of July 16 to pick up some of the baby's belongings. She was found dead in the apartment that afternoon, after being beaten, stabbed, and strangled to death. Jablonski was arrested and spent twelve years in prison. In 1982, while he was still incarcerated, he met and married Carol Spadoni after he had placed an ad in the newspaper.

Jablonski was released in 1990. On April 23, 1991, Spadoni and Eva Petersen, her mother, were killed in their home. Spadoni had been shot, stabbed, and suffocated with tape. Her mother was sexually assaulted before she was shot to death.

Jablonski attended community college as part of his parole and met Fathyma Vann, a recent widow, there. Her body was found in a shallow ditch on April 22, 1991. She had been sexually assaulted and shot in the head. The words "I Love Jesus" had been carved into the skin on her back. Other mutilations included the removal of her ears and her eyes.

On April 27, 1991, Margie Rogers, fifty-eight, was sexually assaulted and shot in the head twice in Grand County, Utah. She had also been robbed.

Jablonski was identified as the main suspect in the killings and arrested on April 28, 1991.

Trial

Following his trial, Jablonski was convicted of the first-degree murders of Carol Spadoni and Eva Petersen. Special circumstances also included that Jablonski had been in the commission, or attempted commission, of the rape and sodomy of Petersen. A sanity trial was held, which found him sane at the time of the murders, so the jury returned a death sentence on each count.

Outcome

In January of 2006, the California Supreme Court upheld the death sentence on appeal. Jablonski is currently on death row.

Trivia

Pen Pal advertisement:

I ask your indulgence male and female and promise to be brief as possible, allow me to introduce myself as Death Row Teddy.

I am 58 years old. My DOB is January 3rd, 1946.

I have been on death row for 11 years. (Aug.1994)

I am seeking for a female/male Teddy Bear.

I lost once my heart scarcely used by one careless owner.

As I saw it last, it was throbbing in your direction.

Caucasian male - seeking an open minded male/female for unconditional correspondence on mature and honest level, that has a caring heart to create a special friendship build from the heart.

Why choose me?

I am a professional artist, photography, amateur poet, writer, masseur, college educated, not a rude person, like to party, travel. My home town is Joshua Tree, CA. I am very understanding and loving. I believe in giving a second chance. People describe me as a gentle giant.

I love cats, dogs, parrots, horses and teddy bears.

What I like in a friend? I like it if you like to travel, party. Someone who is mature and wants a honest friendship. Someone who is able to discuss personal issues on a mature level and is not scared of Frank discussion.

What I miss the most: Traveling, photography male and female company, giving massages, partying, walking in the rain, romantic walks on the beach, romantic candle light dinners, cuddling in front of a roaring fire, soft music.

Let's share our thoughts and feelings (good or bad) lets learn about one another freely and watch our friendship bloom like a rose and be strong as a castle wall which can't be broken.

A loving heart is worth more than a mountain of gold.

Love communicates on any subject or issue.

Write me please you won't be disappointed.

Don't let my situation stop you from writing me. Pick up your pen and pay me a visit.

Guaranteed response.

Sincerely,

Phillip

M. JAISHANKAR

Date of birth: 1977

Aliases/Nicknames: Psycho Shankar

Characteristics: Serial rapist

Number of victims: 19 - 21

Date of murders: 2006 - 2009, 2011

Date of arrest: October 2009 - Escaped March 18, 2011 - Arrested on May 5, 2011 - Escaped on September 2, 2013 - Arrested on September 6, 2013

Victim profile: Women

Method of murder: Stabbing with a machete

Location: Tamil Nadu, Karnataka, India

Status: Sentenced to 10 years in prison on April 24, 2013. Currently facing trial for more than 20 murder cases.

Background

Jaishankar was from the Kanniyanpatti village of Salem district, Tamil Nadu, and was the son of Maarimuttu. He worked as a truck driver and was married with three daughters. Little else is known about his background.

Murders

Jaishankar began his criminal activities around 2008. The first reported crime occurred on July 3, 2009, when he attempted to rape and kill P.Shyamala Perandahalli, forty-five. By August of the same year, after a matter of weeks, he had killed twelve women and raped a further six. He was known to carry a black handbag which held his machete. He would often kidnap prostitutes near roadside restaurants, then rape and murder them. He would also target victims who lived in rural areas, such as in farmhouses.

On August 23, 2009, police constable M. Jayamani, thirty-nine, was raped and murdered by Jaishankar. She had been on temporary duty at Perumanallur that night, instead of at the all-women police station she normally worked at. Jaishankar kidnapped her, raped her several times, and then murdered her. The body was found on September 19.

On September 10, 2009, Jaishankar and his criminal partner, P. Mohan Selvam, were charged with murdering K. Thangammal Ponnaya. They finally located him on October 19 and arrested him. By now, he was charged with thirteen counts of rape and murder. While in custody, he stated he enjoyed torturing the women before he raped and murdered them.

Jaishankar was being transported to court on March 17, 2011; that evening, on the return trip, he managed to escape. He fled to Karnataka and resumed his raping and killing, accumulating six more victims in a month. He also killed a child and a man. The last week of April 2011, police traced his phone to Delhi.

On the night of May 4, 2011, Jaishankar arrived in Elagi village in Karnataka. A woman, Chandrakala Hotagi, was working by herself in a field, and he approached her asking for food and water. He then tried to rape her, but she managed to get the attention of her husband who, along with a friend, came to her rescue. Jaishankar tried to run, but he was caught and taken to the police on May 5, 2011.

While in jail, Jaishankar was given psychiatric treatment. On August 31, 2013, he was taken to court. After he returned, he said he felt uneasy and was taken to the prison hospital. He had managed to get a duplicate key, and on September 1, at 2 a.m., he escaped.

Jaishankar fractured his leg during the escape, but that didn't stop him from fleeing. However, an informant lured him to a building in Bangalore with the offer of a motorbike to help him with his escape. Once there, he was arrested.

Jaishankar received surgery and treatment for his leg injury, and then was sent to Central Prison. He was housed in a high-security cell with CCTV monitoring 24/7 and extra lighting. The cell lock was designed so that he couldn't reach it, and it was decided that if he fell ill, he would be treated in his cell. Whenever he had to leave the prison, extra security was deployed.

Trial

After his arrest in 2011, Jaishankar was found guilty and sentenced to twenty-seven years in prison. In 2013, he was given a further ten-year sentence.

Outcome

Jaishankar tried to escape once more on February 25, 2018, but he was unsuccessful. He was then placed in solitary confinement. Two days later, he slit his throat with a shaving blade. The staff found him in a pool of blood. Though he was still alive, he died in the hospital a few hours later.

Trivia

M. Jaishankar is one of India's most notorious serial killers of the twenty-first century.

VINCENT JOHNSON

Date of birth: January 6, 1969

Aliases/Nicknames: The Brooklyn Strangler, The Williamsburg Strangler

Characteristics: Homeless, drug addiction, targeted prostitutes

Number of victims: 5 - 6

Date of murders: 1999 - 2000

Date of arrest: August 5, 2000

Victim profile: Patricia Sullivan; Rhonda Tucker; Joanne Feliciano; Elizabeth Tuppeny; Vivian Caraballo; Laura Nusser

Method of murder: Ligature strangulation

Location: New York City, New York, USA

Status: Sentenced to life in prison without parole on March 10, 2001.

Background

Johnson's childhood led him to develop a deep hatred for his mother. As a child, he was sent to foster care, only to later be abandoned by his foster mother as well. By the time he was twenty-one, he was living with his girlfriend, Patricia Carter. The relationship was violent. But it lasted about five years before Patricia kicked him out.

As an adult, Johnson was homeless and addicted to crack. He panhandled to get the money to pay for his drugs, and his feelings toward his mother (and women in general) increasingly worsened. Between the summer of 1999 and 2000, a number of prostitutes were murdered in the Williamsburg and Bedford -Stuyvesant areas of Brooklyn. The police investigation involved questioning and DNA testing of numerous homeless men who were known to frequent the area; this ultimately led to the identification of Johnson as the man responsible.

Murders

The first victim was Vivian Carabello, twenty-six. Her body was found in the elevator room on the roof of 237 South Second Street, Williamsburg, on August 26, 1999. A piece of cloth had been used to strangle her to death. On September 16, 1999, the body of Joann Feliciano, thirty-five, was discovered on the roof of 171 South Fourth Street. The killer had used speaker wire and shoelaces to strangle her.

The next murder victim was Rhonda Tucker, twenty-one. Her body was found on September 25, 1999, this time in her apartment on Park Avenue in Bedford-Stuyvesant. She had been strangled with the drawstring that had been taken from her own pants.

Just over a week later, the fourth victim was found. Katrina Niles, thirty-four, was found in an apartment on Marcy Avenue in Bedford-Stuyvesant. This time, not only was she strangled with an electrical cord, she had also had her throat cut.

When firefighters responded to a fire in a large utility room four months later, they found the decomposing body of a female. Under the Williamsburg Bridge lay the body of Laura G. Nusser, forty-three, who had last been seen with Johnson, and who had actually previously lived with him in the room. An electrical cord had been used to strangle her.

The final known victim was forty-eight-year-old Patricia Sullivan. Her body was discovered on a dirty mattress in a vacant lot on Marcy Avenue on June 22. Shoelaces had been used to strangle her to death.

Police were able to link the murders together relatively quickly and they were on the hunt for a serial killer. One of the men brought in whose DNA was tested was excluded as the killer, but he was able to direct police to another suspect. He told them about a homeless man who he thought was obsessed with sadomasochistic sex. The man was Johnson.

Investigators tracked down Johnson, but he refused to provide a DNA sample and denied he had known any of the victims. A keen-eyed detective spotted Johnson spitting on the street, however, and managed to retrieve the saliva. This was tested, and the DNA matched samples found on four of the victims. He was subsequently arrested and charged.

Trial

Johnson was charged under a statute that provides for a maximum of either the death penalty or life in prison without parole if more than two people have been murdered separately over a twenty-four month period. Johnson was therefore charged with murder in the four cases where his DNA matched. Police were convinced he was guilty of the other two murders and continued to search for evidence.

Rather than risk the death penalty, Johnson pled guilty and accepted the life imprisonment sentence without parole.

Further evidence led to Johnson being charged with the first-degree murder of Demetrius Johnson (of no relation), whom he had stabbed to death. He was also charged with attempted murder for stabbing Misty Battisti, his former wife. He was convicted of all charges, including the possession of a firearm during the commission of a felony, on March 13, 2018.

Outcome

Currently, Johnson is serving his life sentence in the Clinton Correctional Facility in New York. He will never be released.

Trivia

Johnson's crimes and his arrest were the subject of a number of episodes of the documentary series *Brooklyn North*.

Johnson blamed his mother for his actions, saying, "The thoughts of my childhood and foster care and mom came into my mind."

Regarding the murder of Patricia Sullivan, he said, "I didn't see strangling her as doing something wrong at the time."

His mother had always only taken one day off from work, which happened to be a Thursday. Three of Johnson's victims were murdered on Thursdays.

GILBERT PAUL JORDAN

Date of birth: December 12, 1931

Aliases/Nicknames: The Boozing Barber, The Alcohol Murders

Characteristics: Alcoholic, rape

Number of victims: 8 - 10

Date of murders: 1965 - 1987

Date of arrest: October 23, 1987

Victim profile: Ivy Rose; Mary Johnson; Barbara Paul; Mary Johns; Patricia Thomas; Patricia Andrew; Vera Harry; Vanessa Lee Buckner

Method of murder: Alcohol poisoning

Location: Vancouver, British Columbia, Canada

Status: Sentenced to fifteen years in prison in 1988, reduced on appeal to nine years. Released in 1994. Died on July 7, 2006.

Background

A former barber, Jordan was the first person in Canada to use alcohol to kill. He was linked to up to ten deaths of aboriginal women between 1965 and 1988. But he had been in trouble with the law much earlier, with a criminal record dating back to 1952. Some of his convictions had been for rape, indecent assault, hit and run, abduction, car theft, and drunk driving.

In 1976, Dr. Tibor Bezeredi examined Jordan as part of a court procedure and diagnosed him with an antisocial personality.

Murders

Jordan would find women in bars, usually aboriginals who were often dependent on alcohol. He would buy them drinks or pay them for sex. He encouraged them to go back to his room and drink with him. After the women blacked out from too much alcohol, he would pour more alcohol directly down their throats. The deaths were reported as alcohol poisoning, so the police did not pay a lot of attention to it.

The first known victim to have died by alcohol poisoning while with Jordan was Ivy Rose in 1965. Rose was a switchboard operator and had been persuaded to join Jordan in a hotel room for drinks. She was naked when she died, and her alcohol level was 0.51.

Other alleged victims were:

Mary Johnson: She died on November 30, 1980, at the Aylmer Hotel. Her blood alcohol level was 0.34
Barbara Paul: She died on September 11, 1981, at the Glenaird Hotel. Her blood alcohol level was 0.41
Mary Johns: She died on July 30, 1982, at 2503 Kingsway (Jordan's barbershop). Her blood alcohol level was 0.76
Patricia Thomas: She died on December 15, 1984, at 2503 Kingsway (Jordan's barbershop). Her blood alcohol level was 0.51
Patricia Andrew: She died on June 28, 1985, at 2503 Kingsway (Jordan's barbershop). Her blood alcohol level was 0.79
Vera Harry: She died on November 19, 1986, at the Clifton Hotel. Her blood alcohol level was 0.04

The naked body of Vanessa Lee Buckner was found on the floor of the Niagara Hotel on October 12, 1987. She had been drinking with Jordan, and his fingerprints were found in the room. A month later, another woman, Edna Shade, was found in similar circumstances in a different hotel.

Jordan was questioned about Buckner's death but wasn't charged. Suspicious, police surveilled Jordan between October 12 and November 26, 1987. As a result, they managed to rescue four women before they could succumb to Jordan's deadly ministrations. They were:

- Rosemary Wilson, November 20, 1987, at the Balmoral Hotel; Blood alcohol level: 0.52

- Verna Chartrand, November 21, 1987, at the Pacific Hotel; Blood alcohol level: 0.43

- Sheila Joe, November 25, 1987, at the Rainbow Hotel; Blood alcohol level: unknown

- Mabel Olson, November 26, 1987, at the Pacific Hotel; Blood alcohol level: unknown

Trial

Investigators gathered enough evidence to charge Jordan with manslaughter in the death of Buckner. The prosecution brought forward evidence of "similar fact" regarding the number of women who had died while drinking with Jordan. He was found guilty and sentenced to serve fifteen years in prison. He appealed, and the sentence was reduced to nine years.

In the end, Jordan only served six years. Upon release, he was placed on restrictive probation which meant he had to stay on Vancouver Island. His criminal activities didn't stop, however. In June of 2000, he was charged with sexual assault, assault, administering a noxious substance (alcohol), and negligence causing bodily harm. That same year he tried to change his name, choosing to go by Paul Pearce. But he dropped the application once he discovered he would have to provide his fingerprints or a criminal check.

In 2002, he was arrested for breach of probation when he was caught drinking alcohol with a woman—something he was forbidden to do. He received a sentence of fifteen months in prison and three years' probation.

Jordan was arrested again on August 11, 2004, for violating his probation order. He had been at the York Hotel in Saskatchewan on August 9, drinking with Barb Burkley. Burkley was a resident of the hotel and had a serious problem with alcohol. A friend found her in a terrible condition and took her to the hospital. Though the friend identified Jordan as being present, he was acquitted of any wrongdoing in 2005.

Outcome

After Jordan was released from prison, the police issued a warning to the public as follows:

JORDAN, Gilbert Paul, age 73, is the subject of this alert. JORDAN is 175cm (5'9") tall and weighs 79kgs (174lbs) [sic]. He is partially bald with grey hair and a grey goatee. He has blue eyes and wears glasses. JORDAN is currently in the Victoria area but has no fixed address. JORDAN has a significant criminal record including manslaughter and indecent assault of a female. He uses alcohol to lure his victims. JORDAN's target victim group is adult females. JORDAN is subject to court-ordered conditions, including:

Abstain absolutely from the consumption of alcohol.

Not to be in the company of any female person or persons in any place where alcohol is being either consumed or possessed by that person or persons.

If you observe the subject in violation of any of the above conditions, please call the Saanich Police Department at 475-4321, 911 or your local police agency. If you have questions concerning the public notification process please contact the BC Corrections Branch at 250-387-6366.

Trivia

The Canadian television program *Exhibit A: Secrets of Forensic Science* had an episode called "Dead Drunk," which was about Jordan and the forensic techniques that helped authorities convict him.

Playwright Marie Clements wrote a play called *The Unnatural and Accidental Women*, with the story focused on the victims' stories, to make up for the lack of media attention toward the victims. It was later adapted into a screenplay for the film *Unnatural and Accidental*.

Jordan was the inspiration behind the first several episodes of the program *Da Vinci's Inquest*, which is set in Vancouver, Canada.

JOSEPH AND MICHAEL KALLINGER

Joseph Kallinger

Date of birth: December 11, 1936

Aliases/Nicknames: The Shoemaker

Characteristics: Child abuse, serial rapist, mutilation

Number of victims: 3

Date of murders: 1974 - 1975

Date of arrest: January 17, 1975

Victim profile: Jose Collazo; Joseph Kallinger Jr.; Maria Fasching, 21

Method of murder: Stabbing with knife, drowning

Location: Pennsylvania, New Jersey, USA

Status: Sentenced to life in prison on October 14, 1976. Died in prison on March 26, 1996.

Michael Kallinger

Date of birth: 1962

Aliases/Nicknames: Nil

Characteristics: Under the father's control

Number of victims: 3

Date of murders: 1974 - 1975

Date of arrest: January 17, 1975

Victim profile: Jose Collazo; Joseph Kallinger Jr.; Maria Fasching, 21

Method of murder: Stabbing with knife, drowning

Location: Pennsylvania, New Jersey, USA

Status: Sentenced to a reformatory until he was 21, then released.

Background

Joseph Kallinger was born Joseph Lee Brenner III, but after his father left the family in December 1937, he was placed in foster care. On October 15, 1939, Austrian immigrants Stephen and Anna Kallinger adopted him, but his life wasn't about to improve. Both of his adoptive parents abused him so severely that he developed a hernia at the age of six. Some of the punishments inflicted on Kallinger included making him kneel on sharp rocks, locking him in closets, making him eat feces, burning him with irons, whipping him with belts, starvation, and forced self-injury. At the age of nine, he was also sexually assaulted by a group of boys in the neighborhood.

When Kallinger was fifteen, he began dating Hilda Bergman, but his parents did not want them to see each other. Rebelling, he married her, and they later had two children. Kallinger was violent toward her though so she left him. On April 20, 1958, he remarried, and this union produced five children. He was abusive toward his wife and his children, and they were often forced to endure the same punishments he had when he was a child.

Over the next ten years, Kallinger was in and out of mental institutions for a variety of reasons. These included suicide attempts, arsons, and amnesia.

In 1972, his children went to the police about the treatment they experienced at home and Kallinger was arrested and sent to prison. While he was in prison, he was diagnosed with paranoid schizophrenia, and it was recommended that he have supervised visits with his family. Later, the children recanted the allegations.

Kallinger's son, Joseph Jr., was found dead among rubble in an old building two years later. The insurance company was suspicious of foul play because Kallinger had only taken out insurance policies on his children two weeks prior to the death; they refused to pay out on the claim.

Murders

By the middle of 1974, Kallinger was experiencing constant hallucinations. He was having conversations with a disembodied head and claimed he was receiving personal "orders from God." The demands included he kill young boys and cut off their genitals. He confided these thoughts to his son Michael, who was thirteen at the time. He asked the boy to help him, and Michael was more than happy to assist his father.

Their first victim was killed eleven days later. Jose Collazo, a Puerto Rican youth, was tortured by Kallinger and his son and his penis amputated. Kallinger planned for the next victim to be his own son, Joseph Jr. At first, he tried to get Joseph Jr. to fall off a cliff while taking photographs, but that failed. He then took both Joseph Jr. and Michael with him to commit arson, hoping Joseph Jr. would get trapped in the fire, but that also failed. In the end, they drowned him at a demolition site. The body was found on August 9, 1974. Kallinger was suspected and interviewed, but there was not enough evidence to charge him.

On November 22, father and son broke into a house in Lindenwold, New Jersey, to rob it. Nobody was home at the time. Next, they entered the home of Joan Carty. They tied her to the bed and Kallinger sexually abused her.

Eleven days after the attack on Carty, the Kallingers robbed five hostages at knifepoint. They slashed one of the women in the breast and got away with twenty thousand dollars in jewelry and cash. Next, they held Pamela Jaske hostage in her home. She was forced to perform fellatio on Kallinger at gunpoint. The same was carried out with the next victim, Mary Rudolph on January 6.

On January 8, the Kallingers broke into a home in Leonia, New Jersey, and held eight hostages at gunpoint while they robbed the house. One of the hostages, Nurse Maria Fasching, was stabbed to death after she refused to bite off a male hostage's penis. As the Kallingers made their getaway, Kallinger dropped a shirt with bloodstains on it near the scene. Police officers traced the shirt to Kallinger, and they were both arrested on January 17. Father and son were charged with three counts of murder.

Trial

At his trial, Kallinger pled insanity, stating God had instructed him to kill. After a psychiatric assessment deemed him sane, he was found guilty. Kallinger was sentenced to life in prison on October 14, 1976. Because Michael he was a minor and clearly under the control of his father, he was sent to a reformatory and was released at the age of twenty-one.

Outcome

Kallinger tried to kill himself numerous times while in prison, including an incident where he tried to set himself on fire. Due to his behavior, he was transferred to a mental hospital.

In 1976, he was interviewed by author Flora Rheta Schreiber, and a book was published by Simon & Schuster, with the title *The Shoemaker: The Anatomy of a Psychotic*. A lawsuit was brought forth by the family of one of the victims because Kallinger was receiving royalties for the book. A judge ruled that all earnings from Kallinger, Simon & Schuster, and Schreiber be awarded to the family. This was appealed, and only Kallinger's royalties were awarded.

On March 26, 1996, Joseph Kallinger died from an epileptic seizure. He had been on suicide watch for the last eleven years of his life.

Trivia

For many years, Kallinger sent a Christmas card to Michael Korda, an editor at Simon & Schuster.

Schreiber maintained a relationship with Kallinger until her death in 1988, and they exchanged letters and phone calls.

BÉLA KISS

Date of birth: 1877

Aliases/Nicknames: The Monster of Czinkota, Vampire of Cinkota.

Characteristics: Rape, robbery

Number of victims: 24 +

Date of murders: 1900 - 1914

Date of arrest: Not apprehended

Victim profile: Women

Method of murder: Strangulation

Location: Czinkota, Hungary

Status: Unknown.

Background

Kiss was born in Izsák, Austria, Hungary in 1877. He later lived in Cinkota and worked as a tinsmith. He was apparently interested in occult practices and was an amateur astrologer. Kiss had two marriages and two children. In 1912, when his latest wife left him for someone else, Kiss hired a housekeeper, Mrs. Jakubec.

Jakubec noticed Kiss corresponded with a large number of women, usually through advertisements he placed in newspapers. He offered his services as a fortune teller or a "matrimonial agent." Sometimes he would bring the women back to his house.

Kiss was allegedly well-liked by his neighbors even though they didn't know him that well. It was noted by the community that Kiss collected a lot of metal drums, and when he was questioned by the police, he said he was filling the drums with gasoline in preparation for the rations that would occur in the upcoming war.

In 1914, at the start of World War I, Kiss was conscripted, and while he was away, Jakubec looked after his house. One day his landlord poked a hole in one of the drums and was shocked by the smell of death that emanated from it.

Murders

The landlord notified the police about the discovery of the drums in July of 1916. The constable recalled Kiss saying the drums were filled with gasoline, and with soldiers needing the supply, he escorted them to the property to collect the gasoline. As they tried to open the drums, a horrible smell escaped. Inside and opened drum, they discovered the body of a woman who had been strangled. An inspection of the other six drums revealed that they too contained bodies. A full search of the house yielded twenty-four dead bodies in total.

The military was informed and instructed to arrest Kiss immediately. But the name was very common, and it wasn't certain if he was even still alive. Jakubec was arrested, and the postal service was told to hold on to any letters en route to Kiss in case she had tried to warn him about the discovery. The detective thought Jakubec might have been an accomplice to the murders, especially when they found Kiss' will, which left money to her if he died.

Claiming her innocence, she told the authorities about a secret room that Kiss kept locked and she was told never to enter. A search of the room found lots of correspondence between Kiss and seventy-four women. The letters dated back to 1903, and their contents revealed that Kiss had been defrauding all these women. Most of the books on the shelves were on topics such as strangulation and poisons.

Kiss chose women without nearby relatives so that their disappearance wouldn't be noticed quickly. He convinced them to send them money, promising marriage. Two of the women he had been defrauding initiated court cases against him, but after they disappeared, the cases were dismissed.

All of the women Kiss killed had been strangled, the bodies then "pickled" in alcohol before being sealed in the drums. There were puncture marks on the necks, indicating Kiss had drained their blood, and this led some to believe he was some sort of vampire.

The lead detective received a letter on October 4, 1916, stating Kiss was in a Serbian hospital. But, by the time he got there, Kiss was gone. In his bed was the body of a dead soldier.

Trial

Kiss was never apprehended and therefore never charged with any of the murders.

Outcome

There were numerous sightings of Kiss over the years, but none of the leads panned out. Many believed he had changed his identity, and rumors were rife that maybe he was in a Romanian prison or had died of yellow fever.

A French Foreign Legion soldier reported in 1920 that a fellow legionnaire called Hoffman had boasted he was good at using a garrote. Hoffman was a name Kiss had used in some of his letters to the women. By the time police arrived, he was gone.

In New York City in 1932, a homicide detective was certain he saw Kiss coming out of the subway in Manhattan. There were rumors he was working as a janitor, but when police went to interview him, the janitor had disappeared.

What happened to Kiss remains a mystery to this day. The total number of victims is also unknown—it is likely he continued to kill wherever he went.

Trivia

The story was the inspiration behind *23*, a play by Antonin Artaud.

Bela Kiss: Prologue (a German horror film) was released in 2013.

The novel *Hill House*, written by Gopi Kottoor, was inspired by the life of Kiss.

In "The Alphabet Serial Killer Song," written by Amoree Lovell, Kiss is the letter "B."

TIMOTHY KRAJCIR

Date of birth: November 28, 1944

Aliases/Nicknames: Timothy Wayne McBride

Characteristics: Rape

Number of victims: 9

Date of murders: 1977 - 1982

Date of arrest: August 29, 2007

Victim profile: Mary Parsh, 58; Brenda Parsh, 27; Sheila Cole, 21; Margie Call, 57; Mildred Wallace, 65; Deborah Sheppard, 23; Virginia Lee Witte, 51; Myrtle Rupp, 51; Joyce Tharp, 29

Method of murder: Shooting, strangulation

Location: Illinois, Missouri, Kentucky, Pennsylvania, USA

Status: Sentence to life in prison in Illinois and Missouri in 2008.

Background

Krajcir was called Timothy Wayne McBride at birth, but his mother later remarried and her new husband adopted him. From then on he used the surname Krajcir. By the age of ten, he had developed an unhealthy obsession with his mother that was both emotional and sexual in nature. He had become a voyeur and exhibitionist by the time he was thirteen.

The first time Krajcir came into contact with police was on July 7, 1951. He was charged with petty theft after stealing a bicycle. Then in 1960, when he was fifteen, he was again charged with petty theft. He later joined the navy but was discharged dishonorably after fourteen months for committing a sexual assault. In 1963, he was convicted of rape and was given his first prison sentence. From then onward, he was in and out of prison—mostly for sex crimes.

Murders

When Krajcir began killing, he traveled to towns where no connection could be made with him. He would choose a victim, stalk them, then break into their home and wait for their return. Some of his victims were found tied up in their beds, while others were abducted and driven across state lines before they were murdered. Nearly all of the victims were raped, and he would also force them to perform other sexual acts. The methods of murder varied, from stabbing, asphyxiation, and gunshots to the head.

Because the crimes were far and wide, there was little evidence that they were linked in any way. At the time, little forensic technology existed in DNA testing, so it was almost impossible to connect the deaths to one killer.

Known and suspected victims:

Deborah Sheppard, twenty-three
Mary Parsh, fifty-eight
Brenda Parsh, twenty-seven
Sheila Cole, twenty-one
Virginia Lee Witte, fifty-one
Myrtle Rupp, fifty-one
Joyce Tharp, twenty-nine
Mildred Wallace, sixty-five
Margie Call, fifty-seven

Eventually, with the advancement of DNA technology, the police were finally able to connect a murder to Krajcir.

Trial

On December 10, 2007, Krajcir was convicted of killing Deborah Sheppard in 1982. He was sentenced to forty years in prison. He was then charged with five other murders and three counts of rape. He pled guilty to the murder of Virginia Lee Witte on January 18, 2008, and received another forty-year sentence to be served consecutively. He then pled guilty to five murders and seven sexual assaults as well as a robbery. He received thirteen life terms.

At his sentencing in April, Krajcir stated, "I don't know if I could have been so generous if I were in the same situation. Thank you for sparing my life."

Outcome

Currently, Krajcir is serving his sentence at the Pontiac Correctional Center in Illinois.

Trivia

Krajcir attained a BA in the Administration of Justice from Southern Illinois University Carbondale. His minor was in psychology.

"It's scary," Krajcir told a newspaper in a phone interview from his cell. "I've done a lot of terrible things to this community, and I imagine there is a lot of anger and hate here toward me. But believe it or not, I'm the type of person that likes to be liked."

"I regret doing all of it, but its 30 years ago. I wish a lot of things could have been different, but that's the way it was. It's like I'm two different people. I worked for the ambulance service saving lives, and here I was taking them."

"I have felt emotional about my victims at times, and I'm not the same person I was 30 years ago. They told us in therapy to try to feel what our victims and their families were feeling, and I've done that. But I can't say for sure that I wouldn't do anything again."

PETER KÜRTEN

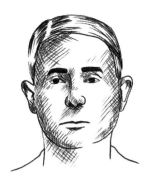

Date of birth: May 26, 1883

Aliases/Nicknames: The Vampire of Düsseldorf

Characteristics: Sadist, rape

Number of victims: 10 (more than 31 attempted)

Date of murders: 1913 - 1929

Date of arrest: May 24, 1930

Victim profile: Christine Klein, 9; Gertrud Franken, 17; Rose Ohliger, 9; Rudolf Scheer, 45; Maria Hahn; Gertrude Hamacher, 5; Luise Lenzen, 14; Ida Reuter, 31; Elizabeth Dörrier, 22; Gertrude Albermann, 5

Method of murder: Stabbing with a knife, hitting with a hammer, strangulation

Location: Prussia Rhine Province, Germany

Status: Executed by guillotine in Cologne on July 2, 1931.

Background

Kürten, one of thirteen children, was born into a poor and abusive family. Both of his parents were alcoholics, and the whole family lived in a one-room apartment. The children and their mother were regularly beaten by Mr. Kürten. He would often gather all the children into the room and make them watch as he had sex with their mother. In 1894, Mr. Kürten was sent to prison for fifteen months for being incestuous with his elder daughter, who was only thirteen at the time.

At the age of five, Peter Kürten attempted to kill one of his play friends by trying to drown him. When he was nine, he often went out with the local dogcatcher who liked to torture and kill animals. Before long, Kürten was willingly participating. He claimed that, at this same age, he killed a boy by pushing him off a log raft, knowing the boy couldn't swim. When another boy tried to save the drowning boy, Kürten held his head under water until he also drowned. At the time, the deaths were ruled accidental.

His experiences with his father's torrid abuse led to him regularly running away from home. While out on the streets, he learned a variety of petty crimes. At thirteen, he developed a relationship with a girl, and although she let him fondle her, she refused to have sexual intercourse with him. Kürten began engaging in bestiality with goats, sheep, and pigs to relieve his urges. He achieved the biggest sense of elation when he stabbed them just before he had an orgasm. Around this time, he also tried to rape his sister, the same one his father had molested.

After leaving school, Kürten got an apprenticeship as a molder, which lasted for two years. Robbing his employer, he took all the money he could find at home, and ran away to Koblenz. A month later, he was caught and charged with theft and breaking and entering and spent a month in prison. Upon his release, he went back to his old ways of committing petty crime.

Murders

Kürten later told investigators that his first murder was that of an eighteen-year-old girl in November of 1899. He said that after they had sex he strangled her to death with his hands. There were no reports of this murder; it was possible the girl had actually survived and not reported it.

The first confirmed murder took place on May 25, 1913. While robbing a tavern, Kürten came across Christine Klein, nine, asleep. He strangled the little girl, slashed her throat with a pocket knife, and as he listened to the blood dripping onto the floor, he ejaculated. The next day, he went to the tavern across the road so he could hear what people were saying about the murder. He would later occasionally return to her grave; he claimed that when he touched the soil on the grave he would ejaculate.

Two months after this murder, Kürten came across Gertrud Franken, seventeen, during the robbery of a home he had broken into. He strangled her with his hands, and as blood came out of her mouth, he ejaculated. Days later, on July 14, he was arrested for arsons and burglaries and sent to prison for six years. His behavior in prison added two more years to his sentence.

After his release in April of 1921, he moved to Altenburg and lived with his sister for a while. Through her, he met a slightly older woman, Auguste Scharf, who had previously killed her fiancé. They married two years after meeting, and Kürten later said that he could only have sex with her if she initiated it, and he would fantasize about violence the whole time.

Kürten and his wife moved back to Düsseldorf in 1925. He then began an affair with Tiede, a servant girl, and Mech, a housemaid. When his wife found out, Tiede reported him to the police, saying he had seduced her. Mech then alleged she had been raped by him. The report resulted in another prison sentence of eight months, but he only served six.

On February 3, 1929, Kürten stalked an elderly woman, Apollonia Kühn. He grabbed her and dragged her into nearby bushes and stabbed her with a pair of scissors twenty-four times. Several of the wounds went so deep they entered her bones. Miraculously, she survived.

Five days later, on February 8, he strangled Rosa Ohliger, nine, until she was unconscious. He then stabbed her with a pair of scissors in the temple, genitals, heart, and stomach. As he plunged the knife into her body he ejaculated, which he then inserted into her vagina with his fingers. He left her body beneath a hedge, and several hours later he set her on fire. When he saw the flames, he had another orgasm. Her body was discovered the following day. On February 13, Kürten murdered Rudolf Scheer, forty-five, stabbing him twenty times—mostly about the head, eyes, and back.

Between March and July of 1929, Kürten tried to strangle four more women and claimed he had thrown one of them into the river. But there were no further murders until August 11, when he raped, strangled, and stabbed Maria Hahn multiple times. They had arranged to go on a date, and he led her into a meadow. He said she pleaded with him repeatedly to let her go as he killed her. From start to finish, it took around one hour for her to die. He buried her body in a cornfield. Several weeks later, he came back with a plan to nail her body to a tree to disgust the public. But the body was too heavy for him, so he caressed the remains, embracing them as he lay beneath them, and then buried them again.

He sent an anonymous letter to the police three months later, confessing to the murder and leaving instructions on how to find her remains. The police found her body on November 15.

Kürten embarked on a spree of violence on August 21. He attacked three people, stabbing an eighteen-year-old girl, a thirty-seven-year-old woman, and a thirty-year-old man. All were seriously injured but survived. At a fairground three days later, he noticed two sisters walking home. He approached them and sent the older girl, Luise Lenzen, fourteen, on an errand to buy him cigarettes with the promise of some money when she returned. He then picked the other girl, Gertrude Hamacher, five, off the ground by her neck. He strangled her until she was unconscious, and then cut her throat. When Lenzen returned, he strangled her, stabbed her (this included a wound to her aorta), and bit her throat, sucking the blood from the wounds.

The next day he assaulted Gertrude Schulte, twenty-seven, when she refused to have sex with him. He stabbed her repeatedly in the head, back, shoulder, and neck, but she survived. Unfortunately, she was unable to describe him to investigators. In September, he attempted to murder two more people. He then decided a hammer would be a good weapon to use in the future.

On September 30, Kürten crossed paths with Ida Reuter, a thirty-one-year-old servant, at the train station. He convinced her to go for a walk and then struck her in the head with the hammer. He raped her and then hit her again. He continued to strike her in the head until she died.

He came across another servant girl, Elizabeth Dörrier, twenty-two, outside a theater on October 11, and persuaded her to go for a drink with him. They traveled to Grafenberg by train, and as they walked along the Kleine Düssel River, he struck her in the temple with the hammer. He raped her and then continued to beat her with the hammer. She was found the next morning, still alive, but she died the following day without ever waking up. Kürten attacked two more women on October 25, but they both survived—in one case, because the hammer broke.

On November 7, 1929, he met five-year-old Gertrude Albermann and convinced her to follow him to an area of deserted plots. He strangled her and stabbed her in the temple with scissors. Then he stabbed her thirty-four more times.

Multiple nonfatal hammer attacks took place between February and May of 1930. Ten victims were attacked, and some were able to describe the man who had attacked them.

On May 14, Kürten came across a man and a woman arguing at the train station. Maria Budlick, twenty, was being bothered by a stranger. As they argued, Kürten approached and asked Maria if she was being bothered. When she nodded, the stranger left. Kürten invited her to his apartment and, guessing what he was wanting, she informed him she wasn't interested in sex. After agreeing to take her to a hotel, he directed her into the Grafenberg Woods. There, he grabbed her by the throat and, as he raped her, he tried to strangle her. She started to scream and, for some reason, he let her go.

Maria didn't report the attack to the police, but she did write a letter to a friend detailing what had happened. Because the address on the letter was incorrect, it was opened at the post office and forwarded on to the police. Chief Inspector Gennat thought she might have been a victim of the Düsseldorf murderer and organized an interview with her. Maria remembered where Kürten lived and led Gennat to the address. Gennat spoke to the landlady and was given the name of Kürten.

Trial

Gennat searched Kürten's home, and Kürten, who had noticed him standing in the communal hallway, promptly left. Now that the police were on to him, he went back to his wife and told her he had raped Maria. He moved to another property for a while and returned to his wife on May 23. Then he confessed he was the "Vampire of Düsseldorf" and urged her to turn him in so she could get the reward that was being offered.

The following day, his wife contacted the police and told them he was willing to turn himself in. That afternoon, he was arrested. He confessed immediately to all of the crimes the police knew about, and then told them about the murders of Klein and Franken in 1913. He admitted to ten murders, thirty attempted murders, and sixty-eight crimes in total.

Kürten's trial took place on April 13, 1931, and he was formally charged with nine murders and seven attempted murders. Not surprisingly, he pled not guilty to all by reason of insanity. An assessment, however, declared him sane. The trial went on for just ten days, and on April 22, the jury returned their verdict - he was guilty of all counts. Kürten was sentenced to death. In his final address to the court, he stated he now saw his crimes as being "so ghastly that [he did] not want to make any sort of excuse for them."

Outcome

Although he didn't appeal his conviction, Kürten did submit a petition for a pardon which was rejected on July 1. He wrote letters of apology to the families of his victims and his wife.

Kürten was served his final meal on the evening of July 1, 1931. He dined on fried potatoes and Wiener schnitzel and a bottle of white wine. The following morning, at 6 a.m., he was beheaded by guillotine. When he was asked if he had any last words, he simply said no.

Trivia

Just before he was executed by guillotine, Peter Kürten, the so-called Vampire of Dusseldorf, asked the prison psychiatrist: "Tell me, after my head has been chopped off will I still be able to hear; at least for a moment, the sound of my own blood gushing from the stump of my neck?"

When the doctor replied that his brain and ears would probably function for several seconds after he was struck by the blade, Kurten replied: "That would be the pleasure to end all pleasures."

After his execution, his head was dissected and preserved, and his brain was analyzed forensically to try to determine a medical reason for his shocking behavior and personality. But no abnormalities were detected.

An autopsy concluded that, apart from having an enlarged thymus gland, Kürten had no other physical problems or abnormalities.

The interviews Kürten took part in with Dr. Karl Berg in 1930 and 1931 were the first psychological, sexual serial killer study. The interviews formed the basis of Berg's book, *The Sadist*, as well.

After World War II ended, Kürten's head was taken to America. It is currently on display at the Ripley's Believe it or Not! Museum in Wisconsin.

Film

- The first film to be inspired by the murders committed by Kürten, *M*, was released in May of 1931. The director was Fritz Lang, and it starred Peter Lorre as a fictional child killer named Hans Beckert. It was also inspired by Fritz Haarmann and Carl Großmann.

- The thriller *Le Vampire de Düsseldorf* (translated to "The Vampire of Düsseldorf"), produced in 1965, is based on the case of Kürten.

- The film *Normal* is based on the story of Kürten. It is a film adaptation of the play *Normal: The Düsseldorf Ripper*.

ALLAN JOSEPH LEGERE

Date of birth: February 13th, 1948

Aliases/Nicknames: The Monster of the Miramichi

Characteristics: Rape, robbery

Number of victims: 5

Date of murders: June 21, 1986 - November 24, 1989

Date of arrest: November 24, 1989

Victim profile: John Glendenning; Annie Flam, 75; Sisters Donna and Linda Lou Daughney, 45 and 41; Rev. James Smith, 69

Method of murder: Beating

Location: Miramichi, New Brunswick, Canada

Status: Sentenced to life in prison with eligibility for parole in 18 years on January 22, 1987. Escaped May 3, 1989. Sentenced to life in prison on November 3, 1991.

Background

Legere's behavior was sexually deviant from an early age. He had to share a small bedroom with his older sisters, and as they undressed, he would often masturbate. As he got older, he progressed to peeping into women's windows while masturbating.

He had an obsession of sorts with religion, and once ran into a church proclaiming he was the one true path to God. He told the worshippers that they could only be granted passage into heaven if they accepted him as their true savior.

In 1979, he was arrested after a fight where he stabbed a man in the face with a broken bottle, nearly severing the victim's cheek. When the police came to arrest him, he pulled a knife on them, but was subsequently overcome and arrested. This was just the beginning of a violent spree to come.

Murders

On the evening of June 21, 1986, Legere, along with companions Scott Curtis and Todd Matchett, broke into a store belonging to elderly couple John Glendenning and his wife, Mary. They beat the couple repeatedly and then fled. When Mary regained consciousness, she realized her husband was dead. She phoned the police, who promptly tracked the three men down and arrested them. They were charged and convicted.

On May 3, 1989, while Legere was serving his sentence, he was transported to a local hospital, to have an ear infection treated. He managed to escape and went on the run. He avoided capture for seven months, during which time he killed four more people.

Legere broke into the home of Annie Flam, seventy-five, and her sister-in-law Nina Flam, sixty-one, who owned a small grocery store. Both women were raped and severely beaten, then the home was set on fire. When firefighters responded, they found Nina alive, but Annie was dead in her bedroom.

The similarity between the murders of the Glendennings and the Flams was becoming apparent to authorities, and Legere was the prime suspect. But they couldn't yet prove he was involved.

On September 30, Morrissy Doran, seventy, interrupted an intruder in his home and was shot in the back, but survived. The following day, the home of seniors Edwin and Evangeline Russell was broken into; they were both assaulted.

Early in the morning of October 14, firefighters were called to the home of Linda Daughney, forty-one, and her sister Donna, forty-five. They found the bodies of the sisters in the house, and examinations showed they had both been raped and then beaten to death. The scene was almost identical to the other murders, and once police learned Legere and Linda had previously been involved in a relationship, they were certain he was the man they were looking for.

On the night of November 16, the priest of the Blessed Virgin Mary Church, Father James Smith, sixty-nine, failed to show up for mass. When a parishioner went to check on him, he was found beaten to death in his residence. The safe had been robbed, and his car had been stolen.

Police located Legere on November 24, 1989, and he was arrested.

Crimeline

June 22, 1986: John Glendenning was beaten to death; his wife was beaten, sexually assaulted, and left to die.

January 22, 1987: Legere was convicted of second-degree murder and received a sentence of life in prison with eligibility for parole in eighteen years.

May 3, 1989: Legere escaped from the Dr. Georges L. Dumont Hospital in Moncton after being taken there from the Atlantic Institution at Renous for an ear infection.

May 29, 1989: Annie Flam was beaten to death. Nina Flam was beaten and raped.

October 13, 1989: Donna and Linda Daughney were sexually assaulted and beaten to death in their home. The home was set on fire.

November 24, 1989: James Smith was found beaten to death in the rectory of the Nativity of the Blessed Virgin Mary Church.

November 24, 1989: Legere was recaptured by RCMP near Nelson-Miramichi.

Trial

Legere's trial on the charges surrounding his escape from custody ended in August of 1990. He was sentenced to a further nine years in prison. His trial for the murders began in November of 1990. For the first time in Canada, DNA fingerprinting was used for a conviction rather than exoneration. Legere was convicted of the murders in November of 1991 and sentenced to life in prison.

Outcome

Legere was transferred from the super-maximum security penitentiary in Sante-Anne-des-Plaines, Quebec, to the Edmonton Institution in Alberta in 2015.

Trivia

The jail in Fredericton was closed in 1996, and it became a science museum in 1999. Legere's former cell now holds a DNA fingerprinting exhibit.

Legere's case was one of the first times in Canadian judicial history where DNA evidence contributed to a conviction.

There is a special digital archive at the University of New Brunswick's law department which is all about New Brunswick's worst serial killer, Legere.

EDWARD 'EDDIE' LEONSKI

Date of birth: December 12, 1918

Aliases/Nicknames: The Brown-Out Strangler

Characteristics: Rape

Number of victims: 3

Date of murders: May 3 - 18, 1942

Date of arrest: May 22, 1942

Victim profile: Ivy Violet McLeod, 40; Pauline Thompson, 31; Gladys Lilian Hosking, 41

Method of murder: Strangulation

Location: Melbourne, Victoria, Australia

Status: Executed by hanging at Pentridge Prison on November 9, 1942.

Background

Like many others, Leonski grew up in a family plagued with abuse and alcoholism. His mother was controlling and overprotective, and Leonski was regularly bullied by other children for being a "mama's boy." Later, a psychologist deemed his crimes were the result of his intense hatred and resentment toward his mother.

In February of 1941, Leonski was called up by the U.S. Army; he was transferred to Melbourne, Australia in 1942. When he started his military duty, he left behind a family that included a mentally unstable mother, a brother in a mental institution and two brothers who had been in prison. Up until 1942, no reports of violence had been exhibited by Leonski.

Murders

The body of Ivy Violet McLeod, forty, was found in a park in Melbourne on May 3, 1942. She had been beaten before being strangled to death. Because her purse was untouched, it was clear the motivation wasn't robbery.

Just six days later, another woman was found dead. Pauline Thompson, thirty-one, had been on a night out and was last seen with a young man who had an American accent. She had also been strangled to death. Then, on May 18, Gladys Hosking, forty, was killed while walking home from work. A witness claimed an American man had approached her that night for directions. She described him as disheveled, covered with mud, and out of breath. This description matched that of the man seen with Pauline Thompson before her murder.

There had been a number of survivors of similar attacks, and when they were shown a lineup of American servicemen, they picked out Leonski. He was subsequently arrested and charged with the three killings.

Trial

Even though the murders had occurred in Australia, the trial had to be conducted under American military law because he was an American serviceman. Leonski confessed to the murders and was convicted. He was sentenced to death on July 17, 1942. The sentence was confirmed on October 14 by General Douglas MacArthur, and a further review upheld the sentence on October 28.

On November 4, MacArthur signed the order of execution.

Outcome

On November 9, Leonski was executed by hanging at Pentridge Prison. His remains were interred on a temporary basis at several cemeteries in Australia until they were finally interred at Schofield Barracks Post Cemetery in O'ahu, Hawaii.

Trivia

The film *Death of a Soldier,* released in 1986, is based on Leonski, with the main character played by actor Reb Brown.

An episode of *Inside the Mind of a Serial Killer* featured Leonski.

The gallows used to hang Leonski were the same ones used to hang notorious bushranger, Ned Kelly.

Leonski is the only foreign citizen in history to be executed in Australia under another country's law.

Leonski said of his victim Thompson: "She told me I had a baby face, but I was wicked underneath."

SAMUEL LITTLE

Date of birth: June 7, 1940

Aliases/Nicknames: Samuel McDowell

Characteristics: Robbery, rape

Number of victims: 34 – 90

Date of murders: 1970 – 82, 1989 – 2005

Date of arrest: September 5, 2012

Victim profile: Carol Elford; Guadalupe Abodaca; Audrey Nelson; Denise Christie Brothers; Melinda LaPree, 22; Patricia Mount, 26; Melissa Thomas; Brenda Alexander; Fredonia Smith, 18; Dorothy Richards, 55; Daisy McGuire, 40; Julia Critchfield, 36; Nancy Carol Stevens, 46; Evelyn Weston, 19; Rosie Hill, 20; Linda Sue Boards, 23; Martha Cunningham, 34; plus many more

Method of murder: Strangulation

Location: California, Texas

Status: Life imprisonment.

Background

It is possible Little was born while his mother was completing one of her many stints in prison. He later said his mother was a "lady of the night," a prostitute, and he was brought up by his grandmother during most of his childhood. While he was at high school, he was arrested and convicted for breaking and entering and was sent to a juvenile offender institution. When he was released, he spent most of his time on the streets, working part-time as a laborer and relying on petty theft to support himself.

In 1961, Little was arrested for breaking into a furniture store. He was sentenced to three years in prison and was released in 1964. By 1975, he had been arrested a staggering twenty-six times in eleven different states. The charges included assault, theft, attempted rape, attacks on government officials, and fraud.

Little was arrested in 1982 for the murder of Melinda LaPree, twenty-two, a prostitute who had disappeared in September. When it went to the grand jury, they declined to indict him for the murder. While he was being investigated, Little was transferred to Florida and charged with the murder of

Patricia Mount, twenty-six, whose body had also been found in September. Due to issues with witnesses, he was acquitted in January of 1984.

In October that year, he was arrested again for attacking two prostitutes and beating them. He was sent to jail for two and a half years and was released in February of 1987. From there, he moved to Los Angeles and committed a number of murders.

Murders

On September 5, 2012, Little was arrested in Louisville, Kentucky, after DNA evidence had linked him to three murders. Carol Elford was murdered on July 13, 1987; Guadalupe Apodaca was killed on September 3, 1987; and Audrey Nelson was killed on August 14, 1989.

Little was extradited to Los Angeles, where he was charged on January 7, 2013, for the three murders. The investigation was ongoing, however. Ultimately, he was investigated in regard to sixty murders.

The FBI stated that Little had confessed to the murders of the following individuals. He even provided sketches for sixteen of them. These individuals have not been confirmed to be linked to specific, known murders, but their somewhat scant details are as follows:

1970–71: Unnamed white female, Homestead, Florida, age unknown.

1971: "Linda," Miami, Florida, black female, approximately twenty-two.

1971–72: "Marianne/Mary Ann," Miami, Florida, black female, approximately eighteen. *Little provided a sketch of this victim.*

1971–72: Unnamed female, Miami, Florida, black female, possibly affiliated with the air force.

1972: Unnamed white female, Prince George's County, Maryland, aged twenty to twenty-five. Little's confession was matched to a known Jane Doe case. Possibly from Massachusetts. *Little provided a sketch of this victim.*

1973: Unnamed white female, Kendall, Florida, about forty-five, possibly from Massachusetts. Both 1973 victims could possibly have the first name, "Sarah."

1973: Unnamed black female, New Orleans, Louisiana, age unknown. Possibly worked at a local restaurant.

1974: Unnamed black female, Savannah, Georgia, approximately twenty-two or twenty-three.

1974: Unnamed black female, Cincinnati, Ohio, age unknown.

Mid-1970s: "Emily," Miami, Florida, black female, approximately twenty-three or twenty-four. Possibly worked at the University of Miami.

1975: Unnamed black female, Knoxville, Tennessee, approximately twenty-five.

1976–77: Unnamed black female, Wichita Falls, Texas, age unknown. Disposal location of body unspecified, but stated to be near this city. *Little provided a sketch of this victim.*

1976–79: "Jo," Granite City, Illinois, black female, approximately twenty-six. May have picked her up in St. Louis, Missouri. *Little provided a sketch of this victim.*

1976-79: Unnamed black female, East St. Louis, Illinois, age unknown. Possibly picked up in St. Louis, Missouri.

1976–79 or 1993: Unnamed black female, Houston, Texas, age unknown. *Little provided a sketch of this victim.*

1977: Unnamed black female, Macon, Georgia , approximately thirty to forty. This confession was matched to an existing Jane Doe case.

1977: Unnamed black female, Pascagoula, Mississippi, approximately thirty-five to forty-five.

Possibly met in Gulfport, but native to Pascagoula and worked at a shipyard. Confession matched to an existing Jane Doe case.

1977–78: Unnamed black female, Plant City, Florida, age unknown. Apparently met in the city of Clearwater.

1977 or 1982: Unnamed black female, Charleston, South Carolina, approximately twenty-eight.

1980–81: Unnamed black female, Dade County, Georgia, approximately twenty-five to thirty. This confession was matched to a known Jane Doe case.

1980–84: Unnamed black female, Gulfport, Mississippi, approximately twenty-two.

1981: Unnamed black female, Atlanta, Georgia, approximately thirty-five to forty. *Little provided a sketch of this victim.*

1982: Unnamed white female, New Orleans, Louisiana, age unknown.

1983–84: Unnamed white female, Atlanta, Georgia, approximately twenty-six; she may have been from Griffin, Georgia. *Little provided a sketch of this victim.*

1984: Unnamed black female, Atlanta, Georgia, approximately twenty-three to twenty-five, and possibly a college student. *Little provided a sketch of this victim.*

1984: Unnamed white female, Northern Kentucky, age unknown. Possibly picked up from Columbus, Ohio. *Little provided a sketch of this victim.*

1984-mid 1990s: Unnamed black female, West Memphis, Arkansas, approximately twenty-eight or twenty-nine. May have been picked up in Memphis, Tennessee. *Little provided a sketch of this victim.* Confession matched to a known Jane Doe case. The sketch was recognized by the family of Zena Maria. A man named Anthony Jones also said that the sketch looked like his mother, who had been killed in 1997.

1984: Unnamed black female, San Bernardino, California, approximately eighteen to twenty-three.

1984: Unnamed black female, Fort Myers, Florida, age unknown.

1984: Unnamed black female, Tampa Bay, Florida, age unknown.

1984: Unnamed black female, Savannah, Georgia, approximately twenty-three.

1987: Unnamed black female, Los Angeles, California, age unknown.

1987: Unnamed black female, Los Angeles, California, age unknown.

1987: Unnamed black female, Los Angeles, California, approximately nineteen.

1987: "Granny," Los Angeles, California, black female, approximately fifty.

1987: Unnamed black female, Los Angeles, California, approximately twenty-two or twenty-three.

1987: Unnamed black female, Los Angeles, California, approximately twenty-six or twenty-seven.

1987 – early 1990s: Unnamed black female, Monroe, Louisiana, approximately twenty-four. *Little provided a sketch of this victim.*

1988 or 1996: Unnamed Hispanic female, Phoenix, Arizona, approximately in her forties. May have been native to the area. *Little provided a sketch of this victim.*

1990–97: Unnamed black female, Pine Bluff, Arkansas, age unknown.

1990-91: "Alice," Los Angeles, California, black female, approximately forty to forty-five.

1991–92: Unnamed black female, Los Angeles, California, approximately twenty to twenty-two. May have been from San Francisco.

1992: Unnamed black female, Los Angeles, California, age unknown.

1992–93: Unnamed black female, Los Angeles, California, age unknown.

1992–93: Unnamed Hispanic female, Los Angeles, California, approximately twenty-four or twenty-five. May have been from Phoenix.

1992–93: Unnamed black female, North Little Rock, Arkansas, age unknown.

1996: Unnamed black female, Los Angeles, California, approximately twenty-three to twenty-five.

1996: "T-Money," Los Angeles, California, black female, approximately twenty-three or twenty-four.

1996: Unnamed white female, Los Angeles, California, approximately twenty-three to twenty-five. *Little provided a sketch of this victim.*

1996: Unnamed black female, Los Angeles, California, approximately twenty-five.

1997: "Ann," Phoenix, Arizona, white female, age unknown. *Little provided a sketch of this victim.*

Trial

Little's trial for the murders of Elford, Nelson, and Apodaca began in September of 2014; DNA evidence was presented as well as witness testimony. Some of these witnesses were survivors of attacks by Little. On September 25, he was convicted of all charges. He received a sentence of life in prison without parole. He faced a further indictment in December of 2018 for the murder of Linda Sue Boards, twenty-three, who had been strangled to death in May of 1981 in Kentucky.

Another of his victims was identified in December 2018. Martha Cunningham, thirty-four, had been murdered in 1975.

Outcome

In November of 2018, Little began to make a number of confessions. These included:

1996: Melissa Thomas
1994: Denise Christie Brothers
1979: Brenda Alexander
1977: Unidentified woman
1982: Fredonia Smith
1982: Dorothy Richards
1996: Daisy McGuire
1978: Julia Critchfield
2005: Nancy Carol Stevens
1978: Evelyn Weston
1982: Rosie Hill

On November 13, 2018, the Wise County Sheriff's Office announced that Little might have committed over ninety murders between 1970 and 2005. It was also announced on that day that Little was being charged with the murder of Denise Christie Brothers. He pled guilty on December 13 and received another term of life in prison.

On November 20, law enforcement officials in Lee County announced that the case for the murder of Nancy Carol Stevens would be presented to a grand jury in January of 2019. The FBI announced on November 27 that thirty-four of Little's confessions had been confirmed, and they were still working to identify the other cases.

To help the FBI solve the cases, Little began doing sketches of his victims. These were released in the media. In their report, the FBI stated that "With no stab marks or bullet wounds, many of these deaths were not classified as homicides but attributed to drug overdoses, accidents, or natural causes."

Trivia

Little has a heart condition and diabetes and mobilizes using a wheelchair.

Little's girlfriend Jean had financially supported them by shoplifting and had done so for many years.

HENRY LEE LUCAS

Date of birth: August 23, 1936

Aliases/Nicknames: The Confession Killer, The Highway Stalker

Characteristics: Cannibalism, necrophilia

Number of victims: 11 - 600

Date of murders: 1960 - 1983

Date of arrest: June 11, 1983

Victim profile: Viola Dixon Lucas, 74; Becky Powell, 15; Kate Rich, 82; Linda Phillips, 26; Officer Clemmie E. Curtis, 30; Lillie Pearl Darty, 18; "Orange Socks"; Dianna Lynn Bryant, 17; Glenna Bailey Biggers; Laura Marie Purchase; Laura Jean Donez, 16

Method of murder: Various

Location: Michigan, Texas, Louisiana, California, New York

Status: Sentenced to death, later commuted to life.

Background

When Lucas was ten, he developed an eye infection after getting into a fight; he lost the eye as a result. An associate from his childhood described him as exhibiting "frighteningly strange" behavior to get attention. His mother, a prostitute, would force him to watch her engage in sex with her clients and would often cross-dress him and send him out in public.

In December of 1949, Lucas' father—who had previously lost both legs in an accident—died of hypothermia after collapsing outside the home, drunk, during a blizzard. Not long after the death of his father, Lucas ran away from home. He later claimed he committed his first murder in 1951 when he strangled Laura Burnsley, seventeen, after she refused to have sex with him. He later retracted his confession.

Lucas was convicted on June 10, 1954, of more than a dozen burglary charges and was sentenced to four years in prison. In 1957, escaped and was caught again three days later. He was released in September of 1959.

On January 11, 1960, Lucas and his mother were engaged in an argument that turned violent. He claimed she had hit him over the head with a broom, so he stabbed her in the neck. Thinking she was dead, he fled. His sister came home, found their mother, and called for help, but she died. Lucas was sentenced to twenty to forty years. He served only ten years though due to overcrowding and was released in June of 1970.

Lucas was charged with attempting to abduct three schoolgirls in 1971 and was convicted. While in prison, he started corresponding with a family friend who was also a single mother. When he was released in 1975, they married. He left two years later, after his stepdaughter made accusations he had been sexually abusing her.

At this time, he met Ottis Toole; they lived in Jacksonville, Florida with Toole's parents. Lucas became close with Toole's teenage niece, Frieda "Becky" Powell, who was mildly mentally impaired. He worked for a while as a roofer and fixed cars and seemed settled.

In 1982, Powell was put into state care after her mother and grandmother died, and Lucas convinced her to run away with him and live on the road. They moved to California and ended up working for Kate Rich, eighty-two. They were thrown out, however, when they were accused of stealing money. While hitchhiking, they received a ride by the minister of a religious commune. The minister thought they were a married couple, so he allowed them to stay on the commune and got Lucas a job as a roofer. According to Lucas, Powell got homesick and left.

Murders

In June of 1983, Lucas was arrested for the unlawful possession of a firearm. After being in custody for four days, he confessed he had killed Rich, and then Powell. He then began confessing to numerous cases. Investigators initially thought he was credible, especially since he had already confessed to actual murders.

In November, he was transferred to a jail in Williamson County, Texas, and he continued to confess to many unsolved murders. Investigators thought they could corroborate twenty-eight of the murders, so they developed the "Lucas Task Force" to further investigate his confessions. Apparently, because of Lucas' confessions, they were able to clear two hundred thirteen cases that had previously been unsolved.

Claimed Murders but not convicted:

Laura Burnley, seventeen
Naomi Miller, fifty-four
Deborah Sue Williamson, eighteen
Vickie Lee Schneider, nineteen
Tammy Jo Alexander, sixteen
Mildred H. McKinney, seventy-three
Beverly Luttrell, forty-six
Deion Marie Wilkinson, twenty-two
Estella Montoya
Ruth Kaiser, seventy-nine

Alleged Mutual Victims with Ottis Toole - Cleared

Curby Reeves, sixty-nine
Linda Beicher, nineteen
James Carpellotti, forty-nine
Katherine L. Robinson, fifteen
John Watley, seventy-four
Faye Watley, sixty-eight
Elizabeth Anne Price, forty-five
Sima Warren, twenty-nine

Stephanie Lee Smith, twenty-four
Tine Williams, seventeen
Yolanda Hernandez Garcia, twenty-four
Arley Bell Killian, twenty-three
Sharon Shelling
Russell Curtis King
Sandra Dubbs, thirty
Harold Schlesinger, fifty-three
Molly Schlesinger
Helene Prunszky, twenty-one
Nanette Warren, fifty-seven

Trial

In the end, Lucas was convicted of eleven murders and was sentenced to death, but this was later commuted to life.

Outcome

One of the cases he was convicted of was the murder of an unidentified woman known as "Orange Socks." In this case, his confession had been recorded. When it was shown in court, it seemed it had a considerable amount of editing, which led critics to think Lucas had been coached on the crime details.

It was later determined that it was highly unlikely Lucas had been involved in the murder of Orange Socks. Lucas later stated he had confessed to it as an attempt to commit "legal suicide," that it would guarantee a death penalty because he wanted to die.

On March 12, 2001, Lucas died from heart failure at the age of sixty-four. He is buried in an unmarked grave in Captain Joe Byrd Cemetery in Huntsville, Texas.

Trivia

There have been a number of books written about Lucas, as well as documentaries, which include:

- *Confessions of a Serial Killer*
- *Henry: Portrait of a Serial Killer*, played by Michael Rooker
- *Henry: Portrait of a Serial Killer, Part II*
- 2009 film *Drifter: Henry Lee Lucas*
- *The Serial Killers*
- *Henry Lee Lucas: The Confession Killer*

An episode of *A&E Biography* that featured Lucas was broadcast in 2005.

*"I hated all my life. I hated everybody. When I first grew up and can remember, I was dressed as a girl by my mother. And I stayed that way for two or three years. And after that, I was treated like what I call the dog of the family. I was beaten. I was made to do things that no human bein' would want to do." - **Lucas***

MAOUPA CEDRIC MAAKE

Date of birth: 1965

Aliases/Nicknames: Wemmer Pan Killer, Hammer Killer, Deranged Killer

Characteristics: Rape, robbery

Number of victims: 27 +

Date of murders: 1996 - 1997

Date of arrest: December 23, 1997

Victim profile: Men and women

Method of murder: Beating with rocks, shooting, hitting with a hammer

Location: Johannesburg area, South Africa

Status: Sentenced to 27 life sentences, plus 1159 years and 3 months imprisonment, on September 6, 2000. In total, his sentence amounted to 1,340 years in prison.

Background

Maake was given the nickname the "Wemmer Pan Killer" because he targeted the majority of his victims in this area of Johannesburg. He had no preferences for his victims, killing individuals of any age, race, or gender. Sometimes he used a gun and other times he used a knife. His only objective was to hurt and kill. By the time he was caught, he had killed at least twenty-seven victims in about eighteen months.

Murders

The first group of victims was bludgeoned to death with rocks while they were walking alone. The next group consisted of couples sitting in cars. With these victims, Maake would shoot the men and rape the women.

At first—due to the differences in victims, weapons, and locations—the police thought the murders were the actions of two separate killers. Then the killer started targeting tailors who were beaten to death with hammers in their shops. This led to the belief that there were two perpetrators: the Wemmer Pan Killer and the Hammer Killer. Police had no idea they were all committed by the same person. It wasn't until January 12, 1998, that various murders were finally connected.

The police finally identified Maake as the killer and arrested him in December of 1997. He initially admitted he was responsible for the crimes, and took officers around locations to point out where he had killed people.

Trial

Maake was charged with thirty-six counts of murder and twenty-eight counts of attempted murder. He was also charged with fifteen counts of rape and forty-six counts of aggravated robbery, as well as charges of unlawful possession of firearms. He pled not guilty to all charges, even though he had previously admitted he was responsible.

The trial involved brutal testimony from surviving female victims who explained how Makke would kick them and shout obscenities at them while they were on the ground. Experts detailed how Maake crushed the skulls of his male victims using large rocks. His own behavior in court was shocking, with verbal outbursts, crying when he saw his mother, and slamming his head against the dock. He even threatened a female prosecutor, saying she would get the same treatment as his victims.

As he was being pronounced guilty of killing Jose de Caires, he slept. Maake's behavior was so appalling that the judge ordered him to be removed at one point. He was prescribed tranquilizers at one stage, but he refused to take them.

The judge said that Maake had shown no remorse for the pain and suffering he had inflicted on society.

Outcome

On September 6, 2000, Maake was convicted of twenty-seven murders, twenty-six attempted murders, fourteen rapes, and forty-one aggravated robberies, as well some less serious charges. In total, he was charged with one hundred thirty-four crimes and convicted of one hundred fourteen of them. He was sentenced to twenty-seven life sentences, plus 1,159 years and three months in prison for the other counts.

Trivia

Cedric Maake was the topic of a factual television series, *Criminal Minds*.

Maake would watch couples have sex before he would kill the man and then rape his female companion.

PATRICK MACKAY

Date of birth: September 25, 1952

Aliases/Nicknames: Nil

Characteristics: Robbery, psychopath

Number of victims: 3 - 11

Date of murders: 1973 - 1975

Date of arrest: March 23, 1975

Victim profile: Isabella Griffiths, 87; Adele Price, 89; Father Anthony Crean, 63

Method of murder: Stabbing with knife

Location: England, United Kingdom

Status: Sentenced to life in prison in November of 1975.

Background

Mackay's father was a violent alcoholic, yet after his death when Mackay was ten, Mackay struggled to deal with the grief. He even refused to attend the funeral. He quickly took on the role vacated by his father and began beating his mother and sisters regularly. Police were called to the house up to four times a week and, between the ages of twelve and twenty-two, Mackay was removed from the house by police on eighteen occasions.

Mackay was put into specialist schools, prisons, and institutions; one of his teachers, as well as a female police officer, actually predicted he would one day be a killer. Later on in his youth, he indulged in cruelty to animals and liked to light fires. He threw extreme tantrums and violent bouts of anger and was a bully to younger children. He would break into homes, especially those belonging to the elderly, and rob them.

At one point, Mackay tried to kill his mother and his aunt but was unsuccessful. He also attempted to kill a younger boy but was effectively restrained by others. When Mackay was sixteen, a psychiatrist diagnosed him as a psychopath, and predicted that he would become a "cold, psychopathic killer." Mackay was committed to a mental hospital in October of 1968 and wasn't released until 1972.

As a young adult, Mackay became fascinated with Nazism. He started calling himself "Franklin Bollvolt the First" and his flat was full of Nazi materials and memorabilia. He indulged in drugs and alcohol and was living in London at the time. In 1973, he was in Kent near his mother's house and met a priest, Father Anthony Crean. Though they became friends, Mackay still robbed him. He was arrested and charged with the theft and ordered to pay compensation, but he didn't. At this time, Mackay returned to London. He later claimed to have drowned a homeless person in the River Thames during this time period.

Murders

On March 21, 1975, Mackay went back to Father Crean's home and killed him with an axe. He stood and watched the man bleed to death from the horrific injuries inflicted on his skull. Mackay was quickly arrested, as one of the responding officers recalled the previous theft. Soon after he was in custody, police began to suspect he had been responsible for up to a dozen other murders. Mackay told authorities he had killed eleven people. Some of his known victims were:

Heidi Mnilk
Heidi was stabbed to death and thrown from a train in July of 1973.

Mary Hynes
Mary was murdered in her apartment in July of 1973. She had been beaten to death.

Stephanie Britton and her Grandson
Stephanie was stabbed to death, along with her four-year-old grandson, in January of 1974.

Homeless Person
A homeless person was killed after being thrown off a bridge in January of 1974.

Isabella Griffiths
She was strangled and then stabbed to death in February of 1974.

Tobacconist
A sixty-two-year-old tobacconist was killed in 1974. A lead pipe had been used to bludgeon him.

Sarah Rodwell
Sarah, ninety-two, was beaten to death in 1974.

Ivy Davies
Ivy was killed with an axe in 1974.

Adele Price
Adele was murdered in her apartment in March of 1975. She had been strangled to death.

Father Crean
On March 21, 1975, Father Crean was murdered with an axe.

Trial

Mackay was initially charged with five murders, but this was reduced to three due to a lack of evidence in two of the cases. He was convicted of manslaughter due to diminished responsibility in November of 1975, and he received a sentence of life imprisonment.

Outcome

He is still incarcerated and is apparently one of only fifty or so inmates in the United Kingdom that has a whole life tariff—meaning he is unlikely to ever be released back into society.

Trivia

*"I shan't shed a tear. Life is full of shocks of all descriptions and they have to be faced." - **Mackay***

MICHAEL MADISON

Date of birth: October 15, 1977

Aliases/Nicknames: Nil.

Characteristics: Convicted sex offender, kidnapping, rape, necrophilia

Number of victims: 3

Date of murders: September 2012 - July 2013

Date of arrest: July 19, 2013

Victim profile: Shetisha Sheeley, 28; Angela Deskins, 38; Shirellda Helen Terry, 18

Method of murder: Ligature strangulation

Location: East Cleveland, Cuyahoga County, Ohio, USA

Status: Sentenced to death.

Background

On October 15, 1977, Madison was born as the result of an accidental pregnancy. John Baldwin, who was named as his father, denied he was the father and therefore played no part in Madison's life.

Murders

Police were called on July 19, 2013, to investigate reports of a foul odor coming from a garage that was leased to Madison. Inside, they found a decomposing body. The following day, during a search nearby, they found two more bodies. One was in a backyard, and the second was in the basement of a vacant house. All three bodies were within one hundred and two hundred yards apart. Each of the bodies was wrapped in plastic bags.

Police obtained a warrant to search Madison's apartment, and they found more evidence of decomposition inside. A standoff between Madison and the police ensued, but he was eventually taken into custody without any incident.

The victims were identified as:

Angela Deskins, thirty-eight, who had been reported missing in June of 2013.

Shetisha Sheeley, twenty-eight, who had been missing since September of 2012.

Shirellda Helen Terry, eighteen, was last seen July 10, 2013, leaving a Cleveland elementary school where she was working for the summer.

Trial

Madison was charged with three counts of aggravated murder on July 22, 2013. He waived his right to a preliminary hearing, and his bail was set at six million dollars, so there was no way he would be released.

The defense didn't argue Madison was innocent. Instead, in a move to spare him from execution, they argued that the murders had not been premeditated. A not guilty plea was entered on October 31, 2013, and it was announced by the prosecution that they intended to seek the death penalty. The indictment was updated to include two counts of aggravated murder for each victim, three counts of kidnapping, three counts of gross abuse of a corpse, one count of rape, and one count of weapon possession by a former convict.

Madison had previously been registered as a sex offender after four years in prison for attempted rape in 2002.

Outcome

Madison was found guilty of the murders on May 5, 2016. The jury took less than a day to come to a verdict. On May 20, the jury recommended that Madison should receive the death penalty. On June 2, the sentence of death was given to Mackay.

Trivia

An ex-girlfriend took the witness stand and recalled times when she would notice a horrible smell when she walked into Madison's apartment. When she questioned him about it, he told her there were dead raccoons in his closet.

In 1980, when Madison was aged two, it was discovered that his mother had stuffed food down his throat, which caused him to vomit. After he vomited, she would put him in a tub of hot water. If he screamed, she took him out of the bath and used an extension cord to beat him.

By the age of sixteen, he was roaming the streets and sleeping anywhere he could.

At seventeen, he was charged with delinquency for inappropriately touching a classmate.

RAMADAN ABDEL REHIM MANSOUR

Date of birth: 1980

Aliases/Nicknames: al-Tourbini, The Butcher of Gharbia

Characteristics: Rape, torture

Number of victims: 8 - 20 +

Date of murders: 2004 - 2006

Date of arrest: November 29, 2006

Victim profile: Children aged between 10 and 14 years (predominantly males)

Method of murder: Shooting

Location: Several locations, Egypt

Status: Sentenced to death on May 23, 2007.

Background

At an early age, Mansour left his home and joined a street gang. The leaders of the gang taught him how to survive, and allegedly used razors to cut him when he made mistakes. He would later become a leader of the gang himself.

Murders

Mansour raped and murdered at least thirty-two children over a seven-year period in Cairo, Alexandria, Beni Suef, and Qalyubia in Egypt. The victims were all aged between ten and fourteen, and the majority of them were boys. Mansour was arrested in 2006, along with six accomplices.

During his confession, he stated he had learned that to get back at those who crossed him, he would rape them. He killed anyone who threatened to go to the police. One of his victims was Ahmed Nagui, twelve, who was a member of his gang. When Mansour attempted to sexually assault him, Nagui went to the police. Due to lack of evidence, Mansour was released, and soon after he raped and killed Nagui.

He often traveled between Cairo and Alexandria by train and said he preferred Alexandria because there were less police there. Mansour and his associates would lure street children onto the roof of the train carriage, then strip them, rape them, torture them, and throw their naked bodies onto the tracks. Some of the victims were thrown into the Nile, and others were buried alive.

Trial

After police arrested Mansour, he told prosecutors repeatedly that he was possessed by a female "jinn," a spirit, who ordered him to commit the crimes. At his trial he was convicted and sentenced to death.

Outcome

In 2010, Mansour was executed.

Trivia

Commercialization of the nickname al-Tourbini.

An Egyptian newspaper reported after Mansour's arrest that some of the products available in Egypt were being renamed after his nickname. Some of the restaurants in Tanta, his home town, began selling the "al-Tourbini sandwich." The name was also applied to large lambs, and some drivers named their tuk-tuks after the murderer. Even stranger, certain supermarkets renamed their stores "al-Tourbini: The Butcher of Gharbia."

DAVID MASON

Date of birth: December 2, 1956

Aliases/Nicknames: Nil

Characteristics: Robbery

Number of victims: 6

Date of murders: March 6, 1980 - December 2, 1982

Date of arrest: February 1981

Victim profile: Joan Pickard, 71; Arthur Jennings, 83; Antoinette Brown, 75; Dorothy Lang, 72; Robert Groff, 55; Boyd Wayne Johnson, 24

Method of murder: Strangulation, shooting, garroted with a towel

Location: California, USA

Status: Executed by asphyxiation gas in California on August 24, 1993.

Background

Mason's strict fundamentalist Christian parents inflicted such severe physical, psychological, and verbal abuse on him that he tried to commit suicide when he was just five years old. (He swallowed a bottle of pills and set himself on fire.) This would be the first of at least twenty-five attempts to take his own life.

From an early age, Mason's behavior was described as uncontrollable. He lit fires and attacked other children. When he was eight, he was discovered standing with a knife over his brother's crib. As a result, his parents started to lock him in a room that had the windows nailed shut, which they referred to as "the dungeon." At the age of eleven, Mason soiled himself, and as punishment his mother pinned the baby's soiled diaper to him and made him wear his dirty underwear on his head. Another time, his father tied him to a bench and beat him until he was unconscious. Not surprisingly, Mason was later diagnosed with PTSD.

In July of 1977, Mason robbed a store and stabbed the store clerk. He then threatened that if she notified police or testified against him, he would kill her. She didn't heed the threat, and he was arrested and convicted, receiving a sentence of thirty-six months in prison.

Mason assaulted a victim in March of 1980 and attempted to rob them. The victim fought back, so Mason struck them on the head with a gun. In December of 1980, he managed to convince an elderly couple to let him into their home, pretending to be selling firewood. He handcuffed them to chairs and robbed them of coins and jewelry worth forty-seven thousand dollars.

Murders

Mason killed four people in 1980 and then killed his cellmate in 1982. The known victims were (they were not named):

Victim #1 – seventy-three-year-old female
The victim had known Mason for a number of years. He had worked for her doing odd jobs and had even been invited into her apartment. She had shown him her alarm system, including the panic buttons. On March 6, 1980, Mason entered her home, choked her when she tried to escape to activate the alarm, robbed her, tied her up, and then beat and strangled her to death.

Victim #2 – seventy-five-year-old male
On August 18, 1980, Mason beat, strangled, and robbed a victim whom he may have known previously.

Victim #3 – seventy-two-year-old female
On November 11, 1980, Mason strangled the woman and beat her over the head with a wrench. On examination, it was noted that her vaginal tissue was cut and bruised.

Victim #4 – seventy-five-year-old female
On December 6, 1980, Mason beat, strangled, and robbed the woman. She had bruises and cuts over most of her body, and her clothes were partially ripped off.

Victim #5 - Male cellmate at Alameda County Jail
With help from another inmate, Mason beat and garroted his cellmate to death with a knotted towel on May 9, 1982. He then hung the victim from a heavy shower rod to try to make the murder look like a suicide.

Trial

Mason gave his parents a tape recording labeled, "David Mason-Epitaph," which contained his confessions regarding the murders. His parents contacted police, and when they questioned him, he confessed again and provided details that only the police and the killer would know. Later, he recanted, saying he only confessed because he wanted to die following the death of his lover.

Mason was found guilty of the murders and sentenced to death on January 27, 1984.

In March of 1993, Mason indicated that he wanted to discontinue any appeals that had been filed on his behalf. A psychiatric review was requested to determine his ability to make an informed decision and, having viewed the results, the judge ruled in Mason's favor.

In June of 1993, the court issued the execution order for the date requested by Mason: August 24, 1993.

Outcome

As requested, Mason was executed on August 24, 1993, in the gas chamber. Because he had requested the date, a federal judge called the prison a few minutes before the scheduled execution to ensure Mason's attorney was there if he wanted to stop the proceedings.

At 12:08 a.m., the warden asked Mason if he had changed his mind. He said, "No, Warden, I want to proceed; thank you, Warden."

Trivia

Mason was the first inmate in California to drop all of his appeals and just accept his death sentence. This meant his life was cut short by a minimum of three years.

The afternoon before his execution, Mason feasted on sandwiches with his family. This was his last meal. That evening, by request, he only had ice water.

GENNADY MIKHASEVICH

Date of birth: April 7, 1947

Aliases/Nicknames: Nil

Characteristics: Rape

Number of victims: 38

Date of murders: 1971 - 1985

Date of arrest: December 9, 1985

Victim profile: Unnamed women

Method of murder: Strangulation

Location: Belarus

Status: Executed by firing squad on February 3, 1988.

Background

Mikhasevich was born in Ist, Belarus, and served in the army as an adult. He was described as a good family man who drank little alcohol and was good to his two children. He was also a member of the Communist Party and the Voluntary People's Druzhina.

He later explained that his killing spree began after discovering—when he left the army—that his girlfriend had married someone else.

Murders

His first murder occurred on May 14, 1971. He met a young woman and decided to kill her because of his anger toward his girlfriend. In October of 1971, he killed again, and then in 1972, he strangled two women to death. He got married in 1976, but continued to kill.

Mikhasevich killed largely so he could rape. He would usually smother his victims or strangle them. He didn't carry any weapons with him, so he would use whatever was available. After his victims were dead, he would rob them of their cash and valuables. Strangely, he would also take odd household items such as scissors.

In the 1980s, the investigation into the murders began to gain speed, with the investigator in charge believing that all the murders were linked to one killer. The police believed the killer was driving a particular car, a red "Zaporozhets," so they began checking everyone who owned one. Because Mikhasevich was a druzhinnik (a member of the Voluntary People's Druzhina), he helped police with this and was basically searching for himself. This enabled him to gain information so that he could stay one step ahead.

In 1985, he killed twelve women, so he certainly wasn't slowing down. But he made one major mistake. He tried to derail the investigation by sending an anonymous letter to the newspaper claiming an imaginary group, the "Patriots of Vitebsk," was responsible for the killings. He then left a handwritten note next to his latest victim, again claiming the group was responsible.

Investigators decided to analyze the handwriting of all male residents in the area, resulting in the check of 556,000 samples. This led them to Mikhasevich, and once they had uncovered other evidence, he was arrested.

Trial

In December of 1985, Mikhasevich was arrested. At first, he denied he was the killer, but he eventually confessed. He was sentenced to death and executed in 1987 by firing squad. By the time he was arrested, fourteen other people had been convicted of the murders he had committed.

Outcome

The case became notorious for pointing out the incompetence and corruption of the law enforcement agencies. The fourteen men already convicted had been tortured to force them to confess to crimes they hadn't committed. At least two had been executed.

Trivia

In his spare time, Mikhasevich was a police volunteer.

While helping police, he interrogated drivers of the cars they were searching—ironic, since he was the killer all along.

BLANCHE TAYLOR MOORE

Date of birth: February 17, 1933

Aliases/Nicknames: Nil

Characteristics: Poisoner

Number of victims: 1 - 4

Date of murders: 1968 - 1986

Date of arrest: July 18, 1989

Victim profile: P. D. Kiser; Isla Taylor; James N. Taylor; Raymond Reid

Method of murder: Arsenic poisoning

Location: Alamance County, North Carolina, USA

Status: Sentenced to death on January 18, 1991.

Background

Moore's father was an ordained Baptist minister and allegedly an alcoholic who forced her to prostitute herself to pay his gambling debts. Moore was known to switch conversational topics from Scripture to explicitly sexual themes in one breath. In 1968, her father reportedly died from a heart attack.

In 1952, she married James Napoleon Taylor, and they had two children, the first in 1952 and the second in 1959. She began working as a cashier at Kroger in 1954, and by 1959 she was promoted to the position of head cashier, which was the highest-paid female job at Kroger at the time. Moore began an affair with the store manager, Raymond Reid, in 1962.

James died in 1971, and the cause of death was reported as a heart attack, just like Moore's father. Soon after, Moore and Reid went public with their relationship. But, by 1985, the relationship was going downhill. She had allegedly started dating the regional manager for Kroger's, Kevin Denton. When that relationship ended, she filed a sexual harassment lawsuit against Denton and Kroger in October of 1985. As a result, Denton was forced to resign from his job, and two years later, Kroger settled the case for two hundred seventy-five thousand dollars.

The same year, Moore met Rev. Dwight Moore, and a relationship developed between them. She had to keep it secret, however, until after her lawsuit was settled. While she was dating him, she asked him to get her some arsenic-based ant killer.

Murders

In 1986, Reid became ill, supposedly with shingles. He ended up in the hospital in April and was dead by October 7. After his death, Moore and the reverend went public with their relationship. They intended to marry, but postponed their plans when Moore was diagnosed in 1987 with breast cancer. They then decided to marry in November of 1988, but the reverend became ill with an intestinal issue and had to have two surgeries. The couple finally married on April 19, 1989.

They honeymooned over a long weekend. Within days, the reverend became severely ill and collapsed after eating food Moore had given him. He was admitted to hospital after several days. The reverend's health continued to deteriorate, and Moore told the doctors he had been working with an herbicide in the garden. A toxicology screening test was performed, which showed he had twenty times the lethal dosage of arsenic in his system. Remarkably, he survived.

The hospital notified both the police and the State Bureau of Investigation of the toxicology results, and the reverend was interviewed. He mentioned that Moore's former boyfriend had died due to Guillain-Barre syndrome, the symptoms of which are very similar to arsenic poisoning. As they investigated, they found Moore had tried to have the reverend's pension changed so that she was the main beneficiary.

A picture was starting to form, so Moore's first husband, James Taylor, lover Raymond Reid, and her father, Parker Kiser were exhumed and tested. High levels of arsenic were found in all three bodies. Moore tried to explain these results away by saying that both the reverend and Reid had been depressed and maybe they had taken the poison themselves.

To make things look even worse, Moore had the reverend's hair cut short, so it couldn't be sampled for arsenic testing. Pubic hair was taken instead, so her attempts were foiled. Moore was arrested on July 18, 1989, and charged with two counts of first-degree murder for the deaths of Taylor and Reid.

Trial

On October 21, 1990, the trial began. Moore denied she had given Reid any food in the hospital, but the prosecution had fifty-three witnesses that stated otherwise. On November 14, she was convicted, and three days later, the jury recommended the death penalty. The presiding judge agreed, and on January 18, 1991, she was sentenced to death.

Outcome

Moore is still waiting for her execution by lethal injection. She spends most of her time in prison writing poetry, and she still claims she is innocent. In 2010, a motion was filed to convert Moore's sentence—along with that of other death row inmates—to life because of the Racial Injustice Act, which was related to the racial composition of the jury.

There has been a lot of speculation that Moore may have killed others. There were a number of mysterious deaths surrounding Moore, with some having symptoms of arsenic poisoning. One of the potential victims was Isla Taylor, her former mother-in-law.

Trivia

Book and film

The book *Preacher's Girl* was written by Jim Schutze in 1993. In the book, the author claimed to have uncovered evidence that Moore had set up the sexual harassment suit against Denton, and that she may have lit the two fires intentionally.

Actress Elizabeth Montgomery portrayed Moore in the television film based on the book, *Black Widow Murders: The Blanche Taylor Moore Story*.

David Tamer, one of Moore's attorneys, was charged with misappropriation of client funds, including hers, and was convicted of embezzlement. He had a history of mental health issues.

Due to health issues, Moore has received chemotherapy and radiotherapy treatments while in prison.

PETER MOORE

Date of birth: 1940

Aliases/Nicknames: The Man in Black

Characteristics: Mutilation

Number of victims: 4

Date of murders: September - December of 1995

Date of arrest: December of 1995

Victim profile: Henry Roberts, 56; Edward Carthy, 28; Keith Randles, 49; Anthony Davies, 40

Method of murder: Stabbing with knife

Location: North Wales, Wales, United Kingdom

Status: Sentenced to life imprisonment in November of 1996.

Background

Moore had an extremely close relationship with his mother, who doted on him and called him her miracle son because she had believed she couldn't have children. They lived in a nice part of town, and his upbringing was rather privileged. He was always fascinated by film and video, and he later owned four small cinemas.

At his cinemas, he ran a "Saturday Club" so children could watch films and buy sweets for a reasonable cost. Moore was well respected within his community, but there was something about him none of his acquaintances ever suspected.

Murders

Between the months of September and December of 1995, Moore mutilated and stabbed to death four men. In September, the body of Henry Roberts, fifty-six, was found in the yard outside a farmhouse near Holyhead. He had been stabbed twenty-seven times. Roberts was considered a bit of an eccentric in the community and was the kind of man who wouldn't hurt anyone or anything. The community was completely stunned that someone would kill him, let alone so brutally.

Moore met his next victim in a gay bar in Liverpool in October. Edward Carthy, twenty-eight, was a drug and alcohol addict. Moore and Carthy drove to Clocaenog Forest in North Wales, where Moore stabbed the man to death. His body was the last one found, and it was only located with the help of Moore after his arrest.

In November, Moore killed traffic manager Keith Randles, forty-nine, who had been living in a caravan on a construction site near Llangefni. Randles was last seen at the local fish and chip shop on November 29. His body was discovered the following morning with multiple stab wounds.

Anthony Davies, forty, was the next victim. He was killed in December after driving to a nearby beach that was a common spot for gay men to meet. Moore stabbed him to death on the beach. Later, Moore told investigators that he targeted Davies after he saw him expose himself while cruising the area.

Police had found blood at the scene and tested it; the DNA results were a match to Moore. He was arrested in December.

Trial

At the opening of the trial, prosecution barrister Alex Carlile QC referred to Moore as "The man in black - black thoughts and the blackest of deeds." Moore claimed during his trial that a homosexual lover named Jason had committed the murders. But this person was completely fictitious. He had called this imaginary person Jason after the *Friday the 13th* horror film character.

Moore was found guilty on all counts.

Outcome

In November of 1996, Moore was sentenced to life in prison with the recommendation he never be released. During the investigation, it was discovered he had committed thirty-nine other sex attacks on men over a period of twenty years.

Trivia

While in Wakefield Prison, Moore became friends with Harold Shipman, who later hanged himself in January of 2004.

Moore was told in June of 2008 that he would spend the rest of his life in prison without release. He challenged the ruling in March of 2011, in the European Court of Human Rights (ECHR). His appeal failed, but in July of 2013, the ECHR ruled there had to be both a review and possibility of release compatible with human rights.

The ECHR was challenged by murderer Arthur Hutchinson, and in February of 2015, it announced that whole life orders were lawful under exceptional circumstances.

Other

There was a false report on October 13, 2011, that Moore had died at Broadmoor hospital on 30 July 2011.

Moore contacted police while in prison and claimed he knew the identity of the Clocaenog Forest Man, but because the dates were conflicting, it was ruled out.

DONTAE MORRIS

Date of birth: August 24, 1985

Aliases/Nicknames: Nil

Characteristics: Drug deals

Number of victims: 5 - 7

Date of murders: May 2010 - June 2010

Date of arrest: July 2, 2010

Victim profile: Derek Anderson, 21; Rodney Jones, 42; Harold Wright, 25; Police Officer Jeffrey Kocab; Police Officer David Curtis

Method of murder: Shooting

Location: Florida

Status: He was initially sentenced to life imprisonment until mid-2015, when he was resentenced to the death penalty three times.

Background

Morris' mother was just sixteen years old when he was born, and when he was two, his father was murdered. The crime was never solved. His grandmother helped raise him, and he often changed schools throughout his childhood. His mother entered a new relationship that bore two more children.

It is believed Morris was a member of the "Bloods" street gang, and at some point, he fathered a child. His aunt was employed with the Tampa Police Department, and in July of 2010, she was released due to withholding information that could have led to a quicker arrest of Morris.

Murders

On May 18, 2010, Morris shot and killed Derek Anderson in front of his home. They had previously been involved in an argument on a basketball court. His next victim was Rodney Jones, whom he shot dead on May 31, while Jones was leaving the Cotton Club Bar. Then he killed Harold Wright and robbed him.

Morris and his girlfriend were pulled over by police officers for missing license plates on June 29, 2010. Officer David Curtis discovered there was a warrant for Morris' arrest and called for his partner Officer Jeffrey Kocab to assist him. When Morris was asked to put his hands behind his back, he shot both officers in the head, killing them.

The patrol car had a dashcam which recorded the whole event, so Morris was quickly identified as the killer. The search became the biggest manhunt in Tampa's history, with more than one thousand police officers and staff from twenty-two agencies involved, as well as the FBI, ATF, and SWAT teams. Armored vehicles were deployed, along with dog teams and helicopters.

Morris was finally arrested on July 2, 2010, and was taken to jail.

Trial

The first trial was for the murder of Jones and it began in July of 2012. Morris was convicted of murder and attempted robbery in March of 2013 and was sentenced to life without parole and a further twenty-five years.

Morris' next trial began in November of 2013, for the murders of Curtis and Kocab. Because he had been filmed carrying out the murders, it only took four hours for the jury to find him guilty. In May of 2014, he was sentenced to death.

The third trial was to begin on July 20, 2015, for the murder of Anderson. That same month he was convicted and received another death sentence.

In December of 2015, the prosecutor announced that Morris would not be put on trial for the murder of Wright.

Outcome

Morris appealed the death penalty in the case of the murders of the police officers, and in April of 2017, this was rejected. In January of 2018, his death penalty for murdering Anderson was reversed on the grounds that the verdict by the jury had not been unanimous.

He still awaits his execution.

Trivia

During his trial, the defense stated that despite having a difficult childhood, including a murdered father, Morris was able to take care of his younger siblings.

Defense witnesses testified that Morris was physically abused by his stepfather. He formed a parental relationship with his step-grandfather, but the older man became addicted to drugs and died after he was burned by chemicals in an accident.

HERBERT MULLIN

Date of birth: April 18, 1947

Aliases/Nicknames: Nil

Characteristics: Mutilation, delusional

Number of victims: 11 - 13

Date of murders: October 13, 1972 - February 13, 1973

Date of arrest: February 13, 1973

Victim profile: Lawrence White, 55; Mary Guilfoyle, 24; Rev. Henri Tomei, 64; James Gianera, 24; Joan Gianera, 23; Kathleen Prentiss, (aka Kathy Francis), 30; David Hughes, 9; Daemon Francis, 4; Robert Spector, 18; David Oliker, 18; Brian Scott Card, 19; Mark Dreibelbis, 19; Fred Perez, 72

Method of murder: Beating, stabbing with a knife, shooting

Location: Santa Cruz, California, USA

Status: Sentenced to life in prison in August 1973, with the possibility of parole in 2025.

Background

Mullin grew up with a strict war veteran father, but there was no abuse in the family. At school he was voted by his classmates as "Most Likely to Succeed." Not long after he graduated high school, his best friend was killed in a car accident, leaving Mullin devastated to the point that he created a shrine in his friend's memory in his bedroom.

When Mullin was twenty-one, he was willingly committed to a mental hospital, and over the next few years, he was in and out of a variety of institutions. He attempted to enter the priesthood at one point, would stub cigarettes out on his skin, and was evicted from an apartment for shouting at imaginary people.

At the age of twenty-five, he moved back home with his parents. By now, he was now hearing voices. The voices told him that an earthquake was imminent, and the only way to save California was through human sacrifice. His birthday happened to be the anniversary of the 1906 San Francisco earthquake, so he thought this was hugely significant.

Mullin believed that earthquakes had been delayed by all the bloodshed during the Vietnam War, and now that the war was winding down, he would need to kill people to create enough death to stop an earthquake from occurring.

Murders

On October 13, 1972, Mullin came across homeless man Lawrence "Whitey" White, fifty-five, who was hitchhiking on Highway 9. Mullin tricked White into taking a look at his car's engine, and as he did so, Mullin struck him in the head. He later stated that White was really Jonah from the Bible and he had telepathically told Mullin: "Pick me up and throw me over the boat. Kill me so that others will be saved."

Mary Guilfoyle, a twenty-four-year-old college student, was the next to meet her death at the hands of Mullin. Mullin picked her up as she hitchhiked on October 24, 1972. Once in the car, he stabbed her in the chest and the back, before cutting up her body and scattering her remains alongside a road.

Mullin went to the St. Mary's Catholic Church on November 2, 1972, to confess his sins. However, he was in a delusional state, and he believed that Father Henri Tomei wanted to be his next sacrifice. So, Mullin beat, kicked and finally stabbed Tomei to death.

Mullin attempted to join the Marines at this point and remarkably managed to pass the psychiatric tests. But, when it was discovered he had been arrested multiple times for bizarre behavior, he was rejected. This fed his paranoid delusions of conspiracy, and he believed a group of hippies was behind it all.

In January of 1973, Mullin made the decision to stop using drugs, believing that they were the reason behind his problems. He then decided to kill a friend from high school who had sold him marijuana, Jim Gianera. He bought some guns and, on January 25, went to where he believed Gianera lived. However, he found the house was occupied by Kathy Francis and her children, and she gave Mullin the new address for Gianera.

Mullin traveled to Gianera's new home and proceeded to kill both Gianera and his wife. He shot them both in the head and stabbed them multiple times. Then he went back to the old house and killed Francis and her children, Daemon, aged nine, and David aged four.

On February 10, Mullin was walking through Henry Cowell Redwoods State Park and came across four teenage boys who were illegally camping. He told them he was a park ranger and ordered them to leave, but they refused. So he shot them all. Their bodies weren't found until the following week.

Three days later, as Mullin was driving on the Santa Cruz west side, he noticed Fred Perez weeding his lawn. For no reason, he turned his car around, drove back, and shot Perez through the heart, killing him instantly. Then he got back into the car and drove away. However, there were witnesses, and they gave the license plate to the police. Just a few minutes later, Mullin was stopped and arrested.

Trial

Once in custody, Mullin confessed to the murders and told police that voices had instructed him to kill to prevent a major earthquake. He was charged with ten murders, and his trial began on July 30, 1973. Because he had confessed to the crimes, the purpose of the trial was to determine his sanity at the time of the killings. Because he had made an effort to cover his tracks at some of the murders, and some also showed premeditation, he was declared sane despite his paranoid schizophrenia.

Mullin was convicted of first-degree murder on August 19, 1973, for the murders of Gianera and Francis. For the other eight murders he was found guilty of second-degree murder. He was due to go on trial for the murder of Tomei in Santa Clara on December 11, 1973, but he pled guilty to second-degree murder and was convicted without trial.

Outcome

Mullin was sentenced to life imprisonment, and since 1980, he has been denied parole ten times. He is currently incarcerated at the Mule Creek State Prison in Ione, California.

Trivia

In the horror film *The Coed Killer*, Mullin was portrayed by actor Andy E. Horne.

Mullin was featured in an episode of *Born to Kill*.

Mullin had some interaction in prison with Edmund Kemper, another serial killer active in the same area and at the same time as Mullin. They had adjoining cells. Kemper recalled, "Well, [Mullin] had a habit of singing and bothering people when somebody tried to watch TV. So I threw water on him to shut him up. Then, when he was a good boy, I'd give him some peanuts. Herbie liked peanuts. That was effective because pretty soon he asked permission to sing. That's called behavior modification treatment."

ROBERT NAPPER

Date of birth: February 25, 1966

Aliases/Nicknames: The Plumstead Ripper, The Green Chain Rapist

Characteristics: Rape, mutilation

Number of victims: 3

Date of murders: July 15, 1992, November of 1993

Date of arrest: May of 1994

Victim profile: Rachel Nickell, 23; Samantha Bisset, 27; Samantha's daughter, Jazmine, 4

Method of murder: Stabbing with a knife, smothering

Location: London, England, United Kingdom

Status: Remanded in Broadmoor Hospital indefinitely on 18 December 2008.

Background

Napper was yet another who grew up in a violent household, with his father violently attacking his mother. When he was nine, his parents divorced, and Napper and his siblings were placed into foster care. They all received psychiatric treatment, with Napper receiving counseling for six years.

Napper was sexually assaulted at the age of thirteen by a family friend, and it is said that his personality changed. He became obsessive about tidiness, introverted, and reclusive. He began spying on his sister while she was undressed and bullied his siblings.

He first came to the attention of police in 1986, when he was arrested and convicted of an air gun offense. His mother contacted the police in October of 1989 to inform them that Napper had admitted committing rape. But the police had no case on file that matched, so they dismissed the information. It was later found that there had indeed been a rape, and at that point, Napper's mother ceased all contact with him.

Murders

On July 15, 1992, Napper attacked Rachel Nickell, stabbing her forty-nine times while her two-year-old son clung to her. The following year, in November, he stabbed Samantha Bisset in her chest and neck, killing her. Then he sexually assaulted and smothered her daughter, Jazmine Jemima Bisset, who was just four years old. Napper mutilated Samantha's body and took part of her with him as trophies. The scene of the crime was so horrific that the police photographer had to take leave for two years.

A fingerprint was found at the scene that matched to Napper. Police located Napper and arrested him, charging him in May of 1994 with the murders of Samantha and her daughter.

Trial

When Napper went on trial, details about his delusions were laid out before the court. He had been diagnosed a paranoid schizophrenic, and he believed he could communicate telepathically. A psychiatrist who was treating Napper while he was in custody also diagnosed him with Asperger's syndrome. Napper believed he had a Nobel Peace Prize and a degree in math, as well as medals from fighting in Angola. He also believed he had millions of dollars in the bank. Another bizarre delusion was that changes had been made to the calendar and he believed this meant unusual things were occurring.

Napper had stated he had once been kneecapped by the IRA and had fingers blown off by an IRA bomb, but they had grown back as some sort of miracle. The psychiatrist stated Napper felt untouchable, that he could get away with anything, and she felt Napper would most likely never be let out of Broadmoor.

In October of 1995, he was convicted of the murders of Samantha and her daughter.

Outcome

While in custody, Napper confessed to two rapes and two attempted rapes. He was questioned about the murder of Nickell but denied he was responsible. Investigators believe Napper was the "Green Chain Rapist," a savage rapist who committed at least seventy attacks over four years. The earliest attacks were linked to Napper, and he admitted to those in 1995.

In 2004, Napper was linked to Nickell's murder by DNA profiling. On December 18, 2008, he was found guilty of manslaughter on the grounds of diminished responsibility. He was incarcerated indefinitely at Broadmoor Hospital for the criminally insane.

Trivia

Napper had planned out his murders in fine detail, including taking note of any paths, surveillance spots, and potential fox holes on his maps.

Napper is suspected of having committed as many as eighty-six rapes in total.

Napper was featured on *Born to Kill?* in 2014.

NATIONAL SOCIALIST UNDERGROUND

Date of birth: N/A

Aliases/Nicknames: Bosphorus Serial Murders, Kebab Murders

Characteristics: Neo-Nazi terror group

Number of victims: 10

Date of murders: 9 September 2000 to 25 April 2007

Date of arrest: November of 2011

Victim profile: Enver Şimşek, 38; Abdurrahim Özüdoğru; Süleyman Taşköprü, 31; Habil Kılıç, 38; Mehmet Turgut; İsmail Yaşar, 50; Theodoros Boulgarides; Mehmet Kubaşık; Halit Yozgat; Michèle Kiesewetter, 22

Method of murder: Shooting

Location: Germany

Status: Sentenced to between two years and life imprisonment - multiple offenders.

Background

Beate Zschäpe, Uwe Böhnhardt, and Uwe Mundlos were the founding members of the National Socialist Underground. They had grown up in Jena in Thuringia, the former East Germany state. In the 1990s, they became involved in the neo-Nazi scene, engaging in street fights with anti-fascists and attending far-right concerts; they even made SS uniforms and wore them to the former concentration camp Buchenwald. As they became more radical, they joined the Thuringia Home Guard, a neo-Nazi group.

The local police in Jena received a tip about Zschäpe, Mundlos, and Böhnhardt, and they raided a storage unit the trio had rented. The raid occurred in 1998; the police discovered bomb-making materials and anti-Semitic material, but the trio had gone into hiding, fleeing to Saxony.

Over the next thirteen years, a number of race-related murders occurred, including eight Turkish-Germans, one Greek, and a German police officer. The same rare Ceska 83 pistol had been used in all but one of the murders.

Murders

Enver Şimşek, thirty-eight, was a businessman with Turkish roots who ran several flower stalls in southern Germany. Şimşek stepped in when his employee running the stall in Nuremberg went on holidays, and on the afternoon of September 9, 2000, he was shot in the face by two gunmen. He died two days later.

On June 13, 2001, Abdurrahim Özüdoğru was shot in the head twice with the same gun used in the murder of Enver Şimşek. Özüdoğru, a machinist, had been helping out in a tailor's shop. A passerby looked through the shop window and saw the bloody body sitting in the back of the shop.

On June 27, 2001, Süleyman Taşköprü, thirty-one, was killed in his shop in Hamburg-Bahrenfeld—shot three times in the head. The bullets retrieved matched the guns that were used in the first murder.

Habil Kılıç became the fourth victim on August 29, 2001. Kılıç, aged thirty-eight, was shot at point-blank range in his greengrocer's shop in Munich-Ramersdorf.

In Rostock-Toitenwinkel, on the morning of February 25, 2004, Mehmet Turgut was shot in the head and neck three times with a silenced CZ 83 and died instantly. Turgut, who was living in Hamburg illegally at the time, had been asked by an acquaintance to open up a doner kebab shop in Rostock that day. Because there was a link between Rostock and Hamburg, a connection was made to the third victim, Süleyman Taşköprü, by the police, and the term "doner murder" was established.

On June 9, 2005, İsmail Yaşar, fifty, who had come from Suruç, Turkey to Nuremberg, and owned a kebab shop in Scharrerstrasse, was found dead with five gunshot wounds.

On June 15, 2005, locksmith Theodoros Boulgarides was killed in his shop. He was a Greek and the first victim who wasn't a Turk.

On the afternoon of April 4, 2006, kiosk vendor Mehmet Kubaşık, a German citizen with Turkish origins, was found murdered in his store. Like the majority of the victims, Kubaşık had been shot in the head.

Two days after Kubaşık was murdered, on April 6, 2006, Halit Yozgat became the last victim of Turkish ethnicity. Yozgat ran an Internet café in Kassel, Hesse, and like the other victims, was shot in the head. On this occasion, an agent of the Hessian Office for the Protection of the Constitution was present. At first, he claimed he had left the premises just before the murder, but when shown evidence of witnesses who had seen him present when the murder occurred, he later changed his statement. His involvement created suspicions that government agencies may be linked to the group responsible for the murders.

On April 25, 2007, police officer Michèle Kiesewetter and her partner were attacked during their lunch break. Kiesewetter, twenty-two, was killed; her partner was critically wounded but survived with no memory of the attack. Both were shot in the head at point-blank range while sitting in their patrol car. The shooters had approached their vehicle from both sides. Kiesewetter died on-site, and her male partner was in a coma for several weeks. It is uncertain why Kiesewetter and her partner were attacked as they didn't fit the profile of the other murders.

Trial

On November 4, 2011, after a bank robbery in Eisenach, Mundlos and Böhnhardt were found shot dead in a caravan, which had been set on fire. Police believed they had set it alight and then killed themselves. Inside the service pistol (HK P2000) of murdered policewoman, Michèle Kiesewetter was found.

Zschäpe set fire to the apartment she had shared with Böhnhardt and Mundlos in Saxony and then turned herself in to police. At that time, a video was circulating that linked the murders to the group, the National Socialist Underground.

On May 6, 2013, the trial began. It would last for four years due to the massive amount of information and evidence.

Zschäpe was charged with nine murders, an attack on police, and a further murder, arson, two attempted murders, and membership in a terrorist organization.

André Eminger was charged with providing assistance in a nail bomb attack in Cologne.

Holger Gerlach was charged with providing assistance to NSU members.

Carsten Schultze was charged with providing weapons to NSU members.

Ralf Wolleben was charged with providing weapons to NSU members.

The defense attorneys argued that Zschäpe was innocent of all charges and that they had been committed by Mundlos and Böhnhardt. She hadn't spoken for two years and gave her testimony in the form of a written statement which was then read out to the court by her attorney. She said in the statement that she felt regret that she was unable to do anything to stop her associates from murdering their loved ones.

Outcome

On July 11, 2018, Beate Zschäpe was convicted of ten counts of murder, membership in a terrorist organization, and arson. She was sentenced to life imprisonment. Her accomplices were convicted as follows:

Wolleben: Guilty – Convicted of aiding and abetting nine murders by procuring the pistol used. Sentenced to ten years in prison.

Eminger: Guilty – Convicted of aiding a terrorist organization. Sentenced to two and a half years in prison.

Gerlach: Guilty – Also convicted of aiding a terrorist organization. Sentenced to three years in prison.

Schulze: Guilty – Convicted of aiding and abetting in nine counts of murder. Sentenced to three years of juvenile detention as he was only twenty years old at the time of the murders.

Ralf Wolleben, thirty-eight, and Carsten Schultze, thirty-three, were found guilty of being accessories to murder in the killing of the nine male victims. Prosecutors alleged that they had supplied the gun and silencer used in the killings. Wolleben had previously been a member of Germany's far-right National Democratic Party, which held seats in two state parliaments located in eastern Germany.

Andre Eminger, thirty-three, was found guilty of being an accessory in two of the bank robberies and the Cologne bombing in 2001. He was also found guilty of two counts of supporting a terrorist organization.

Holger Gerlach, thirty-eight, was found guilty of three counts of supporting a terrorist organization.

Trivia

In November of 2011, German Chancellor Angela Merkel stated that *"the cold-blooded murder of nine immigrant shopkeepers by Neo-Nazis is an inconceivable crime for Germany and a national disgrace."*

EARLE NELSON

Date of birth: May 12, 1897

Aliases/Nicknames: The Gorilla Killer, The Dark Strangler

Characteristics: Rape, necrophilia, mutilation

Number of victims: 22 - 25

Date of murders: 1926 - 1927

Date of arrest: June 10, 1927

Victim profile: Clara Newman, 60; Laura Beale, 63; Lillian St. Mary, 63; Ollie Russell, 53; Mary Nisbet, 52; Beata Withers, 35; Virginia Grant, 59; Mabel Fluke; Anna Edmonds, 56; Blanche Myers; Florence Monks; Almira Berard, 41; Bonnie Pace, 23; Germania Harpin, 28, and her 8-month-old son Robert; Mary McConnell, 53; Jennie Randolph, 53; Fannie May; Maureen Atorthy; Mary Cecila Sietsma, 27; Lola Cowan, 14; Emily Patterson

Method of murder: Strangulation

Location: USA, Canada

Status: Executed by hanging in Winnipeg, Canada, on January 13, 1928.

Background

By the time he was two, Nelson was an orphan—both of his parents had died of syphilis. He went to live with his grandmother who was devoutly religious, and he was raised beside her younger children. From a young age, he showed morbid behavior and self-loathing, and he was expelled from primary school at the age of seven. When he was around ten, he was struck by a streetcar while riding his bicycle and was in a coma for six days. From then on, his behavior became more erratic; he suffered from memory loss and frequent headaches.

Some of Nelson's odd behaviors included talking to people who weren't there and quoting Bible passages. He also liked to watch female family members undress. His grandmother later said that he would go to school in fresh, clean clothes and return in rags, as though he had swapped his clothes with a homeless person.

In his early teens, Nelson began going to bars and brothels regularly, and at one point he contracted a venereal disease. His criminal career started when he was young, with his first prison sentence (for breaking and entering) taking place in 1915. He was paroled in September of 1916 but was back behind bars by March 9, 1917. After serving six months, he was released and then arrested for burglary. Five months later, he escaped from jail.

Nelson enlisted in the military in late 1917, but deserted after serving just six weeks. He went on to enlist in different branches of the military under different names, but each time he deserted soon after enlisting. He was committed to a mental hospital in 1918, while in the Navy, for odd and erratic behavior.

The psychiatrist who treated him said that he didn't appear to be homicidal, violent, or destructive. Also, Nelson had spoken of paranoid delusions and hallucinations. The doctor stated, "He has seen faces, heard music, and at times believed people were poisoning him. Voices sometimes whisper to him to kill himself. Says that if he were kept in jail, he would get something sharp and cut the veins in his wrists."

While in the mental hospital, Nelson escaped three times. Eventually, the staff stopped looking for him. He was discharged from the Navy on May 17, 1919.

While working at St. Mary's Hospital as a janitor, Nelson met Mary Martin, sixty, who was working in administration. They were married in August of 1919, but the union was short-lived. Martin later said he made her life a living hell, with bizarre sexual demands, jealous rages, religious delusions, and behavior that was becoming increasingly violent. They separated after just six months.

On May 19, 1921, Nelson entered a home in San Francisco under the pretense of being a plumber. In reality, he was there because of Mary Summers, twelve, whom he had planned to molest. When she started screaming, her elder brother came running to her aid, and Nelson fled. He was caught hours later and was sent back to the mental hospital. He escaped two more times before he was discharged in 1925.

Murders

Nelson embarked on his murderous spree in early 1926. His first victim, Clara Newman, sixty, was a wealthy landlady in San Francisco. He entered her property on February 20, 1926, posing as a potential tenant. He strangled Newman to death, then raped her and hid her body in an empty apartment in the building.

His next victim was Laura Beale, sixty-three. He entered her San Jose home on March 2, and strangled her with a silken cord. It was wound so tightly that it had embedded in the flesh of her neck.

Nelson strangled and then raped Lillian St. Mary, sixty-three, on June 26, in San Francisco. Then two weeks later, he strangled Ollie Russell, fifty-three, in her boardinghouse. She had been sexually assaulted after her death. On August 16, the husband of Mary Nisbet, fifty-two, found her body in the bathroom of a vacant apartment in the building they owned. She had been strangled and then raped. A witness described the offender as a man with long arms and large hands, which led to the nickname the "Gorilla Man" or "Gorilla Killer."

Nelson moved to Portland, Oregon, and on October 19, he raped and killed landlady Beata Withers, thirty-five. Her body was found inside a steamer trunk in the attic by her teenage son. The next day, Nelson murdered Virginia Grant, fifty-nine, and hid her body behind the furnace in the basement. Two days later, on October 21, landlady Mabel Fluke went missing from her home. Several days later, her body was found in the attic; she had been strangled to death with her scarf.

Nelson went back to San Francisco where he raped and killed Anna Edmonds, fifty-six, on November 18. The next day, a pregnant woman was showing her home to a potential buyer when she was attacked. The twenty-eight-year-old woman survived and was able to give a description. On November 29, Blanche Myers was murdered by Nelson in her home, and police managed to recover fingerprints.

As theories and fear ran rampant, a woman called the police to say a suspicious man had stayed at her boardinghouse for a number of days. On the day of Myers' murder, the man had told the woman he was leaving and wouldn't be back. He gave her some jewelry as a gift, and police later identified it as belonging to Florence Monks, who had been murdered and raped in Seattle on November 23.

The body of Amira Berard, forty-one, was found inside her home in Iowa on December 23. She had been garroted with a shirt, and she had been raped. On December 27, Bonnie Pace, twenty-three, of Kansas City, was strangled and raped in her home. Her husband found her body. On the following day, Germania Harpin and her infant son were found murdered in their Kansas City home. Germania had been raped after her death. Both had been strangled, the baby with a diaper.

Nelson moved on to Philadelphia, and on April 27, he murdered and raped Mary McConnell, another landlady. Then, he went to Buffalo, New York, on May 27 and rented a room from Jennie Randolph using the alias "Charles Harrison." Randolph's body was found three days later stuffed under a bed. Like the others, she had been strangled and then raped after death.

In Detroit, Michigan, boardinghouse manager Fannie May and boarder Maureen Atorthy were found murdered and raped on June 1. An electrical cord had been cut from a table lamp and used to garrote May. Mary Cecilia Sietsma was killed by Nelson two days later in Chicago.

On June 8, 1927, Lola Cowan, fourteen, went missing in Winnipeg, Manitoba, Canada, after going out to sell flowers from door-to-door. Two days later, Emily Patterson (from the same area) went missing; she was found later that night by her husband. She had been strangled and raped and shoved underneath her son's bed. She had also been beaten with a claw hammer.

Police in Winnipeg conducted a search of all boardinghouses in the city on June 12, during which they found the nude and decomposing body of Cowan under the bed in the room Nelson had been staying in. Unlike the other victims, Cowan had been mutilated.

On June 16, police in Killarney near Manitoba stopped a man who fit the description of Nelson, but who was going by the name "Virgil Wilson." They took him to the local jail, and he escaped that night. Nelson happened to catch the same train that was being used to transport Winnipeg police officers, however, and he was recaptured within twelve hours of his escape.

Police took photographs of Nelson and sent them out to all police departments throughout America; this resulted in a number of positive identifications in California and Illinois. When fingerprints were sent to the San Francisco Police Department, they were matched, and his identity was confirmed as Nelson. The same fingerprints had been found at a number of crime scenes.

At first, Nelson confessed to the crimes, saying to reporters, "I only do my lady killings on Saturday nights." But he quickly recanted and claimed he was innocent.

Trial

When Nelson was arrested, he was a wanted man in six cities across the U.S. He was held so that he could be tried in Manitoba for the murders of Paterson and Cowan. Other charges included two attempted molestations and one burglary. The trial was meant to start on June 27, 1927, but it was delayed until November 1.

Nelson's ex-wife took the stand and testified that he was completely insane. Another sixty people from both the U.S. and Canada testified, linking him to the scenes or to the property he had stolen from the victims. A guard at the jail noted that Nelson became obsessed with a passage from the Book of Proverbs:

My son, give me thine heart,
and let thine eyes observe my ways.
For a whore is a deep ditch;
and a strange woman is a narrow pit.

She also lieth in wait as for a prey,
and increaseth the transgressors among men.

On November 5, 1927, closing statements were made in Nelson's trial. The jury only took forty minutes to deliberate before returning a verdict of guilty. Nelson was sentenced to death. In late December, a thirty-page document was submitted to the minister of justice petitioning for clemency on insanity grounds. Despite the extent of the document, the appeal was denied.

Outcome

On January 13, 1928, Nelson was hanged at the Vaughan Street Jail in Winnipeg. His last statements before the trap was sprung, were, "I am innocent. I stand innocent before God and man. I forgive those who have wronged me and ask forgiveness of those I have injured. God have mercy! I forgive those who have wronged me."

Trivia

Nelson was the first serial killer to have gained widespread attention in the media, including radio, magazines, and newspapers, in American history.

His confirmed murder count, more than twenty, was the highest for nearly fifty years, until the discovery of Dean Corll's crimes in 1973. Crime historians Harold Schechter and David Everitt claim Nelson was the first serial sex murderer in twentieth-century America.

Alfred Hitchcock's film *Shadow of a Doubt* was inspired by Nelson's murder spree.

NEW BEDFORD HIGHWAY KILLER

Date of birth: Unknown

Aliases/Nicknames: Nil

Characteristics: Targeted prostitutes, drug addicts

Number of victims: 9 - 11

Date of murders: 1988 - 1989

Date of arrest: Never apprehended.

Victim profile: Robbin Rhodes, 28; Rochelle Clifford Dopierala, 28; Debroh Lynn McConnell, 25; Debra Medeiros, 30; Christine Monteiro, 19; Marilyn Roberts, 34; Nancy Paiva, 36; Debra DeMello, 35; Mary Rose Santos, 26; Sandra Botelho, 24; Dawn Mendes, 25,

Method of murder: Strangulation

Location: New Bedford, Massachusetts, USA

Status: Unknown.

Background

This serial killer was responsible for the murders of at least nine women, and the disappearances of two others in New Bedford, Massachusetts between July of 1988 and June of 1989. There were a number of assaults as well. The majority of the victims were either drug addicts or prostitutes, and despite them being taken from New Bedford, their bodies were found in nearby towns that followed along the path of Route 140.

Murders

Murders that are possibly due to the New Bedford Highway Killer are:

Robbin Rhodes, twenty-eight. She was last seen in New Bedford, March/April 1988. Her body was found on March 28, 1989, along Route 140.

Rochelle Clifford Dopierala, twenty-eight. She was last seen in New Bedford, late April of 1988. Her body was found on December 10, 1988, along Reed Road, two miles from Interstate 195.

Debroh Lynn McConnell, twenty-five. She was last seen in New Bedford, May of 1988. Her body was found on December 1, 1988, off Route 140.

Debra Medeiros, thirty. She was last seen in New Bedford, May 27, 1988. Her body was found on July 3, 1988, on Route 140.

Christine Monteiro, nineteen. She was last seen in New Bedford, late May of 1988.

Marilyn Roberts, thirty-four. She was last seen in New Bedford, June of 1988.

Nancy Paiva, thirty-six. She was last seen in New Bedford, July 7, 1988. Her body was found on July 30, 1988, alongside Interstate 195.

Debra DeMello, thirty-five. She was last seen in New Bedford, July 11, 1988. Her body was found on November 8, 1988, alongside Interstate 195.

Mary Rose Santos, twenty-six. She was last seen in New Bedford, July 16, 1988. Her body was found on March 31, 1989, along Route 88.

Sandra Botelho, twenty-four. She was last seen in New Bedford, August 11, 1988. Her body was found on April 24, 1989, along Interstate 195.

Dawn Mendes, twenty-five. She was last seen in New Bedford, September 4, 1988. Her body was found on November 29, 1988, alongside Interstate 195.

Trial

Although nobody has ever been caught and charged with the murders, there were a number of suspects.

Anthony DeGrazia

A local prostitute identified DeGrazia from a photograph shown to her by a young detective. The prostitute didn't name him as a positive suspect but said he looked similar to the man who had assaulted her. He was later accused of seventeen rapes and assaults. Because of the allegations, DeGrazia was brought in for questioning about the rapes and then charged while being investigated as the murder suspect. DeGrazia spent fifteen months in jail and attended court eighteen times before being released in January of 1990 on bail. He committed suicide.

Kenneth C. Ponte

Ponte was indicted by a grand jury in August of 1990 in the murder of Rochelle Clifford Dopierala, who had been beaten to death. Ponte was a drug user and had been involved in a previous incident with Dopierala. On July 29, 1991, the murder charges against Ponte were dropped due to lack of evidence.

In May of 2009, Ponte was back in the news. Police had dug up the patio and driveway of his former home in New Bedford but found nothing. On January 27, 2010, he was found dead in his home with foul play ruled out.

Daniel Tavares Jr.

While Tavares was incarcerated for murdering his mother, he sent a letter to one of the staff at the prison that indirectly suggested he was the Highway Killer. He had lived in New Bedford and knew where the body of another murder victim, Gayle Botelho, was buried. Tavares was also convicted of killing Brian and Bev Muack and then convicted of killing Botelho. Her body was buried under a tree in his yard.

Outcome

Of all the murders that are known, only nine of the bodies have been recovered. Three decades from the start of the killings, the identity of the killer has still not been uncovered.

Trivia

Most of the victims were prostitutes and drug addicts, and between them they left behind fifteen children.

COLIN NORRIS

Date of birth: February 12, 1976

Aliases/Nicknames: Nil

Characteristics: "Angel of Death" nurse

Number of victims: 4 - 7

Date of murders: 2001 - 2002

Date of arrest: October 12, 2005

Victim profile: Doris Ludlam, 80; Bridget Bourke, 88; Irene Crookes, 79; Ethel Hall, 86

Method of murder: Insulin poisoning

Location: Leeds, West Yorkshire, England

Status: Sentenced to life imprisonment, with a minimum term of thirty years in prison, on March 4, 2008.

Background

Norris was a nurse from Glasgow, Scotland, who became notorious for killing his elderly patients. His first contact with elderly patients occurred while he was placed on Ward Seven at the Royal Victoria Hospital in Dundee, in 1998.

Norris had complained to a friend that he didn't like elderly patients because he preferred the excitement of trauma. He was later sent to the Riverside View Nursing Home in Dundee, but reported in sick after three days and never returned.

He told a colleague: "When I was bathing female patients and washing them down below, I found it difficult to start with, especially because they were the same age as my grandmother."

Four months after he qualified as a nurse, he gained employment on Ward 36 at the Leeds General Infirmary. What followed was a killing spree that would last six months.

Murders

Crimeline:

May 2, 2002: Vera Wilby, ninety, broke her hip and after surgery was admitted to ward 36 at Leeds General Infirmary. As she was recovering, her condition deteriorated.

May 17, 2002: Mrs. Wilby was given a dose of the powerful painkiller morphine by Norris to make her sleepy. He then administered more medication to her, and she was found semi-unconscious after suffering a sudden hypoglycemic attack ninety minutes after Norris finished his shift at the hospital. She survived the attack.

June 12, 2002: Doris Ludlam, eighty, from Pudsey, West Yorkshire, broke her hip after a fall while in Chapel Allerton Hospital in Leeds where she had been admitted for a heart condition. She was transferred to ward 36 at Leeds General Infirmary for surgery.

June 16, 2002: Bridget Bourke, eighty-eight, of Holbeck, Leeds, broke her hip and was admitted to ward 36 at Leeds General Infirmary.

June 17, 2002: Mrs. Bourke underwent surgery for her hip. She was weak and confused, with bleeding in her brain and complications from a stroke. She then developed a serious bacterial infection.

June 25, 2002: Mrs. Ludlam was administered an "unnecessary" dose of diamorphine by Norris, which was double the recommended dose. She became drowsy, and Norris then gave her medications that reduced her blood sugar level before he finished work. She was discovered about forty minutes later in a coma.

June 27, 2002: Mrs. Ludlam died.

July 20, 2002: Mrs. Bourke fell out of bed.

July 21, 2002: Norris claimed to have found Mrs. Bourke slumped in bed at 3:10 a.m. Doctors were called, and she was found to have suffered a hypoglycemic attack, despite not being diabetic, and was deeply unconscious.

July 22, 2002: Mrs. Bourke never recovered and died shortly after midnight. The cause of death on the certificate was a stroke.

October 2002: Mrs. Wilby was discharged from the hospital and went to live at a nursing home. The following year she died from unrelated causes.

October 10, 2002: Irene Crookes, seventy-nine, from Hunslet, Leeds, broke her hip after a fall and was admitted to ward 36 at St James's Hospital. She was treated by Norris for several days, and although she was breathless and requiring oxygen, and had to use a walker, there was no cause for concern. Norris recorded in his notes that her condition was improving.

October 19, 2002: Norris reported finding Mrs. Crookes "totally unresponsive" shortly before 6 a.m. She had suffered a hypoglycemic attack though she was not diabetic.

October 20, 2002: Mrs. Crookes died.

November 2002: Ethel Hall, eighty-six, of Calverley, Leeds, broke her hip and was admitted to ward 36 at Leeds General Infirmary for surgical repair. The surgery went well, and she appeared to be recovering and able to walk with a little assistance.

November 19, 2002: Ethel Hall had a fainting spell, which was unusual for her.

November 20, 2002: Ethel Hall took a "very serious turn for the worse" in the early hours of the morning after she was found choking. Her blood sugar levels were found to be very low, and blood tests showed levels of insulin that were very high. On December 6, 2002, the West Yorkshire Police were called in to investigate.

December 11, 2002: Ethel Hall died of irreversible brain damage without ever regaining consciousness.

December 2002: During questioning by the police, Norris told officers "he seemed to have been unlucky over the last twelve months," but denied murdering his patients.

September 2003: Mrs. Bourke's body was exhumed fourteen months after her death, by detectives who were investigating Norris. An autopsy determined her cause of death to be a coma induced by insulin.

Suspicions were raised when Norris predicted change in the condition of a patient, without any medical indications, in a conversation with colleagues, saying: "Whenever I did nights someone always died." He continued: "It was always in the morning when things go wrong - about 5:15 a.m."

When it was reported to police, they brought Norris in for questioning. When asked about the deaths, Norris stated he seemed to have been unlucky over the past twelve months. Police investigated a total of seventy-two deaths before charging him with four murders, carried out with high dosages of insulin.

Trial

The trial lasted for nineteen weeks, and after deliberating for four days, Norris was convicted on March 3, 2008, of four murders and another attempted murder. He received a sentence of life imprisonment with the minimum period set at thirty years. The judge rejected the suggestion that Norris had euthanized the patients because none of them had been terminally ill. Judge Mr. Justice Griffith stated, "You are, I have absolutely no doubt, a thoroughly evil and dangerous man. You are an arrogant and manipulative man with a real dislike of elderly patients. The most telling evidence was that observation of one of your patients, Bridget Tarpey, who said 'he did not like us old women.'"

Outcome

In October of 2011, a number of concerns were brought up about whether Norris was really guilty or not. An expert in insulin poisoning, Professor Vincent Marks, said the jury was misled that a cluster of hypoglycemic incidents in people who were not diabetic had to be sinister. According to Marks, the four patients who died were at a high risk of developing hypoglycemia due to their risk factors, which included infection, multi-organ failure, and malnutrition.

Without the medical evidence, the case against Norris would collapse due to the lack of any other evidence or a motive.

In January of 2015, the jury foreman from the trial said he now believed Norris was innocent, along with another jury member.

Trivia

Norris had been a boy scout, and he helped look after mentally handicapped people and was involved in amateur dramatics.

He once said to a colleague that "someone always died" when he was on the night shift. Apparently, he became so arrogant that he predicted the next death (Ethel Hall's), to within fifteen minutes of the actual time of death. When she was discovered in a coma, Norris pointed to his watch and said to a staff nurse: "I told you so."

ORIGINAL NIGHT STALKER - GOLDEN STATE KILLER

Date of birth: November 8, 1945

Aliases/Nicknames: Golden State Killer, Joseph James DeAngelo, East Area Rapist, Visalia Ransacker, Diamond Knot Killer, East Bay Rapist

Characteristics: Rape, robbery

Number of victims: 13 +

Date of murders: 1974 - 1986

Date of arrest: April 24, 2018

Victim profile: Janelle Lisa Cruz, 18; Greg Sanchez, 27; Cheri Domingo, 35; Keith Eli Harrington, 24; Patrice Briscoe Harrington, 27; Brian Maggiore, 21; Katie Maggiore, 20; Dr. Robert Offerman, 44; Debra Alexandria Manning, 35; Lyman Smith, 43; Charlene Smith, 33; Claude Snelling, 45; Manuela Witthuhn, 28

Method of murder: Shooting, bludgeoning

Location: California, USA

Status: Awaiting trial.

Background

When DeAngelo was around nine years old, he witnessed the rape of his seven-year-old sister by two airmen at a base warehouse in Germany. He graduated from high school in 1964 and joined the Navy. During the Vietnam War he served on cruisers as a damage control man and received medals for his service.

After leaving the Navy, he went to college and graduated with an associate degree in police science in June of 1970. The following year, he studied criminal law at Sacramento State University and received a bachelor's degree in criminal justice. Then he completed a police internship at the Roseville Police Department.

He married in November of 1971 and had three daughters; the marriage ended in 1991. Between May 18, 1973 and August of 1976, he worked as a police officer in Exeter. DeAngelo was promoted to sergeant by 1976 and was in charge of the "Joint Attack on Burglary" program for the Exeter Police department. He was later caught shoplifting dog repellent and a hammer and received six months' probation in October of 1979, ending his police career.

Murders

On October 1, 1979, an intruder broke in and tied up a couple in Goleta. Alarmed by hearing him say "I'll kill 'em" to himself, the couple attempted to escape when he left the room with the woman screaming. Knowing the screaming would arouse the neighbors, the intruder jumped on his bicycle and rode away. A neighbor who happened to be an FBI agent gave chase but was unable to catch him. The attack was later linked to the Offerman–Manning murders by the shoe prints left behind and the type of twine used to tie up the victims.

On December 30, Robert Offerman and Debra Alexandra Manning were found shot to death at Offerman's condominium in Goleta. Offerman's bindings were untied, indicating that he had lunged at the attacker. The neighbors had heard the gunshots, and paw prints from a large dog were found at the scene, suggesting the killer may have brought a dog with him.

On March 13, 1980, Charlene Smith and Lyman Smith were found murdered in their home in Ventura. Charlene had been viciously raped before she was murdered. A log from the woodpile outside the house had been used to bludgeon the Smiths to death. A cord had been used to tie their ankles and wrists. An unusual Chinese knot, called a diamond knot, was used on Charlene's wrists.

On August 19, Keith Eli Harrington and Patrice Briscoe Harrington were found bludgeoned to death in their home in Dana Point's Niguel Shores gated community. Patrice had also been raped. Although their wrists and ankles had been bound, no ligatures or murder weapon were found.

On February 6, 1981, Manuela Witthuhn was raped and murdered in her home in Irvine. Witthuhn's body showed signs of being tied, but no ligatures or a murder weapon were located at the scene.

On July 27, Cheri Domingo and Gregory Sanchez were attacked in Domingo's residence in Goleta. The killer had climbed through a small bathroom window to get into the house. Sanchez wasn't tied up; he had suffered a gunshot to the cheek before he was beaten to death with a garden tool. Sanchez's head was then covered with clothing that had been pulled out of the closet. Domingo was raped and bludgeoned, and bruises on her wrists and ankles indicated that she had been tied. The restraints were missing from the scene.

On May 4, 1986, Janelle Lisa Cruz was found after she had been raped and bludgeoned to death in her home in Irvine. The murder weapon was thought to be a pipe wrench that was missing.

Investigators did not initially consider the murders that occurred in southern California to be linked to the others. Each police department seemed to think that their cases were the work of someone in their own area. Decades later, the cases were linked almost entirely by DNA testing.

Trial

DeAngelo was formally arrested on April 24, 2018, by the Sacramento County Sheriff's Department. The now seventy-two-year-old man was subsequently charged with eight counts of first-degree murder with special circumstances. He was then charged with four more counts of first-degree murder on May 10 by the Santa Barbara County District Attorney.

Four months earlier, police had uploaded the killer's DNA profile to a website GEDmatch. Ten to twenty distant relatives were then identified through the site, and five investigators worked with a genealogist to create a family tree. Through this, they identified two potential suspects. One was ruled out, and the other was DeAngelo.

To confirm his DNA, investigators managed to collect a sample from the door handle of a car he had been driving. They then collected a tissue from his garbage can. Both samples matched.

Because of the statute of limitations on rape and burglary, DeAngelo can't be charged for those crimes. But he has been charged with murder and kidnapping. On August 13, 2018, it was announced that DeAngelo would be charged with the murder of Claude Snelling in 1975.

Outcome

It was announced in March of 2019 that the death sentence would be sought in DeAngelo's case.

Trivia

Letters and other writings:

In December of 1977, letters containing a poem entitled "Excitement's Crave" by an individual claiming to be the East Area Rapist were sent to the editor of the *Sacramento Bee*, the Sacramento mayor's office, and the KVIE TV station. It read as follows:

"Excitement's Crave"

All those mortal's [sic] surviving birth / Upon facing maturity,
Take inventory of their worth / To prevailing society.
Choosing values becomes a task; / Oneself must seek satisfaction.
The selected route will unmask / Character when plans take action.
Accepting some work to perform / At fixed pay, but promise for more,
Is a recognized social norm, / As is decorum, seeking lore.
Achieving while others lifting / Should be cause for deserving fame.
Leisure tempts excitement seeking, / What's right and expected seems tame.
"Jessie James" has been seen by all, / And "Son of Sam" has an author.
Others now feel temptations [sic] call. / Sacramento should make an offer.
To make a movie of my life / That will pay for my planned exile.
Just now I'd like to add the wife / Of a Mafia lord to my file.
Your East Area Rapist
And deserving pest.
See you in the press or on T.V.

Phone calls:

"I'm the East Side Rapist" (March 18, 1977)

Three calls were received by the Sacramento County Sheriff's Office on March 18, 1977. The man making the calls claimed he was the East Area Rapist. He just laughed during the first two calls, then hung up the phone. During the third call, he said: "I'm the East Side Rapist, and I have my next victim already stalked, and you guys can't catch me."

"Never gonna catch me" (December 2, 1977)

The Sacramento Police received a call saying: "You're never gonna catch me, East Area Rapist, you dumb fuckers, I'm gonna fuck again tonight. Careful!" The next victim of the rapist was attacked the same night.

"Watt Avenue" (December 10, 1977)

Both the City of Sacramento's Police Department and the County of Sacramento's Sheriff's Department received calls on the same night, with the caller saying: "I am going to hit tonight. Watt Avenue."

"Gonna kill you" (January 2, 1978)

A call was made to the first victim of the East Side Rapist on January 2, 1978, and the caller said: "Gonna kill you ... gonna kill you ... gonna kill you ... bitch ... bitch ... bitch ... bitch ... fuckin' whore."

Later calls (1982–1991)

One of the earlier victims was working at a restaurant in 1982 and received a call there from the rapist. He told her he was going to rape her again. It's believed the victim was recognized by the rapist while he was at the restaurant.

RUDOLF PLEIL

Date of birth: July 7, 1924

Aliases/Nicknames: The Deathmaker

Characteristics: Rape, robbery

Number of victims: 10 - 25

Date of murders: 1946 - 1947

Date of arrest: April of 1947

Victim profile: One man and nine women (unnamed)

Method of murder: Blows to the head with various objects

Location: Germany

Status: Sentenced to 12 years in prison for manslaughter in ax murder of a salesman, 1947. Sentenced to life in prison for nine further murders involving rape in 1950. Hung himself in prison on February 18, 1958.

Background

Pleil was born in a small village near the border of former Czechoslovakia. His father was a communist, and when the Nazis seized control, he was arrested. The family moved to Vejprty, and from the age of nine, Pleil supported his unemployed parents through border smuggling. He was arrested multiple times. When Pleil was thirteen, he had his first sexual experience with a prostitute.

At the age of fifteen, in 1939, he began working as a butcher; this job lasted only a few weeks. Then he worked as a shipboy on barges, all the while operating illegal businesses. During the Second World War, Pleil was found to be unfit to serve due to his epilepsy. He was supposed to be sterilized, which was the law at the time for those with epilepsy. But a few days before he was meant to have the procedure, the operating room was destroyed by a bombing attack. He did apparently father a child who was raised by his sister.

Pleil worked in a labor camp as a cook and used to eat cats. After the Red Army invaded, he worked as an auxiliary policeman in his village. He married but found that this didn't satisfy his urges, so he started attacking women at night. He later said he had started killing in 1945, but there was no proof of this.

From 1946 to 1947, Pleil helped paying customers to cross illegally to East and West. During the two-year period, he, along with accomplices Karl Hoffmann and Konrad Schüßler, killed twelve women.

Murders

On July 19, 1946, Pleil abused and killed a woman, who was around twenty-five years old, in the forest between Walkenried and Ellrich on the edge of southern Harz. He used a hammer to commit the murder.

On August 19, Pleil and accomplice Karl Hoffmann convinced a young woman to accompany them to a freight depot in the Upper Franconian border town of Hof. Once there, her head was bashed in with a knife by Hoffmann as she was assaulted. They killed her by slitting her throat.

A twenty-five-year-old woman crossed the path of Pleil and Hoffman on September 2, at the border crossing at Bergen. Using a fieldstone, Pleil beat her to death. Her body was then buried in the forest by Hoffman.

The next victim was a young woman who was crossing the border from Trappstadt in the middle of September. In the forest, they robbed her and then murdered her. After she was dead, they cut off her head.

At the end of November, Pleil offered his assistance to a young woman who wanted to get across the border. She was guided to the forest between Walkenried and Ellrich, at which point Pleil later claimed he had suffered a seizure. He stated that when he regained consciousness, the girl was lying beside him dead.

A widow, fifty-five, was robbed by Pleil and Schüßler near Nordhausen on December 12. They beat her with clubs. Despite leaving her for dead, she survived. She later testified at the trial.

Two days later, a woman was murdered by Pleil in the guard booth of Vienenburg while Schüßler watched on. Her body was tossed down a well. Then on December 19, Pleil killed a forty-four-year-old widow, and her body was also put down the well.

On January 16, 1947, Pleil and Hoffmann offered to take a young woman to the East Zone. Pleil killed her near the road that runs between Abbenrode and Stapelburg. They disposed of her body in a nearby stream.

The next victim was attacked in mid-February near Dudersieben. After Pleil killed the forty-nine-year-old woman, Hoffman robbed her body of her valuables.

Pleil and Hoffman carried out their next killing at the beginning of March, near Zorge, which was in the Soviet occupation zone. The woman was slaughtered by Hoffman with a knife and then decapitated. They moved her body to the British zone, where it was later found.

When Pleil was finally arrested, it wasn't for the murders of the women, but for the murder of merchant Hermann Bennen in a border crossing crash. Pleil was charged with manslaughter because he was intoxicated at the time of the crime. While he was in custody, he finally confessed to the other murders. In total, he claimed he had killed twenty-five people.

Trial

The trial was set to begin on October 31, 1950. Pleil had already received a twelve-year sentence for the manslaughter. In court, he exaggerated the details of his crimes without any shame, because he loved the attention he was getting in the press. By now, his total had climbed to an alleged forty murders. He tried to convince the court he was insane but failed. On November 17, 1950, Pleil and his accomplices were found guilty and each sentenced to life imprisonment.

Outcome

On February 16, 1958, Pleil hanged himself in his prison cell. Hoffman died in prison in 1976, and Schüßler was later pardoned in the late 1970s.

Trivia

"You underrate me; I am Germany's greatest killer. I put others, both here and abroad, to shame." - *Pleil*

Documentary film *Der Totmacher Rudolf Pleil* was released in 2007 and was based on the life of Pleil.

Pleil had a strange set of ethics when it came to murder. While he didn't see anything wrong ethically with raping and murdering women, he was against anyone decapitating the bodies. He thought decapitation was a disgusting act, and on at least one occasion, he beat an accomplice for attempting to cut off the victim's head.

While he was in prison, he wrote his life story and called it *Mein Kampf*. He signed it "by Rudolf Pleil, death dealer (retired)."

During his trial it became known that Pleil had once applied for the hangman's job. He had written in his application that if they wanted proof of his skills, they should look in a particular well. Those who were checking the applications thought it was some sort of joke, and they ignored it. However, when the well was later checked, a corpse was found that showed signs of strangulation.

Throughout his trial, Pleil constantly interrupted the proceedings, and he demanded he be charged with twenty-five murders, which he claimed to have committed, not the nine he was being charged with.

STEPHEN PORT

Date of birth: February 22, 1975

Aliases/Nicknames: The Grindr Killer

Characteristics: Serial rapist, poisoner

Number of victims: 4

Date of murders: June 2014 - September 2015

Date of arrest: October 15, 2015

Victim profile: Anthony Walgate, 23; Gabriel Kovari, 22; Daniel Whitworth, 21; Jack Taylor, 25

Method of murder: GHB poisoning (gamma-Hydroxybutyric acid)

Location: Barking, London, England, United Kingdom

Status: Port received a life sentence with a whole life order on November 25, 2016, meaning he is unlikely to ever be released from prison.

Background

Born in Southend-On-Sea, Port and his family moved to Dagenham, where they remain today. At school, Port was described as a loner, and a neighbor said he had a strange childlike personality. As a grown man, he was witnessed playing with children's toys. In the mid-2000s he came out as gay and was living by himself in a flat in Barking, London. He was working as a chef when he started meeting men through gay online social networks.

Murders

His first victim was Anthony Walgate, twenty-three, a fashion student who also worked occasionally as an escort. Port contacted him on June 17, 2014, and hired his services as an escort for eight hundred pounds. They met at Barking station and returned to Port's home. Two days later, Port called emergency services anonymously saying there was a young man collapsed outside his flat. Walgate was pronounced dead. Although Port wasn't considered a suspect in the death, he was convicted of perverting the course of justice in March of 2015 and sentenced to eight months in jail. However, he was released the following June.

From August of 2014 until September of 2015, Port murdered three more men. Gabriel Kovari, twenty-two, had lived with Port briefly before he was murdered. Daniel Whitworth, twenty-one, was also a chef and lived in Gravesend in Kent. The last victim was Jack Taylor, twenty-five, who was living with his parents in Dagenham. Of the four murders, three bodies were found in the graveyard at the church of St. Margaret of Antioch in Barking. Beside the body of Whitworth was a fake suicide note left by Port. The note also suggested Whitworth was responsible for one of the other murders.

The initial inquests into the deaths returned open verdicts, but the coroner, Nadia Persaud, said she still had some concerns with Daniel's death that hadn't been answered by the police investigation. She said, "most concerning are the findings by the pathologist of manual handling prior to his death" and noted that "the bed sheet that he was found wrapped in was not forensically analyzed, and the bottle of GBL which was found near him was also not tested for fingerprints or DNA."

It was the murder of Jack Taylor that brought about Port's undoing. The two men were captured by CCTV footage on the night of the murder as they left the Barking station, and when this footage was released, Port was identified and arrested.

Trial

During his trial, the drugs used by Port on his victims were discussed. He had used a range of drugs and narcotics, including amyl nitrate, Viagra, meow meow, crystal meth, and GHB or GHL. The autopsies of the four victims all had high levels of GHB, leading to overdoses.

Port was convicted on November 23, 2016, of the penetration, rapes, and murders of the four victims. He was also convicted of three other rapes, ten counts of administering a substance with intent, and four sexual assaults. In total, there were eleven victims. Port was given a whole life order, so he will never be released.

Outcome

Malcolm McHaffie, Deputy Chief Crown Prosecutor for CPS London, said:

"Over a period of three years, the defendant committed a series of murders and serious sexual offenses against young men. Port manipulated and controlled these men through the chilling and calculated use of the drug GHB, which he administered without their permission ... This was a technically challenging case, complicated by a significant amount of evidence taken from the numerous social media sites Port used."

Trivia

Despite the evidence, Port's family continued to believe that he was an innocent man. His mother said: "I know he's my son – he's a kind boy. He said all along, 'I didn't murder anyone Mum,' he said. Honest truth. 'I didn't murder anyone' - that's what he told me last Sunday on the telephone."

When advertising or trying to pick up men, he used the names "top fun Joe," "shyguy," and 'Basketballguy," among others. He said he preferred slim men who were under thirty years of age. On one of his many profiles he claimed he had graduated from Oxford University. In another, he claimed he was a special needs teacher.

"I am a shy, polite guy. Enjoy keeping in shape, love to have a good time. I am romantic, caring, and would take good care of my partner. I am successful, educated and determined," he wrote. "I'm looking for fun/date/bf who is between 18-24, slim, smooth twink type, not too camp tho .... who has plenty of energy and enjoys a good time." - Port

DOROTHEA PUENTE

Date of birth: January 9, 1929

Aliases/Nicknames: Nil

Characteristics: Robbery, killed boarders for money

Number of victims: 9 - 15

Date of murders: 1982 – 1988

Date of arrest: November 11, 1988

Victim profile: Ruth Munroe, 61; Everson Gillmouth, 77; Alvaro "Bert" Montoya, 51; Dorothy Miller, 64; Benjamin Fink, 55; Betty Palmer, 78; Leona Carpenter, 78; James Gallop, 62; Vera Faye Martin, 64

Method of murder: Medication poisoning

Location: Sacramento, California, USA

Status: Sentenced to life in prison without parole on December 11, 1993. Died in prison on March 27, 2011.

Background

Puente was born Dorothea Helen Gray. In 1931, when she was eight, her father died of tuberculosis. A year later, when her mother was killed in a car accident, Puente was sent to an orphanage. When she was sixteen, she married a soldier, Fred McFaul, and she had two daughters. One of the girls was given up for adoption, and the other was sent to live with relatives. The marriage ended in 1948 after McFaul left her.

Not long after, she was arrested and convicted of forging checks and served six months of a twelve-month sentence. Following her release, she became pregnant to a man she hardly knew, and the baby was put up for adoption. She married again in 1952, to Axel Johanson, and though their marriage lasted fourteen years, it was very turbulent.

She was arrested in the 1960s for managing and owning a brothel and was sentenced to ninety days in jail. As soon as she was released, she was arrested again for vagrancy and sentenced to another ninety days. Upon release, she began working as a nurse's aide, taking care of elderly and disabled people in their homes. Before long, she began managing boarding houses.

Johanson and Puente divorced in 1966, and she then married Roberto Puente who was nineteen years younger than her. This marriage lasted two years. Puente then took over a sixteen-bedroom care home at 2100 F Street in Sacramento. She married again in 1976 to violent alcoholic Pedro Montalvo, and this union ended a few months later. Puente began hanging out in bars looking for older men who were receiving benefits. She would then forge their signature and steal their money. She was arrested and charged with thirty-four counts of treasury fraud and received probation.

Murders

Puente rented an apartment at 1426 F Street, and the murders started not long after. In April of 1982, her friend and business partner Ruth Monroe moved into the apartment. Shortly after, she died from an overdose of acetaminophen and codeine. Puente told police Monroe was depressed because her husband was terminally ill, and they believed her.

A few weeks after Monroe's death, police came back, due to a complaint by Malcolm McKenzie, a seventy-four-year-old pensioner, who claimed Puente was drugging him and stealing his money. She was charged and convicted on August 18, 1982 and sentenced to five years in prison. While behind bars, Puente began corresponding with Everson Gillmouth, seventy-seven, who lived in Oregon. When she was released in 1985, he was there to pick her up in his red Ford pickup truck. Before long, they were making plans for a wedding.

In November of 1985, Puente hired handyman Ismael Florez to install some wood paneling. As a bonus, she gave him a red Ford pickup, telling him it belonged to her boyfriend in Los Angeles who he didn't need it anymore. She then asked Florez to build a box, six feet by three feet by two feet. She said she wanted it for storing books and things. She asked him to transport it to a storage depot, and she joined him on the trip.

While they were driving on the Garden Highway in Sutter County, however, she instructed Florez to pull over and dump the box on the riverbank where there was an unofficial dumping site. A fisherman saw the box on January 1, 1986, and notified police. Inside was the badly decomposed body of an elderly man. For three years, he remained unidentified.

Neighbors first became suspicious when they noticed Puente had taken on as a handyman to do odd jobs around the property. Known as "Chief," Puente had made him dig the soil out of the basement and cart it away. The floor was then covered with a concrete slab. Next, he took down a garage that was in the backyard and installed a new concrete slab there as well. Not long afterward, Chief disappeared.

A social worker notified police of the disappearance of Alberto Montoya, a developmentally disabled schizophrenic who was living on the property. Police inquired at the property on November 11, 1988 and noticed soil disturbance. Upon digging, they located the body of Leona Carpenter, seventy-eight, who had been a tenant. In total, seven bodies were found on the property.

Trial

Puente was charged with nine murders in total. The trial started in October of 1992 and finished a year later. Over one hundred thirty witnesses were called by the prosecution. The case put forward was that Puente would drug the tenants until they were unconscious and then suffocate them. To dispose of the bodies, she hired convicts to dig holes in the yard.

Despite the defense calling several witnesses to testify to Puente's kind and generous manner, some of the testimony wasn't as helpful as they expected it to be. Some agreed that she had an evil side that would come out from time to time.

Outcome

Puente was convicted of three murders; the jury couldn't reach a decision on the other six. A mistrial was declared when the jury said they would not change their minds. As a result, Puente received life without the possibility of parole. She was sent to the Central California Women's Facility in Chowchilla, California.

Puente continued to maintain her innocence for the rest of her life and insisted the tenants had died of natural causes.

On March 27, 2011, Puente herself died of natural causes at the elderly age of eighty-two years.

Trivia

Puente has been featured on many true crime television shows including *Crime Stories*, *Deadly Women*, *A Stranger In My Home* and *World's Most Evil Killers*.

Puente began exchanging letters with Shane Bugbee in 1998, and as a result, they created a recipe book called *Cooking with a Serial Killer*, which was published in 2004. Included in the book was an interview with Puente, some artwork she had created while in prison, and nearly fifty recipes.

Puente's crimes and the recipe book were mentioned in the novel *House Rules* by Jodi Picoult.

The Sacramento Old City Association held a home tour in 2013, and the house at 1426 F Street was included. A documentary in 2015 mentioned the house in a short titled *The House is Innocent*. As a result, the house was open for tour groups to visit for one day while the documentary was being screened.

In 2017, the house was investigated by Zak Bagans and his ghost hunting team along with a psychic medium. It was screened as an episode of *Ghost Adventures*.

WANG QIANG

Date of birth: January 16, 1975
Aliases/Nicknames: Nil
Characteristics: Rape, necrophilia
Number of victims: 45 +
Date of murders: 1995 – 2003
Date of arrest: July 14, 2003
Victim profile: Young girls, women (unnamed)
Method of murder: Stabbing, slashing
Location: China
Status: Executed November 17, 2005.

Background

Qiang was from Budayuan Town, Kuandian Manchu Autonomous County, Liaoning, China, and was one of the most sadistic and notorious rapists and murderers in Chinese history. He lived his childhood in a small village called Kaiyuan. His father was addicted to alcohol and gambling and was very abusive. He would not let Qiang go to school. His mother had abandoned him, leaving him with his father.

Murders

Qiang's first known murder occurred on January 22, 1995, and he continued to rape and kill for a further nine years. The majority of his victims were mutilated, with many being disemboweled. As is customary with Chinese serial killers, there is not a lot of information about the killer or the crimes available.

Trial

Qiang was arrested on July 14, 2003. He was charged and convicted of forty-five murders and ten rapes, some of which occurred postmortem.

Outcome

He was sentenced to death and executed in November of 2005.

Trivia

The demented man went on to say that he never lost sleep or his appetite after his heinous actions.

ÁNGEL MATURINO RESÉNDIZ

Date of birth: August 1, 1960

Aliases/Nicknames: Railroad Killer

Characteristics: Rape, robbery

Number of victims: 15

Date of murders: 1986 - 1999

Date of arrest: July 13, 1999 - Surrendered

Victim profile: Michael White, 22; Jesse Howell, 19; Wendy Von Huben, 16; Christopher Maier, 21; Leafie Mason, 87; Fannie Whitney Byers, 81; Claudia Benton, 39; Norman J. Sirnic, 46; Karen Sirnic, 47; Noemi Dominguez, 26; Josephine Konvicka, 73; George Morber Sr., 80; Carolyn Frederick, 52; others unknown

Method of murder: Stabbing with a knife, beating

Location: Texas, Illinois, Florida, Kentucky, California, Georgia, USA

Status: Executed by lethal injection in Texas on June 27, 2006.

Background

Reséndiz was born in Izúcar de Matamoros, Puebla, Mexico, in 1960. The name listed on his birth certificate was Ángel Leoncio Reyes Recendis, and he was known to use many different aliases as an adult. At some point, he entered America illegally and lived an itinerant lifestyle.

He was suspected of committing twenty-three murders across America and Mexico during the 1990s. He was known as the Railroad Killer because most of his crimes were committed near railroads where he had jumped off trains.

He was the four hundred fifty-seventh fugitive listed by the FBI on its Ten Most Wanted Fugitives list briefly on June 21, 1999. He was removed from the list following his surrender.

Murders

Reséndiz killed at least fifteen victims using a variety of objects, including rocks, blunt objects, and a pickaxe. The victims were often killed in their homes, and he would hang around for a while after the deed and sometimes eat what he could find. He would look at the victim's personal belongings and identification to learn about the person he had just killed. Then he would steal valuables and later give them to his mother and wife. He didn't always take the money though. His female victims were raped, but that wasn't his main intent. Many of the victims were found covered.

Unknown date in 1986 - Unidentified woman, Bexar County, Texas

Shot four times, her body was dumped in an abandoned farmhouse. Reséndiz said he met the woman at a homeless shelter. They took a motorcycle trip together, and Reséndiz said that he shot and killed the woman for disrespecting him.

Unknown date in 1986 - Unidentified man, Bexar County, Texas

This victim had allegedly been the previous victim's boyfriend. He was shot and killed by Reséndiz, and his body was disposed of in a creek located between Uvalde and San Antonio. According to Reséndiz, he killed him because he was involved in black magic. The body has never been found.

July 19, 1991 - Michael White, twenty-two, San Antonio, Texas

Reséndiz used a brick to beat White to death. He then left the man's body in the front yard of an empty house. He claimed he murdered White because he was gay.

March 23, 1997 - Jesse Howell, nineteen, Ocala, Florida

An air hose coupling was used to bludgeon Howell to death, and his body was dumped next to railroad tracks.

March 23, 1997 - Wendy Von Huben, sixteen, Ocala, Florida

Von Huben had been Howell's fiancé. Reséndiz raped her, tried to strangle her, and then suffocated her manually until she was dead. He buried her body in a shallow grave in Sumter County, Florida.

July 1997 - Unidentified man, Colton, California

A transient was beaten to death with a piece of plywood in a rail yard.

August 29, 1997 - Christopher Maier, twenty-one, Lexington, Kentucky

Maier was walking along railroad tracks with his girlfriend, Holly Dunn Pendleton, twenty, when they were attacked by Reséndiz. Using a fifty-pound rock, Reséndiz beat him to death. Pendleton was severely beaten and raped, but she survived.

October 4, 1998 - Leafie Mason, eighty-seven, Hughes Springs, Texas

An antique flat iron was used to beat Mason to death. He had gained access to her home through a window before attacking her.

December 10, 1998 - Fannie Whitney Byers, eighty-one, Carl, Georgia

Byers was beaten to death with a tire rim in her home, which was located near railroad tracks. At first, a couple from Lexington was charged with her murder, but they were released after Reséndiz confessed to an FBI agent.

December 17, 1998 - Claudia Benton, thirty-nine, West University Place, Texas

Benton was a pediatric neurologist. Reséndiz gained entry to her home and then brutalized her. He raped her, stabbed her, and then beat her to death with a statue. Her vehicle was found in San Antonio, and his fingerprints were found inside on the steering column.

May 2, 1999 - Norman J. Sirnic, forty-six, Karen Sirnic, forty-seven, Weimar, Texas

The Sirnics were bludgeoned to death with a sledgehammer in a parsonage of the United Church of Christ, where Norman was a pastor. The building was beside the Union Pacific Railroad. The Sirnics' red Mazda was found in San Antonio three weeks later, and fingerprints linked their case with Claudia Benton's murder.

June 4, 1999 - Noemi Dominguez, twenty-six, Houston, Texas

Dominguez, a schoolteacher, was bludgeoned to death with a pickaxe in her apartment. Her vehicle, a white Honda Civic, was located by state troopers a week later on the International Bridge in Del Rio, Texas.

June 4, 1999 - Josephine Konvicka, seventy-three, Fayette County, Texas

Konvicka was bludgeoned in her farmhouse near Weimar (where the Sirnics were murdered) with the same pickaxe used to kill Dominguez. Reséndiz also tried to steal her car but couldn't find the car keys.

June 15, 1999 - George Morber Sr., eighty, Gorham, Illinois

Morber was shot in the head with a shotgun. The house was located only one hundred yards from a railroad track. Later police found his red pickup truck in Cairo, Illinois. Fingerprints found in Morber's ransacked home positively identified Reséndiz as the killer.

June 15, 1999 - Carolyn Frederick, fifty-two, Gorham, Illinois

Frederick was bludgeoned to death with the same shotgun.

Reséndiz also confessed to seven other killings, which he said occurred in Mexico.

Trial

Police located his sister, who had seen the Most Wanted poster and was worried her brother might be killed by the FBI or another agency, and she agreed to help catch her brother. On July 12, 1999, his sister, a Texas Ranger and a spiritual guide, met with Reséndiz on a bridge between El Paso, Texas and Ciudad Juárez, Chihuahua, and he surrendered.

During an appearance in court, Reséndiz accused the Texas Ranger of lying under oath. He stated his family was given the impression that he would be spared the death penalty. His fate would depend on the jury, however, not the Texas Rangers.

Reséndiz went on trial for the murder of Claudia Benton and was found guilty. He was sentenced to death.

Outcome

A judge ruled on June 21, 2006, that Reséndiz was mentally competent to be executed. On hearing the ruling, Reséndiz said, "I don't believe in death. I know the body is going to go to waste. But me, as a person, I'm eternal. I'm going to be alive forever."

On June 27, 2006, Reséndiz was executed by lethal injection. In his final statement, he said, "I want to ask if it is in your heart to forgive me. You don't have to. I know I allowed the Devil to rule my life. I just ask you to forgive me and ask the Lord to forgive me for allowing the devil to deceive me. I thank God for having patience in me. I don't deserve to cause you pain. You do not deserve this. I deserve what I am getting."

The husband of victim Claudia Benton was present at the execution. He stated that Reséndiz was "evil contained in human form, a creature without a soul, no conscience, no sense of remorse, no regard for the sanctity of human life."

Trivia

The Reséndiz case was featured in four criminal documentaries:

- *Crime Stories* on the Discovery Channel

- *Infamous Murders*, "Death in the Country," on the History Channel

- *Murder She Solved: True Crime*, "Episode 13: Railway Killer", on the Oprah Winfrey Network (Canadian TV channel)

- *The FBI Files*, "Tracks of a Killer," on the Biography Channel (2003)

- An episode of *48 Hours* called "Live to Tell: The Railroad Killer" (which aired in December of 2010), focused on the crimes committed by Reséndiz. One of his survivors, Holly Dunn Pendleton, gave an interview for the program during which she discussed her attack and the murder of her boyfriend, Christopher Maier.

Reséndiz was also the feature of a television program called *Dates from Hell*.

The "Catching Out" episode of the television program *Criminal Minds* featured a serial killer by the name of Armando Ruis Salinas. This character was very similar to Reséndiz, including his Hispanic heritage and drifter status, and his victims were mostly bludgeoned to death, as the killer traveled by railroad.

There were a total of sixteen podcasts about Reséndiz by journalist Alex Hannaford between October of 2018 and February of 2019. They were called *Dead Man Talking*, and were based on interviews Hannaford recorded with Reséndiz in 2003. In the interview, he said he had committed a lot more murders than were known about and that there were innocent people in prison wrongfully convicted for his murders.

RIPPER CREW

Robin Gecht

Date of birth: November 30, 1953

Aliases/Nicknames: The Chicago Rippers

Characteristics: Gang, mutilation, rape, cannibalism

Number of victims: 6 - 18

Date of murders: May 23, 1981 - October 8, 1982

Date of arrest: October 20, 1982

Victim profile: Linda Sutton, 28; Lorraine Borowski, 21; Shui Mak, 30; Sandra Delaware; Rose Davis, 31; Beverley Washington, 20

Method of murder: Stabbing, strangulation

Location: Illinois

Status: Sentenced to three 60 year sentences plus a 30-year sentence.

Edward Spreitzer

Date of birth: January 5, 1961

Aliases/Nicknames: The Chicago Rippers

Characteristics: Gang, mutilation, rape, cannibalism

Number of victims: 6 - 18

Date of murders: May 23, 1981 - October 8, 1982

Date of arrest: November 5, 1982

Victim profile: Linda Sutton, 28; Lorraine Borowski, 21; Shui Mak, 30; Sandra Delaware; Rose Davis, 31; Beverley Washington, 20

Method of murder: Stabbing, strangulation

Location: Illinois

Status: Sentenced to 6 life terms plus over 400 years for other crimes.

Andrew Kokoraleis

Date of birth: 1961

Aliases/Nicknames: The Chicago Rippers

Characteristics: Gang, mutilation, rape, cannibalism

Number of victims: 6 - 18

Date of murders: May 23, 1981 - October 8, 1982

Date of arrest: November 5, 1982

Victim profile: Linda Sutton, 28; Lorraine Borowski, 21; Shui Mak, 30; Sandra Delaware; Rose Davis, 31, Beverley Washington, 20

Method of murder: Stabbing, strangulation

Location: Illinois

Status: Sentenced to death. Executed by lethal injection.

Thomas Kokoraleis

Date of birth: 1958

Aliases/Nicknames: The Chicago Rippers

Characteristics: Gang, mutilation, rape, cannibalism

Number of victims: 6 - 18

Date of murders: May 23, 1981 - October 8, 1982

Date of arrest: November 5, 1982

Victim profile: Linda Sutton, 28; Lorraine Borowski, 21; Shui Mak, 30; Sandra Delaware; Rose Davis, 31; Beverley Washington, 20

Method of murder: Stabbing, strangulation

Location: Illinois

Status: Sentenced to 70 years. Released in March of 2019.

Background

The Ripper Crew, sometimes known as the Chicago Rippers, was an organized crime group and a satanic cult. The members were Robin Gecht, Edward Spreitzer, and Andrew and Thomas Kokoraleis. The group was a suspect in the disappearances of eighteen women in 1981 and 1982 in Illinois.

Murders

On May 23, 1981, the gang abducted Linda Sutton, twenty. Ten days later, her body was found in a field. Her left breast had been cut off, and the rest of her body was mutilated. The gang was quiet for nearly a year before they killed their next victim. Lorraine Borowski was abducted by them on May 15, 1982. She had been about to open the door to the office where she worked when she was kidnapped. Five months later, her body was found in a cemetery in Clarendon Hills.

The gang next abducted Shui Mak on May 29 from Hanover Park. It was four months before her body was discovered. Two weeks after the murder of Mak, they picked up Angel York and handcuffed her in the back of their van. They slashed her breast and tossed her out of the vehicle, alive.

Two months later, on August 28, 1982, the body of Sandra Delaware was found on the Chicago River bank. She had been strangled, stabbed, and her left breast had been removed. Then on September 8, Rose Davis was found dead in an alley with almost identical injuries.

The last victim was Beverley Washington. She was found by a railroad track on December 8. Her left breast had been amputated, and the right breast slashed severely. Despite these and other injuries, she survived and was able to give descriptions of her assailants.

The men were also suspected of being involved in the disappearance of Carole Pappas. She went missing on September 11, 1982, and her body was found five years later.

Gecht was the first to be arrested, but he was released soon after due to lack of evidence. Police continued investigating him and learned he had rented a motel room in 1981, along with three friends. The manager of the hotel said they had loud parties and seemed to be in some sort of cult. Investigators found the others, Spreitzer and the Kokoraleis brothers. Under interrogation, Thomas Kokoraleis confessed that they had taken women back to Gecht's place, raped and tortured them, and then cut off their breasts with a wire garrote. He further stated that they would eat parts of the breasts as a sacrament and Gecht would masturbate into the breasts before putting them in a box. He claimed he had seen fifteen breasts in the box.

Trial

The only one not to confess was Gecht, who claimed he was innocent. A series of trials ensued, after which Thomas Kokoraleis was convicted of murder. Because of his initial confession, he was rewarded with a sentence of life imprisonment. He was later given a parole component and was released on March 29, 2019.

Outcome

Andrew Kokoraleis was convicted and sentenced to death.

Gecht was found guilty of attempted murder, rape, deviate sexual assault, armed violence, and aggravated battery. He was sentenced to one hundred twenty years in prison.

Spreitzer was convicted and sentenced to death, but this was later commuted.

Trivia

"A black female was picked up, blindfolded and gagged. Robin shot her point blank in the head. Put chains around her neck and legs, attached two bowling balls and threw her in the water. I understand her body was not found." — **Edward Spreitzer**

JAMES DALE RITCHIE

Date of birth: November 4, 1976

Aliases/Nicknames: The Midnight Sun Killer, Anchorage Serial Killer

Characteristics: Always committed murders near midnight

Number of victims: 5 +

Date of murders: July 2016 - August 2016

Date of arrest: Killed during a shootout

Victim profile: Brianna Foisy, 20; Jason Netter Sr., 41; Treyveonkindell Thompson, 21; Kevin Turner, 34; Bryant De Husson, 25

Method of murder: Shooting

Location: Alaska

Status: Shot and killed by police on November 12, 2016.

Background

As a high school student, Ritchie was very athletic; he played in the state championship football and basketball teams in 1994. He was a close friend of Bobby and Quincy Thompson and spent a lot of time with their family throughout his teens. Quincy died in 1994; the following day, Ritchie was recruited by West Virginia University to play for their football team.

Ritchie lasted only one semester before dropping out and returning to Alaska. He became involved in dogfighting and dealing drugs in 1995. His street name was Tiny, and over the next seven years he was arrested numerous times—mainly for drug offenses. In 2005, he was arrested while undertaking a home invasion. He spent two years in custody.

Ritchie moved to Broadway, Virginia in 2013. After breaking up with his girlfriend in March of 2016, he again returned to Alaska. He sought mental health treatment, but there was no record of a diagnosis.

Murders

Early in the morning on July 3, 2016, Ritchie committed his first murders. On a bike path near Ship Creek, a cyclist found the dead bodies of Brianna Foisy, twenty, and Jason Netter Sr., forty-one. Netter was known for his drug activity, and Foisy was a drug addict who was homeless.

On July 29, Ritchie shot and killed the son of his childhood friend. Treyveonkindell Thompson, twenty-one, was the son of Bobby Thompson. Ritchie shot him multiple times as he was riding his bicycle home from work. He then took the bicycle and fled from the scene.

Kevin Turner, thirty-four, and Bryant De Husson, twenty-five, were shot and killed by Ritchie early on the morning of August 28. Police were alerted by a female who was walking through Valley of the Moon Park and came across the body of De Husson. Turner was homeless at the time and suffered from mental illness. De Husson was an environmental activist, and it was thought that he was on a late-night bicycle ride.

After Thompson was murdered, Mandy Premo, his mother, did her own investigation in an effort to find her son's murderer. She searched low-income neighborhoods and homeless camps looking for clues. In October of 2016, near the Alaska Regional Hospital, she found Ritchie, who was armed with a gun. She notified the police that she had found the man who had killed her son.

Trial

When police approached Ritchie on November 12, 2016, a gunfight ensued. Police Officer Arn Salao had responded to a report of a man who hadn't paid his taxi fare, and he stopped when he saw Ritchie walking down the street. When the officer asked Ritchie to stop, he kept on walking. Suddenly, Ritchie turned around, walked back to the police car, and opened fire on Salao. He was shot four times, suffering damage to his liver, intestines, and bones. Salao got out of the car and fired back, and then a physical fight occurred. Sergeant Marc Patzke saw what was happening and opened fire on Ritchie, killing him.

Outcome

After he died, police found a handgun on his body, a Colt Python, and this was linked to the murders he had committed over the two-month period.

Salao spent seven hours in surgery, but doctors saved his life.

Trivia

"He was a happy, positive person in high school. It's shocking to me," said Mao Tosi, a teammate from high school.

Ritchie wrote a letter to the judge presiding over one of his cases that said he would "lay in bed every night thinking about how I've ruined my life. Then I sit up crying wishing I could go back to when I was in high school."

MICHAEL BRUCE ROSS

Date of birth: July 26, 1959

Aliases/Nicknames: The Egg Man, The Roadside Strangler

Characteristics: Rape

Number of victims: 8

Date of murders: 1981 - 1984

Date of arrest: June 28, 1984

Victim profile: Dzung Ngoc Tu, 25; Paula Perrera, 16; Tammy Williams, 17; Debra Smith Taylor, 23; Robin Stavinksy, 19; April Brunias, 14; Leslie Shelley, 14; Wendy Baribeault, 17

Method of murder: Strangulation

Location: Connecticut, USA

Status: Executed by lethal injection in Connecticut on May 13, 2005.

Background

Ross came from a dysfunctional home; his mother beat all of the children, but him most of all. She had been institutionalized at some stage and abandoned the family on at least one occasion. Later, it was suggested by some family members that Ross may have been molested by his uncle who killed himself when Ross was six years old.

At school, he performed well. He graduated from high school in 1977, and then went to Cornell University where he studied agriculture. He graduated from the university in May of 1981. From there, he became an insurance salesman. Ross had shown signs of antisocial behavior from a young age, but his behavior deteriorated more when he was in college. He committed his first rape during his senior year, with his first murder not too far behind.

Murders

Ross murdered eight females between 1981 and 1984. They ranged in age between fourteen and twenty-five. Seven of them had also been raped. His victims were:

Dzung Ngoc Tu, twenty-five: May 12, 1981, a student at Cornell University.

Tammy Williams, seventeen: January 5, 1982, from Brooklyn, Connecticut.
Paula Perrera, sixteen: March 1, 1982, from Wallkill, New York.
Debra Smith Taylor, twenty-three: June 15, 1982, from Griswold.
Robin Dawn Stavinksy, nineteen: October 23, 1983, from Norwich.
April Brunias, fourteen: April 22, 1984, from Griswold.
Leslie Shelley, fourteen: April 22, 1984, from Griswold.
Wendy Baribeault, seventeen: June 13, 1984, from Griswold.

Trial

Ross confessed to all of the murders when questioned by police. At his trial, he was convicted of four of the murders: Stavinksy, Brunias, Shelley, and Baribeault. On July 6, 1987, he was sentenced to death.

Outcome

While Ross was incarcerated he met Susan Powers and they became engaged. She ended the relationship in 2003, but continued to visit him until he was executed. He met with priests regularly and became a devout Catholic. He learned to translate braille, took on the role of a big brother for other inmates, and even sponsored a child from the Dominican Republic.

In the last year of his life, Ross supported his death sentence, saying he wanted to spare the families of his victims any further pain. However, an hour before he was to be executed, his lawyer obtained a two-day stay of execution. He was then scheduled to be executed on January 29, 2005. Earlier that day, there was some question about Ross' mental competency and the execution was postponed again.

On May 13, 2005, the execution went ahead. Ross didn't request a special meal, instead eating the same meal as the rest of the inmates. When asked if he wanted to make a final statement, he said no. His remains were buried at the Benedictine Grange Cemetery.

Trivia

After his execution, psychiatrist Dr. Stuart Grassian, who had argued Ross wasn't competent to waive appeal, received a letter from Ross dated May 10, 2005, which read "Check, and mate. You never had a chance!"

The execution of Ross was the first to occur in Connecticut since 1960. It was also the only lethal injection execution in Connecticut to date.

One of his alleged rape victims, Vivian Dobson, became one of his loudest supporters by opposing the death penalty so that his life would be saved.

Ross was also a suspect in other rapes and murders in the state of Indiana.

Pop culture

Ross was featured in a British television series about serial killers in 1995. The producers of the segment gave him the nickname "The Roadside Strangler" because other killers in the series had nicknames.

The book *The Man in the Monster: An Intimate Portrait of a Serial Killer*, was published by Penguin Press.

SERGEI RYAKHOVSKY

Date of birth: December 29, 1962

Aliases/Nicknames: The Hippopotamus, The Balashikha Ripper

Characteristics: Necrophilia, mutilation

Number of victims: 19

Date of murders: 1989 - 1993

Date of arrest: April 13, 1993

Victim profile: Vladimir Zaitsev, 16; Osipova, 73; Anna Feodorovna Narsisyan, 62; Osipovich Nicholas Belkin, 60; Oleg Boldin, 38; Tatiana Alexandrovna Norkin, 48; Vilkin Shuyko, 55; Rinat Khabibulin, 13; Shumakova, 45; Claudia Khokhlova, 70; others unnamed

Method of murder: Stabbing, bludgeoning, strangulation

Location: Moscow, Russia

Status: Sentenced to death by firing squad in July of 1995. A moratorium on executions was imposed in Russia in 1996, and his sentence was commuted to life imprisonment. He died in prison in 2005 from tuberculosis.

Background

Ryakhovsky was born in the Saltykovka area of Balashikha, Moscow Oblast, which is less than a mile east of Moscow. As an adult, he stood six feet six inches in height and weighed two hundred eighty pounds. He claimed that, in 1982, he began to feel "an irresistible desire for intimacy with a woman." This drove him to attempt to rape elderly women, and he was arrested and convicted of hooliganism and sent to prison for four years.

Murders

Ryakhovsky killed a homosexual man in 1988, in Bitsa, on the outskirts of Moscow. That same year he murdered another three homosexual men, which he later claimed was due to his mission to "cleanse" society by ridding it of homosexuals and prostitutes. With the exception of five women and two teenagers, however, his victims were elderly women.

His main methods of committing the murders were by stabbing or strangling his victims, either with his hands or a rope. Once the victim was dead he would mutilate the body, especially in the genitals. In some cases, he would perform sexual acts with the corpses.

Ryakhovsky killed a seventy-eight-year-old man in January of 1993. He beheaded the elderly man with a hunting knife, and then returned on the following day to cut off his leg. The next victim was a sixty-five-year-old woman; he used a pyrotechnical device to rupture her abdomen. His final victim was a sixteen-year-old boy. He hanged him, then decapitated him, and eviscerated the body.

As police were searching a crime scene area, they noticed a shack that had a noose attached to the ceiling. They thought it might be preparatory work for another murder, so they set an ambush. Ryakhovsky arrived at the shack on April 13, 1993, and was promptly arrested. Even though he was a very strong man, he put up no fight, and later admitted that when he saw the weapons on the officers he became "frozen with fear."

He cooperated with investigators and showed them where crime scenes were located and the method he used to kill each victim. He stated that the majority of the murders were unplanned, except for the three homosexuals he killed in 1988.

Ryakhovsky was assessed by psychiatrists who determined he had a malfunction in his central nervous system that led him to commit necrophiliac acts. He was found sane and competent to stand trial. Ryakhovsky was angry at the diagnosis, and he stopped being cooperative and revoked his confessions.

Trial

Ryakhovsky was sentenced to death in July of 1995. When the verdict was given, he simply said: "I will be back." In 1996, a moratorium on executions was imposed in Russia, and Ryakhovsky's sentence was commuted to life imprisonment.

Outcome

On January 21, 2005, Ryakhovsky died from tuberculosis, which he had been suffering from for a long time without treatment.

Trivia

Ryakhovsky was known as "The Hippopotamus" because of his size and his thick neck.

Ryakhovsky wrote a letter to Alexander Rutskoy during the Russian constitutional crisis in 1993, claiming he was an innocent victim of the "anti-national authority."

ALTEMIO SANCHEZ

Date of birth: January 19, 1958

Aliases/Nicknames: The Bike Path Rapist

Characteristics: Serial rapist

Number of victims: 3 +

Date of murders: 1990, 1992, 2006

Date of arrest: January 15, 2007

Victim profile: Linda S. Yalem, 22; Majane Mazur, 32; Joan Diver, 45

Method of murder: Strangulation

Location: Erie County, New York, USA

Status: Sentenced to 75 years in prison with no chance of parole on August 15, 2007.

Background

Sanchez and his family moved to the United States when he was aged two. When he was young, his father died, and his mother went on to remarry. An aunt described him as a nice kid who was quiet and serious.

As an adult, Sanchez married and had two sons. He coached basketball teams and Little League baseball teams. His neighbors liked him and found him charismatic, and Sanchez was very involved in the community. Sanchez, however, had been in trouble with the law on at least two occasions for soliciting prostitutes in 1991 and 1999.

Murders

Sanchez murdered at least three women and possibly more; he also committed a number of rapes. He remained undetected for more than ten years, and if it wasn't for DNA testing, he might have remained at large.

VICTIMS LINKED BY DNA

Joan Diver, fourty-five

Means of Attack: She was strangled and bludgeoned with a blunt object.

Her body was found at 276 Military Road, behind a junkyard, near the Hertel Avenue in the Riverside section of Buffalo.

Unnamed high school student, fourteen

Means of Attack: The victim was grabbed from behind and strangled. The killer used rope and tape.

Her body was found in a field located off Exchange Street in Buffalo.

Majane Mazur, thirty-two

Means of Attack: She was grabbed from behind. The killer used rope and tape.

She was found on a bicycle path at Ellicott Creek, in the Town of Amherst.

Linda S. Yalem, twenty-two

Means of Attack: Her body was discovered near a path in thick brush. Yalem had been raped before she was strangled to death. The official cause of death was asphyxiation due to strangulation by ligature. The killer had taped up her mouth and nose.

The murder occurred on a shortcut path near a high school in Hamburg.

Unnamed victim, thirty-two

Means of Attack: He grabbed the victim from behind, tightening a cord around her neck until she was unconscious. He then dragged her to a clear area in the underbrush; she remained unconscious throughout the attack.

She was found on the bicycle path at Willow Ridge, in the Town of Amherst.

Unnamed victim, fifteen

Means of Attack: She was attacked from behind using a rope that he tightened around her neck to control her. He forced her to a clear area, and then he tied her hands behind her back. White, adhesive tape was used to bind her hands and cover her eyes and mouth. While attacking her, he repeatedly brought the victim in and out of consciousness before leaving her for dead.

The attack occurred on a shortcut path to Riverside High School in Buffalo.

Unnamed victim, fifteen

Means of Attack: As he walked past her on the path, he smiled and then grabbed her. He wrapped a rope around her neck and forced her to a vacant building. There, he used white tape to cover her eyes before he attacked her.

The attack occurred on a shortcut path to Riverside High School in Buffalo.

Unnamed victim, sixteen

Means of Attack: The victim thought the assailant had used wire to attack her. He forced her about six hundred feet along the path to a junkyard. Once there, he taped up her mouth with duct tape.

She was attacked on a shortcut path near a high school in Hamburg.

Unnamed victim, seventeen

Means of Attack: The victim was attacked from behind, and a clothesline was placed around her neck. It was then tightened so he could get control over her. She was forced about three hundred thirty yards along the path to a cutoff.

The attacked occurred in Delaware Park, Buffalo.

Unnamed victim, forty-four

Means of Attack: She was grabbed from behind, and a cord was tightened around her neck to gain control over her. He then forced her to some underbrush by the path. He tightened the cord until she was unconscious.

Trial

Sanchez was arrested on January 15, 2007, by a police task force in Erie County, New York. He was charged with the murders of Yalem, Mazur, and Diver. Due to the statute of limitations, he wasn't charged with many of the rapes he had committed.

On May 17, 2007, Sanchez pled guilty to the three murders in a confession that came as a surprise. He cried as he gave his confession in court. On August 15, 2007, he was sentenced to seventy-five years to life in prison. Investigations into some of his potential crimes are ongoing.

Outcome

In March of 2007, a man who had been incarcerated for twenty-two years for two rapes was set free. Anthony Capozzi had been convicted of rapes that were committed by Sanchez. When Sanchez's DNA came back as a match, the police realized the wrong man was behind bars. This led to the exoneration of Capozzi. A civil lawsuit was filed and a settlement of $4.25 million was awarded to Capozzi for the wrongful conviction.

Trivia

Sanchez was mentioned on the television crime drama *Criminal Minds*, in the season four episode called "Zoe's Reprise."

He had signed up to run in the Linda Yalem Safety Run, a run that was dedicated to its namesake, a murder victim—ironically, a victim of Sanchez.

*"I just wanted to mention that whatever sentence I get today, I deserve. I know I'm going to be spending life behind bars, never to see the streets again. But... I did these crimes, and I should pay for these crimes." — **Sanchez***

GERARD JOHN SCHAEFER

Date of birth: March 25, 1946

Aliases/Nicknames: Nil

Characteristics: Sheriff's deputy, rape, mutilation

Number of victims: 2 - 9 +

Date of murders: 1969 - 1973

Date of arrest: April 7, 1973

Victim profile: Leigh Hainline Bonadies, 25; Carmen Marie Hallock, 22; Belinda Hutchens, 22; Collette Goodenough, 19; Barbara Ann Wilcox, 19; Susan Place, 17; Georgia Jessup, 16; Mary Alice Briscolina, 14; Elsie Lina Farmer, 14

Method of murder: Shooting, strangulation

Location: Florida, USA

Status: Sentenced to two concurrent terms of life imprisonment in October of 1973. On December 3, 1995, Schaefer was found stabbed to death in his cell, killed by fellow inmate Vincent Faustino Rivera.

Background

Schaefer was born to Catholic parents and didn't get along with his father very well, with Schaefer believing his father favored his sister over him. As a teenager, he became obsessed with women's underwear and started peeping at women through windows. He began spying on a neighbor, Leigh Hainline. When she was murdered, Schaefer became the main suspect. He later admitted to killing animals when he was young and cross-dressing.

He went to college and married, and in 1969 he became a teacher. He was fired due to "totally inappropriate behavior" and then tried to enter the priesthood. Rejected, he decided to change his career to law enforcement. At the end of 1971, Schaefer had graduated as a police patrolman.

While he was on patrol on July 21, 1972, he picked up two teenage hitchhikers. He took the girls to a forest and tied them to trees. He threatened he was either going to sell them into prostitution or kill them. Before he could do anything else, duty called, and he had to leave, vowing to the girls, he would return.

The girls managed to escape and went to the nearest police station, which happened to be Schaefer's. Meanwhile, Schaefer went back to the forest and noticed the girls were gone. He called the station and said he had done something foolish. He said he had pretended to abduct the girls to scare them away from hitchhiking. His boss didn't believe his story and charged him with false imprisonment and assault and stripped him of his badge.

Schaefer posted bail and was released, and two months later, two young girls were murdered. Susan Place, seventeen, and Georgia Jessup, sixteen, were abducted, tortured, and murdered on September 27, 1972.

Schaefer went to court in December of 1972 for the charges relating to the abductions. He struck a plea bargain and pled guilty to one charge of aggravated assault, with a sentence of one year.

Murders

Six months after they vanished, in April of 1973, the decomposing and mutilated remains of Place and Jessup were discovered. They had been abducted while hitchhiking, and tied to a tree at some point. Because of the similarities with the other case Schaefer had been convicted of, a search warrant was obtained to search his home.

During the search, they found stories Schaefer had written about the torture, rape, and murder of women. They also found a number of personal items from females, including jewelry, diaries, and teeth. It was discovered that some of the jewelry had belonged to Leigh Hainline Bonadies. There was also a purse that had belonged to Place.

ALLEGED VICTIMS:

- Nancy Leichner and Pamela Ann Nater, twenty, both of whom went missing on October 2, 1966.

- Debora Sue Lowe, thirteen, went missing on February 29, 1972. She was known to Schaefer, and her family has always believed he was involved in her disappearance.

- Carmen Marie Hallock, twenty-two, went missing on December 18, 1969.

- Peggy Rahn and Wendy Stevenson, both of whom went missing on December 29, 1969. Schaefer confessed to killing them in a letter he wrote to his girlfriend. Their bodies have not been found.

Trial

On May 18, 1973, Schaefer was indicted for the murders of Place and Jessup. He was subsequently convicted of two counts of first-degree murder in October of 1973. He was sentenced to two terms of life imprisonment. All of his appeals were rejected.

Outcome

Schaefer was found stabbed to death in his cell on December 3, 1995. Inmate Vincent Rivera was convicted of the murder and received a further fifty-three years and ten months added on to his sentence. No motive was given, and he didn't confess.

At the time of his death, homicide detectives at Broward County were preparing to bring about charges for three more unsolved murders.

Trivia

Schaefer recalled, "I discovered women's underwear panties. Sometimes I wore them. I wanted to hurt myself. "

"Doing doubles is far more difficult than doing singles, but on the other hand, it also puts one in a position to have twice as much fun." — *Schaefer*

Fiction

Schaefer's high school girlfriend, Sondra London, interviewed him in prison after his conviction. He had written some short stories, and she published them, along with some of his drawings, in a book titled *Killer Fiction* in 1990. She wrote a second book, *Beyond Killer Fiction*, two years after the first book. Schaefer's stories contained graphic and savage torture of women who were then murdered; they were written from the perspective the killer. In many of the stories, the killer was a police officer who had gone rogue.

After Schaefer's death, a second edition of *Killer Fiction* that had been revised was released. This book contained articles and stories from the previous books. It also contained a letter that Schaefer had written claiming he had killed thirty-four females; additionally, he bragged that Ted Bundy, a fellow inmate at the time, was impressed with him.

While Schaefer was writing to London, she noticed him telling the rest of the world he was innocent and had threatened to sue any writers or journalists who named him as a serial killer. Yet in a letter to her, he said he had been killing since 1965, at the age of nineteen. In another letter, he bragged of cannibalizing schoolgirls, Wendy Stevenson and Peggy Rahn, in December of 1965. But in public, he denied having killed anyone.

In 1991, London stopped corresponding with Schaefer. She told him that he was indeed a serial killer. In response, he threatened to kill her multiple times and filed a lawsuit against her for saying he was a serial killer in printed materials.

CHARLES SCHMID

Date of birth: July 8, 1942

Aliases/Nicknames: The Pied Piper of Tucson, Smitty

Characteristics: Rape

Number of victims: 3

Date of murders: 1964 - 1965

Date of arrest: November 10, 1965

Victim profile: Alleen Rowe, 15; Gretchen Fritz, 17; Wendy Fritz, 13

Method of murder: Strangulation

Location: Tucson, Arizona, USA

Status: Sentenced to death in 1966. When the state of Arizona temporarily abolished the death penalty in 1971, his sentence was commuted to 50 years in prison. On March 10, 1975, Schmid was stabbed 47 times by two fellow prisoners. He lost an eye and a kidney. He died 20 days later.

Background

Schmid was adopted and had a difficult relationship with his adoptive father. At one point, he tried to meet his birth mother, but she got angry and told him never to return. Just before he graduated from high school, he stole some tools from the school's machine shop and was suspended. He never went back to school; instead, he lived on an allowance from his parents each month. He spent most of his time drinking with friends and picking up girls.

A short man, Schmid would stuff his cowboy boots with flattened cans and newspapers to give the appearance of being taller. He used pancake makeup, lip balm, and drew a mole on his cheek. He even used a clothespin to stretch his bottom lip to look more like Elvis Presley. His nickname was the Pied Piper because he was so charismatic.

Murders

Schmid decided on May 31, 1964, that he wanted to murder high school student Alleen Rowe. His current girlfriend Mary French convinced Rose to go out with John Saunders, Schmid's friend. But the intention all along was for Schmid to kill Rowe. He apparently wanted to know what it would feel like to take someone's life.

Rowe was taken to the desert by Schmid and his friends. Schmid told Saunders to rape Rowe, but he was gay. Then she was killed. French sat in the car listening to the radio while this occurred. They then buried Rowe in the desert.

Another girlfriend of Schmid's was Gretchen Fritz. He had told her of Rowe's murder, and there were rumors that she also knew of an earlier murder he may have committed, but this was never proven. Schmid decided to break up with Fritz, and she threatened to tell the authorities about Rowe. In response, Schmid strangled her and her sister Wendy on August 16, 1965.

Schmid told Richard Bruns, his friend, that he had killed the sisters and buried them in the desert. He showed him where the bodies were. Bruns became fearful Schmid would murder his girlfriend, so he went to stay with his grandparents in Ohio. He told them everything he knew, and the authorities were notified.

Trial

Schmid was arrested and went on trial in 1966. He was found guilty of murder and received a death sentence. In 1967, Rowe's remains were found. In 1971, Arizona abolished the death penalty temporarily, and Schmid's sentence was commuted to fifty years.

Outcome

On several occasions, Schmid tried to escape from prison. He succeeded on November 11, 1972, along with another inmate, Raymond Hudgens. For a while, they held four people hostage on a ranch and then split. Both were recaptured and returned to prison.

On March 10, 1975, Schmid was attacked by two inmates and stabbed forty-seven times. He lost a kidney and an eye as a result. He died on March 30, 1975, due to the injuries he had sustained. Strangely, his body was stolen from the morgue. He was given a Catholic funeral at the prison even though there was no body.

Trivia

"The oddest thing was his boots. He'd had them special-made according to his own design. They were black and laced all the way up the back, with a tall cowboy heel and pointed toes. These he would stuff to make himself taller, although he didn't mind exploiting his bantam height to convince girls he'd once been crippled. That often made them pliable…and easy."

He used makeup to darken his skin, and the ChapStick he applied was so thick it made his lips appear white.

Books and Media

The short story "Where Are You Going, Where Have You Been?" about a teenage girl being charmed and menaced by a predatory man, was written and published by Joyce Carol Oates. She stated she was inspired, in part, by the Schmid case. The story is dedicated to Bob Dylan because Oates was also inspired by his song "It's All Over Now, Baby Blue." The story was adapted into a 1986 film *Smooth Talk*, in which Schmid's character, Arnold Friend, is played by Treat Williams.

The movie *The Todd Killings*, released in 1971, was based on the Schmid case.

The film *Dead Beat*, released in 1994, was based on the case.

The film *The Lost*, released in 2005, was adapted from a novel by Jack Ketchum.

The thriller *Half in Love with Death*, written by Emily Ross, was inspired by the Schmid case.

Childhood friend Richard Bruns wrote *I, a Squealer: The Insider's Account of the "Pied Piper of Tucson" Murders* which gives a firsthand account of the crimes. Bruns later provided the information to the police that led to his arrest and subsequent conviction.

JUAN SEGUNDO

Date of birth: January 25, 1963

Aliases/Nicknames: Nil

Characteristics: Rape

Number of victims: 4 +

Date of murders: August 3, 1986 - June 17, 1995

Date of arrest: April 19, 2005

Victim profile: Vanessa Villa, 11; Melissa Badillo, 23; Francis Williams; Maria Reyna Navarro, 32

Method of murder: Strangulation

Location: Tarrant County, Texas, USA

Status: Sentenced to death on February 15, 2007.

Background

Segundo, born Juan Ramon Segundo Meza, was a rapist and serial killer who operated in Fort Worth, Texas. He was convicted of one murder and linked to three others by DNA.

Murders

His first known victim was Vanessa Villa, eleven. On the night of August 3, 1986, Segundo broke into her home, raped her, and strangled her to death. She was pronounced dead in the early hours of August 4. On August 10, a wake for Vanessa was held, and Segundo allegedly attended, as he was a friend of the family. He was questioned by police but cleared, and Vanessa's mother had defended him as not being the type to kill.

His next known attack occurred on October 6, 1987. A woman woke to find Segundo fondling her. He assaulted her, and when her daughter woke, he fled. She was able to identify him as they had previously worked together. In June of 1988, he was convicted of burglary for the incident and sentenced to ten years. He was released a year later.

Through DNA testing, Segundo was further linked to three cold cases. These murders had occurred during a nine-month period during the 1990s.

- Melissa Badillo, twenty-three: She was abducted and murdered in September of 1994. The link was made to Segundo while he was on death row in 2010.

- Francis Williams. She was found dead in a drainage ditch on November 15, 1994.

- Maria Reyna Navarro, thirty-two. She was abducted on June 16, 1995. Her body was found the next day in Buck Sansom Park. In December of 2005, the link was made to Segundo.

Trial

Forensic investigators matched Segundo's DNA to samples found at the scene of Vanessa's murder in early 2005. He was subsequently arrested on April 19. Segundo was not willing to talk and refused interviews. In December of 2006, he was found guilty of the charges relating to Vanessa's murder. He was sentenced to death.

Outcome

Segundo's last appeal was denied in February of 2017. He was given an execution date for October of 2018. Because of concerns regarding how intellectual disability was determined, the execution date was stayed once again. To date, he remains in prison on death row.

Trivia

According to his brother, Segundo fell down some stairs when he was a baby, and after that accident, he had always appeared to be in a daze and seemed to be slow. When his IQ was tested, he scored seventy-five, which was a borderline legal result for intellectual disability.

Segundo had been diagnosed as intellectually disabled by multiple professionals due to his IQ scores being consistently low. He was unable to tell which side was left and which was right, and he couldn't tell the time on a clock.

TOMMY LYNN SELLS

Date of birth: June 28, 1964

Aliases/Nicknames: Coast to Coast Killer

Characteristics: Rape

Number of victims: 1 - 13 +

Date of murders: 1980 - 1999

Date of arrest: January 2, 2000

Victim profile: Kaylene "Katy" Harris, 13; other victims not confirmed or prosecuted

Method of murder: Cutting her throat

Location: Missouri, New York, Illinois, Texas, USA

Status: Sentenced to death in Texas on November 8, 2000. Executed by lethal injection in Texas on April 3, 2014.

Background

When Sells and his twin sister were eighteen months old, they contracted meningitis; he survived, but his sister did not. Soon afterward, he was sent to live with his aunt. At the age of five, he went back to live with his mother.

Sells was eight years old when a man named Willis Clark began molesting him. Appallingly, his mother had given this man consent. Sells later said this abuse greatly affected him, and while he was committing his crimes, he would relive the experiences of the molestation.

From 1978 to 1999, Sells train-hopped and hitchhiked across the country. He used drugs, alcohol, and committed a variety of crimes, which landed him in prison on several occasions. He stole a truck in 1990 and was sentenced to sixteen months in prison. At this time, he was diagnosed with a personality disorder which included schizoid, borderline and antisocial features, major depressive disorder, psychosis, and bipolar disorder.

On May 13, 1992, Sells was panhandling under an overpass and carrying a sign saying he would work for food. A young woman took pity on him and took him back to her house, then asked him to wait outside while she got him something to eat. Sells entered the home anyway. When she turned her back to him, he grabbed a knife from the kitchen and trapped her in a bedroom. He raped her repeatedly at knifepoint. The woman hit him in the head with a ceramic ornament, so Sells used a piano stool to beat her. He then stabbed her a total of eighteen times. Remarkably, she survived. Sells was arrested and charged in September of 1992. He took a plea deal and received two to ten years' imprisonment.

While incarcerated, he married Nora Price. In 1997, he was released from prison and moved to Tennessee. He soon left Price and went back to traveling across the country.

Murders

Sells told police that his first murder occurred when he was fifteen years old. He said he had broken into a house and found a man performing fellatio on a boy, so he killed him. This has not been confirmed.

In July of 1985, Sells met Ena Cordt, twenty-eight, while working at a carnival in Forsyth, Missouri. She had a son, Rory, who was four. Cordt invited Sells to her house, and he said he had sex with her and fell asleep. When he woke, she was stealing from his backpack. He used her son's baseball bat to beat her to death. Then he killed the little boy to stop him from being a witness. The bodies were found three days later.

On December 31, 1999, Sells sexually assaulted Kaylene "Katy" Harris, thirteen. Afterwards, he stabbed her and slit her throat. He also slit the throat of Krystal Surles, ten, but she managed to survive after traveling a quarter-mile to her neighbors with a severed trachea. She described Sells, and a sketch was made, which led to his identification.

Sells is suspected of these crimes:

May 1987: The murder of Suzanne Korcz (February 2, 1960 – disappeared & presumed dead May of 1987) in New York

November 17, 1987: The murders of four members of the Dardeen family in Illinois

September 11, 1988: The murder of Melissa Tremblay (March 1, 1977 – September 11, 1988) in Lawrence, Massachusetts

1989: The murder of a co-worker in Texas

October 13, 1997: The murder of ten-year-old Joel Kirkpatrick in Lawrenceville, Illinois

November 18, 1997: The murder of Stephanie Mahaney (June 20, 1984 – November 18, 1997) near Springfield, Missouri

April 18, 1999: The murder of nine-year-old Mary Beatrice Perez (April 7, 1990 – April 18, 1999) in San Antonio, Texas, a murder for which Sells was ultimately convicted

May 23, 1999: The sexual assault and murder of Haley McHone (August 14, 1985 – May 23, 1999) in Lexington, Kentucky

December 31, 1999: The sexual assault and murder of Kaylene Jo "Katy" Harris (September 27, 1986 – December 31, 1999)

Trial

While Sells was in custody, police were not convinced that all of his confessions were actually true. Maybe he was trying to work the system? The state's attorney in Jefferson County decided not to charge him with the Dardeen family murders in 1987 because his confession wasn't completely accurate.

On February 8, 2000, Sells was indicted by Texas for the murder of Kaylene Harris in 1999. He was convicted of capital murder on September 18, 2000. He was sentenced to death.

Though he appealed his conviction and sentence, the Texas Court of Criminal Appeals rejected his appeal on March 12, 2003.

Outcome

In 2004, Sells confessed that on October 13, 1997, he entered a home and stabbed a little boy to death, then fought with the mother. The details were consistent with the case of Julie Rea Harper, who had initially been convicted of her son's murder before being acquitted in 2006.

On April 3, 2014, Sells was executed. He declined to make a final statement.

Trivia

"Uh, you all haven't asked this, but I will go ahead and tell you this. Do I think I'm the one that killed this kid? Yes...Uh, if it wasn't this kid I killed, then there's a murder out there that, that we still ain't undug yet." **-Tommy Lynn Sells**

"I don't know what love is. Two words I don't like to use is 'love' and 'sorry,' because I'm about hate." **-Tommy Lynn Sells**

In media

Sells was interviewed for the documentary series *Most Evil* eight years before his death. He was interviewed for the program by forensic psychiatrist Dr. Michael Stone, during which Sells claimed he had murdered over seventy people.

ANTHONY ALLEN SHORE

Date of birth: June 25, 1962

Aliases/Nicknames: The Strangler, Tourniquet Killer

Characteristics: Rape

Number of victims: 4 - 5

Date of murders: 1986, 1992 - 1995

Date of arrest: October 24, 2003

Victim profile: Laurie Lee Tremblay, 15; Maria Del Carmen Estrada, 21; Diana Rebollar, 9; Dana Sanchez, 16

Method of murder: Strangulation

Location: Harris County, Texas, USA

Status: Sentenced to death on November 15, 2004.

Background

Shore was a talented musician and songwriter, who played both the piano and the guitar. People saw him as trustworthy and charming, but they didn't know the real Shore. He was a stalker and a bit of a control freak; for some people, there was something creepy about him.

He married a woman much younger than himself. She left two years into the marriage,, after waking up and finding his hands around her throat.

Murders

Laurie Tremblay, fourteen, was Shore's first known victim. She was murdered on September 26, 1986, while on her way to school. Shore tried to sexually assault her before strangling her to death. He dumped her body behind a restaurant.

On April 16, 1992, Maria del Carmen Estrada, twenty-one, was killed. She had been sexually assaulted and strangled. Her body was left behind a Dairy Queen the day she was killed.

Shore broke into the home of Selma Janske, fourteen, on October 19, 1993. He tied the girl up and sexually assaulted her, but didn't kill her.

Diana Rebollar, nine, went missing after leaving a grocery store on August 8, 1994. The following day, her body was discovered on a loading dock behind a building. She had been sexually assaulted, beaten, and strangled with a rope with a bamboo stick attached—the same as Estrada.

On July 6, 1995, Dana Sanchez, sixteen, was killed. Shore had offered to give her a ride in his van, and when she resisted his advances, he strangled her. Shore made an anonymous call seven days later telling police where to find her body.

In 1998, Shore was convicted of molesting his daughters. Because of the conviction, he had to provide a DNA sample to police. In 2000, Estrada's murder was given another look over. Evidence that had been found beneath her fingernails and stored was tested for DNA. There were issues with the laboratory, which ended up closed in 2002, so the samples were sent to another laboratory to be tested again. In 2003, the match was made with Shore.

Shore was arrested and interrogated, and after eleven hours, he confessed to the murders of Estrada, Rebollar, and Sanchez. Then he confessed to killing Tremblay and raping another teenage girl in 1994. Tremblay's murder hadn't been linked to the others because he had used a ligature with her murder. He explained the change by saying, "because I hurt my finger while murdering Tremblay."

Trial

Even though Shore had confessed to a total of four murders and a separate rape, Kelly Siegler, the prosecutor, decided he would only be charged with Estrada's murder because there was more forensic evidence in that case.

Shore's trial began in October of 2004. He was found guilty of capital murder, and the jury recommended the death penalty. Shore had actually asked to be put to death as well. Therefore, he was sentenced to death on November 15, 2004.

Outcome

On January 18, 2018, Shore was executed by lethal injection.

Trivia

His final statement was as follows:

"I like to take a moment to say I'm sorry. No amount of words could ever undo what I've done. To the family of my victims, I wish I could undo the past. It is what it is. God bless all of you. I will die with a clear conscious. I made my peace. There is no others. I will like to wish a happy birthday to Barbara Carrol. Today is her birthday. I would like to specifically thank those that have helped me, you know who you are. God bless everybody, until we meet again. I'm ready, warden."

His last words were "Ooh-ee, I can feel that!"

ANGUS SINCLAIR

Date of birth: 1945

Aliases/Nicknames: World's End Murders

Characteristics: Serial rape

Number of victims: 4 - 8

Date of murders: 1961, 1977, 1978

Date of arrest: March 31, 2005

Victim profile: Catherine Reehill, 7; Frances Barker, 37; Hilda McAuley, 36; Agnes Cooney, 23; Anna Kenny, 20; Christine Eadie, 17; Helen Scott, 17; Mary Gallacher, 17

Method of murder: Strangulation

Location: Wales, United Kingdom

Status: Sentenced to 10 years in prison in 1961. Served 6 years. Pleaded guilty to rape and sexual assault of 11 children aged 6 to 14 in 1982. Sentenced to life in prison. Sentenced to a minimum of 37 years in prison on November 14, 2014.

Background

When Sinclair was sixteen, he raped and killed his neighbor, Catherine Reehill, who was only seven years old at the time. He had lured the little girl into a stairwell before attacking her. Police were shocked by the methods employed by Sinclair to dispose of the body and try to cover his tracks. But his methods weren't good enough, and he was sentenced to ten years in prison, of which he served six.

In 1978, he murdered Mary Gallacher, seventeen, and then called an ambulance saying "a wee girl has fallen down the stairs." He wasn't arrested for that murder until 2001.

Murders

Christine Eadie and Helen Scott were last seen leaving The World's End pub on the night of October 15, 1977. The next day, Eadie's body was found in Gosford Bay. Then, six miles away, Scott's body was found in a field. The girls had been gagged, tied up, raped, beaten, and then strangled. Their bodies were left out in the open with no attempt to hide them.

A number of witnesses had reported seeing the two girls with two men on the night of their murders. On November 25, 2004, Sinclair was detained, and DNA swabs were taken. He was then arrested on

March 31, 2005, and charged with the rape and murder of the two girls.

Trial

The trial began on August 27, 2007. The indictment alleged that Sinclair and his now-deceased brother-in-law Gordon Hamilton had forced or persuaded the girls into a motor vehicle and held them against their will. They then allegedly drove Eadie to Gosford Bay, stripped her, gagged her with her underwear, and tied her wrists. She was then raped and killed. The indictment alleged Sinclair then raped and killed Scott in a similar manner before disposing of her body in the field.

Sinclair pled not guilty. He stated that sexual activity with the girls had been consensual. He also claimed that if they had come to any harm, it was at the hands of Hamilton.

The DNA testing was finalized, and both Sinclair and Hamilton were a match. On September 7, 2007, a submission was made by the defense that there was no case to answer due to insufficient evidence. Following legal arguments, the trial judge upheld the submission and formally acquitted Sinclair on September 10, 2007.

In October of 2013, eight days of court time were set aside by three judges to hear a bid from the prosecutors for Sinclair to stand trial for a second time. The bid was successful. On April 15, 2014, permission was granted for a trial to commence.

On October 13, 2014, the trial began. Sinclair was convicted of the rapes and murders of Eadie and Scott on November 14, 2014.

Outcome

Sinclair was sentenced to life imprisonment with the possibility of parole after thirty-seven years. He is unlikely to get out because, by the time his parole period comes around, he would be one hundred six years old.

Trivia

The case led to a systematic review of Scottish criminal procedure. On November 20, 2007, the Cabinet Secretary for Justice, Kenny MacAskill, MSP, referred several issues to the Scottish Law Commission for investigation.

On June 30, 2010, the Scottish Parliament passed the Criminal Justice and Licensing (Scotland) Act 2010.

On March 22, 2011, in direct response to the Scottish Law Commissions findings on the issue of double jeopardy, the Scottish Parliament passed the Double Jeopardy (Scotland) Act 2011. The act makes various provisions for circumstances when a person convicted or acquitted of an offense can be prosecuted anew.

MOSES SITHOLE

Date of birth: November 17, 1964

Aliases/Nicknames: The ABC Murderer, The Gauteng Killer

Characteristics: Serial rapist

Number of victims: 38

Date of murders: 1994 - 1995

Date of arrest: October 18, 1995

Victim profile: Marina Monene Monama, 18; Amanda Kebofile Thethe, 26; Joyce Thakane Mashabela, 32; Refilwe Amanda Mokale, 24; Rose Rebothile Mogotsi, 22; Beauty Nuku Soko, 27; Sara Matlakala Mokono, 25; Nikiwe Diko; Letta Nomthandazo Ndlangamandla, 25; Sibusiso Nomthandazo Ndlangamandla, 2; Esther Moshibudi Mainetja, 29; Granny Dimakatso Ramela, 21; Elizabeth Granny Mathetsa, 19; Mildred Ntiya Lepule, 28; Francina Nomsa Sithebe, 25; Ernestina Mohadi Mosebo, 30; Elsie Khoti Masango, 25; Josephine Mantsali Mlangeni, 25; Oscarina Vuyokazi Jakalase, 30; Makoba Tryphina Mogotsi, 26; Nelisiwe Nontobeko Zulu, 26; Amelia Dikamakatso Rapodile, 43; Monica Gabisile Vilakazi, 31; Hazel Nozipho Madikizela, 21; Tsidi Malekoae Matela, 45; Agnes Sibongile Mbuli, 20; Beauty Ntombi Ndabeni; others unknown

Method of murder: Ligature strangulation

Location: Pretoria, Gauteng, South Africa

Status: Sentenced to 50 years' imprisonment for each of the 38 murders, 12 years imprisonment for each of the 40 rapes, and 5 years' imprisonment for each of the 6 robberies. Since his sentences run consecutively, the total effective sentence was thus one of 2,410 years. His sentencing took place on December 5, 1997.

Background

Sithole was born in 1964, in a poor neighborhood of Boksburg, called Vosloorus, in South Africa. His father died when he was five years old, and soon after, his mother abandoned him and his siblings. The children went to live in an orphanage for three years, and later he claimed they were mistreated there. He ended up running away and went back to his mother, but she returned him to the orphanage. Eventually, he went to live with an older brother.

Sithole began committing rapes in his twenties. His third victim testified against him, and he went to prison. While incarcerated, he was sexually assaulted by other inmates. Shortly after he was released, he began committing murders.

Murders

To gain access to victims, Sithole posed as a businessman offering employment. He even went to the extreme of inventing a fictional charity organization. Once Sithole had gained the victim's trust, he would offer to walk them through a field to the "headquarters." As soon as they were out of sight and hearing range, he would rape and then strangle them. Sithole had claimed more than thirty victims by 1995. Sometimes he would telephone the family of the victim and taunt them.

In August of 1995, a witness identified Sithole as being seen with one of the victims. Police then discovered the details of his fake business and his history of conviction for rape. Sithole went on the run, but also contacted a journalist and said he was the killer.

The third time Sithole called the journalist, he gave her a number so she could call him back. She gave the number to the police. They quickly located the payphone he had called from, but he was already gone. Soon after, Sithole contacted his brother-in-law who arranged a meeting with him to give him a gun. Instead, he notified the police. Sithole thought it might have been a trap and tried to run. When police approached, he ran at them with an axe and was shot twice. Though wounded, his injuries weren't serious, and he was taken into custody.

Trial

Once he was arrested, Sithole confessed to the murders. On December 5, 1997, he received a fifty-year sentence for each of the thirty-eight murders. He was also sentenced to twelve years for each of the forty rapes. For each of the six robberies he committed he received a sentence of five years in prison.

Outcome

Sithole is imprisoned in Pretoria Central Prison in the C-Max (maximum security) section. He has subsequently been diagnosed HIV positive. He is provided with treatment for HIV, but his family wasn't so lucky. His wife and child died from the disease because they didn't qualify for health care coverage.

Trivia

Sithole said that he had two accomplices named "Tito" and "Mandla." Adding to the confusion, Sithole used the alias "Mandla" when he made a taunting call to the grandmother of one of his victims while he was already under police custody. Likewise, someone who claimed to be named "Martin," a recurring alias of Sithole's, called the workplace of one of the victims attributed to Sithole, to inform the workers that she would not go to work that day because she had suffered an accident.

ERNO SOTO

Date of birth: Unknown

Aliases/Nicknames: Charlie Chopoff

Characteristics: Pedophilia, rape, genital mutilation

Number of victims: 4

Date of murders: 1972 - 1973

Date of arrest: May 25, 1974

Victim profile: Douglas Owens, 8; Wendell Hubbard, 9; Luis Ortiz, 9; Steven Cropper, 8

Method of murder: Stabbing with knife

Location: New York City, New York, USA

Status: Found incompetent for trial. Committed to a mental institution for the criminally insane in 1974.

Background

The root of Soto's problems seemed to be his marriage. After he and his wife had separated, Soto attempted to reconcile with her. But he discovered that she had conceived a child while they were apart. The child was black, and the Sotos were Puerto Rican, so it was clear the child was not his.

Soto pretended he didn't care about the child that wasn't his, but by the time the child was eight, Soto became more erratic in his behavior. He was committed to the State Hospital in 1969 and 1970.

From then onwards, he would periodically go back to the hospital for treatment. Soto found more relief when he was stalking small, dark boys on the streets of New York.

Murders

The first child Soto murdered was Douglas Owens, aged eight. His body was found on March 9, 1972, two blocks from his home. He had been stabbed a total of thirty-eight times in the chest, back, and neck. His penis had been cut but was still attached. Police received an anonymous call on March 23 suggesting Soto was the killer, but they didn't follow up on it.

On April 20, another black boy who was ten years old was attacked. He was stabbed in the back and the neck, and his penis was severed and taken away. The boy surprisingly survived and was able to give a description. However, because of the trauma inflicted upon him, his value as a witness was limited.

Wendell Hubbard, nine, was murdered on October 23. He was stabbed seventeen times in the chest, abdomen, and neck, and his penis was cut off and taken away as well. Then on March 7, 1973, Luis Ortiz, nine, disappeared while on his way to the corner store. His body was later found in the basement of an apartment house. He had been stabbed thirty-eight times in the chest, back, and neck and his severed penis was missing.

Soto seemed to break pattern with his next victim. On August 17, 1973, eight-year-old Steven Cropper was murdered on a rooftop like many of the others. But he wasn't stabbed to death. He had been slashed with a razor, and his penis was still intact. The differences led police to believe there was a second killer. Later, they decided it would be unusual to have two killers with similar methods. The murders, they decided, were most likely the work of one perpetrator.

Soto was arrested on May 25, 1974, after he tried to kidnap a nine-year-old boy. He was surrounded by neighbors of the boy and held until the police arrived. Once in custody, he confessed to the murder of Cropper. Unfortunately, his only surviving victim refused to pick him out of a lineup.

The state hospital initially gave Soto an alibi, saying he was in the hospital at the time of the murder. But later they admitted that sometimes he got away unnoticed. Soto was found to be insane and was sent back to the hospital, where he was guarded more closely.

Trial

Soto was diagnosed with schizophrenia and therefore found not guilty by reason of insanity. The files on the murders are still officially open. While he is incompetent to stand trial, the murder cases may not be cleared. However, the crimes stopped once he was incarcerated at the hospital.

Outcome

Soto will remain in the mental hospital until such time as he is found fit and competent to stand trial.

Trivia

"God told me to make little boys into little girls." - Soto

Soto has an alibi for at least one of the killings, as he was in a mental institution on the same date. He could have "jumped the wall," committed the crime, then come back, but it hasn't been proven either way.

LYDA SOUTHARD

Date of birth: October 16, 1892

Aliases/Nicknames: Flypaper Lyda, The Black Widow, Lyda Trueblood, Lydia Keller

Characteristics: Killed for insurance money

Number of victims: 6

Date of murders: 1915 - 1920

Date of arrest: May 1921

Victim profile: Robert Dooley; William McHaffle; Harlan Lewis; Ed Myer; Paul Vance Southard; Lorraine Dooley, 4

Method of murder: Arsenic poisoning

Location: Idaho, Montana

Status: Sentenced to a term of 10 years to life in Idaho in 1921. Paroled on October 3, 1941. Died on February 5, 1958.

Background

Born Lydia Keller, Southard grew up in Keytesville, Missouri. Her family was close to another local family, the Dooleys, and Robert Dooley fell in love with her. They married in Twin Falls, Idaho in 1912. The couple was focused on security, so Robert and his brother Edward both had life insurance policies. If either of them died, one thousand dollars would go to the surviving brother, and the same amount would go to Southard.

Murders

Southard and Dooley were happily married and had a baby they called Lorraine. The girl died suddenly at the age of four, and things went downhill from there. Edward, who had been living with them, also died. Then, in October of 1915, Dooley died—apparently from typhoid fever.

Two years after the deaths, Southard remarried and moved to her new husband's home in Montana. But on October 1, 1918, her husband William G. McHaffle died, by what was thought to be complications from diphtheria and influenza. Southard had now been widowed twice by the time she was twenty-five.

Southard met a new man, Harlan C. Lewis, and within four months he too was dead, supposedly from complications related to gastroenteritis. Next, she married Edward F. Meyer. Sadly for Meyer, he was dead a month later from typhoid.

The local chemist in Twin Falls, Earl Dooley, who happened to be related to Southard's first husband, became suspicious about the number of deaths surrounding her and began to study them. With the help of another chemist and a physician, they determined that both Dooley brothers had been killed by arsenic poisoning. The county prosecutor began exhuming the bodies of Southard's husbands, her daughter, and her brother-in-law. Arsenic was detected in some of the bodies, and it was presumed the others had died from the same poisoning as their bodies were so well preserved.

On further investigation, they discovered that all of the dead men had held life insurance policies that Southard the beneficiary. Over the years, she had collected seven thousand dollars from her dead husbands. When law enforcement found her, she was living in Honolulu and was married to fifth husband, Navy petty officer Paul Southard. She was extradited to Idaho.

Husband Insurance Money

Robert Dooley $4,600
William McHaffle $500
Harlan Lewis $3,000
Ed Myer $10,000
Paul Vance Southard $10,000

Trial

Southard's trial lasted six weeks. At the end of it, she was convicted of second-degree murder. She received a sentence of ten years to life in prison. On May 4, 1931, she escaped and began working as a housekeeper for Harry Whitlock in Denver, Colorado. She married him in March of 1932, but he eventually helped police recapture her on July 31, 1932.

In October of 1941, Southard was released on probation. In 1942, she received a final pardon. Then she was sent back to Idaho to face trial for the murder of Meyer. She pled not guilty but was convicted of murdering her husband for the insurance money.

Outcome

Southard was sentenced to ten years to life in prison. On February 5, 1958, Southard died of a heart attack.

Trivia

Warden Rudd:

Once back in prison, Southard had one last trick up her sleeve. This time she convinced George Rudd, the prison warden, to grant her special privileges such as day trips to a local resort and special visitations to see her sick mother. When an investigation into prison conditions was performed, and the truth came out about her getting special treatment, Rudd was forced to resign.

RICHARD SPECK

Date of birth: December 6, 1941

Aliases/Nicknames: Nil

Characteristics: Hostage, rape

Number of victims: 8 +

Date of murders: July 14, 1966

Date of arrest: July 18, 1966

Victim profile: Gloria Davy, 22; Patricia Matusek, 20; Nina Schmale, 24; Pamela Wilkening, 20; Suzanne Farris, 21; Mary Ann Jordan, 20; Merlita Gargullo, 22; Valentina Pasion, 23

Method of murder: Strangulation, stabbing with knife

Location: Chicago, Illinois, USA

Status: Sentenced to death on June 5, 1967. Resentenced to 400 to 1,200 years in prison (8 consecutive sentences of 50 to 150 years) on November 21, 1972. Sentence reduced in 1973 to a new statutory maximum of 300 years. Died in prison on December 5, 1991.

Background

Speck was close to his father, who died from a heart attack when he was just six years old. His mother later remarried, but Speck didn't like his stepfather, a drunk who abused him psychologically. Speck had a lot of difficulty at school and dropped out after he turned sixteen. By that stage, he had already been drinking alcohol for four years and had spent most of the previous year drunk every day.

The first contact Speck had with the police was when he was thirteen, and he was arrested for trespassing. Dozens of further arrests occurred over the next several years, mainly for misdemeanors. In October of 1961, Speck met fifteen-year-old Shirley Malone. Within three weeks, she was pregnant. They married on January 19, 1962.

Speck continued to commit crimes, and in July 1963, he was arrested for forging a check. Then he robbed a grocery store. For these two crimes, he was given a sentence of three years in prison. He was paroled after sixteen months.

A week after he was released, on January 9, 1965, Speck attacked a woman with a carving knife in the parking lot of her apartment building. He ran when she screamed, but was apprehended minutes later by police. He received a sixteen-month sentence for aggravated assault. Due to an error, he was released six months into his sentence.

Speck's wife filed for divorce in January of 1966. Within that same month, Speck stabbed a man during a knife fight. He was again charged with aggravated assault, but his attorney got it reduced to disturbing the peace, and he spent three days in jail for not paying the imposed fine of ten dollars.

He continued to rob grocery stores and attack women, but his actions on the night of July 13, 1966 changed multiple lives forever.

Murders

Speck broke into a townhouse that was being used as a dormitory for student nurses at 11:00 pm. Using a knife, he killed Patricia Matusek, Gloria Davy, Nina Jo Schmale, Suzanne Farris, Pamela Wilkening, Merlita Gargullo, Valentina Pasion, and Mary Ann Jordan. He first held them hostage in one room for hours, and then led them out one at a time. He stabbed or strangled each woman, and the last victim, Gloria Davy, was also raped. One of the women, Corazon Amurao, managed to hide and survived the attack. Fingerprints were found that were a match to Speck.

Two days later, a drifter named Claude Lunsford identified Speck. He recognized the sketch of the murderer in the paper and notified police. It's unknown why, but the police didn't respond. At the Starr Hotel, Speck tried to commit suicide and was taken to a hospital. There, he was recognized by one of the doctors as the wanted man due to his tattoo "Born to Raise Hell." The doctor called the police and Speck was arrested.

Trial

A panel was convened to determine Speck's mental state at the time of the crime and his competence to stand trial. The conclusion was that he was sane and competent. While awaiting his trial, however, he was seen twice a week by jail psychiatrist Dr. Marvin Ziporyn. He diagnosed Speck with organic brain syndrome. He stated Speck was competent to stand trial but had been insane at the time of the murders. When it came to the trial, neither side used the doctor to testify as they had discovered he was writing a book about Speck for financial gain and could thus be biased.

On April 3, 1967, the trial by jury began. A gag order was put on the press. During the trial, survivor Amurao identified Speck as the killer. On April 15, he was found guilty after the jury deliberated for just forty-nine minutes. The jury recommended the death penalty. He was sentenced to death.

Outcome

The U.S. Supreme Court upheld his conviction but reversed his death sentence on June 28, 1971. The reason was that more than two hundred fifty potential jurors had been unconstitutionally excluded. On June 29, 1972, the death penalty was declared unconstitutional, so Speck needed to be resentenced again. Finally, on November 21, 1972, Speck was sentenced to four hundred to twelve hundred years in prison. He was rejected at every parole hearing he attended.

While in prison, Speck was given the nickname "Birdman." Like the character of the same name in the film *Birdman of Alcatraz*, Speck kept a pair of sparrows in his cell.

On December 5, 1991, Speck died of a heart attack. He would have turned fifty the following day. His sister was concerned his grave would be desecrated, so he was cremated and the ashes scattered.

Trivia

In films

The film *Naked Massacre* is a fictional version of Speck's murder spree, set in Northern Ireland.

The film *Speck* portrays Speck's murders from his perspective.

The film *Chicago Massacre: Richard Speck* portrays Speck's crimes.

The film *100 Ghost Street: The Return of Richard Speck* follows investigators who attempt to capture Speck's ghost on film at the site of the murders.

In television

Speck was featured on the documentary series *A Crime to Remember* in the episode, "And Then There Was One."

An episode of *Mindhunter* involves interviews with Richard Speck as he talks about the murders of the nurses.

Speck was the feature of an episode of *Murder Made Me Famous*.

In music

A report of Speck's grand jury indictment is among the news bulletins read in "7 O'clock News/Silent Night," a song from Simon and Garfunkel's 1966 album *Parsley, Sage, Rosemary, and Thyme*.

Cheap Trick wrote a song about Speck called "The Ballad of TV Violence (I'm Not the Only Boy)." The song was originally titled "The Ballad of Richard Speck," but according to drummer Bun E. Carlos, "The legal department said we could call it that if we wanted, but 'the estate will sue and you'll have to give all your royalties to them' - can't profit from a crime and all that."

Former Marilyn Manson keyboardist Zsa Zsa Speck followed the group's stage name tradition of mixing pop culture icons with serial killers by adopting the names of Zsa Zsa Gabor and Richard Speck.

Garage rock band, The Chesterfield Kings, wrote the song "Richard Speck" for their 1989 album *Berlin Wall of Sound*.

Metal band Macabre has a song about Speck called "What the Heck, Richard Speck" on their 1993 album *Sinister Slaughter*.

Doom metal band, Church Of Misery, wrote a song about Speck, called "Born to Raise Hell," on their 2009 album *Houses of the Unholy*.

In art

Photographs of the eight nurses Speck murdered were the basis of *Eight Student Nurses* (1966), a painting series by German artist Gerhard Richter.

ALEXANDER SPESIVTSEV

Date of birth: March 1, 1970

Aliases/Nicknames: The Cannibal of Siberia, Sasha, Novokuznetsk Monster, Siberian Ripper

Characteristics: Former mental patient, cannibalism

Number of victims: 19 - 82 +

Date of murders: 1991 - 1996

Date of arrest: October 26, 1996

Victim profile: Street children (whom he saw as the detritus of society)

Method of murder: Stabbing with knife

Location: Novokuznetsk, Siberia, Russia

Status: Ruled insane by a court and committed to a psychiatric hospital on October 5, 1999.

Background

Spesivtsev was raised in central Novokuznetsk, Soviet Union, and was often sickly as a child. He didn't have any friends and was bullied at school. He had a strong but unusual relationship with his mother. From a young age, she would often show him photographs of corpses in books. They shared a bed until Spesivtsev was twelve years old.

As he grew up, he showed increasing sadistic tendencies, and he was admitted to a mental hospital in 1988.

Murders

Spesivtsev began a one-man war against street children because he believed they were detrimental to society. He killed at least nineteen children after he had taken them back to his home. Then he cooked the flesh and ate it with his mother.

In the summer of 1996, he started getting rid of body parts by throwing them in the Aba River. This alerted police to the possibility of a serial killer operating in the area. But, because the victims were homeless children, there wasn't a lot of effort put into the investigation. Even after multiple complaints from his neighbors about the stench coming from his apartment, police still failed to react.

A year later, the police finally went to the apartment to investigate. Inside they found Olga Galtseva, fifteen, on the couch with multiple stab wounds to her chest and abdomen. She was barely alive. She managed to tell police that she had come to the apartment with two friends who had helped Spesivtsev's mother carry some bags. Once inside, they were trapped. The police assumed the other two children were dead, but because of a lack of funding, they were unable to conduct a full search.

As they looked around, though, they came across body parts all over the apartment. A headless corpse was in the bathroom and on the floor in the living room was a rib cage. They found enough evidence to determine there had been nineteen murders. They also uncovered more than eighty pieces of bloodstained clothing.

Spesivtsev and his mother were arrested on October 26, 1996.

Trial

Spesivtsev had previously been committed to a mental institution after killing his girlfriend. The court ruled him insane, and he was committed to a psychiatric hospital.

Outcome

The young girl found on his couch, Olga Galtseva, died the day after she was rescued.

Trivia

He spends his days in prison writing poems about "the evils of democracy," and he undergoes psychiatric testing regularly. When asked how he could justify his crimes, he said, "How many people have our democracy destroyed? ... If people thought about that, there wouldn't be any of this filth. But what can you do?"

Spesivtsev wants to sell his head to an institute so they can study his brain, and he wants to be paid "in advance, in cigarettes."

GERALD STANO

Date of birth: September 12, 1951

Aliases/Nicknames: Paul Zeininger

Characteristics: Rape

Number of victims: 9 - 41 +

Date of murders: 1969 - 1980

Date of arrest: April 1, 1980

Victim profile: Cathy Lee Scharf, 17; Mary Carol Maher; Toni Vann Haddocks; Nancy Heard; Linda Hamilton; Ramona Neal; Susan Hamilton; Susan Bacile; Mary Kathleen Muldoon; Sandra Dubose; Barbara Bauer; Susan Bickrest

Method of murder: Stabbing with knife, strangulation

Location: Florida, Pennsylvania, New Jersey, USA

Status: Executed by electrocution in Florida on March 23, 1998.

Background

Stano—born Paul Zeininger—was neglected so severely that when his mother went to give him up for adoption, the doctors declared he wasn't adoptable. He was apparently functioning at what they called an "animalistic level," and was even eating his own feces just to survive. He was eventually adopted by Norma Stano, a nurse, who gave him the name Gerald Eugene Stano.

Stano certainly had a number of issues growing up. He continued to wet the bed until he was ten years old. He was a compulsive liar and would steal from his adoptive father. He was bullied at school and didn't graduate high school until he was twenty-one years old. He couldn't hold down a job, usually getting fired for stealing money or constant lateness.

Murders

Between December of 1973 and January of 1974, Stano murdered Cathy Lee Scharf, seventeen, who was hitchhiking. She was stabbed to death, and her body was found in an isolated area of Brevard County. Stano stated he choked her repeatedly before dumping her in a drainage ditch. Then he went roller-skating.

Stano confessed to killing Mary Carol Maher. He said he stabbed her in the chest, back, and thigh, and that when he stabbed her in the chest, he did it as hard as he could. Her autopsy later showed a broken sternum. Stano wrapped her body in foam padding and left her near the airport covered in palm branches.

The next victim he confessed to killing was Toni Vann Haddocks. Her body was found around April 6, 1980, in an area where Stano used to live. Her body had also been covered with tree branches in an attempt to hide it.

Other victims he confessed to killing were:

Nancy Heard
Linda Hamilton
Ramona Neal
Susan Hamilton
Jane Doe
Susan Bacile
Mary Kathleen Muldoon
Sandra Dubose
Barbara Bauer
Susan Bickrest

Trial

Stano was arrested after a woman went to the police station and stated Stano had sliced her. The woman, Donna Hensley, was still bleeding. Under interrogation, Stano admitted that he had committed his first murder in 1969 in New Jersey. He then added he had killed six women in Pennsylvania. After moving to Florida, he killed thirty or more women.

Stano used a variety of methods to kill his victims, including gunshots, stabbing, and strangulation. He didn't rape his victims. He was in prison by his twenty-ninth birthday for murdering forty-one women.

Outcome

Stano was convicted of killing nine women. He received the death penalty in one case and eight life sentences. For a while, he was housed with Ted Bundy until the latter was executed.

There has been some controversy over Stano's guilt or whether he was what is called a "serial confessor." Some believe he was fed details about the crimes, so his confessions seemed more legitimate. To further enhance this argument, in 2007, a lab report from the FBI concluded the pubic hairs found on the body of Scharf did not belong to Stano.

On March 23, 1998, Stano was executed by electric chair. The pubic hair evidence was destroyed after his death.

Trivia

For his final meal Stano requested Delmonico steak, a baked potato with sour cream and bacon bits, tossed salad with blue cheese dressing, lima beans, a half-gallon of mint chocolate chip ice cream, and two liters of Pepsi.

Stano's final statement proclaimed innocence and directed blame for his false confessions at the lead investigator, Paul Crow. He stated:

"I am innocent. I am frightened. I was threatened, and I was held month after month without any real legal representation. I confessed to crimes I did not commit."

*"I hate a bitchy chick." - **Stano***

Stano wrote to a friend a month before his execution, stating "I'll get by this date like the ones before. There's no need to worry. There's no way they'll execute me."

He often referred to himself as a "REAL ITALLION STALLION."

PAUL MICHAEL STEPHANI

Date of birth: September 8, 1944

Aliases/Nicknames: The Weepy-Voiced Killer

Characteristics: Tearful phone calls taunting police

Number of victims: 3

Date of murders: 1981 - 1982

Date of arrest: 1982

Victim profile: Kimberly Compton, 18; Kathy Greening, 33; Barbara Simons, 40

Method of murder: Stabbing 61 times with an ice pick, drowning, stabbing with a knife more than 100 times

Location: Minneapolis, St. Paul, Minnesota, USA

Status: Sentenced to 40 years in prison on one count in 1983.

Background

Stephani was one of ten children in a family that was very religious. He later married Beverly Lider and had a daughter. He had a history of mental illness and had once been convicted of an aggravated assault. His serial killings started on New Year's Eve, 1980.

Murders

Karen Potack had been at a party with her sisters and left just after midnight, wandering around the city drunk. Police received a call a few hours later saying a girl was hurt near the Malberg Manufacturing Company. When they arrived, they found Potack lying in the snow near railroad tracks, naked. She had been beaten so ferociously her skull was cracked. She survived but suffered brain trauma.

Police received another call from the same man months later saying he had stabbed someone with an ice pick. Soon after, the body of Kimberly Compton was found. She was lying near an unfinished freeway and had been stabbed with an ice pick.

The body of Barbara Simmons was found fourteen months later, and she had also been stabbed. Stephani called fire emergency two days later claiming he was responsible and that he was sorry for what he had done. Meanwhile, a waitress from a bar identified Stephani as the last person she had seen with Simmons the night of her murder.

Police began monitoring Stephani. Even so, he managed to solicit a prostitute, Denise Williams, and take her back to his apartment for sex. Then he offered to drive her back to her district, and she accepted. But he took her down a secluded road instead, claiming it was a shortcut. Williams was suspicious and planned to use a glass bottle if she had to defend herself. When they reached the end of the road, he stabbed her in the stomach, and she hit him with the bottle. She managed to open the door but was stabbed several more times. Her screaming woke a man nearby who scared off Stephani.

Later that night, Stephani called for help to stop his bleeding, and the emergency services recognized his voice.

Trial

Stephani was arrested and subsequently convicted of the attempted murder. He was then charged with the murder of Simmons. Police couldn't link him to the other murders because the only evidence they had was the recordings of his voice, which wasn't enough.

After Stephani was diagnosed with skin cancer, he decided to confess to the murder of Compton, the attempted murder of Potack, and another victim, Kathy Greening, who had been drowned.

Outcome

When Stephani was diagnosed with skin cancer in 1997, he was given less than a year to live. He died on June 12, 1998.

Trivia

Phone quotes:

"I'm sorry I killed that girl. I stabbed her forty times. Kimberly Compton was the first one over in St. Paul. I don't know what's the matter with me. I'm sick. I'm going to kill myself, I think. I'm just going to... If somebody dies with a red shirt on it's me. I've killed more people... I'll never make it to heaven!"

"God damn, will you find me? I just stabbed somebody with an ice pick. I can't stop myself. I keep killing somebody."

*"Killing was, seemed to me, the thing you were supposed to do that was part of life. Driving a car was part of life. Eating food was part of life. To me, it seemed like killing was part of life until I did it." — **Stephani***

JOHN STRAFFEN

Date of birth: February 26, 1930

Aliases/Nicknames: Nil

Characteristics: Hatred and resentment toward the police, child Killer

Number of victims: 3

Date of murders: 1951 - 1952

Date of arrest: August 9, 1951

Victim profile: Brenda Goddard, 6; Cicely Batstone, 9; Linda Bowyer, 5

Method of murder: Strangulation

Location: Somerset, Berkshire, England, United Kingdom

Status: Sentenced to death on July 25, 1952. Home Secretary Sir David Maxwell-Fyfe commuted the sentence to life imprisonment because Straffen was "feeble-minded" on August 29, 1952. Died in prison on November 20, 2007.

Background

Straffen came into contact with law enforcement at a young age. His first time in court was in June of 1939, for stealing a purse. He received two years' probation. His probation officer noticed Straffen didn't understand the difference between right or wrong, let alone understand what probation meant. The probation officer took Straffen to see a psychiatrist who certified him as a "mental defective" under the Mental Deficiency Act 1927.

In 1940, his IQ measured as fifty-eight, and his mental age was deemed around six. From then onwards, he was sent to a school for mentally defective children. When he was sixteen, his mental capacity was measured again. This time, his IQ recorded as sixty-four and his mental age was nine years and six months.

In early 1947, Straffen began entering unoccupied homes and stealing small items. He didn't take the items home or give them to anyone else, he would just hide them somewhere. He wasn't stealing for financial gain, he just liked taking things.

Police responded to a report on July 27, 1947, by a thirteen-year-old girl who said a boy named John had assaulted her, put his hand over her mouth, and said, "What would you do if I killed you? I have done it before." This wasn't connected to Straffen until much later.

Weeks after that incident, Straffen strangled chickens belonging to the father of a girl he had argued with. Once arrested, Straffen began confessing to other crimes and incidents he had been involved with, none of which had been connected to him. He was remanded and examined by a medical officer, who determined he was mentally retarded. He was subsequently committed to Hortham Colony in Bristol under the Mental Deficiency Act.

Murders

Straffen went to the cinema unescorted on July 15, 1951, and came across Brenda Goddard, five. He noticed her picking flowers and offered to show her a place that was better. He lifted her up over a fence, and she fell and struck her head on a stone, which rendered her unconscious. Straffen strangled her and left her body out in the open. Then he went back to the cinema and watched a film. Police hadn't considered Straffen to be violent, but they did question him about the murder.

On August 8, he went to the cinema again and met Cicely Batstone, nine. He took her to another cinema where they watched a film, and then they took a bus ride to a meadow on the outskirts of Bath. He strangled her to death. Several witnesses had seen him with the girl, and he was arrested on August 9.

Trial

When he was questioned, he admitted to killing Batstone and Goddard, saying, "The other girl, I did her the same." A two-day hearing was held, and he was committed for trial for the murder of Goddard.

His trial began on October 17, 1951. The only witness to speak was the medical officer at Horfield Prison, who stated Straffen was unfit to plead. The jury agreed, and he was taken to Broadmoor Institution.

Outcome

On April 29, 1952, Straffen—along with another patient and an attendant—went to clean some outbuildings near the external wall. Beside the wall was a low shed. Straffen asked if he could shake his duster and went into the yard. He climbed up onto the shed's roof and over the wall. Within twenty minutes, he approached Doris Spencer, who was in her drive, and asked for some water, which she gave him. Then he left.

He came across Linda Bowyer, five, who was riding her bicycle around the village, and within thirty minutes, he had killed her. Straffen went to another house for a cup of tea, and the woman agreed to take him to a bus stop. They saw police near the bus stop, and Straffen jumped out of the car and ran. He was captured within a few minutes.

On May 1, he was charged with the murder. The trial began on July 21, and he pled not guilty. His sanity was once again in question, but this time he was deemed to be sane. He was subsequently found guilty, and he was sentenced to death. On August 29, it was announced that the Home Secretary had recommended he be reprieved.

Straffen died at Frankland Prison in County Durham on November 19, 2007 at the age of seventy-seven.

Trivia

Until his death, Straffen had been incarcerated for fifty-five years—a record in Britain. Following Straffen's death, Ian Brady became the longest-serving prisoner until his own death.

After his arrest and the killing of Cicely Bartstone, Straffen said, "Is it about the little girl I took to the pictures last night? When I left her, she was dead under the hedge."

He also confessed to Brenda's murder, saying: "She never screamed when I squeezed her neck, so I bashed her against a tree. I didn't feel sorry."

WILLIAM SUFF

Date of birth: August 20, 1950

Aliases/Nicknames: The Riverside Prostitute Killer, The Lake Elsinore Killer

Characteristics: Rape, mutilation

Number of victims: 13 - 20 +

Date of murders: 1974, 1986 - 1991

Date of arrest: January 9, 1992

Victim profile: Janet Suff, his 2-month-old daughter; Michelle Yvette Gutierrez, 23; Charlotte Jean Palmer, 24; Linda Ann Ortega, 37; Martha Bess Young, 27; Linda Mae Ruiz, 37; Kimberely Lyttle; Judy Lynn Angel, 36; Christina Tina Leal, 23; Daria Jane Ferguson, 27; Carol Lynn Miller, 35; Cheryl Coker, 33; Susan Melissa Sternfeld, 27; Kathleen Leslie Milne, 42; Cherie Michelle Payseur, 24; Sherry Ann Latham, 37; Kelly Marie Hammond, 23; Catherine McDonald, 30; Delliah Zamora Wallace, 35; Eleanore Ojeda Casares, 39

Method of murder: Beating, strangulation, stabbing with knife

Location: Texas, California, USA

Status: Sentenced to 70 years in prison in 1974. Paroled in March of 1984. Sentenced to death on August 17, 1995.

Background

Suff was described by neighbors as someone who was always doing things to help people and a nerd. He worked as a government stock clerk and had an affinity for impersonating police officers. He also liked to drive flashy cars, write books, and do work in the community.

What his neighbors didn't know was that during the 1970s, he had been imprisoned for a while for beating his two-month-old child to death.

Murders

Between June 28, 1989, and December 23, 1991, Suff raped, tortured, stabbed, strangled, and occasionally mutilated a dozen or more sex workers.

Michelle Yvette Gutierrez, twenty-three

Found: October 30, 1986

The body of Michelle Yvette Gutierrez, of Corpus Christi, Texas, showed injuries to her genitals and anus, and there were indications she had been strangled.

Charlotte Jean Palmer, twenty-four

Found: December 11, 1986

The body of Charlotte Jean Palmer was found close to Matthews Road and Highway 74 in Romoland. Because her body had decomposed so quickly, an autopsy couldn't show the cause of death.

Linda Ann Ortega, thirty-seven

Found: Early 1987

Suff's third victim was Linda Ann Ortega. Her naked body was found tortured and stabbed off a dirt road near Franklin Street and Ridge Road. There were high levels of cocaine and alcohol in her blood, and there was evidence she had died three days before she was found.

Martha Bess Young, twenty-seven

Found: May 2, 1987

Martha Bess Young was found spread-eagled and nude in a gully adjacent to Franklin Street. She was identified by dental records. She had been deceased for at least three weeks and had been strangled. She had a high level of amphetamines in her blood.

Linda Mae Ruiz, thirty-seven

Found: January 17, 1989

The body of Linda Mae Ruiz was discovered on the beach of Lake Elsinore about one hundred twenty feet from the water. There were no physical signs to suggest she had struggled, and she had been strangled. Her head had been forcefully pushed into the sand, and she had been smothered. She had a high level of alcohol in her blood.

Kimberely Lyttle

Found: June 28, 1989

Her body was located in Cottonwood Canyon south of Canyon Lake, and the autopsy showed she had been strangled.

Judy Lynn Angel, thirty-six

Found: November 11, 1989

Her naked and beaten body was found northwest of Lake Elsinore. A pathologist was able to conclude, by the deep cuts on her arms and hands, that she had fought against her killer.

Christina Tina Leal, twenty-three

Found: December 13, 1989

Christina Tina Leal was found off Goetz Road in Quail Valley. The autopsy showed signs that she was sexually assaulted before being strangled, and there was a stab wound to her heart.

Daria Jane Ferguson

Found: January 18, 1990

The nude body of Daria Jane was found at Grape Street.

Carol Lynn Miller, thirty-five

Found: February 8, 1990

Her naked body was discovered by workers in an orchard, at Mt. Vernon Avenue and Pigeon Pass Road in Highgrove. She had been asphyxiated and stabbed stabbed multiple times in the chest, leading to her death.

Cheryl Coker, thirty-three

Found: November 6, 1990

Police determined that Cheryl Coker suffered the most gruesome death of all. Her remains were discovered near a dumpster enclosure northeast Riverside, adjacent to where Miller's body was found. She was naked and had been suffocated. Her right breast had been cut off and was lying next to her body.

Susan Melissa Sternfeld, twenty-seven

Found: December 21, 1990

Behind an industrial complex on Iowa Avenue, the nude body of Susan Melissa Sternfeld was found in a dumpster. She had been strangled.

Kathleen Leslie Milne, forty-two

Found: January 19, 1991

The pathologist determined Kathleen Leslie Milne "was rendered unconscious by several blows to the head and then strangled." Her body was dumped amid discarded beer cans and old tires.

Cherie Michelle Payseur, twenty-four

Found: April 27, 1991

Her nude body was found at the rear of the Concourse Bowling Center on Arlington Avenue in Riverside. A toilet plunger had been inserted in her vagina.

Sherry Ann Latham, thirty-seven

Found: July 1991

Her body was found outstretched in a patch of grass; she had been strangled.

Kelly Marie Hammond, twenty-three

Found: August 1991

Her naked body was found by a truck driver near the intersection of Sampson Avenue and Delilah Street, south of Highway 91. Her corpse was still warm.

Catherine McDonald, thirty

Found: September 13, 1991

Her body was discovered off a dirt road near a barren construction site in the Tuscany Hills section of Lake Elsinore.

Delliah Zamora Wallace, thirty-five

Found: October 30, 1991

Her nude body was found in undergrowth on the dirt shoulder of an intersection in Mira Loma, northwest of Riverside.

Eleanore Ojeda Casares, thirty-nine

Found: December 23, 1991

Her nude body was found by an orange grove worker close to the intersection of Jefferson Street and Victoria Avenue. The Riverside police station was only a half-mile away.

Trial

On January 9, 1992, Suff was arrested following a routine traffic stop after an officer found a bloodstained knife and objects believed to be related to the killings in his vehicle.

Suff was found guilty of twelve murders and one attempted murder on July 19, 1995. Police suspected he was responsible for twenty-two murders but couldn't get enough evidence to prove it. On August 17, he was sentenced to death.

Outcome

Suff is currently on death row at San Quentin State Prison. His appeal in 2014 was rejected, and his death penalty was upheld.

Trivia

During the investigation, the task force had some furniture delivered by none other than Suff, who was working as a furniture delivery man at the time.

It was alleged he once used the breast of one of his victims in a chili contest and won.

Book and TV

The Riverside Killer, by Christine Keers and Dennis St Pierre, was published in 1996.

The book *Cat and Mouse - Mind Games with a Serial Killer* was written by Brian Alan Lane after Suff told him his story. Included in the book are poems and short stories Suff had written, along with photos of some of his victims.

Suff is featured in an episode of program *Real Detective*. The program includes interviews with the lead detective from the case; it was broadcast on March 9, 2017.

IGOR SUPRUNYUCK AND VIKTOR SAYENKO

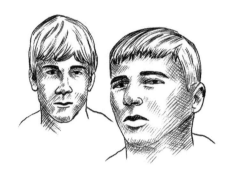

Igor Suprunyuck

Date of birth: April 20, 1988

Aliases/Nicknames: The Dnepropetrovsk Maniac

Characteristics: The killers had a plan to get rich from the murder videos that they recorded, torture, mutilation

Number of victims: 21

Date of murders: June 25, 2007 - July 16, 2007

Date of arrest: July 23, 2007

Victim profile: Ekaterina Ilchenko, 33; Roman Tatarevich; Evgeniya Grischenko; Nikolai Serchuk; Egor Nechvoloda; Elena Shram, 28; Valentina Hanzha; Andrei Sidyuck, 14; Sergei Yatzenko, 48; Natalia Mamarchuk, 45; others unnamed

Method of murder: Hitting with hammers and steel construction bars, stabbing with knife

Location: Dnepropetrovsk, Ukraine

Status: Sentenced to life in prison on February 11, 2009.

Viktor Sayenko

Date of birth: March 1, 1988

Aliases/Nicknames: The Dnepropetrovsk Maniac

Characteristics: The killers had a plan to get rich from the murder videos that they recorded, torture, mutilation

Number of victims: 18

Date of murders: June 25, 2007 - July 16, 2007

Date of arrest: July 23, 2007

Victim profile: Ekaterina Ilchenko, 33; Roman Tatarevich; Evgeniya Grischenko; Nikolai Serchuk; Egor Nechvoloda; Elena Shram, 28; Valentina Hanzha; Andrei Sidyuck, 14; Sergei Yatzenko, 48; Natalia Mamarchuk, 45; others unnamed

Method of murder: Hitting with hammers and steel construction bars, stabbing with a knife

Location: Dnepropetrovsk, Ukraine

Status: Sentenced to life in prison on February 11, 2009.

Background

Suprunyuck, Sayenko, and their friend Hanzha all went to school together and came from influential and wealthy families. All three of them had some sort of phobia, including a fear of heights and, in the case of Hanzha, a fear of blood. Suprunyuck suggested to Hanzha that he could overcome his fear of blood by killing stray dogs. They proceeded to do so, taking photos of themselves next to the dead animals.

At the age of seventeen, Suprunyuck beat up a boy and stole his bicycle, selling it to Sayenko. They were both arrested, but due to their age, they didn't go to jail. When they finished school, Hanzha drifted from job to job, Sayenko went to a metallurgy institute part-time, and Suprunyuck started driving his car as an unlicensed taxi. They would rob his passengers, but eventually, the thrill of stealing wore off. At one point, Sayenko and Suprunyuck decided to start killing people just for the excitement of it.

Murders

Late on June 25, 2007, the first two murders took place. The first victim that night was Ekaterina Ilchenko, who was walking home from a friend's house. As she walked past Suprunyuck, he turned around and struck her in the side of the head with a hammer. An hour later, they attacked Roman Tatarevich as he lay asleep on a bench. Using blunt objects, they smashed his head and face until he was unrecognizable.

Two more victims were killed by Suprunyuck and Sayenko on July 1. Evgeniya Grischenko and Nikolai Serchuk were found dead in Novomoskovsk. Five nights later, on July 6, three people were murdered in Dnipropetrovsk. One of these victims was Egor Nechvoloda, a former army recruit, who was killed while walking home from a nightclub. Yelena Shram, a night guard, was killed just around the corner, and then Valentina Hanzha was killed.

On July 7, two fourteen-year-old boys were attacked while they were fishing. Andrei Sidyuk was killed, but Vadim Lyakhov managed to escape and hid in the woods. The next victim was Sergei Yatzenko, killed on July 12. Then, two days later, Natalia Mamarchuk was knocked off her scooter and beaten to death with either a pipe or a hammer.

A further twelve people were killed, sometimes more than one in a single day. Between July 14 and 16, two victims were killed each day. The majority of the victims were vulnerable people, such as the elderly, children, vagrants, or those who had been drinking alcohol. Some of the victims had their eyes gouged out while they were still alive; they even cut a fetus from a woman's womb.

Until the July 7 attack on the two boys, there had been no official link between the murders. But the survivor of that attack, who was originally put under arrest for killing his friend, was eventually listened to by police. He was able to help create sketches of the men who had attacked him and his friend.

On July 23, 2007, Suprunyuck tried to sell a victim's mobile phone to a pawn shop, and law enforcement tracked the location of the shop. Both Suprunyuck and Sayenko were arrested at the shop. They arrested Hanzha at his home; Hanzha had reportedly flushed a number of stolen items down the toilet.

Trial

Suprunyuck was charged with twenty-one counts of capital murder, eight armed robberies, and one count of animal cruelty, while Sayenko was charged with eighteen murders, five robberies, and one of animal cruelty. Hanzha was charged with two counts of armed robbery.

The three men confessed to their crimes quickly, though Suprunyuck later withdrew his confession. In June 2008, their trial began. Both Hanzha and Sayenko pled guilty, but Suprunyuck pled not guilty, attempting to plead insanity, a bid which failed.

On February 11, 2009, Sayenko and Suprunyuck were found guilty, and both were sentenced to life imprisonment. Both also were given fifteen-year sentences for the robbery counts. Hanzha was found guilty of robbery and received a sentence of nine years. Hanzha later said, "If I had known the atrocities that they were capable of committing, I would have not gone near them at gunpoint."

Outcome

It took two days to read out the court's verdict, as it was several hundred pages long. The parents of both Suprunyuck and Sayenko were convinced that their sons were innocent and set about trying to persuade the authorities. Despite all of the photographic and video evidence showing them committing a number of atrocities, the perpetrators' parents claimed their sons had been tortured by the authorities and that they were scapegoats.

An appeal was lodged on August 18, 2009. On November 24, the life sentences were upheld. Hanzha didn't appeal his sentence.

Trivia

Chilean documentary

Chilean television channel MEGA broadcast a documentary on August 2, 2010, about the murders. The name of the documentary was *Los maníacos del Martillo*, which in English translates to *The Hammer Maniacs*. It was part of a series called *Aquí en Vivo*, which is *Here, Live*, and a number of people involved in the case were interviewed by journalist Michele Canale. The documentary ran for an hour and twenty-five minutes.

Alleged copycat case in Irkutsk

Two young men from Russia, Nikita Lytkin and Artyom Anoufriev, later known as the "Academy Maniacs," were arrested on April 5, 2011, for attacks and several murders in Akademgorodok in Irkutsk. Using a knife and a hammer, they had begun killing in December of 2010. A video recording was discovered on Lytkin's uncle's phone, which showed them mutilating a woman's body with a knife. The uncle had become suspicious of his nephew and his friend and somehow obtained the horrific video. Lytkin and Anoufriev later said they had been influenced by the Dnepropetrovsk maniacs after reading about the case online. Both were examined by a psychiatrist and deemed sane. They claimed they had targeted weak people because they were easy victims. Lytkin was sentenced to twenty-four years in prison, and Anoufriev received a life sentence.

Quote from the video:

Suprunyuck: "What, he's still alive?"

Sayenko: "He's still moving his arms after I ripped up his intestines."
— Video of Sergei Yatzenko murder

AHMAD SURADJI

Date of birth: January 10, 1949

Aliases/Nicknames: Nasib Kelewang, Datuk Maringgi

Characteristics: Traditional sorcerer, the bodies were buried around his house in an attempt to increase his magical powers

Number of victims: 42

Date of murders: 1986 - 1997

Date of arrest: May 2, 1997

Victim profile: Women ranging in ages from 11 to 30 years (women who came to him to ask for supernatural help in making themselves richer or more attractive)

Method of murder: Ligature strangulation

Location: Medan, Indonesia

Status: Executed by firing squad on July 10, 2008.

Background

Suradji was employed as a cattle breeder in Indonesia when his father appeared to him in a dream in 1986. His father commanded him to increase his occult powers; to do so, he had to drink the saliva of seventy dead young women. By doing this, he would become a mystic healer. Suradji thought it would take too long to come across seventy dead women, so he decided to kill them himself.

Murders

Because many local women came to his home to buy love charms and other items, it wasn't hard for Suradji to find his victims. His method was first to charge the victim a fee, ranging from two hundred to four hundred dollars, then he would lead them to a sugar plantation nearby. Digging a hole, he would bury the woman up to her waist. Once she was unable to move, he would use an electrical cord to strangle her and then drink the saliva. Then he would remove the clothing from the body and bury it with the head aimed toward his home. This was to supposedly channel the mystical powers from the spirit.

If there weren't enough customers coming to his home, he would hire prostitutes and kill them.

Trial

On April 28, 1997, three bodies were found on the plantation, and Suradji was arrested and brought in for questioning. He confessed to killing sixteen women over a five-year period, but a search of his home proved otherwise. Police found items belonging to twenty-five missing women. Eventually, he confessed to killing forty-two women over eleven years. In addition to Suradji, the police also arrested his three wives. Two of the wives were released, but one was kept in custody after she confessed to assisting her husband with the murders.

In total, police found forty bodies on the plantation. Around eighty families had reported females missing, and the victims ranged in age from twelve to thirty years. Suradji and his wife were charged with forty-two counts of murder and went on trial on December 21, 1997.

Outcome

Suradji was convicted on April 27, 1998, and sentenced to death by firing squad. His wife was sentenced to life in prison.

Suradji was executed on July 10, 2008.

Trivia

Suradji stated the following to the police:

"My father did not specifically advise me to kill people. So I was thinking, it would take ages if I have to wait to get seventy women. I was trying to get to it as fast as possible, I took my own initiative to kill."

JOSEPH TABORSKY

Date of birth: March 23, 1924

Aliases/Nicknames: Mad Dog

Characteristics: Robbery

Number of victims: 7

Date of murders: 1951, 1956 - 1957

Date of arrest: February 23, 1957

Victim profile: Louis Wolfson; Edward Kurpewski; Daniel Janowski; Samuel Cohn; Bernard "Buster" Speyer; Ruth Speyer; John M. Rosenthal

Method of murder: Shooting

Location: Connecticut, USA

Status: Executed by electrocution in Connecticut on May 17, 1960.

Background

Taborsky had been a troubled teen, and by the time he was in his early twenties, he already had a long history with the police for crimes such as stealing and robbery. He decided to celebrate his twenty-fifth birthday, on March 23, 1950, by indulging in a night of crime with Albert, his younger brother. They went to a liquor store, robbed the owner, and shot him.

Albert turned himself in months later and made a full confession, telling them his brother had been involved in the murder of the store owner. Both brothers were convicted, with Albert receiving a life sentence and Taborsky the death penalty. Taborsky sat on death row for four years, until Albert ended up in an insane asylum. This lead to the state throwing out the case and Taborsky's sentence being revoked, and he was released. He told a reporter at the time," You can't beat the law. From now on, I'm not even going to get a parking ticket." This didn't last long.

Murders

Along with a new partner, Arthur Culombe, Taborsky embarked on a spree of violence in early December of 1956. They robbed businesses, murdering or violently assaulting the owners in many communities in Connecticut. Taborsky was given the nickname of Mad Dog by the media, due to the brutal nature of the killings. Nearly all of the murders were carried out with gunshots to the back of the head.

One surviving victim from a shoe store told police the man who shot him had asked for a pair of size twelve shoes. When this information was cross-referenced against ex-convicts, Taborsky became the prime suspect. Taborsky and Culombe were arrested, and Culombe confessed to being an accomplice almost immediately. The murders, he claimed, were purely the work of Taborsky.

Trial

In June of 1957, Taborsky was convicted. He was the only criminal in the history of Connecticut to be sentenced to death twice.

Outcome

Taborsky had his final meal on May 17, 1960. It consisted of a banana split, cherry soda, and some cigarettes. Then he was taken to the execution chamber, where he was executed by the electric chair.

Trivia

Taborsky was the last person to be executed in the "Old Sparky" electric chair in Connecticut.

Taborsky was the last person put to death in Connecticut until Michael Bruce Ross' execution in 2005.

He is the only convict to be sent to death row twice, for different crimes.

Taborsky donated his body to the Yale School of Medicine, and his ashes were later buried in the garden of Christ Church Cathedral.

SERHIY TKACH

Date of birth: September 12, 1952

Aliases/Nicknames: The Pologovsky Maniac

Characteristics: Necrophilia, former police criminal investigator

Number of victims: 29 - 100

Date of murders: 1980 - 2005

Date of arrest: August of 2005

Victim profile: Girls and young women aged between 8 and 18

Method of murder: Suffocation, Strangulation

Location: Crimea, Zaporozhye, Dnipropetrovsk and Kharkov regions, Ukraine

Status: Sentenced to life in prison on December 23, 2008.

Background

Tkach was born in the Soviet Union and served in the Soviet Army. He had told neighbors he was a veteran of the invasion of Afghanistan. Out of the military, he worked as a police criminal investigator. He had been recommended to attend the Ministry of Internal Affairs School, but he was caught falsifying evidence and was forced to resign. He then worked in a number of jobs before he moved to Ukraine in 2002. He then began working as a police criminal investigator in the Dnipropetrovsk region.

Murders

Young women and girls began disappearing in Kharkiv Oblast, Zaporizhia Oblast, Dnipropetrovsk, and Crimea, in 1984—the same areas Tkach was living and working in. The victims ranged in age between eight and eighteen. He would rape the victim first, and then suffocate them. Once they were dead, he would perform necrophiliac acts on the body. He used his police knowledge to mislead investigators.

Trial

Tkach attended the funeral of one of his victims in August of 2005. Children at the funeral claimed they had seen Tkach with the victim just before her murder. He was then arrested at his home and confessed to his crimes. He claimed he had killed over one hundred people. He also demanded the death penalty.

His trial lasted a year, and in 2008, he was sentenced to life imprisonment for the murder of thirty-seven victims.

Outcome

On November 4, 2018, Tkach died in prison; the cause of death was determined to be heart failure. Three days later, his body had not been claimed by relatives, so he was buried by staff at the prison.

Trivia

When police arrived at his door, he surrendered and said that he had been waiting for them all these years.

"He told us that he was a military officer and that he was in Afghanistan, he even showed us his wounds. Other neighbors say that he was a very smart man, very quiet. No one could have thought that he was the man police were looking for," said his former neighbor.

Tkach had four children and had been married three times. According to his friends and coworkers, he had never spoken badly about women, and he was not known to treat them badly either.

OTTIS TOOLE

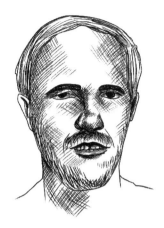

Date of birth: March 5, 1947

Aliases/Nicknames: The Jacksonville Cannibal

Characteristics: Rape, cannibalism, serial arsonist

Number of victims: 6 - 65

Date of murders: 1961 - 1983

Date of arrest: June 15, 1983

Victim profile: Ada Johnson, 19; George Sonnenberg, 65; Silvia Rogers, 19,

Method of murder: Stabbing with knife, shooting, setting fire

Location: Texas, Florida, USA

Status: Sentenced to death in Florida, 1984. Commuted to life imprisonment. Died in prison on September 15, 1996.

Background

According to Toole, his alcoholic father abandoned him, and his mother used to call him Susan and dress him in girl's clothing. He claimed he was sexually abused by many relatives and acquaintances as a young child, including a neighbor and his older sister. His grandmother was allegedly a Satanist, called him "Devil's Child," and taught him about self-mutilation, rituals, and robbing graves.

Toole regularly ran away from home. From a young age, he realized he was sexually aroused by fire, subsequently becoming a serial arsonist. His IQ was measured at seventy-five, meaning he was mildly retarded.

He claimed that at the age of five, he was forced to have sex with a friend of his father, and at the age of twelve, he was involved in a sexual relationship with a boy. Toole said he was a prostitute as a teen, and claimed he had committed his first murder when he was just fourteen years old. Toole's first arrest, for loitering, occurred when he was seventeen.

Toole became the prime suspect in the murder of Patricia Webb in 1974 in Nebraska. Just after the murder, he moved to Boulder, Colorado, and a month later, was the prime suspect in the murder of Ellen Holman, killed on October 14, 1974. Toole then decided to go back to Jacksonville.

Toole married an older woman on January 14, 1976, later stating that he married her to hide the fact he was gay. The marriage lasted only three days, after she discovered the truth about his sexuality.

In 1976, Toole met Henry Lee Lucas in a soup kitchen, and they became lovers. They would later become accomplices in numerous homicides around the country.

Murders

On January 4, 1982, George Sonnenberg was barricaded in a boarding house by Toole in Jacksonville. Toole set the house on fire and Sonnenberg was so badly injured, he died a week later. Toole was arrested in April of 1983 for another arson and was sentenced to twenty years in prison. While he was in custody, he confessed to the murder of Sonnenberg. He claimed they had been in a sexual relationship and he had set the fire after an argument.

Lucas was arrested two months later, in June, for firearm possession. Lucas began talking about the murders the two of them had allegedly committed, and before long, Toole started to back up the claims.

Murders for which Toole claimed responsibility, though he was cleared of (or never convicted of) almost all of them:

circa 1961, unspecified location:
Ran an unnamed traveling salesman over with a vehicle and killed him.
Strangled an unidentified woman to death.

September 24, 1968, Savannah, Georgia:
Strangled an unidentified woman and then burned her body.

April 18, 1974, Lincoln, Nebraska:
Shot and killed Patricia Webb, twenty-four.

September 19, 1974, Colorado Springs, Colorado:
Stabbed Yun Lee, slashed her throat, and set her on fire, but she survived.
Raped Sun Ok Cousin, stabbed her, shot her, and then set her on fire.

October 10, 1974, Pueblo County, Colorado:
Shot Ellen Holman, thirty-one, with a .38 three times in the head.

July 31, 1976, Milwaukee, Wisconsin:
Robbed Alice Daubon, seventy, and then used a toilet plunger to sexually assault her. Strangled her to death with a wire.

August 16, 1976, Pueblo, Colorado:
Sexually assaulted Sharon Marie Copp, thirty-five, tortured her, and beat her to death. Her body was then dismembered.

February 12, 1977, Houston, Texas:
Used a frying pan and his fists to beat Bernice Price Erdman, seventy-six, to death.

March 1, 1977, Waldo, Florida:
Shot Julie Cohen.

November 30, 1977, Oklahoma City, Oklahoma:
Shot Tina Williams, seventeen, with a .38 twice in the head.

December 19, 1977, Houston, Texas:
Used a shotgun to shoot John Carter Swint, sixty-six, in the back of the head.

January 18, 1979, Houston, Texas:
Alfredo Trevizo was stabbed multiple times in the stomach, thigh, and chest.

February 6, 1980, Pensacola, Florida:
David Schallart, nineteen, was shot in the head five times.

July 27, 1981, Hollywood, Florida:
Adam Walsh, six, was asphyxiated, and then a machete was used to decapitate him. The same machete was allegedly used to slash Joana Holter, forty-six, to death.

January 12, 1982, Jacksonville, Florida:
George Sonnenberg, sixty-five, was trapped in a house that was then set on fire.

February of 1983, Fort Walton Beach, Florida:
Ada Johnson, nineteen, was shot in the head.

February of 1983, Tallahassee, Florida:
Silvia Rogers, nineteen, was strangled to death.

Trial

While on trial for the murder of Sonnenberg, Toole claimed he hadn't lit the fire and had only signed the confession so he would be extradited back to Jacksonville. On April 28, 1984, he was found guilty of first-degree murder and was sentenced to death. Later in the year, he was found guilty of another murder and was given another death sentence. He appealed both death sentences and was successful, with his sentences commuted to life in prison.

While incarcerated, he pled guilty to four more murders in 1991. He was given four more life sentences.

Outcome

Toole died in prison on September 15, 1996, from cirrhosis of the liver. Nobody claimed his body, so he was buried in the Florida State Prison Cemetery.

Trivia

Conversation with Lucas, taped by Texas Rangers in November of 1983:

TOOLE: Remember that one time I said I wanted me some ribs? Did that make me a cannibal?

LUCAS: You wasn't a cannibal. It's the force of the devil, something forced on us that we can't change. There's no reason denying what we become. We know what we are.

TOOLE: Remember how I liked to pour some blood out of them?

LUCAS: Ottis, you and I have become something people look on as an animal. There's no way of changing what we done, but we can stop it and not allow other people to become what we have. And the only way to do that is by honesty.

In popular culture

In *Henry: Portrait of a Serial Killer*, Tom Towles portrayed a character that was based on Toole.

Toole and the murder of Adam Walsh are mentioned in "Execution," an episode of the third season of *Law & Order: Special Victims Unit*.

JANE TOPPAN

Date of birth: August 17, 1854

Aliases/Nicknames: Honora Kelley

Characteristics: Poisoner

Number of victims: 31 +

Date of murders: 1887 - 1901

Date of arrest: October 29, 1901

Victim profile: Israel Dunham, 83; Lovely Dunham, 87; Elizabeth Brigham, 70; Mary McNear, 70; Florence Calkins, 45; William Ingraham, 70; Sarah (Myra) Connors, 48; Mattie Davis, 62; Genevieve Gordon (Annie); Alden Davis, 64; Mary (Minnie) Gibbs, 40; Edna Bannister, 77

Method of murder: Morphine and atropine poisoning

Location: Middlesex County, Suffolk County, Massachusetts, USA

Status: Found not guilty by reason of insanity on June 23, 1902, and committed for life in the Taunton Insane Hospital. Died on August 17, 1938.

Background

Toppan, born Honora Kelley, lost her mother to tuberculosis when she was very young. Her abusive alcoholic father took Toppan and her sister to the Boston Female Asylum, an orphanage, in 1863. They never saw their father again.

Two years later, Toppan was sent to work in the home of Mrs. Ann C. Toppan as an indentured servant, a labor system where people worked for someone for a fixed term to earn their passage to the New World. Although the family never adopted her formally, she took on the Toppan surname. She got along very well with their daughter, Elizabeth.

Toppan started training as a nurse in 1885, at Cambridge Hospital, where she was described as brilliant, bright, and friendly. Her nickname was "Jolly Jane." During her residency at the hospital, she experimented with atropine and morphine on her patients to see what it would do to their nervous system.

Murders

Toppan shifted to Massachusetts General Hospital in 1889 but was fired a year later. She then went back to Cambridge Hospital. She was fired there as well—for recklessly administering opiates to her patients. Her next career step was as a private nurse.

In 1895, she began poisoning people in earnest, starting with Israel Dunham (her landlord) and his wife. She murdered Elizabeth Toppan in 1899 with strychnine. In 1901, she went to live with Alden Davis, an elderly man, and his family to take care of him after his wife Mattie had died. (Toppan had actually murdered Mattie was well.) Davis was murdered within weeks, along with his sister Genevieve, and his daughters Edna and Minnie.

Members of the Davis family ordered a toxicology test on Minnie, which found she had been poisoned. Police immediately suspected Toppan and began to surveil her. She was arrested on October 29, 1901, and charged with murder. By the following year, she had confessed to killing thirty-one people.

Trial

Under questioning, Toppan admitted she got a sexual thrill when her patients were near death, then brought back to life, and then near death again. She would lie in bed with them, holding them as they died. She felt immense satisfaction staring into their eyes as their life ebbed away.

At her trial, Toppan tried very hard to convince the jury that she was sane, but they didn't agree. She was declared insane and committed to a mental hospital for life on June 23.

Outcome

Toppan is often called an "angel of death," a killer who kills dependent patients she is taking care of. There were a variety of motivating factors, such as jealousy or personal gain. Toppan described it as a "paralysis of thought and reason," a very strong urge to poison and kill.

Trivia

The character of Jane Toppan in the film "American Nightmare" was inspired by Toppan. In the film, the character is a nurse who murders multiple characters by a variety of methods.

Toppan was the subject of one of six monologues in the play *Murderess* by Anne Bertram. She was portrayed by Laura Wiebers in the segment "The Truth About Miss Toppan," directed by Mishia Burns Edwards. Minneapolis *Star Tribune* theater critic William Randall Beard called the Toppan segment "a chilling portrait of a sociopath nurse."

Toppan was featured in an episode of program *Deadly Women*.

Toppan is widely believed to have been the inspiration for "the Incomparable Bessie Denker," a character in William March's novel *The Bad Seed*, which later became a film. Like Toppan, Denker was a serial poisoner who began killing at a young age.

Her ambition was "to have killed more people — helpless people — than any other man or woman who ever lived..."

CHESTER TURNER

Date of birth: November 5, 1966

Aliases/Nicknames: Nil

Characteristics: Rape

Number of victims: 14 +

Date of murders: 1987 - 1998

Date of arrest: September 2003

Victim profile: Paula Vance, 24; Brenda Bries, 39; Diane Johnson, 21; Annette Ernest, 26; Anita Fishman, 31; Regina Washington, 27; Andrea Tripplett, 29; Desarae Jones, 29; Natalie Price, 31; Mildred Beasley, 45;Tammie Christmas; Deborah Williams, 32; Mary Edwards, 42; Elandra Bunn, 33; Cynthia Annette Johnson, 30

Method of murder: Strangulation

Location: Los Angeles, California, USA

Status: Sentenced to death on July 10, 2007.

Background

Turner's parents separated when he was five years old, and he moved to Los Angeles with his mother. After he left high school, he began working as a delivery person. When his mother moved to Utah, he drifted around different missions and homeless shelters in Los Angeles. Between 1995 and 2002, he went to jail seven times for a variety of crimes, including assault.

Murders

Nine of the murders occurred in a four-block-wide corridor that ran on either side of Figueroa Street between Gage Avenue and 108th Street.

Diane Johnson, twenty-one, was found partially nude and strangled in March of 1987 in a roadway construction area west of the Harbor Freeway.

Annette Ernest, twenty-six, was friends with Jerri Johnson Triplett, the mother of Turner's fourth victim Andrea Triplett. Her body was found lying on a shoulder of a road in October of 1987, partially nude and strangled.

Anita Fishman, thirty-one, was strangled and left partially nude outside a garage in an alley off Figueroa Street in January of 1989.

Regina Washington, twenty-seven, was found inside a garage off Figueroa Street, partially nude and strangled to death, in September of 1989. At the time of her murder, she was six months pregnant. The death of the fetus was ruled a homicide after it was attributed to the strangulation of the mother.

Andrea Tripplett, twenty-nine, was strangled. Her partially naked body was discovered behind an empty building on Figueroa Street in April of 1993. She was pregnant, but at the time California law did not consider a five-and-half--month-old fetus viable, so it wasn't considered a homicidal death.

Desarae Jones, twenty-nine, was found strangled to death in a backyard in May of 1993.

Natalie Price, thirty-one, was found partially nude and strangled next to a vacant residence in February of 1995.

Mildred Beasley, forty-five, was found partially nude and strangled; she was left amongst the bushes alongside the 110 Freeway in November of 1996.

The last two murders occurred outside of this area:

Paula Vance, twenty-four, was found in the business premises of Olympia Tool, in Azusa in February of 1998. The murder of Vance had been witnessed by someone at a trailer park next door.

Brenda Bries, thirty-nine, was found strangled to death in a portable toilet near Little Tokyo in April of 1998. Her body was discovered just fifty yards away from Turner's hotel.

Turner was convicted of sexually assaulting a woman in March of 2002 and received an eight-year sentence. He had to provide a DNA sample as a result, and in September 2003, he was matched to DNA found on the bodies of Vance and Beasley. In total, nine murders were matched to him through DNA.

Trial

In 2007, Turner was found guilty of ten murders of women plus one count for the murder of the unborn fetus. He was sentenced to death.

On June 19, 2014, he was found guilty of four more murders: Cynthia Annette Johnson, Elandra Bunn, Mary Edwards, and Deborah Williams. He received another death sentence.

Outcome

While investigating these murders, detectives discovered that David Allen Jones had been wrongfully convicted of three murders. Jones had been questioned with an attorney present and had told police he had used drugs with the victims in the same areas their bodies were discovered. After eleven years in prison, he was exonerated. He was released in March of 2004 and received $720,000 in compensation.

Trivia

Turner once worked as a cook and deliveryman for Domino's Pizza.

Turner's attorney, Jon Roberts, said Turner was prepared to hear the verdict. Roberts said, "Turner acted in a way that suggested he wanted to be caught, leaving his DNA on victims or at crime scenes and leaving alive his last rape victim, a woman who knew him." He further said that Turner had followed her when she reported his attack to the police.

"For me, that was sufficient evidence that he was trying to seek redemption in any way that he could. I don't know how you do that when you're a serial killer other than by getting yourself stopped," Roberts said. "I think he's definitely on the path to redemption, and I can only pray and hope that he finds it one day."

JACK UNTERWEGER

Date of birth: August 16, 1951

Aliases/Nicknames: Vienna Woods Killer

Characteristics: Rape, prostitutes

Number of victims: 12 +

Date of murders: 1976, 1990 - 1992

Date of arrest: February 27, 1992

Victim profile: Margaret Schäfer, 18; Blanka Bockova; Brunhilde Masser, 39; Heidi Hammerer, 31; Elfriede Schrempf, 35; Silvia Zagler, 23; Sabine Moitzl, 25; Karin Eroglu, 25; Regina Prem, 32; Shannon Exley, 35; Irene Rodriguez, 33; Peggy Booth, 26

Method of murder: Strangulation

Location: Austria, California, USA, Czechoslovakia

Status: Sentenced on June 29, 1994, to life in prison without the possibility of parole. Hung himself in his cell the night of his sentencing.

Background

Unterweger grew up with his alcoholic grandfather and never knew who his father was. He committed crimes from a young age; his first arrest at sixteen was for a violent assault toward a prostitute. Later, when he was incarcerated for his first murder, he became a writer, producing a novel, an autobiography, and poems. This would eventually lead him to America, but not before he killed multiple women in Austria and Czechoslovakia.

Murders

On September 15, 1990, some people walking along the Vitava River in Czechoslovakia discovered the body of a young woman. Blanka Bockova was Unterweger's first victim. She was nude, lying on her back with her legs open. Her grey stockings were tied around her neck, and she was covered with leaves.

Weeks later, a prostitute from Graz, Brunhilde Masser, was reported as missing. Then in early December, prostitute Heidemarie Hammerer disappeared. On New Year's eve, her body was discovered in the woods outside of town. She was on her back and covered with leaves. It was clear she had been dressed and dragged along the ground. A piece of fabric from her slip was shoved inside her mouth. A pair of tights had been used to strangle her, and marks on her wrists suggested she had been tied up for a while.

The body of Masser was found a few days later in woods in Bregenz. The way in which she had been killed and left behind mirrored the previous murders. On March 7, 1991, prostitute Elfriede Schrempf disappeared. Her body was found on October 5, in the woods outside of Graz. She had been killed in the same manner as the others and covered in leaves. With the next murders, it became clear to police that they were dealing with a serial killer.

Within the space of a month, four prostitutes vanished from Vienna. They were Silviz Zagler, Regina Prem, Sabine Moitzl, and Karin Eroglu. The body of Moitzl was found on May 20, 1992, and then Ergolu's body was discovered. They had both been strangled and dumped in the woods outside of Vienna. Their clothing had been used to strangle and asphyxiate them.

Retired investigator August Schenner made the connection between these murders and ones he had seen in the 1970s. For those killings, Unterweger had been imprisoned. Schenner contacted Barbara Scholz, a prostitute, who told him she had helped Unterweger abduct Margaret Schaefer. She said they had taken her to the woods where they tied her up, and Unterweger assaulted her. When she refused sex, he bludgeoned her to death then strangled her, leaving her body nude and lying face up, covered with leaves.

Unterweger had been freed from prison on May 23, 1990. The following year, he was sent to Los Angeles by an Austrian magazine to write about crime there, including how prostitution was managed and how people saw prostitutes there versus in Austria. While he was in Los Angeles, three sex workers had been killed: Shannon Exley, Irene Rodriguez, and Peggy Booth. All had been sexually assaulted with tree branches, beaten, and strangled with their own clothing.

Unterweger, the prime suspect in Austria, was tracked down and arrested by U.S. Marshals. When his apartment in Los Angeles was searched, a number of incriminating items were found that linked him to the prostitutes who had been murdered in that city.

At first, Unterweger wanted to be tried in California because there were only three victims there. Once he realized he could be executed, however, he agreed to be extradited to Austria. This occurred on May 28, 1992.

Trial

Unterweger went on trial in Graz, Austria, in June of 1994. He was tried for all murders, including those that had occurred in Los Angeles. He tried to portray to the jury that a man like him, who had fame and money, was unlikely to destroy his "privileged" life by killing women.

But there was plenty of physical evidence against him, such as lab reports on the ligature knots, hair found in his car belonging to Bockova, and fibers from his scarf on Massar's body. At the end of the trial, he was found guilty of nine counts of murder and sentenced to life in prison.

Outcome

Unterweger decided not to serve out his sentence. On the same night he was sentenced, he hung himself while the guards weren't looking.

Trivia

Due to an Austrian law technicality, Unterweger's death before his sentencing began meant that he had to be considered innocent even though there had been a verdict of guilty. Because of this, a review of the law involved Unterweger's case.

DARREN DEON VANN

Date of birth: March 21, 1971

Aliases/Nicknames: Nil

Characteristics: Serial rapist

Number of victims: 7

Date of murders: July 2013 - October 2014

Date of arrest: October 18, 2014

Victim profile: Anith Jones, 35; Teaira Batey, 28; Kristine Williams, 36; Afrikka Hardy, 19; Tracy Martin, 41; Sonya Billingsley, 53; Tanya Gatlin, 27

Method of murder: Strangulation

Location: Gary, Hammond, Indiana, USA

Status: sentenced to seven concurrent life sentences without parole.

Background

Vann enlisted in the U.S. Marine Corps in 1991, but was discharged in 1993—and not in an "honorable" way. Though little information is available, it may have had to do with his behavior. At one point, he spent ninety days in jail for threatening to kill his girlfriend.

Vann had been married to a woman thirty years older than him for sixteen years, until she filed for divorce in August of 2009. This coincided with a conviction he received on September 28, 2009, for sexual assault. He was given a five-year sentence and was released from prison on July 5, 2013.

Murders

Thomas Hargrove, a reporter, used an algorithm in August of 2010 to analyze crime data in Gary, Indiana, which suggested there was a serial killer operating in the area. He took the information to police and urged them to look into fifteen suspicious deaths. The police denied there was such a killer.

There are seven victims Vann is suspected of killing:

Tanya Gatlin

Tanya Gatlin, twenty-seven, had been missing since January of 2014. Her body was discovered in an empty house, along with the body of victim Sonya Billingsley, on October 19, at 413 East 43rd Avenue in Gary.

Teaira Batey

Teaira Batey, twenty-eight, left to meet a friend on January 13, 2014, and never returned. Her body was discovered in an empty house on October 19, at 1800 East 19th Avenue.

Kristine Williams

Kristine Williams, aged thirty-six, was reported missing after her mother-in-law stated that she had not heard from her since February of 2014. Her body was discovered in an empty house at 4330 Massachusetts Street in Gary on October 19.

Sonya Billingsley

Sonya Billingsley, fifty-three, had been reported missing on February 7, 2014. Her body was discovered in an empty house, along with the body of Tanya Gatlin, on October 19, at 413 East 43rd Avenue in Gary.

Tracy Martin

Tracy Martin, forty-one, had been reported missing on June 26, 2014. Her body was discovered in an empty house on October 19, at 2200 Massachusetts Street in Gary.

Anith Jones

Anith Jones, thirty-five, was reported missing on October 10, 2014, after she hadn't been seen for two days. Following Vann's arrest on October 18, he showed police the empty house at 415 East 43rd Avenue in Gary where her body was located.

Afrikka Hardy

Vann hired nineteen-year-old Afrikka Hardy as an escort, and they met at a motel in Hammond, Indiana. On October 17, 2014, her dead body was found in the bathtub of the motel room.

Police used Hardy's phone records and located Vann. When he was arrested, Vann had Hardy's phone as well as other items of evidence. While under interrogation, he not only confessed to being involved in Hardy's murder but also confessed his involvement in other murders.

Trial

Vann's first court hearing was due to take place on October 22, but he was held in contempt of court. The next hearing occurred on October 28, and he pled not guilty to the charges of murder in the deaths of Anith Jones and Afrikka Hardy.

Over the next couple of years, there were numerous delays to his trial for a variety of reasons—including a motion his defense team filed stating the death penalty was unconstitutional. This was eventually rejected, and his trial was set for October 22, 2018.

Outcome

As part of a plea deal to take the death penalty off the table, Vann pled guilty to seven murders. On May 25, 2018, he was sentenced to seven concurrent life sentences without the possibility of parole.

Trivia

Vann called himself "Big Boy Appetite," when calling escort agencies.

Vann had a history of involvement with Indiana police even before registering as a sex offender. In 2004, he was charged with residential entry and intimidation from an incident during which he allegedly threatened to set himself on fire.

ROBERT JOE WAGNER

Date of birth: November 28, 1971

Aliases/Nicknames: The Snowtown Murders, The Bodies in Barrels Murders

Characteristics: Cannibalism, torture

Number of victims: 10

Date of murders: 1992 - 1999

Date of arrest: May 20, 1999

Victim profile: Clinton Trezise, 22; Ray Davies, 26; Michael Gardiner, 19; Barry Lane, 42; Thomas Trevilyan, 18; Gavin Porter, 29; Troy Youde, 21; Frederick Brooks, 18; Gary O'Dwyer, 29; Elizabeth Haydon, 37; David Johnson, 24

Method of murder: Shooting, strangulation

Location: Snowtown, South Australia

Status: Sentenced to ten consecutive sentences of life imprisonment without the possibility of parole on September 8, 2003.

Background

A number of murders that occurred between August of 1992 and May of 1999 in Adelaide, South Australia, became known as the Snowtown Murders. Wagner, John Bunting, and James Vlassakis were a group that worked together to target pedophiles and homosexuals and kill them. Mark Haydon, the fourth person in the group, was convicted for aiding in the disposal of the victims' bodies. Ironically, Wagner's romantic partner was a male cross-dresser, Barry Lane, who had a history of being a pedophile.

Murders

The murders were as follows:

Clinton Trezise, twenty-two, murdered on August 31, 1992, body discovered on August 16, 1994

Trezise was found buried in a shallow grave at Lower Light. He had been murdered at Bunting's home in Salisbury North. The killers had invited him to visit and then used a shovel to bash him to death.

Ray Davies, twenty-six, murdered in December of 1995, body discovered on May 26, 1999

Davies was a mentally handicapped man who lived in a caravan behind Suzanne Allen's house. He became a target after she made the accusation that he was a pedophile. He was tortured before he was killed, and was never reported missing.

Suzanne Allen, forty-seven, died November of 1996, body discovered on May 23, 1999

Allen died sometime after Davies; her remains were found buried above his in the garden of the house at Salisbury North, her body wrapped in eleven plastic bags. Her death had been concealed by the killers, and they continued to collect her pension. Later, when questioned about her death, they claimed she had died of a heart attack.

Michael "Michelle" Gardiner, nineteen, murdered in September of 1997, body discovered on May 20, 1999

Gardiner was an openly gay man whom they murdered after they became suspicious that he was a pedophile.

Barry "Vanessa" Lane, forty-two, murdered in October of 1997, body discovered on May 20, 1999

Lane, a gay man and crossdresser, had been in a relationship with Wagner at the time Bunting first met them in 1991. Lane's toes had been crushed with pliers.

Thomas Trevilyan, eighteen, murdered on November 5, 1997, body discovered on November 5, 1997

Trevilyan was found near Kersbrook in the Adelaide Hills, hanging from a tree. At first, it was presumed he had killed himself. He had assisted with murdering Barry Lane, but kept talking about it to others, so he was killed. He suffered from paranoid schizophrenia and was easily persuaded by people.

Gavin Porter, twenty-nine, murdered in April of 1998, body discovered on May 20, 1999

Porter was a heroin addict and a friend of Vlassakis. After Bunting, Harvey, Vlassakis, and Youde moved to Murray Bridge, South Australia, Porter moved into the house with them. It was decided Porter would be the next victim because Bunting had been pricked by a syringe Porter left in the couch. Porter was strangled in his car while it was parked on the property.

Troy Youde, twenty-one, murdered in August of 1998, body discovered on May 20, 1999

Vlassakis' half-brother Troy was living with them at Bunting's house when he was murdered. They dragged him from his bed while he was sleeping and killed him. This was the first time Vlassakis had participated in a murder.

Frederick Brooks, eighteen, murdered in September of 1998, body discovered on May 20, 1999

Brooks was the intellectually disabled son of a woman in love with Bunting, Jodie Elliott. Bunting saw him as an easy victim. Brooks suffered brutal torture before he was killed at Bunting's house.

Gary O'Dwyer, twenty-nine, murdered in October of 1998, body discovered on May 20, 1999

O'Dwyer had been disabled in a car accident and was on a pension. He was a stranger to the killers and was picked as an easy target. He was killed in his home on Frances Street, Murray Bridge, by Bunting, Wagner, and Vlassakis.

Elizabeth Haydon, thirty-seven, murdered on November 21, 1998, body discovered on May 20, 1999

Mark Haydon's wife was killed by Bunting and Wagner in her home while her husband was out.

David Johnson, twenty-four, murdered on May 9, 1999, body discovered May 20, 1999

Vlassakis' half-brother; he was killed by Bunting in the bank building (Snowtown), having been lured there by Vlassakis. He was the only victim who actually was killed at Snowtown.

Trial

Wagner, Bunting, and Haydon were all charged with the murders. Vlassakis pled guilty to four murders, and for a lesser sentence he agreed to provide testimony against the others.

Wagner and Bunting's trial lasted nearly twelve months—the longest trial in the history of South Australia. In December of 2003, Wagner was convicted of ten murders, having confessed to three. Bunting was convicted of eleven murders. Hayden was convicted in 2004 on five counts of assisting with the murders.

Outcome

Wagner was sentenced to ten consecutive terms of life in prison without parole. Bunting received eleven terms of life without parole, Vlassakis received four consecutive life sentences with a non-parole period of twenty-six years, and Hayden was sentenced to twenty-five years with the possibility of parole after eighteen years.

Trivia

At his sentencing, Wagner rose in the dock and stated:

> *"Pedophiles were doing terrible things to children. The authorities didn't do anything about it. I decided to take action. I took that action. Thank you."*

Community impact

Bizarrely, the notoriety of the crimes led to a short-term economic boost from tourists visiting Snowtown. It also created a lasting stigma, with newspaper *The Age* reporting in 2011 that Snowtown would be "forever stigmatized" because it was associated with the horrible murders.

Soon after the discovery of the bodies in Snowtown, the community considered changing the name to "Rosetown," but this never came about.

A store in Snowtown was selling souvenirs of the murders in an effort to cash in on the town's notoriety.

The South Australian Housing Trust demolished Bunting's house in Salisbury North, where two of the victims had been buried.

In February of 2012, the bank, along with the attached house, was put up for auction. It didn't reach the reserve price of two hundred thousand dollars and so remained unsold. An open house was then held, with an entrance fee charged to potential buyers. The money raised went to charity. Later that year, the bank and house finally sold. The new owners had planned to run a business from the bank and live in the house. A commemoration plaque was to be installed to acknowledge the victims.

Films

Snowtown, a feature film based on the life of John Bunting, was released in Australia on May 19, 2011.

Music

Comedian Eddie Perfect, the host of the 2011 Inside Film Awards in Australia, had planned to broadcast a song he had written for *Snowtown the Musical*. It wasn't broadcast, however, most likely because it was in such bad taste.

Documentaries

The case was featured on *Crimes That Shook Australia*. The episode "Snowtown: The Bodies in the Barrels Murders" aired in 2013.

The case was featured on *Crime Investigation Australia*. – The episode "Snowtown: Bodies in the Barrels"aired in 2005.

WEST MESA KILLER

Date of birth: Unknown

Aliases/Nicknames: West Mesa Bone Collector

Characteristics: Targeted drug addicts and prostitutes

Number of victims: 11

Date of murders: 2001–2005

Date of arrest: Not apprehended

Victim profile: Jamie Barela, 15; Monica Candelaria, 22; Victoria Chavez, 26; Virginia Cloven, 24; Syllania Edwards, 15; Cinnamon Elks, 32; Doreen Marquez, 24; Julie Nieto, 24; Veronica Romero, 28; Evelyn Salazar, 27; Michelle Valdez, 22

Method of murder: Undetermined

Location: Albuquerque, New Mexico, U.S.

Status: Unknown.

Background

The bodies of eleven women were discovered buried in Albuquerque's West Mesa between 2001 and 2005. Exactly who killed them or buried them remains a complete mystery to this day.

The bodies were discovered after a retaining wall, built to channel stormwater to a detention pond, exposed the bones.

Murders

A woman walking her dog on February 2, 2009, came across a human bone and reported it to the authorities. Upon further inspection of the area, the remains of eleven women, two girls, and a fetus were discovered. Most of the victims were Hispanic and ranged in ages from fifteen to thirty-two years. Most of them had been involved with sex work and drugs.

Police believe the deaths and burials were the result of one person, most likely a serial killer. They also think the murders may be linked to the annual state fair, which attracts a high number of sex workers to the area during the fall.

The victims:

Jamie Barela and her cousin Evelyn Salazar had last been seen in April of 2004, on their way to a park.

Victoria Chavez was the first set of remains identified.

Syllania Edwards had no family or friends and had run away from foster care. She was the only African American victim.

Cinnamon Elks was thirty-two when she disappeared; she had a long list of solicitation and prostitution arrests and convictions. She was friends with three other victims: Michelle Valdez, Julie Nieto, and Victoria Chavez.

Doreen Marquez had gone from a doting mother to a drug user.

Julie Nieto had always been small. From the age of nineteen, she had been a regular drug user.

Veronica Romero was reported missing by her family on February 14, 2004. She was the eleventh victim found on West Mesa.

Evelyn Salazar was reported missing by her family on April 3, 2004; she was the tenth victim identified.

Trial

No suspect has been officially identified. A reward of up to one hundred thousand dollars was offered in 2010 for information leading to the arrest and conviction of the person or persons who were responsible for the murders.

Outcome

There have been some suspects over time who have attracted the attention of the police:

Fred Reynolds

Reynolds was a pimp who knew at least one of the missing women. He reportedly had photos of missing sex workers in his possession. He died in January of 2009 from natural causes.

Lorenzo Montoya

He lived just three miles from the burial site. Tire tracks were reportedly seen leading from his trailer to the site in 2006. Montoya strangled a teenager in his trailer in December of 2006 and was shot dead by her boyfriend.

Scott Lee Kimball

Scott Lee Kimball, convicted serial killer, stated in December of 2010 that he was being investigated for the murders but denied any involvement.

Trivia

Dan Valdez served as the unofficial spokesperson for the victims' families over the years until his death in 2015 from cancer and liver disease.

CHRISTOPHER WILDER

Date of birth: March 13, 1945

Aliases/Nicknames: The Beauty Queen Killer

Characteristics: Rape, torture

Number of victims: 8 +

Date of murders: February - April 1984

Date of arrest: Not apprehended due to his death

Victim profile: Rosario Gonzalez; Elisabeth A. Kenyon, 23; Terry Ferguson, 21; Terry Walden, 24; Suzanne Logan, 21; Sheryl Bonaventura, 18; Michelle Korfman, 17; Beth Dodge, 33

Method of murder: Stabbing with knife, shooting

Location: Florida, Texas, Oklahoma, Nevada, California, New York, USA

Status: Shot himself to death during a scuffle with state troopers to avoid capture on April 13, 1984.

Background

Wilder was born in Australia in 1945. His father was an American naval officer, and his mother was Australian. In 1962 or 1963, he was convicted of gang-raping a woman at a beach in Sydney and was sentenced to probation. During this time, he was given electroshock therapy. There is some evidence that this treatment may have made his violent sexual tendencies worse.

He moved to the U.S. in 1969 and lived in Florida. He had an interest in photography and was a successful real estate agent. Between 1971 and 1975, he was charged with multiple counts of sexual misconduct, culminating in the rape of a young woman he had tricked into thinking he was photographing for a modeling contract. Remarkably, he never received any jail time for these offenses.

Wilder attacked Carla Hendry, seventeen, on April 13, 1980, and tried to abduct her, but she managed to escape. He visited his parents in Australia in 1982 and was charged with sexual offenses for forcing two fifteen-year-old girls to pose nude. His bail was posted by his parents, and he returned to Florida. Due to court delays, and his subsequent death, he never went to trial.

In the early months of 1984, Wilder went on a six-week crime spree across the country that left several females dead.

Murders

The first known victim of Wilder was Rosario Gonzalez. She had been working as a model at the Miami Grand Prix on February 26, 1984, when she disappeared. Wilder had been at the event racing a Porsche. Wilder's ex-girlfriend, Elizabeth Kenyon, disappeared on March 5. The bodies of these two women have never been found.

On March 18, Wilder persuaded Theresa Wait Ferguson to leave the Merritt Square Mall with him. After he killed her, he disposed of her body at Canaveral Groves. Her remains were found on March 23. Then on March 20, he attempted to abduct Linda Grover from the Governor's Square Mall in Tallahassee. He attacked her in the mall parking lot, tied her hands, wrapped her up in a blanket, and put her in his trunk. He drove her to a motel and raped her. Then he used superglue and a hairdryer to blind her. He electrocuted her through copper wires on her feet. She tried to run, but he beat her, so she locked herself in the bathroom. She began pounding on the walls, and Wilder fled.

The following day, Terry Walden was approached by Wilder, who suggested having her pose as a model. She declined the offer, and when they crossed paths two days later, he abducted her. He then stabbed her to death. Her body was found in a canal on March 26. The day before, he had abducted Suzanne Logan from a shopping mall in Oklahoma City. He drove her to Newton, Kansas, where they stayed in a motel. He drove to Milford Reservoir the next morning, stabbed her to death, and left her body beneath a tree.

Wilder kidnapped Sheryl Bonaventura on March 29. Two days later, he shot her to death near the Kanab River in Utah. Her body was found on May 3. The next victim was Michelle Korfman. He abducted her from a modeling competition at a shopping mall. Her body wasn't found until May 11, and it was mid-June before she was identified. A photograph had been taken at the mall of Wilder stalking her.

Wilder took photographs of Tina Marie Riscio before kidnapping her and assaulting her. He decided she might be useful in helping him get other victims though, so he kept her alive. They traveled to Merrillville, Indiana, and she helped him abduct Dawnette Wilt. She was raped several times while Riscio drove them to New York. Wilder then took Wilt into the woods and tried to suffocate her before stabbing her twice. Thinking she was dead, he left.

But Wilt was still alive. A truck driver found her and took her to the hospital. She informed the police that Wilder was heading to Canada. Meanwhile, Wilder kidnapped Beth Dodge at the Eastview Mall in New York. After driving a short distance, he shot Dodge and dumped her body in a gravel pit. Wilder and Riscio then went to the Logan Airport in Boston, and Wilder bought a ticket to Los Angeles for Riscio.

State troopers noticed Wilder at a service station on April 13. When they approached him, Wilder went to his car and grabbed his gun. One trooper managed to grab Wilder from behind, but two shots were fired during the scuffle. The first shot went through Wilder and into the trooper behind him. The second shot struck Wilder in the chest, killing him.

Trial

In addition to the known victims, Wilder was suspected in several other murders and disappearances of women. Some of the remains were found in parts of Florida he was known to visit.

Colleen Orsborn

Orsborn went missing on March 15, 1984. Wilder was staying at a motel in the same area at the time. A few weeks after she went missing, her body was found partially buried.

Wanda Beach Murders - Marianne Schmidt and Christine Sharrock

On January 11, 1965, Schmidt and Sharrock were killed at Wanda Beach near Sydney, Australia. Wilder looked similar to a suspect sketch that was made at the time.

Mary Opitz

Opitz disappeared on January 16, 1981. She had last been seen walking in the direction of a parking lot in Fort Myers, Florida.

Mary Hare

On February 11, 1981, Mary Hare disappeared from the same parking lot. Hare's body was found in June of 1981.

Tina Maria Beebe and Unidentified Woman

The skeletal remains of two women were uncovered in 1982 near a property owned by Wilder in Florida. One of the victims had her fingers cut off and had been dead for one to three years. In 2013, she was identified as Tina Marie Beebe.

Shari Lynne Ball

Ball went missing in October of 1982. Her body was later found in New York.

Nancy Kay Brown

While on vacation in Cocoa Beach, Florida, Brown disappeared. Her remains were found in Canaveral Groves in March of 1984.

Tammy Lynn Leppert

She was last seen in Cocoa Beach on July 6, 1983.

Broward County Jane Doe

Unidentified female remains were discovered on February 18, 1984, in a canal in Davie, Florida.

Outcome

Wilder was cremated. His personal estate was worth more than seven million dollars; the money was divided among the families of his victims after taxes had been paid.

Trivia

Film

The television movie *Easy Prey*, released in 1986, was based on Wilder's story.

Ruled out victims

A man walking his dog in the woods in Key Largo on May 3, 1973, discovered the bodies of Mary and Marguerit Jenkins. They had last been seen hitchhiking the day before, trying to get home to New Jersey. Both victims had been sexually assaulted and bludgeoned before being shot and killed. The authorities investigated the possibility that Wilder had killed them. But DNA found on one of the girls was not a match to Wilder.

The body of Melody Marie Gay, nineteen, was found in a canal on March 10, 1984. She had been abducted from an all-night store where she worked in Collier County. There were similarities between Wilder's other murders and Gay's, and he was temporarily considered a suspect.

PETER WOODCOCK

Date of birth: March 5, 1939

Aliases/Nicknames: David Michael Krueger

Characteristics: Juvenile, child rapist, mutilation

Number of victims: 4

Date of murders: 1956 - 1957, 1991

Date of arrest: January 21, 1957

Victim profile: Wayne Mallette, 7; Gary Morris, 9; Carole Voyce, 4; Dennis Kerr, 27

Method of murder: Stabbing with knife, bludgeoning

Location: Toronto, Ontario, Canada

Status: Declared legally insane and placed in Oak Ridge, an Ontario psychiatric facility, in 1957. Died there on March 5, 2010.

Background

Woodcock was given up for adoption when he was a month old. He lived in a variety of foster homes but wasn't able to bond with anyone. From the time he turned one, he became terrified if anybody approached him. At the age of two, he was abused by a foster parent and was beaten so badly he had to have medical treatment for a neck injury.

When Woodcock was three, he was finally placed in a stable home. He stopped screaming when people approached him when he was about five years old, but he was bullied by neighborhood kids. He was described by the Children's Aid Society at the age of ten as:

Slight in build, neat in appearance, eyes bright, and wide-open, worried facial expression, sometimes screwing up of eyes, walks briskly and erect, moves rapidly, darts ahead, interested and questioning constantly in conversation ... He attributes his wandering to feeling so nervous that he just has to get away. In some ways, Peter has little capacity for self-control. He appears to act out almost everything he thinks and demonstrates excessive affection for his foster mother. Although he verbalizes his resentment for other children, he has never been known to physically attack another child ... Peter apparently has no friends. He plays occasionally with younger children, managing the play. When with children his own age, he is boastful and expresses determinedly ideas which are unacceptable and misunderstood.

Woodcock was sent to a special school for children who were emotionally disturbed. He started acting on his sexual urges with the other children, including intercourse with a twelve-year-old girl when he was thirteen, which he said was consensual. After he moved back home, he spent a lot of time riding his bicycle around, and often sexually assaulted other children.

Murders

On September 15, 1956, Woodcock met Wayne Mallette, seven, at the Exhibition Place. He lured Mallette away from everyone else and strangled him. Mallette's body was found with his face pushed into the ground, and there were two bite marks on his body - one on his buttock and one of his calves. There were no signs he had been raped. Scattered around the body were pennies; Woodcock had also defecated.

Woodcock was riding his bicycle around Cabbagetown on October 6, 1956, when he came across Gary Morris, nine. They rode together to Cherry Beach, where Woodcock strangled Morris and beat him to death. The autopsy showed the cause of death was a ruptured liver, and there was a bite mark on this throat. This time, instead of pennies, there were paper clips scattered around the scene.

The next victim was Carole Voyce, four, who was approached by Woodcock on January 19, 1957. He picked her up, and they rode to a spot under the Bloor Viaduct. He choked her until she was unconscious and then molested her. She was killed by a tree branch that had been shoved inside her vagina.

Woodcock was seen by a teenager as he rode his bicycle away from the murder scene. A composite sketch was created and was put on the front page of the newspaper. Leads from this led to Woodcock, and he was arrested on January 21, 1957. He subsequently confessed to the three killings.

Trial

Woodcock was diagnosed a psychopath while he was imprisoned. He received a variety of psychiatric treatments. He didn't respond well, and he exploited other inmates and engaged in coercive sexual acts. At one point, he created an imaginary gang which he called the Brotherhood.

Woodcock was sent to the Brockville Psychiatric Hospital. While he was there, he legally changed his name to David Michael Krueger. He had a relationship with Bruce Hamill, a killer from Ottawa who was then working at the courthouse as a security guard. He convinced Hamill that his problems would be solved by an alien brotherhood if he helped Woodcock kill Dennis Kerr, another inmate.

Hamill signed out Woodcock on July 13, 1991, for an escorted day outing. Within the first hour, Woodcock had arranged for Kerr to meet him in the woods near the hospital under the pretense of loaning him money. When Kerr arrived, he was struck in the head with a pipe wrench. Woodcock then beat him until he was unconscious. Woodcock and Hamill used a knife and hatchet to stab and hack at Kerr, mutilating his body and almost decapitating him. The two men then stripped and sodomized the deceased Kerr. When they were done, Woodcock walked to a police station and turned himself in.

Outcome

Woodcock was transferred to the Oak Ridge section of the Penetanguishene Mental Health Centre. Sometimes he would try to explain why he had committed the murders, but he couldn't come up with a rational reason. On March 5, 2010, his birthday, Woodcock died of natural causes.

Trivia

Woodcock told other inmates that there was a "mythical" group outside the prison with whom he had contact. If they wanted to become part of it, Woodcock declared, they had to give him cigarettes and perform oral sex on him.

"I'm accused of having no morality, which is a fair assessment because my morality is whatever the system allows," he said in a 1993 interview.

CHRISTOPHER WORRELL AND JAMES MILLER

Christopher Worrell

Date of birth: January 17, 1954

Aliases/Nicknames: Truro Murderer

Characteristics: Rape, bisexual

Number of victims: 7

Date of murders: December 1976 - February 1977

Date of arrest: Died before an arrest

Victim profile: Veronica Knight, 18; Tania Kenny, 15; Juliet Mykyta, 16; Sylvia Pittman, 16; Vickie Howell, 26; Connie Iordanides, 16; Deborah Lamb, 20

Method of murder: Strangulation

Location: Truro, South Australia, Australia

Status: Worrell was killed in a car accident on February 19, 1977.

James Miller

Date of birth: February 2, 1940

Aliases/Nicknames: Truro Murderer

Characteristics: Homosexual

Number of victims: 6 - 7

Date of murders: December 1976 - February 1977

Date of arrest: May 23, 1979

Victim profile: Veronica Knight, 18; Tania Kenny, 15; Juliet Mykyta, 16; Sylvia Pittman, 16; Vickie Howell, 26; Connie Iordanides, 16; Deborah Lamb, 20

Method of murder: Strangulation

Location: Truro, South Australia, Australia

Status: Sentenced to life in prison with a non-parole period of 35 years on March 12, 1980. Died in prison on October 22, 2008.

Background

Worrell and Miller had met while spending time in prison together. Worrell was incarcerated for rape and breaching a suspended sentence for armed robbery, and Miller was in prison for breaking and entering. They developed a relationship where one was dominant and the other submissive. When they were released, they not only worked together, but lived together as well. Miller was infatuated with Worrell. Worrell, however, would read pornographic magazines while Miller performed sexual acts on him. Since Worrell preferred women, the relationship eventually changed to one that was more like brothers.

The series of murders they were involved in became known as The Truro Murders because the remains were found in Truro, South Australia. Police discovered the remains of seven women in Truro, Port Gawler, and Wingfield. They had been killed during a two-month period in 1976 and1977.

Murders

Victims

Veronica Knight - December 23, 1976
Knight accepted a ride home. Miller claimed they convinced her to go for a drive in the Adelaide foothills. After they parked the car, Miller went for a walk and left Worrell and Knight behind. When Miller returned to the car, Knight was dead. Miller claimed he confronted Worrell, but Worrell threatened him with a knife, so he helped dispose of her body at Truro.

Tania Kenny - January 2, 1977
Kenny was picked up by Worrell and Miller just after she had arrived in the city. They drove her to the home of Miller's sister, and while Kenny and Worrell went inside, Miller claimed he stayed in the car. A while later, Worrell returned to the car saying he needed some help. Kenny was dead, so they took her body to Wingfield and buried her.

Juliet Mykyta - January 21, 1977
Mykyta was waiting at a bus stop when Worrell offered her a lift home. Instead, they drove her to Port Wakefield. While Worrell was tying her up, Miller claimed he sat in the car. He then said he was going to go for a walk but heard a sound and turned back. Mykyta had gotten out of the car and fallen over. Worrell began strangling her. Miller said he tried to pull Worrell off but he wasn't strong enough, and Worrell threatened to kill him. Mykyta's remains were also found at Truro.

Sylvia Pittmann - February 6, 1977
Pittman was waiting for a train at the Adelaide Station when the two men picked her up. They drove to the Wingfield area. Again, Miller claimed he went for a walk and left her alone with Worrell. He later helped dump her body at Truro.

Vickie Howell - February 7, 1977
Miller arrived at a local post office, where he met Howell with Worrell. Miller went for a walk, and when he returned, Howell was dead, and Worrell was in a rage. Howell's body was then taken to Truro.

Connie Iordanides (also known as Connie Jordan) - February 9, 1977
Offered a lift home by Worrell and Miller, Iordanides got frightened when they drove in the wrong direction. Miller stopped at Wingfield and Worrell forced her into the back seat while she screamed. Miller made no attempt to stop it. He went for a walk, and after returning, she was dead, so they drove to Truro to get rid of her body.

Deborah Lamb - February 12, 1977
Lamb was hitchhiking when they picked her up and drove her to Port Gawler where Miller went for his usual walk. When he got back to the car, Lamb wasn't there, and Worrell was using his foot to push sand into a large hole. She had been buried alive.

Deborah Skuse - February 19, 1977

Skuse was an ex-girlfriend of one of their friends. She went to Mount Gambier with Miller and Worrell for the weekend, but Worrell got into one of his dark moods, so they decided to return to Adelaide. Worrell was driving when a tire blew, causing the car to roll over several times. All three were thrown out onto the road. Worrell and Skuse died, and Miller broke his shoulder blade.

Trial

After Worrell was killed, Miller became depressed. At Worrell's funeral, a former girlfriend told Miller that Worrell might have had a blood clot in his brain. This caused Miller to make a comment that he wondered if that's why Worrell had the urge to kill. Amelia informed the police about the comment and collected a financial reward.

Miller was questioned on May 23, 1979, and though he initially denied any knowledge, he eventually told police there were three more bodies than the ones they knew about. He was then escorted to the areas where the bodies had been dumped so he could show the detectives exactly where they were.

Outcome

Miller went on trial and was convicted of six murders on March 12, 1980. He received six consecutive terms of life imprisonment.

Miller died on October 21, 2008, at the age of sixty-eight. The primary cause of death was liver failure, which was a complication from having Hepatitis C. He also had cancer in the lung and the prostate.

Trivia

At the time of his death, Miller was one of the longest-serving prisoners in the state.

Miller often visited the graves of Skuse and Worrell at the cemeteries. He couldn't forget about them. One year to the day after their death, Miller placed a few paragraphs in the "In Memoriam" notices in the Adelaide Advertiser which read:

"Worrell, Christopher Robin.
Memories of a very close
friend who died 12 months
ago this week, Your friendship
and thoughtfulness and kindness,
Chris will always be
remembered by me, mate.
What comes after death I can
Hope, as I pray we meet again"

Miller wrote a book called *Don't Call Me Killer.*

At one stage during his incarceration, Miller went on a hunger strike that lasted forty-three days.

ROBERT ZARINSKY

Date of birth: September 2, 1940

Aliases/Nicknames: Nil

Characteristics: Rape

Number of victims: 2 - 10

Date of murders: 1958 - 1974

Date of arrest: February 22, 1975

Victim profile: Young women and a man (New Jersey police officer)

Method of murder: Shooting, strangulation

Location: Monmouth County, New Jersey, USA

Status: Sentenced to life imprisonment, 1975. Died in prison on November 29, 2008.

Background

From adolescence, Zarinsky showed signs of being mentally unstable. By the early 1960s, he was referring to himself as "Lt. Schaefer, the leader of the American Republic Army."

He spent thirteen months in a state psychiatric hospital at one point after he was convicted of grave desecration and arson. He had vandalized Jewish cemeteries and set fire to five lumber yards. Despite being under the watchful eye of trained psychiatrists, he managed to convince them he was well enough to be released.

Murders

On October 25, 1969, Rosemary Calandriello went missing; her body has never been found. Zarinsky later confessed he had killed her accidentally and buried her in northwest New Jersey. But he also told another investigator that he had thrown her body into the ocean.

Officer Charles Bernoskie came across Zarinsky and his associate, Theodore Schiffer, committing a burglary. He was shot and killed, but it is uncertain who fired the gun. Before he was killed, the officer did manage to shoot both Zarinsky and Schiffer. But they weren't badly injured and managed to escape.

Zarinsky's sister Judith Sapsa, who was under investigation for embezzlement, implicated Schiffer in the shooting. She later testified that she had helped her mother remove bullets from Zarinsky and Schiffer on the night Bernoskie was killed.

The last known victim was Jane Durrua, who went missing on November 4, 1968. Her body was found in a field the next morning.

A fingerprint left at the scene of Bernoskie's murder was eventually matched to Schiffer, and this led to the arrest of Zarinsky and Schiffer.

Trial

In 1975, Zarinsky was convicted of killing Calandriello and was sentenced to life imprisonment. He was acquitted of the murder of Bernoskie in 2001. However, Bernoskie's widow filed a wrongful death against him and was successful. He was ordered to pay her $9.5 million. In 2004, one hundred fifty-four thousand dollars was seized from Zarinsky and given to Bernoskie to divide among her children.

A court reversed the decision in July of 2008 and ordered the money given to Bernoskie be given back to Zarinsky. She no longer had the money, and it is unlikely it would ever be paid back.

Zarinsky was indicted by the grand jury on March 11, 2008, for the murder of Durrua.

Outcome

Zarinsky died on November 28, 2008, as he was waiting to go on trial for the murder of Durrua. His cause of death was pulmonary fibrosis.

There are a few other murders Zarinsky is suspected of committing:

- Linda Balabanow, seventeen, in 1969.
- Joanne Delardo, fifteen, in 1974.
- Doreen Carlucci, fourteen, in 1974.

Trivia

Zarinsky's death came as he was awaiting trial for the 1968 murder of thirteen-year-old Jane Durrua of Keansburg.

Zarinsky was the first person in New Jersey to be convicted of murder despite the lack of a body.

Zarinsky denied any role in the Durrua homicide. "I most certainly was not involved in it, as I was not involved in the numerous other allegations made against me over the years," he wrote on May 26, 2007, to the *Star-Ledger* newspaper.

CONCLUSION

It's been a hell of a read, hasn't it?

It was never going to be easy to digest all of the details surrounding the lives, crimes and final outcomes of 150 different serial killers across the world, but we know that you must feel very accomplished at this moment.

In this book, we covered the stories of psychopathic killers who kidnapped and tortured their victims; silent murderers who drugged their patients and made it seem like an accident; angry male rejects who lashed out on innocent women; and furious women who ended the lives of their partners for fun… truly, there is yet to be a case of two serial killers being exactly the same, and these unique stories make for very interesting reads.

Whether you found yourself most absorbed when reading the details of Joe Ball, the Alligator Man who fed his victim's bodies into a pond full of the lizards; Dale S. Hausner, who wrote a poem that he left behind before committing suicide in his cell; Béla Kiss, who became a "vampire" and went missing before any law enforcement officers could stop him; or Wang Qiang, who killed over 45 young girls and women before being executed in 2005; this book will certainly have allowed you to engross yourself with some of the most fascinating serial killer stories available, many of which you will never have heard of.

You will definitely have learned an important lesson, among the many small ones which this book taught you - the world is a dangerous place to live in, and there is always going to be at least one monster out there on the streets when you least expect it.

Furthermore, as we told you in the introduction, we want you to know that the True Crime genre and serial killer books are more than just a method of release for those with morbid curiosity – they are educational books which you should find yourself proud of reading, especially since you're boosting your knowledge in a subject that may be important for your profession!

We've enjoyed creating this book for you and will keep an eye on feedback for improvements and changes for the next installments.

Can't wait? Go to www.JackRosewood.com/books and see all my other true crime novels.

Thanks for reading - see you in the next one!

- Jack Rosewood